ROMANTICISM AND LANGUAGE

ROMANTICISM
AND LANGUAGE

EDITED BY

ARDEN REED

Cornell University Press

ITHACA, NEW YORK

Cornell University Press gratefully acknowledges a grant from the Andrew W. Mellon Foundation that aided in bringing this book to publication.

First published 1984 by Cornell University Press.

"The Mariner Rimed" by Arden Reed was adapted by the author from a chapter in his book *Romantic Weather: The Climates of Coleridge and Baudelaire*, copyright © 1983 by Brown University Press, Providence, Rhode Island. Reprinted by permission of University Press of New England, Hanover, New Hampshire.

International Standard Book Number (cloth) 0-8014-1606-x
International Standard Book Number (paper) 0-8014-9891-0
Library of Congress Catalog Card Number 84-45146
Printed in the United States of America

LIBRARY OF CONGRESS CATALOGING IN PUBLICATION DATA
Main entry under title:

Romanticism and language.

  Bibliography: p.
  Includes index.
    1. English literature—19th century—History and criticism—Addresses, essays, lectures. 2. Romanticism—England—Addresses, essays, lectures. 3. English language—Style—Addresses, essays, lectures. I. Reed, Arden, 1947–
PR468.R65R65 1984   820'.9'145   84-45146
ISBN 0-8014-1606-X (alk. paper)

In memoriam

Earl Wasserman

Any such conception as "Romanticism" is at one or more removes from actual literary experience, in an inner world where ten thousand different things flash upon the inward eye with all the bliss of oversimplification.

—Northrop Frye

We seem to assume all too readily that, when we refer to something called "language" we know what it is we are talking about, although there is probably no word in the language to be found that is as overdetermined, self-evasive, disfigured and disfiguring as "language."

—Paul de Man

CONTENTS

CONTENTS

PREFACE

    Six of these essays originated at meetings devoted to the topic of Romanticism and language at the Modern Language Association gatherings in New York in 1978 and in San Francisco in 1979; Frances Ferguson's paper was delivered in 1981 at an MLA panel titled "Language and the Younger Romantics," chaired by William Keach. All of these papers were subsequently expanded and revised. I solicited three additional essays (Richard Macksey's was presented as a Butler Lecture at the State University of New York at Buffalo in 1981 and Reeve Parker's at the 1982 Wordsworth-Coleridge Association meeting, chaired by Paul Magnuson), more to complicate matters than to complete them. It hardly needs to be said that these essays do not exhaust the topic of Romanticism and language; they were written more in the spirit of opening up fields of inquiry than in the expectation of closing them off. The selection was to some extent determined by the occasion of the MLA panels, and had space permitted I would naturally have liked to include other contributions. For a sampling of related work, the reader may consult the selected bibliography.

    I am grateful to Peter Manning, without whose characteristic kindness the MLA meeting in 1978 would not have taken place, and to Leslie Brisman, who suggested and supported the publication of these essays. Appreciation is also due to Murray Cohen, for his witty and informed response at the San Francisco meeting, and to Pomona College for financial support. My largest debt is to the contributors themselves, for their generosity and patience, and for having composed this book in every sense.

    I gratefully acknowledge permission to quote from *The Collected Poems of Wallace Stevens,* by Wallace Stevens, copyright © 1954 by Alfred A. Knopf, Inc. A few pages of Jerome Christensen's essay appeared in different form in his book *Coleridge's Blessed Machine of Language* (Ithaca: Cornell University Press, 1981), and another version of my essay appeared in my book *Romantic Weather: The Climates of Coleridge and Baudelaire* (Hanover, N.H.: University Press of New England, 1983). It is a pleasure to acknowledge permission to use them here.

A. R.

Edinburgh, Scotland

ROMANTICISM AND LANGUAGE

Introduction

Arden Reed

In his note to "The Thorn," Wordsworth underscores "the interest which the mind attaches to words, not only as symbols of the passion, but as *things,* active and efficient, which are of themselves part of the passion." Similarly, Coleridge describes in his notebook a "focal word" that "has acquired a *feeling* of *reality*—it heats and burns, makes itself to be felt. If we do not grasp it, it seems to grasp us, as with a hand of flesh and blood, and completely counterfeits an immediate presence, an intuitive knowledge. And who can reason against an intuition?" In *Prometheus Unbound,* Shelley calls language "a perpetual Orphic song, / Which rules with Daedal harmony a throng / Of thoughts and forms, which else senseless and / Shapeless were." And Keats in *Hyperion* evokes the image of "hieroglyphics old / Which sages and keen-eyed astrologers / Then living on the earth, with labouring thought / Won from the gaze of many centuries: / Now lost, save what we find on remnants huge / Of stone, or marble swart; their import gone, / Their wisdom long since fled." The differences in persona, tone, and genre among these passages are self-evident, but such differences bring out a common thread that runs through the citations, other appearances of which would be easy to locate. Wordsworth, Coleridge, Keats, and Shelley here exemplify the emergence of language as a topic in English Romantic literature and display the alertness of that literature to its own status as language. Michel Foucault argues that such self-awareness is no aberration but an integral part of a larger historical development: "From the nineteenth century, language began to fold in upon itself, to acquire its own particular density, to deploy a history, an objectivity, and laws of its own. It became one object of knowledge among others, on the same level as living beings, wealth and value, and the history of events and men."[1]

Like the Romantics, literary critics make language an object of knowledge—whether construed as theme, form, style, or, more recently, a way to interrogate the distinction between criticism and its subject (the poem, the text, "Romanticism," and so on). The purpose of the present collection is to bring together this shared interest of Romantic writers and contemporary critics by presenting some concrete, language-oriented perspectives on the period. The contributors write on Wordsworth, Coleridge, Shelley, Keats, and Romantic essayists, and look back as far as Shakespeare and Milton, across the Channel at Rousseau, and forward to Swinburne and Stevens.

From the Romantics onward, the study of literary language has taken several forms: distinctions drawn (and denied) between the language of poetry and that of prose, debates over the diction appropriate to poetry, speculations on the role of meter and other sound effects, investigations of syntactical and grammatical structures, various formal analyses, and traditional exegeses. As recently as the 1950s and 1960s, American critical interest in the language of poetry usually expressed itself in stylistic studies that tended to eschew interpretation in favor of describing technical innovations. The essays gathered here occasionally touch on some of these issues, but in general they are concerned with language in a more radical way, in that they seek to displace our understanding of literature as a representational art form in order to characterize the maneuverings and interferences of the text and so raise questions about the texture of Romantic literature, about its intertextual relations, and about the irreducibility of the signs in which Romantic thought is encoded.

The shape of the present essays may emerge more clearly when they are set against the backdrop of earlier work. In America, modern criticism of the Romantics began in the 1920s and 1930s with an attack on the period by an odd "coalition of modernist poets and conservative thinkers,"[2] including Irving Babbitt, T. S. Eliot, and Ezra Pound, later to be joined by the New Critics. They saw Roman-

---

[1]Michel Foucault, *The Order of Things* (New York: Pantheon Books, 1970), p. 296. For a different view on "the early part of the nineteenth century [which] has a quality so extraordinary that it demands an explanation," and specifically on "the newly created comparative-historical philology," see Hans Aarsleff, *From Locke to Saussure: Essays on the Study of Language and Intellectual History* (Minneapolis: University of Minnesota Press, 1982), pp. 31–32, and also "Wordsworth, Language, and Romanticism," pp. 372–81.

[2]Preface, *Romanticism: Vistas, Instances, Continuities*, ed. David Thorburn and Geoffrey Hartman (Ithaca: Cornell University Press, 1973), p. 7.

ticism as a "spilt religion" that indulged in the cult of the self at the expense of social responsibility and in violation of their own priv-ileged poetics of irony and impersonality. Although they were al-ways making particular exceptions, these critics charged the Roman-tics with naively glorifying the "noble savage" and other forms of the irrational and with producing imagery that was slack, sloppy, and vague. Such blasts produced ironies of their own, for the defenders of Romanticism raided the enemy arsenal and applied the New Crit-ical techniques of close reading to the Romantics with notable re-sults, most strikingly in the case of Keats's odes. At about the same time, Frank Kermode, Murray Krieger, and others began to argue that those very writers who had mounted the attack did so from a position that was itself Romantic. It is generally agreed that the pro-Romantic side carried the day, as witnessed by the attraction that the period has exercised over many critics who in earlier times might have been expected to direct their energies to sixteenth- or seven-teenth-century poetry. But like all battles, this one left its scars. It is worth recalling the long-settled hostility of the 1920s and 1930s because it influenced the form Romantic criticism would take for decades to follow. Thus what purported to be pure description of the period's characteristic features in the works of such critics as René Wellek and Morse Peckham had a prescriptive element, moti-vated by an ideological response to the old charges.

This ideological strain should have been predictable because it was already operating among the Romantics themselves, nowhere more so than in Coleridge's criticism, from which the modern apologists largely took their lead. In such passages as Chapter 14 of *Biographia Literaria* Coleridge formulated what M. H. Abrams in *The Mirror and the Lamp* called the Romantics' distinctive contribution to aesthetic theory—the idea that the imagination is a creative faculty, the locus of genius and the source of originality (all highly problematic terms that critics rarely questioned, at least in a self-conscious way).[3] But this concept of the imagination was not simply inspired or *sui generis*, for Romantic writers also formulated the context that made such a faculty indispensable. Because they frequently represented their world as made up of dualities (subject and object, self and nature, nature and culture, for example), they found it necessary to posit a force that could effect a "balance or reconciliation of opposite or discordant qualities." And from Kant and Hegel to Heidegger, phi-

[3]See the exchange between Abrams and Jonathan Culler in *High Romantic Argu-ment: Essays for M. H. Abrams*, ed. Lawrence Lipking (Ithaca: Cornell University Press, 1981), pp. 149–75.

losophers have likewise assigned this mediating role to art. Appropriating this theory of poetry, modern critics tended to read Romantic lyrics for representations of "the one Life, within us and abroad": the great poem enacts in its own language the same "organic unity" that it portrays in the wedding of, say, man and nature. Integration, they argued, ought to occur both at the level of form (as in Abrams's thesis about the "Greater Romantic Lyric" that "rounds upon itself to end where it began" but with "deepened understanding")[4] and at the level of imagery, principally the symbol, which, Coleridge had said, participates in the very reality it represents. The critics embraced the symbol at the expense of allegory (which they saw as flat and fragmentary), just as they valued the organic over the mechanic—again taking their cue from a statement of Coleridge that the imagination, "while it blends and harmonizes the natural and artificial, still subordinates art to nature."

While critical enthusiasm for the Romantics was producing important work in America (from the grand conceptual schemes of Walter Jackson Bate and Abrams to the narrower but persuasive studies of individual poets by Harold Bloom, Northrop Frye, Geoffrey Hartman, Earl Wasserman, and others), literary studies in Europe were taking different turns that would eventually contribute to the current interest in Romantic language.[5] Most notable, perhaps, was the rise of structuralism, because it introduced Saussurean linguistics into literary studies. It has been argued that this grafting gave rise to a large part of current literary theory by providing a terminology with which one could consider literature apart from those traditional aesthetic and historical categories that had dominated American criticism.[6] By the late 1960s, however, Jacques Derrida had begun his "biblioblitz" (as Barbara Johnson calls it), which contributed to decentering the structuralist project. This is not the place to summarize Derrida's positions—an undertaking that is bound to be in certain ways unsatisfactory, despite the recent emergence of a cottage industry devoted to "streamlining" his thought.[7] Suffice it to

---

[4]"Structure and Style in the Greater Romantic Lyric," in *Romanticism and Consciousness: Essays in Criticism,* ed. Harold Bloom (New York: Norton, 1970), p. 201.

[5]It would, of course, be incorrect to suppose that American academics had been insular before the late 1960s and the 1970s. In addition to the "Geneva School," there was the considerable influence of such immigrant Romance philologists as Erich Auerbach and Leo Spitzer.

[6]Paul de Man, "The Resistance to Theory," *Yale French Studies* 63 (1982): 8.

[7]For succinct attempts fully aware of their necessary limitations, the reader may wish to consult the introduction to Barbara Johnson's translation of *Dissemination* (Chicago: University of Chicago Press, 1981), pp. vii–xxxiii; Jonathan Culler's essay

say that although none of the contributors would consider themselves strict disciples—a relationship that in any case Derrida is always subverting—none of their essays is entirely innocent of the strategies of reading he has formulated, commonly referred to as "deconstruction." One reason for its impact on Romantic studies is that deconstruction offers a way to interrogate the ideologies by which earlier critics had underwritten Romanticism while still allowing for, if not encouraging, a sustained reading of that literature. (Derrida's own relationship to ideology, it goes without saying, is currently a matter of some debate.)

Contemporaneous with these developments, there appeared an influential article informed by Continental philosophy and bringing that learning to bear on European Romanticism and American scholarship, Paul de Man's "Rhetoric of Temporality."[8] By "deconstructing" the opposition that values symbol over allegory in its Coleridgean *locus classicus*, de Man disclosed the vulnerability of the previous generation's defense of Romanticism. The force of his argument follows in part from the synecdochic character of the symbol, a figure that participates in and in fact may be said to sustain the ideological image of Romanticism I have sketched out. Hence, to render suspect the superiority of symbol to allegory was to question the very terms and concepts in which traditional readings of Romanticism had been conducted. The significance of de Man's gesture became clear when he went on to quarrel with Abrams and Wasserman, two readers who agreed that at its heart Romanticism involves a dialectic between subject and object, which it is poetry's task to synthesize. De Man countered that the subject/object relationship is a "pseudo dialectic," a confusion of the critics, while for the poets "the dialectic between subject and object does not designate the main romantic experience, but only one passing moment in a dialectic, and a negative moment at that, since it represents a temptation that has to be overcome." Whether or not one accepts his conclusions, de Man made it difficult for critics to continue using the term "symbol" with the ease and assurance to which they had become accustomed.

A generation ago, contributors to a collection titled *Romanticism*

---

on Derrida in *Structuralism and Since,* ed. John Sturrock (New York: Oxford University Press, 1979), pp. 154–80; or Alan Bass's "'Literature'/Literature," in *Velocities of Change,* ed. Richard Macksey (Baltimore: Johns Hopkins University Press, 1974), pp. 341–53.

[8]The essay appeared in *Interpretation: Theory and Practice,* ed. Charles S. Singleton (Baltimore: Johns Hopkins University Press, 1969), pp. 173–209.

and Language would probably have taken a strictly New Critical approach, and the extent to which that method has been displaced or supplemented testifies to the persuasiveness of de Man's argument. But the shift in approach is also related to access deconstruction provides to texts and readings that were largely unavailable to earlier critics. According to the New Critical model, the successful poem is autonomous and unified. Its unity derives from the integrated sensibility of the poet, which the critic seeks to demonstrate. By exhibiting the poem's unity, the critic guarantees its autonomy, and thus we come full circle. This procedure helps to explain why the New Critics generally preferred short to long poems, and implies that their reservations about so much of Romantic poetry resulted from its resistance to closure, and hence their inability to square that poetry with their view of the proper model of a poem (even though that view is largely an extension of Romantic aesthetics). A fragment, for example, must be a failure unless the critic can somehow establish its internal coherence and self-sufficiency—but in that case it is no longer a fragment. In place of the New Critical values of unity and autonomy, deconstruction underlines, for instance, difference and intertextuality, and thus enables readings of texts that stage no reconciliations.

Deconstruction, however, has no exclusive claim to the topic of Romanticism and language.[9] This volume is not a manifesto, and as their various styles of arguing make clear, its contributors have made no contract to adhere to the same theoretical or methodological assumptions. One virtue of the topic is in fact that it welcomes a wide range of styles (humanist and so-called antihumanist, rhetorical, poststructural) and approaches (from traditional close reading and the history of ideas to the avant-garde). Indeed, that range extends to practices represented in this book only marginally or not at all. Among them one ought to mention the study of influence as aggression in literary history, *Rezeptionsaesthetik*, and the French interpretation of Freud. Perhaps the most powerful approach on the margin of this volume is the historical, and it is at least worth raising the question how far an historical outlook is compatible with such close reading as is practiced here.[10]

[9]Indeed, Rodolphe Gasché has argued against the whole enterprise of "applying" the interpretative strategies of deconstruction to literary texts. See "Deconstruction as Criticism," *Glyph* 6 (1979): 177–215.

[10]The first category would include Walter Jackson Bate, *The Burden of the Past and the English Poet* (New York: Norton, 1972), and the works of Harold Bloom from *The Anxiety of Influence* (New York: Oxford University Press, 1972) to the present; the second refers primarily to the studies of Hans Robert Jauss and Wolfgang Iser; the

It is conventional in introductions such as this to offer an overview that summarizes the essays to follow and explains their interrelations. I shall make no attempt to regulate the contents of this collection, however, because the will to synthesize so often manifest in introductions is itself part of our Romantic inheritance, bound up with a concept of the harmonizing imagination that makes the critics writing here uneasy. Each of the following essays is already engaged in the reinterpretation of literary and critical traditions, and to attempt to mediate among all these intricate readings, if not to resolve them, would be both reductive and wrongheaded. This is to say not that the relationships among the contributions are inconsequential, of course, but that they may best be left for readers to make as they move from one piece to another, getting caught up in the drama of reinterpretation. Is it pure coincidence, for example, that several of the essays fix on the metaphor of theft? What is the relation among stealing property (material or linguistic), stealing the proper meaning of words and substituting counterfeit or figural meaning, and usurping a person's identity so that he becomes a "persona-fiction"? Several of the essays suggest that the Romantic self is forever threatened with collapse into a "mere man of letters" (if that self was ever anything else) and hence may be able only to feign identity through a rhetorical theft. At the least, the use of language to represent the self in that peculiarly Romantic genre of autobiography always seems to entail being used by language as well. If instead of arriving at easy answers or airtight syntheses, the reader comes to perceive ever more complexity in such issues, the essays will perhaps have done their work.

That said, it may still be useful to suggest a response to the debates I have outlined above. First, the contributors do not canvass Romantic poetry for what Robert Penn Warren once called moments of "sacramental vision," in which the natural, the human, and the supernatural all merge into a greater whole. Any such merging depends on the assumption that the Romantic world view is structured in binary oppositions (such as nature/culture, literal/figural, reading/writing), and the contributors are wary of that construct.

---

third has recently been exemplified by Diana Hume George in *Blake and Freud* (Ithaca: Cornell University Press, 1980).

On the question of history see, for example, Jerome J. McGann, *The Romantic Ideology: A Critical Investigation* (Chicago: University of Chicago Press, 1983); the symposium titled "The Problems of Reading in Contemporary American Criticism," published in *boundary 2* 8 (1979); Frank Lentricchia's *After the New Criticism* (Chicago: University of Chicago Press, 1979); and the recent works of Fredric Jameson and Edward Said.

Second, the essayists represented in this collection tend to read Romantic texts intertextually rather than as autonomous entities. How does our understanding of a work of English Romantic poetry or prose change when we read it again in a revised form, or together with another work by the same writer, or in conjunction with a contemporary English work that shares traits of resemblance or significant difference, or with an earlier text to which the text at hand refers, or with a later text that in some way refers to or reiterates it, or when the text is juxtaposed with texts from other genres, other languages, or other "disciplines"—say, a literary text articulated with a historical or philosophical text? What happens, for instance, when, as in this volume, we read Rousseau with Wordsworth, Shakespeare with Coleridge, Swinburne with Shelley, or Stevens with Keats? One result is to view the text as an appropriation and often a reinterpretation of anterior texts, of which citation and plagiarism are only the more obvious indications.

Third, as the title implies, the contributors by and large take a rhetorical as opposed to a mimetic approach to Romantic literature and attempt to record linguistic play that resists reduction to a single meaning. The various readings here understand Romantic literature to be so multivalent that irony (which one might have thought complex) looks straightforward by comparison. As it has been conventionally understood, irony depends on a writer's complete anticipation of the tonal effects of his or her text, but the kinds of textual play described by the following essays register effects that sometimes exceed such authorial control.

Fourth, and relatedly, the essayists practice criticism, in Geoffrey Hartman's words, as "a hermeneutics of indeterminacy,"[11] for they find the dissonances and differences of Romantic literature to be irresolvable. What De Quincey and Poe both record as being said of "a certain German book" becomes true of all books: "er [sic] / lässt sich nicht lesen" ("it does not allow itself to be read"), if by "read" we mean a monolithic, definitive interpretation. Hence the present writers, while striving for argumentative rigor and coherence, eschew interpretive closure. With a pleasure that may be either untroubled or tinged by nostalgia, the contributors dramatize Roland Barthes's observation that "everything signifies ceaselessly and several times, but without being delegated to a great final ensemble, to an ultimate structure."[12] These words (at least in translation) may

[11]Geoffrey Hartman, *Saving the Text* (Baltimore: Johns Hopkins University Press, 1980), p. 106.
[12]Roland Barthes, *S/Z*, trans. Richard Miller (New York: Hill & Wang, 1974), p. 15.

call to mind the end of Wallace Stevens' poem on Santayana, when he invokes the

> Total grandeur of a total edifice,
> Chosen by an inquisitor of structures
> For himself.

In contrast to Barthes, Stevens' philosopher looks like a New Critic who finally achieves his vision. But Stevens himself may be skeptical about such inquisitions, for just as the old man "chooses" to grasp the whole in a unified and magnificent act of mind, Stevens adds a quiet qualification that defers the totality just announced:

> He stops upon this threshold . . .

In a similar way the following essays stop, or more accurately, they are written *upon* a threshold, and with something resembling "wild surmise." Neither comfortably within nor wholly detached from any possible structure, or else as Wordsworth has it "both at once," the essays wind through liminal and labyrinthine passages, reading Romanticism as a kind of language.

1 /

The Language of Interpretation
in Romantic Poetry:
"A Strong Working of the Mind"

Susan J. Wolfson

I

In 1799 William Blake reminded the Reverend Dr. Trusler, "The wisest of the Ancients considerd what is not too Explicit as the fittest for Instruction, because it rouzes the faculties to act."[1] This comment may be applied to the rhetorical activity of much Romantic poetry as well,[2] especially in poems in which logical structures—the plots of an argument, a tale, or an informing legend—are the expected means of instruction. *The Rime of the Ancient Mariner, The Thorn,* "La Belle Dame sans Merci," and "Ode on a Grecian Urn" all unfold mysteries against potential sources of interpretation: moral lessons, arguments, glosses, village testimony, portentous encounters, spectral legends. Yet however much such sources may "rouze" the mind to render intelligible "what is not too Explicit," in these poems, the materials invoked for that purpose themselves become invaded by what Keats calls "uncertainties, Mysteries, doubts."[3] If these poems arouse expectation that there is a secure logic to be discovered for their perplexing circumstances, they tend to dramatize the difficulties of such discovery more than its success.

---

[1]August 23, 1799, *The Complete Poetry and Prose of William Blake,* ed. David V. Erdman (Garden City, N.Y.: Anchor Books, 1982), p. 702.

[2]Though a fascination with "what is not too Explicit" is not original with the Romantics (as eighteenth-century speculations on the sublime remind us), the development of a significant poetic mode and of specific rhetorical figures for "what is not too Explicit" emerges as a conscious, and ultimately central, literary enterprise in the Romantic period.

[3]*The Letters of John Keats,* ed. Hyder E. Rollins, 2 vols. (Cambridge: Harvard University Press, 1958), I:193. Subsequent references are indicated in parentheses in the text.

The Language of Interpretation in Romantic Poetry

These are poems, in other words, about problems in interpretation, involving questions that go to the heart of the Romantic concern with language itself: What is the status of explication or logical argument in poems that appear to frustrate such modes of discourse even as they put them forth? What kind of poem, or poetry, does this activity produce? One effect, certainly, is to cast into doubt the principles of coherence (the causal sequences) on which plots and arguments alike rely[4] and to foreground the less certain, uneasy motions of mind attempting to describe such principles in the circumstances that have compelled its attention. Such stress yields a poetic syntax more psychological than logical in organization, more affective than narrative in its procedures. These poems all show the degree to which interpretation cannot consist simply of deciphering hidden patterns of meaning or discovering causal sequences, but must become an active seeking and generating of meaning.

The Rime of the Ancient Mariner and *The Thorn* dramatize the efforts of their speakers to elucidate mystery through recourse to the logic of moral argument and the logic of narrative, respectively. The Mariner's "Rime" itself involves several kinds of interpretation, but the most blatant sense-making scheme in Coleridge's text—the Marginal Gloss—is amassed against the Mariner's "Rime" as a parallel commentary, making the poem as a whole bear the signature of two distinct intelligences: that of the riming Mariner and that of the Marginal Editor. In *The Thorn*, Wordsworth entertains dilemmas of interpretation in the body of the poem itself; moreover, he diminishes the locutional differences between the narrator of the tale and the voice of his logic-seeking questioner—as if to suggest a unity of enterprise. In both these lyrical ballads, the sources of interpretive authority and the logical patterns they promote or delineate never quite emerge as "points and resting places in reasoning"[5] independent of "the fluxes and refluxes of the mind" trying to interpret.[6]

---

[4]On plot as a "causal sequence," see E. M. Forster, *Aspects of the Novel* (New York: Harcourt, Brace, 1927): "A plot is a narrative of events, the emphasis falling on causality. 'The king died, and then the queen died' is a story. 'The king died, and then the queen died of grief' is a plot. The time-sequence is preserved, but the sense of causality overshadows. . . . If it is a story we ask 'and then?' If it is a plot we ask 'why?'" (p. 130).

[5]The phrase is Keats's (*Letters*, I:281).

[6]Preface to *Lyrical Ballads* (1800), in *Lyrical Ballads: The Text of the 1798 Edition with the Additional 1800 Poems and Prefaces*, ed. R. L. Brett and A. R. Jones (London: Methuen, 1963; reprint, 1965), p. 247. Hereafter this edition will be cited as Brett and Jones.

So psychological an emphasis (and the poetic texture it effects) must have impressed Wordsworth and Coleridge alike as a revolutionary enough experiment in the language of poetry. Yet Coleridge's belief that "the best part of human language . . . is derived from reflection on the acts of the mind itself"[7] was not to be given its most radical poetic treatment until a generation later. Keats explicitly features the questions of interpretation that haunt *The Rime of the Ancient Mariner* and *The Thorn* in his own lyrical ballad "La Belle Dame sans Merci"—a poem that bears a structural resemblance to *The Thorn*. Not long after, he was at work on a series of odes (of which "Ode on a Grecian Urn" is the most striking example) in which he not only makes a premise of the problems of interpretation all these lyrical ballads trace with increasing intensity, but extends that negotiation with uncertainty to the reader's engagement with the play of his rhyme.

II

Today, most readers of *The Rime of the Ancient Mariner* are probably not as bothered as was Coleridge's acquaintance, the poet and essayist Mrs. Barbauld, about the "improbable" nature of his story. The second "fault" of which she complained to the author, however, remains something of a notorious vexation for many modern readers—namely, that the poem "had no moral." Coleridge is willing to cede the point on "probability"; but "as to the want of a moral," he counters, the poem's "chief fault, if I might say so, was the obtrusion of the moral sentiment so openly on the reader as a principle or cause of action in a work of pure imagination."[8] Yet in *The Rime of the Ancient Mariner* Coleridge not only seems to deplore "moral sentiment"; in this work of pure imagination, he seems to want to baffle the effort to discover any principle of action. Indeed, he continues his remarks by declaring that his poem "ought to have no more moral than the *Arabian Nights'* tale of the merchant's sitting down to eat dates by the side of a well and throwing the shells aside, and lo! a genie starts up and says he *must* kill the aforesaid merchant *because* one of the date shells had, it seems, put out the eye of the genie's son." Coleridge emphasizes the causal vocabulary with know-

[7]*Biographia Literaria*, ed. J. Shawcross, 2 vols. (Oxford: Clarendon, 1907), II:39–40.
[8]Table Talk for May 31, 1830, *Specimens of the Table Talk of the Late Samuel Taylor Coleridge*, ed. H. N. Coleridge, 2 vols. (London: John Murray, 1835), II:155–56.

ing irony, for to the mind of the date-eater, the genie has produced moral necessity from a chance event and consequence.

But before considering what kind of moral paradigm that tale offers to the reader of Coleridge's poem, we need to turn to the Mariner himself, who finds moral uncertainties in the central circumstance of his "Rime." The world he describes, as readers from Wordsworth to the present have noted, is one informed by inscrutable forces: nature is unpredictably solicitous or persecutory, benevolent or tyrannous. As in "Dejection," the language that can be read from nature's appearances often seems barely more than the fiction of a desperate imagination. Indeed, the foggy atmosphere from which the Albatross emerges, and which always surrounds its presence, suggests both inner and outer weather:

> At length did cross an Albatross,
> Thorough the fog it came;
> As if it had been a Christian soul,
> We hailed it in God's name.[9]

Despite the appealing rhyme of "Albatross" with "cross" (here and subsequently), the Mariner's "As if" has the effect of raising a question about what "principle or cause of action" (if any) is actually involved. For the conjecture, uttered in fogbound misery, seems to describe primarily the hopes of an anxious crew, rather than anything positive about the bird itself. The Mariner and crew attempt repeatedly to convert conjecture into a syntax of event and consequence that can join the Albatross to the fate of their ship: when the splitting of the ice and the rising of a good south wind follow the advent of the bird, they hail it as the agent of their release; when the fog disperses (along with the ice and snow) after the Mariner kills the bird, the crewmen reinterpret the Albatross as the cause of the fog, and their release into sunshine and fair breezes as a consequence of its death; and when the same breezes fail and the "glorious" sun becomes "bloody," the crewmen imagine themselves plagued by the Mariner's killing of the Albatross and rue that act. What are we to make of this continual shuffling of logic? Even Wordsworth, usually not averse to making the reader "struggle," sides with Coleridge's perplexed readers and against his "Friend" in

[9]Quotations of *The Rime of the Ancient Mariner*, the Arguments of 1798 and 1800, and the Gloss follow *The Poems of Samuel Taylor Coleridge*, ed. E. H. Coleridge (London: Oxford University Press, 1912; reprint, 1960).

25

the "Note to the Ancient Mariner" he wrote for the second edition of *Lyrical Ballads*. He cites, among other difficulties, the "defect" "that the events having no necessary connection do not produce each other."[10] The arbitrary interpretations that gather around the Albatross are a case in point. Each new scheme of causality does not clarify any "necessary connection" between the bird and the state of the weather, as much as all together expose the fiction of interpretive acts: ascertainment of the bird's value emerges after the fact, as a logic of cause and effect is imposed on a mere sequence of events.[11] As in the tale of the genie and the date-eater, cause and effect are matters of convenient collation rather than of inevitable connection. We begin to sense that if the Albatross signifies anything, it is the very ambiguity of signs—that is, the ambiguity with which the external world vexes a desire for interpretive certainty.

The language of cause and consequence not only surrounds the Albatross but is the very principle upon which a narrative must proceed, and so the problem of collation and connection extends to the listener of the Mariner's tale. How is one supposed to coordinate the two key events upon which his story depends: the killing of the Albatross and the blessing of the snakes? The way the Mariner himself represents these acts makes more of their irrationality than of their moral dimensions: "I shot the ALBATROSS" merely joins subject and predicate, rather than explains the act; and even when that act is apparently redeemed by the blessing of the water-snakes, this, too, is given without reference to a conscious motivation: "I blessed them unaware." The parallel syntax of "I shot" and "I blessed" does make a neat pattern for the sampler homily with which the Mariner caps his tale: "He prayeth best, who loveth best / All things both great and small; / For the dear God who loveth us, / He made and loveth all." Nonetheless, a listener cannot escape awareness that this moral is for its bearer embedded in a self-denying context: the Mariner is doomed to eternal exclusion from the love and prayer he preaches. Ironically, he isolates and terrifies his auditors more than he con-

---

[10]Brett and Jones, pp. 276–77.

[11]For alert discussions of the problem of determining motivation, causes, and consequences, see Frances Ferguson, "Coleridge and the Deluded Reader: *The Rime of the Ancient Mariner*," *Georgia Review* 31 (1977):617–35; and Raimonda Modiano, who observes, "The poem teasingly gravitates toward coherent systems of thought, and yet no mythic or philosophic tradition, be it Christian, Egyptian, Neoplatonic, or the like, is large enough to contain it" ("Words and 'Languageless' Meanings: Limits of Expression in *The Rime of the Ancient Mariner*," *Modern Language Quarterly* 38 [1977]:41). These views are elaborated by Anne K. Mellor, *English Romantic Irony* (Cambridge: Harvard University Press, 1980), pp. 137–50.

soles them with any sense of God's inclusive love. The would-be Wedding-Guest's "wiser" state notwithstanding, that listener at least is also left "sadder" for having heard the "Rime"—perhaps more "stunned" than instructed by the Mariner's will over him. Denied the "goodly company" of the marriage feast, the Wedding-Guest's very name is rendered meaningless. Left "of sense forlorn," this student of the Mariner's lesson finds himself, instead, a participant in the Mariner's alienation: listener and tale-teller alike seem at the end of their encounter "forlorn" of common "sense"—the comfort of living in a world of rational cause and consequence.[12] As Coleridge remarks in the "Conclusion" of his own biography, "there is always a consolatory feeling that accompanies the sense of a proportion between antecedents and consequents . . . giv[ing], as it were, a substratum of permanence, of identity, and therefore of reality, to the shadowy flux of Time."[13]

What denies the Mariner and all his listeners this sense of proportion is that the question that is the efficient cause of his narration—"What manner of man art thou?"—eludes certain answering. What is his "substratum" of identity? Is he a killer of an Albatross, a blesser of water-snakes, a preacher of God's love, or an agent of contamination? The question is voiced originally by the Mariner's first auditor, the Hermit, and as we learn, it wrenches the Mariner "With a woful agony" that requires nothing less than a retelling of all the events of his ordeal. Yet as tortured and elaborate as the Mariner's response is, it remains indeterminate: the question generates his "Rime," and his "Rime" regenerates the question. Its conclusion, in fact, gestures toward its perpetual rehearsal in the shadowy flux of time:

[12]Ward Pafford feels "certain that the Wedding-Guest in his turn will become an agent for propagating the values he has learned from this other "sadder and wiser man'" ("Coleridge's Wedding Guest," *Studies in Philology* 60 [1963]:618–26), but Ferguson argues in her survey of criticism that "the possibility of learning from the Mariner's experience depends upon sorting that experience into a more linear and complete pattern than the poem ever agrees to do" (p. 620). Edward Bostetter offers a reply to Robert Penn Warren's famous reading of the poem as evolving a "sacramental vision" of the "One Life" in "The Nightmare World of 'The Ancient Mariner,'" *Studies in Romanticism* 1 (1962):241–54. See also Lionel Stevenson, who attributes a "post hoc ergo propter hoc" reasoning to the Mariner: "The 'morality' of the poem . . . is not Coleridge's, but that of a primitive seaman who has evolved a creed for himself on the basis of terrific experiences, and is therefore fanatically devoted to it. Coleridge's interest is in the universal psychological fact of rationalization. . . . The wedding guest is 'a sadder and a wiser man,' not so much because of the Mariner's didactic assertions as because he has had a horrifying glimpse into human experience of the extremest hardship, the utter antithesis of his own sheltered life" ("'The Ancient Mariner' as a Dramatic Monologue," *Personalist* 30 [1949]:34–44).

[13]*Biographia Literaria,* II:207.

Since then, at an uncertain hour,
That agony returns:
And till my ghastly tale is told,
This heart within me burns.

Endlessly navigating about a core of mysterious events, the Mariner can never capture their informing logic: his text circles about this absent center but always begins and concludes in agonizing uncertainty. Nor does Coleridge's ballad itself secure the tidy closure of "moral sentiment," ending instead with a register of the aftereffect of the Mariner's tale in the mind of his stunned, forlorn auditor. If the Mariner himself "Is gone," he leaves the trace of his mystery in that interior realm, making the truest issue of his "ghastly tale" the way it haunts a listener's imagination. "I was never so affected with any human Tale," Charles Lamb wrote to Wordsworth; "After first reading it, I was totally possessed with it for many days. . . . the feelings of the man under the operation of such scenery dragged me along like Tom Piper's magic Whistle.—"[14] Another listener confessed to feeling "insulated" in the wake of hearing the poem recited by its author: "a sea of wonder and mystery flows round [me] as round the spell-stricken ship itself."[15]

The effect of the Mariner's "Rime" in leaving its readers thus "possessed," despite the patent moral at its close, is amplified by the interpretive apparatus with which Coleridge surrounds the text of the "Rime." The "Argument" at the head of the 1798 poem is primarily descriptive, concerned mainly with the course of the Mariner's ship and alluding only briefly to "the strange things that befell" as if by chance, accident, or inscrutable agency. With the "Argument" of 1800, however, Coleridge introduces terms of moral logic and potential instruction: "the Ancient Mariner cruelly and in contempt of the laws of hospitality killed a Sea-bird and . . . was followed by many and strange Judgements." Yet in the 1802 and 1805 editions of *Lyrical Ballads* Coleridge dropped the "Argument" altogether, as if he had decided not to prejudice his reader with authorial signals, but to let his poem work its own effect. The next publication of the poem in *Sibylline Leaves* (1817) strikes a compromise, supplying a marginal gloss instead of an argument. Like the "Argument" of 1800, the Gloss often brings a moral interpretation

[14]January 30, 1801, *The Letters of Charles and Mary Anne Lamb*, ed. Edwin W. Marrs, Jr., 3 vols. (Ithaca: Cornell University Press, 1975), I:266.
[15]H. N. Coleridge, *Quarterly Review* 52 (1834), reprinted in *Coleridge: The Critical Heritage*, ed. J. R. de J. Jackson (London: Routledge & Kegan Paul, 1970), p. 645.

to bear on the Mariner's story. Unlike the "Argument," however, the Gloss is a parallel text, in effect competing with the "Rime" for the reader's attention, rather than supervising it. It presumes to order the Mariner's ordeal with a logic that his own "Rime" does not disclose—as if supplying the "necessary connection[s]" whose absence Wordsworth, among others, regretted. "And lo! the Albatross proveth a bird of good omen," it declares with the authority of biblical exegesis. "The ancient Mariner inhospitably killeth the pious bird of good omen," it avers, judgment in its every other word. Or taking as a cue the Mariner's fervent hope that "Sure my kind saint took pity on me," the Gloss confidently interprets a necessary connection: "By grace of the holy Mother, the ancient Mariner is refreshed with rain." The voice of the Gloss confronts the reader as the genie does the date-eater, starting up to declare moral necessity at every turn. Yet far from clarifying whatever connections between events the "Rime" may have left obscure, the very presence of a Gloss emphasizes their absence and points to the need for explicit terms of instruction in a circumstance where all is interrogative ("Why look'st thou so?" "wherefore stopp'st thou me?" "What manner of man art thou?"). Indeed the final marginal comment, "an agony constraineth . . . [the Mariner] to teach, by his own example, love and reverence to all things that God made and loveth," gives the rehearsal of that lesson a psychological urgency ("agony") even as it declares a moral principle. Despite the faith readers such as Robert Penn Warren have placed in the authority of the Gloss,[16] it persists as another fiction—a parallel account of the ordeal recounted by the Mariner's "Rime," or an account of another ordeal: the attempt to make sense of the Mariner's language.

There is one frame, however, that Coleridge retains in every edition, namely, the voice of the anonymous balladeer with which the poem begins and ends. Readers tend, as Lionel Stevenson does, to

---

[16]Penn Warren imagines, for example, that the Gloss possesses the supposed oracular powers of Keats's Grecian Urn: "The Gloss tells us all we need to know"; and he willingly endorses its authority: "For the Gloss says here . . ."; "then, as the Gloss puts it . . ."; "As the Gloss explains here . . ." ("A Poem of Pure Imagination: An Experiment in Reading," abridged in *Twentieth-Century Interpretations of "The Rime of the Ancient Mariner,"* ed. James O. Boulger [Englewood Cliffs, N.J.: Prentice-Hall, 1969], pp. 21–47). See also B. R. McElderry, Jr., "Coleridge's Revision of 'The Ancient Mariner,'" *Studies in Philology* 29 (1932):68–94. McElderry argues that the "differences between the two accounts" are "slight" (p. 92) and that the importance of the Gloss lies in its "artistic restatement and ornament of what is obvious in the text" (p. 91); yet he comments that the "elaborations in the gloss contribute to the unity of the action described, though at the same time they make the emphasis of the text itself seem inadequate" (p. 89).

treat this frame voice as no more than a "perfunctory" device.[17] Yet in a poem so fundamentally involved with issues of tale-telling and tale-listening, this view deserves reconsideration. The relative situation of the Mariner's "Rime" is what lyricizes the ballad, making it as much about the feelings the "Rime" develops in its tellers and listeners as about the supernatural character of its events or the moral wisdom of its instruction. Its concluding focus on the Wedding-Guest suggests, furthermore, the frame narrator's muted but overall interest in the relation between "forced" tale-telling and "forced" tale-listening. The Wedding-Guest, now possessed with the "Rime," may have found a motive for narrative similar in power to that which possesses the Mariner with his ordeal. The poem leaves open to question whether this newly haunted listener might himself become a haunted purveyor of the Rime's repetitive life: Will the Wedding-Guest rise the morrow morn, compelled to reach toward an audience of his own, to say in the manner of the ballad's frame narrator, "It is an ancient Mariner, / And he stoppeth one of three"? The ballad's opening word, "It," bears the same sense of perplexed indeterminacy with which the Mariner has left the Wedding-Guest, while the present tense of narration, both here and in the ballad's penultimate stanza ("The Mariner, whose eye is bright, / Whose beard with age is hoar, / Is gone"), suggests the perpetual presence of that figure in the mind that contains his "Rime." The affinity the balladeer's language bears to the psychology of the Mariner's haunted listener is further enhanced by the copresence of their voices in the poem's inaugural stanza, before the actual character of the Wedding-Guest is introduced. The opening two lines flow immediately into a question—"By thy long grey beard and glittering eye, / Now wherefore stopp'st thou me?"—in which the pattern of meter and rhyme and the as-yet-unspecified identity of the questioner momentarily create the sense of a single mind moving from observation to speech.

The self-circling energies of this narrative frame and the would-be containment offered by the poem's interpretive frame (the early Argument or later Gloss) suggest an extended rhetorical figure for the motions of a mind left stunned by the Mariner's "Rime" and

[17]Stevenson, "'Ancient Mariner' as Dramatic Monologue," p. 40. Huntington Brown attributes a "choric function" to the Wedding-Guest and to the author of the Gloss alike, and points to differences in style and to the evident erudition of the editor to argue "that the minstrel [the frame narrator] is certainly not meant to be the author of the gloss" ("The Gloss to *The Rime of the Ancient Mariner*," *Modern Language Quarterly* 6 [1945]:319–24).

attempting to sort out its mystery. Could the interpretive apparatus surrounding what Coleridge thought of as "A Poet's Reverie" be the textual signatures of a previously sense-forlorn auditor trying to make sense by obtruding (for himself and for his own audience) a "principle of action" on the intolerably inconclusive tale that has possessed his imagination? The Latin epigraph that in 1817 takes the place of earlier Arguments and subtitles indeed brings a problematic perspective to bear on the Mariner's mysterious experience. An excerpt from *Archaelogiae Philosophicae* by the Anglican divine, Thomas Burnet, it offers scholarly speculation on the existence of the invisible and the supernatural in the things of the universe. Yet Burnet cautions that in circling about but never attaining knowledge of the unknown, the mind must be vigilant for truth, careful to distinguish the certain from the uncertain. The action of circling about a center that defies final understanding describes the relation of the Mariner's "Rime" to its enigmatic core of events; it also figures the relation of the Gloss to that "Rime": each text surrounds a mystery, attempting to negotiate moral certainty in the face of what haunts and rouses the imagination. And the comprehensive text of Coleridge's 1817 ballad, equivocating between Marginal Gloss and Mariner's "Rime," now poses that problem to the reader.[18] For the *apparatus criticus* and the "Rime" together shape a fuller text that, while denying unambiguous principles of instruction, offers an explicit figure for the ultimate uncertainty of interpretation.

III

In leaving its reader so "struggl[ing] with feelings of strangeness and aukwardness," *The Rime of the Ancient Mariner* achieves one of the revolutionary goals of *Lyrical Ballads*.[19] Deriding the "mere artifices of connection" that characterize the "falsity in the poetic style" of the day, Coleridge points to Wordsworth's contributions to their volume and praises the way such poems reveal compelling "resemblances between that state into which the reader's mind is thrown" by the "confusion of thought from an unaccustomed train of words and images" and "that state which is induced by the . . .

[18]Mellor notes that the Gloss "is printed in the outside margin and would thus normally be read before the text of left-hand pages, after the text on right-hand pages," yielding "a visual emblem" of Coleridge's ambivalence (*English Romantic Irony*, p. 145).

[19]The "Advertisement" to the 1798 *Lyrical Ballads* warns the reader of such a consequence (Brett and Jones, p. 7).

language of empassioned feeling."[20] The reader's "confusion" in the presence of such language is the note on which *The Thorn* begins, and Wordsworth even supplies an interlocutor to give voice to the inevitable protests. The ballad opens plainly enough, with an unspecified speaker reporting a simple fact: "There is a thorn."[21] But as in *The Rime of the Ancient Mariner,* the world of positive fact ("It is . . .") dissolves rather quickly into the shadows of imagination: this is no mere bush, we find out, but one of a mysteriously charged constellation of objects that has taken possession of the speaker's imagination. He hopes a village tale will supply terms by which he can explain "why" this "spot" should produce such impressive effects out of its simple elements. His initial gesture in this direction is to claim that he "saw" a "woman" at this spot, beside that thorn, crying to herself, "Oh misery! oh misery! / "Oh woe is me! oh misery!"—namely Martha Ray: betrothed, seduced, abandoned in pregnancy on her wedding day, bereaved of her child, and perhaps guilty of infanticide at "the spot." The interpretive appeal of this rural legend for the speaker is that it plots an objective chain of events that culminate in the affective power of "the spot," allowing him to displace his obsession with "the spot" to Martha Ray; he is merely an accidental witness.

But as with the Gloss attached to the Mariner's "Rime," here too the very pressures that introduce the cause-and-effect logic of the tale call into question the validity of the proposed explanation. The speaker's insistence that it was Martha Ray whom he "found," "saw," and "heard" "Ere [he] had heard of Martha's name" may indicate no more than a desperate effort to release his imagination from the grip of a mist-bound panic on a lonely, stormy mountain ridge. Stephen Parrish argues persuasively that the credulous and superstitious speaker may have traced into his account of "the spot" the details of Martha Ray's history after the event of his own witnessing, converting mere objects into intelligible signs of her ordeal.[22] A psychological urgency shades the explanation promised by the tale into language that expresses the reach for explanation by a mind invaded by mystery. The questioner in the speaker's audience may plead, "But what's the thorn? and what's the pond? / "And what's

---

[20]*Biographia Literaria,* II:28.
[21]Quotations of *The Thorn* follow the text of Brett and Jones.
[22]"'The Thorn': Wordsworth's Dramatic Monologue," *English Literary History* 24 (1957):153–63. See also my discussion of *The Thorn* as a study of Wordsworth's experiment with the language of question and response: "The Speaker as Questioner in *Lyrical Ballads,* 1798," *Journal of English and Germanic Philology* 77 (1978):546–68.

the hill of moss to her?" But that plea, despite its relentless repetition, fails to make the speaker clarify an account suspended uneasily between what he professes to know, or swears is true, and what he "do[es] not know," "cannot think" or "tell."

That the poem dramatizes the motions of interpretation as much as it displays the materials of interpretation constitutes what Geoffrey Hartman has termed the "double plot" of *The Thorn,* in which "the action narrated and that of the narrator's mind run parallel."[23] The question for the speaker is "why?": what is the connection between the "tale" and "the spot"? But for the reader, that question is compounded with another, about the agent of that second psychological order of action: "What manner of *mind* is this?" we may ask. Wordsworth himself takes up this last question in his own version of the Coleridgean Argument and Gloss: the long Note he appends to the poem in the second edition of *Lyrical Ballads.*[24] Addressed to "Readers who are not accustomed to sympathize with men feeling in that manner or using such language," the Note supplies a sort of second text—that "Introductory Poem" Wordsworth felt he "ought" to have adduced to *The Thorn* "to give this Poem its full effect." But unlike Coleridge's Gloss, Wordsworth's Note is not concerned with clarifying a principle for the "action narrated"; he means instead to clarify his intent to exhibit what happens to the language of discourse in the absence of such a principle—particularly in the case of a "credulous and talkative" discourser with an imagination "prone to superstition." Wordsworth argues that the speaker's particular "manner," especially his "repetition of words" (a chief complaint among the poem's first readers), is meant to dramatize an effort "to communicate impassioned feelings"—an effort spurred by "something of an accompanying consciousness of the inadequateness of [his] powers, or the deficiencies of language" to do so.

The speaker's frustration of plot and his larger struggle with the language of cause and effect thus become a general struggle with all modes of articulation—except the repetition of verbal fragments "which appear successfully to communicate" a feeling, and "the interest" thereby "which the mind attaches to words, not only as symbols of the passion, but as *things,* active and efficient, which are of themselves part of the passion." "During such efforts," Wordsworth explains, "there will be a craving in the mind" which, to the extent

[23]Geoffrey Hartman, *Wordsworth's Poetry: 1798–1814* (New Haven: Yale University Press, 1964), p. 148.
[24]Brett and Jones, pp. 288–89.

that it remains "unsatisfied," will cause the speaker to "cling to the same words." Though Coleridge deplored this effect, the circumstances of his own Mariner's narrative suggest a certain amount of sympathy for its motivation. For the implicit repetition of the Mariner's "Rime," and the actual repetitions in *The Thorn* that play in the voices of both Martha Ray and the ballad's speaker, all describe motions of mind engaged with what is not too explicit: repetition becomes re-petition, re-asking. As such an interrogative attempt, repetition emerges as another version of the questions that provoke the telling of each tale, that "craving in the mind" for a certainty it cannot locate. Indeed, the voice that actually utters questions in *The Thorn* is itself a repetitive one. This voice never quarrels with the narrator but merely echoes his tentative discourse in interrogative tones. Both the echoing locution of this voice, as well as its indeterminate origin, suggest that Wordsworth may even be shading the poetics of dialogue into monologue, as if to represent a colloquy within one intelligence, between a voice seeking fact and reason ("But why . . . ?"), and a voice helplessly burdened with mystery ("I do not know"). The play of these voices, like that between Coleridge's "Rime" and his framing apparatus, becomes an extended figure for the mind's engagement with uncertainty. There is a difference, however, for in Wordsworth's poem the two voices we hear are scarcely distinguishable, and neither presumes interpretive authority.

IV

The effort of Wordsworth and Coleridge in these "lyrical ballads" to dramatize the uncertainties of interpretation opens a field of rhetorical activity in English Romanticism in which the play of interpretive strategies emerges as a primary subject—a "principle of action" in itself. Shelley writes an ode the whole point of which seems to be to question whether "the human mind's imaginings" work against a "vacancy" of information in the external world (*Mont Blanc*); Byron chants playfully: "Apologue, Fable, Poesy, and Parable, / Are false, but may be rendered also true, / By those who sow them in a land that's arable: / 'T is wonderful what Fable will not do! / 'T is said it makes Reality more bearable" (*Don Juan* XV:89). Keats's Odes are perhaps the consummate Romantic instance of a poetic design in which the primary principle of action is a psychological event—a mind exploring and testing its own fictions of interpretation. But narrative, too, becomes arable land for such testing in a poem such as "La Belle Dame Sans Merci," Keats's version of a lyrical ballad. As in *The Thorn* and *The Rime of the Ancient Mariner,* the central event (the perhaps fatal entanglement of a knight with an enigmatic woman of the meads) emerges only as a troubled memory, the primary action becoming instead the exchange between a perplexed questioner and a would-be tale-teller.[25] The poem opens on an explicitly interrogative note, as a voice arrested by a strange impression queries its cause: "O what can ail thee, knight at arms, / Alone and palely loitering?"[26]

Like the questioners of Wordsworth and Coleridge, Keats's balladeer seeks a reason for a peculiar phenomenon: what explains this unexpected sight on the meads, a knight absent from his wonted world of quest and romance? What sort of tale awaits the telling? The tone of the question reflects its speaker's uncertainty, for it suggests at once a moment of puzzled concern for an ailing countryman and a slightly chiding "what-ails-you?" reproach for the appearance of negligence. The description of the landscape that completes the stanza—"The sedge has wither'd from the lake, / And no birds sing"—extends the mood of inquiry by stressing the incongruity of figure and place. Yet there is a gap between the stanza's questions and its voice of description that raises a question for the reader: are the comments on the landscape a cryptic but potentially meaningful reply *to* the questioner or a further effort *by* the questioner to provoke a reply from the knight? That ambiguity, and its mysterious circumstance, persist in the second stanza:

> O what can ail thee, knight at arms,
>   So haggard and so woe-begone?
> The squirrel's granary is full,
>   And the harvest's done.

This stanza compounds rather than clarifies the indefinite relation between question and statement, an ambiguity to which I shall return. For now it is enough to note that both the landscape that

---

[25]Harold Bloom's influential essay "The Internalization of Quest-Romance" (1969) argues that Romantic poetry in general reorganizes the traditional plot of quest-romance into a psychological idiom. This essay is printed in *The Ringers in the Tower* (Chicago: University of Chicago Press, 1971), pp. 13–35.

[26]Quotations of Keats's poetry follow *The Poems of John Keats*, ed. Jack Stillinger (Cambridge: Harvard University Press, 1978). For "La Belle Dame" I use the text of Charles Brown's transcript rather than the one Leigh Hunt printed in *The Indicator* (May 10, 1820). Though there are provocative differences between the two versions of the poem, their dramas of interpretation are substantially the same.

frames the knight and the statements that frame the questions announce a world of depleted vitality, no longer productive of any
harvest, even, apparently, the harvest of inquiry: the field is unyield-
ing for all. The principle of *in*action seems the profoundest absence
of all; indeed, the questioning voice is the singular movement in this
otherwise barren circumstance.

The adjectives "haggard" and "woe-begone" (as well as the previous stanza's "Alone" and "loitering") begin to play against this
vacancy of information, however, by hinting at anterior events:
"woe-begone" and "Alone" suggest diagnoses of an ailment for
which "loitering" may be a symptom, while the etymology of "haggard," along with what Keats might describe as "its original and
modern meaning combined and woven together, with all its shades
of signification,"[27] suggests an intuition of cause. The modern
meaning of "drawn, gaunt, exhausted" is enhanced by the status of
"haggard" as an adjective derived from "hag," implying prior be-
witchment. The word points even more specifically to the effects of
commerce with a "haggard": "a wild or intractable female," and —
with special relevance to Keats's La Belle Dame—with a "'wild' expression of the eyes."[28] May the knight's present "haggard" appearance be the effect of a contagious encounter with some haggard's "wild wild eyes"? The latent efforts at interpretation stirring
in these adjectives emerge in the overtly symbolic imagery that
follows:

> I see a lily on thy brow
>   With anguish moist and fever dew,
> And on thy cheeks a fading rose
>   Fast withereth too.

As Earl Wasserman remarks, this stanza invites a "symbolic reading":[29] the lily is the harbinger of death (Keats in fact wrote "death's
lilly" in an earlier draft [II:95]); the "fading rose" (also originally
"death's fading rose") cannily surmises the fatal fading of romance,
while the repetition of the verb "wither" in reference to the knight's
appearance can now suggest an affinity between him and a here-

---

[27]Keats uses this phrase to describe the "powerful effect" of Milton's use of the
word "reluctant" in *Paradise Lost* IV:58–59: "reluctant flames, the sign / Of wrath
awak't" (*The Romantics on Milton: Formal Essays and Critical Asides*, ed. Joseph Anthony
Wittreich, Jr. [Cleveland: Press of Case Western Reserve University, 1970], p. 559).
    [28]Vol. H of *Oxford English Dictionary* (1971), pp. 18–19.
    [29]Earl Wasserman, *The Finer Tone: Keats' Major Poems.* (Baltimore: Johns Hopkins
University Press, 1953; reprint, 1967), pp. 67–68.

tofore incongruous circumstance. The elaboration of detail has begun to resonate with an obscure significance which promises a logical connection: the imagery of the whole reports a hollow center whose very vacancy has become significant. Everything speaks of absences, withdrawals, depletions, and abandonments.

The questioner has in effect entered the realm of latent narrative, for with the cue of this "symbolic reading," the knight produces a tale whose information confirms all these intuitions and imaginative surmises. Nonetheless, its sequence of events—far from elucidating the original mystery—only deepens its range, for here too details elude definite organization. Wasserman's study of the poem is particularly alert to "the dim sense of mystery and incompleteness" Keats's artistry arouses in us, along with the way certain "overtones" in the "affective and image-making energies of the poem" "drive the mind to ask questions of conceptual intent. What, one wonders, is the larger meaning couched in the absence of song? why a knight-at-arms and an elfin grot? and what are the significances of the cold hill side and the pale warriors?" (p. 65). Like the Marginal Editor of the Mariner's "Rime," Wasserman means to "penetrate [this] mystery" (p. 65), and he thinks he has the answer: La Belle Dame "is the ideal" that entices mortal man "towards heaven's bourne," but which must elude permanent possession in this world (pp. 74–77). Other readers surmise different causes and propose "Circe" as a more accurate key to interpretation.[30]

Yet the knight's tale yields no certain logic either way, for like his questioner, he too is in struggle with indeterminate appearances. "She look'd at me as she did love," he reports, with a syntax that hovers between a confidently durational sense of "as" as "while" and that of less confident conjecture, "as if." His subsequent assertion, "And sure in language strange she said— / I love thee true," bears no more certainty than the Mariner's hopefully proffered "Sure my kind saint took pity on me." In both cases the claim only accentuates the gap between the strangeness of signs and their proposed translations. La Belle Dame escapes logical explication even in retrospect— as the syntax of the knight's tale everywhere demonstrates: his nar-

---

[30]See Morris Dickstein, *Keats and His Poetry* (Chicago: The University of Chicago Press, 1971), p. 108, and, with qualification, David Perkins, *The Quest for Permanence* (Cambridge: Harvard University Press, 1959), p. 263. Most readers ascribe a central ambivalence to Keats's characterization: see Walter Jackson Bate, *John Keats* (Cambridge: Harvard University Press, 1963), pp. 478–81; Stuart Sperry, *Keats the Poet* (Princeton: Princeton University Press, 1973), pp. 233–41; Perkins, *Quest for Permanence*, pp. 260–63; and Charles Patterson, Jr., *The Daemonic in the Poetry of John Keats* (Urbana: University of Illinois Press, 1970), pp. 141–43.

ration merely accretes from "and" to "and"—a word sounded in fact in every stanza of the ballad, more than two dozen times throughout. As in *The Thorn,* the final stanza comes to rest on the original mystery, its terms now intensified by the intervening narrative:

> And this is why I sojourn here,
>   Alone and palely loitering,
> Though the sedge is wither'd from the lake,
>   And no birds sing.

Despite the withering of lush romance into a death-pale aftermath, the cause remains unknown. The knight's summation simply echoes on a syntactic level the absences noted by the questioner. Though he frames an answer in the syntax of explanation ("And this is why . . ."), it is an answer that doesn't produce much, beyond halting present tenses left wandering between two worlds, one dead and one powerless to be *re*born. Lacking a clear antecedent, its "this" belies the stress by voice and meter: there is, finally, no "why" to solve the mystery of La Belle Dame or to dispel its lingering effects. Indeed, the knight's final, haunting repetition of his questioner's voice only magnifies the interrogative mood of the whole, whose irresolution now involves the reader too.

We should not ascribe that questioning voice simply to ballad convention, however, even if it does perform the conventional service of prompting a tale. For the very presence of this questioner on the meads is itself questionable. As in *The Thorn,* the status of the poem's conversation remains ambiguous enough to suggest two voices playing in one intelligence, instead of two dramatically distinct speakers. We note, for instance, a curiously shared attraction to the landscape of barren meads, as well as a shared song—the knight reports being spellbound by "La Belle Dame sans Merci," and the balladeer repeats the spell of that language strange in the title of his own song. Keats enhances these provocative affinities by keeping the identity of the questioner anonymous (more a voice than a character) and by withholding any punctuation that might distinguish two separate speakers.[31] There is a quality to the place and play of these voices, in other words, that implies the self-questioning motions of a divided

---

[31]David Simpson not only seconds my sense that "the second halves of each of the first two stanzas . . . could as well be parts of an answer as parts of a question or statements of context," but he goes on to wonder if "Stanza III ["I see a lily on thy brow . . ."] could be spoken by the wight to the questioner"—as if to suggest a shared and contagious condition of enthrallment (*Irony and Authority in Romantic Poetry* [Totowa, N.J.: Rowman & Littlefield, 1979], pp. 15–17).

consciousness examining its forlorn state. Even the knight's summary statement, "And I awoke and found me here," points to self-division and the need to heal it, with the location of "here" suspended between a situation in the landscape and a situation in the mind. Like *The Thorn*, Keats's lyrical ballad allows a reading of its voices as a dialogue of the mind with itself; by the end of the poem, the question that drew our attention to the knight has been utterly absorbed into his own voice. The status of the ballad's dialogue must of course remain part of its mystery—neither clearly an internal colloquy nor a conversation between distinct *dramatis personae*. But the ambiguity is suggestive, for it points toward the rhetorical play of the odes, which, as many readers remark, is one of internal dialogue and debate.

V

If "La Belle Dame sans Merci" foregrounds a probing question and a perplexed reply against a set of events that haunt about the shape of present speech, "Ode on a Grecian Urn" heightens that drama of interpretation. Instead of a narrative organization of tale, tale-teller, and listener (or reader), Keats concentrates the action of the poem on the motions of a single lyric intelligence engaged with an image: a tableau on an urn, which like "the spot" in *The Thorn* or the appearance of the knight on the meads seems to signify something beyond itself, but for which there is no "legend" forthcoming, problematic or not. Keats's field of action is that of a poet's mind beckoned to interpretation, and the drama he presents concerns the increasingly self-conscious attempts of that mind to describe the significance of the object before it.

Like "La Belle Dame," the Ode begins with a greeting that suggests there is a story to be told, a meaning to be expressed:

> Thou still unravish'd bride of quietness,
>   Thou foster-child of silence and slow time,
> Sylvan historian, who canst thus express
>   A flowery tale more sweetly than our rhyme.

All the vocatives—an "unravish'd bride," a "foster-child," a silent tale-teller—suggest an unfinished circumstance—or from a rhetorical point of view, information on the verge of expression. Keats brilliantly exploits that implication by following these invocations with a series of questions, the syntactic equivalent of these figures of provocative incompletion:

> What leaf-fring'd legend haunts about thy shape
> Of deities or mortals, or of both,
>   In Tempe or the dales of Arcady?
> What men or gods are these? What maidens loth?
> What mad pursuit? What struggle to escape?
> What pipes and timbrels? What wild ecstasy?

If the speaker surmises the urn as a silent Grecian "historian," the questioning of his "rhyme" provides a particularly cooperative voice, for *historia* is the Grecian method of learning by inquiry. Yet the attempt to double the historians on this occasion produces an ironic counterplay in the language of poetic inquiry. Far from recovering the mysterious legend presumably harbored by this "Sylvan historian," the speaker's rhyme doubles back on itself to mirror his own perplexities: he barely launches his greeting before it branches into multiple "or"s, a kind of "wild ecstasy" of syntax that diagrams his "mad pursuit" of his own "maiden loth"—the unravished "what" that might supply the absent meaning of the images he riddles.[32] As Keats's speaker pursues the significance of his object, Keats's rhyme mirrors the course of that pursuit.

Keats's Ode continues to elaborate this double plot, presenting a speaker in pursuit of interpretation in rhyme that expresses, primarily, the ardor of the pursuer. If, however, Keats's readers are inclined to exempt themselves from this mirror-play, they have unwittingly played into an even more subtle irony. For over the course of the Ode, Keats turns the behavior of his rhyme into a dilemma for the reader, fully analogous to the speaker's dilemma of interpretation before the urn. By the conclusion of the Ode, in fact, the reader may have the uneasy feeling that not only have these dilemmas converged, they may even have reversed, for Keats's speaker abandons us with an ambiguously toned "that is all" just before becoming as silent as the urn itself.

The dovetailing of the two dilemmas of interpretation—the speaker's of the urn and the reader's of the rhyme—begins as soon as the speaker stops questioning to muse on the freedom of the urn from any finite significance. If no "legend" can be read into the silent tableau, it may be because "Heard melodies are sweet, but

---

[32]In *Milton's Poetry of Choice and Its Romantic Heirs* (Ithaca: Cornell University Press, 1973), Leslie Brisman foregrounds Keats's "or"s against Milton's. Where Milton uses the word to call for an "act of choice" that will "exclud[e] certain alternatives in affirming others" (p. 12), Brisman notes that the "or"s in Keats's "Ode" produce a "blurring" of alternatives rather than any opportunity for clear choice (p. 94).

those unheard / Are sweeter." With this new premise, the absent "legend" finds a productive counterpart in "unheard" melodies, those "ditties of no tone" played "Not to the sensual ear, but, more endear'd . . . to the spirit." The language of Keats's poetry intensifies that paradox with a play of visual repetitions and half-heard echoes. The word "ear," for instance, reemerges enfolded in "endear'd," as if that repetition were both a visual and auditory figure for the inner audience to which it refers. Furthermore, the sound (as well as the spelling) of "endear'd" resonates as "end ear'd," as if to signify audience beyond the bourn of "the sensual ear"—"just below the threshold of normal sound," as Cleanth Brooks puts it.[33] The slant and sight rhyme of "endear'd" with "unheard" adds a further elaboration to the visual and auditory design of rhyme. As readers, we begin to attend to information that haunts about the shape of rhyme, as well as the information it expresses through the logic of paradox. Language itself becomes a provocative figure of interpretation.

Yet that very elaboration of linguistic surface further perplexes these "ditties of no tone," for the speaker has a tone, or rather tones, that correspond ambivalently to the absences he notes:

> Fair youth, beneath the trees, thou canst not leave
> Thy song, nor ever can those trees be bare;
> Bold lover, never, never canst thou kiss,
> Though winning near the goal   yet, do not grieve;
> She cannot fade, though thou hast not thy bliss,
> For ever wilt thou love, and she be fair!

Any effort to evaluate the syntax of these judgments is thoroughly involved with the speaker's own perplexity before the arrested figures he contemplates. On the one hand, "Fair youth" and "Bold lover" present ideal images of mortals whose special stasis insulates them from the normal attritions of human passion and the vagaries of human inspiration; "the negation of these verbs," Earl Wasserman insists, "creates an infinity of mutable or chronological time."[34] But the dependency of surmise on such negatives may be decreative as well, for the tone of the whole is poised between emphatic celebration and rueful irony: "do not grieve; / She cannot fade." The initially bold assurance of "therefore, ye soft pipes, play on" succumbs

---

[33]Cleanth Brooks, "Keats's Sylvan Historian," in *The Well-Wrought Urn* (New York: Harcourt, Brace, 1947), p. 157.
[34]Wasserman, *The Finer Tone*, p. 34.

to the wavering balance of "Though . . . yet . . . though," while the expansive potential of figures seemingly poised on the verge of action yields figures trapped in an eternity of postponements.[35]

The third stanza heightens these tensions of interpretation, both for the speaker and for us, not with syntactic equivocation this time, but with a univocal insistence on gradations of happiness, where the very repetition of positive value exposes the urgency with which it is being declared:

> Ah, happy, happy boughs! that cannot shed
>   Your leaves, nor ever bid the spring adieu;
> And, happy melodist, unwearied,
>   For ever piping songs for ever new;
> More happy love! more happy, happy love!
>   For ever warm and still to be enjoy'd . . .

Like the repetitions of Wordsworth's Sea Captain in *The Thorn,* here too "words" verge on becoming mere "things" of passionate speech, rather than "symbols." They render a linguistic event that like the branching syntax of stanza 1 or the seesawing sentences of stanza 2 aligns the reader of Keats's "rhyme" ever more sharply with the interpretive dilemma of the beholder before the urn.[36]

This third stanza concludes with a particularly intense convergence of situation and syntax that invariably trips Keats's readers:

> For ever panting, and for ever young;
> All breathing human passion far above,
>   That leaves a heart high-sorrowful and cloy'd,
>   A burning forehead, and a parching tongue.

On a first reading, "All breathing human passion far above" seems to be a summary phrase for the state of "More happy love! . . . For ever panting, and for ever young": the semicolon after "young"

---

[35]For a fuller discussion of these ambivalent motions, see Perkins, *Quest for Permanence,* pp. 236–40.

[36]Readers' sharply contrasting responses to stanza 3 are a telling effect. Wasserman finds the repetitions show how fully Keats has entered into "the dynamically static existence" he contemplates, "participat[ing] in [its] sensations and experiences" (*Finer Tone,* p. 30; cf. p. 24). Brooks is uncomfortable enough with the "tone" of this stanza, but makes a case for it based on "the increased stress on the paradoxical element" of its imagery (p. 158). Perkins, too, finds the tone jarring, but also makes a case by suggesting that Keats is deliberately commenting on the "falseness" of the vision: "It is the obvious sentimentality of directly assigning things a greater value than they merit. It is an attempt to assert and defend a wish in contradiction to fact" (p. 238).

perhaps marks a pause analogous to a comma, like the semicolons after "adieu" and "new" in the same stanza,[37] while, conversely, the comma after "above" temporarily halts our reading in this field of happy surmise. Moreover, the stanza's syntax encourages us to feel that there is no problem in reading "breathing" as a continuation of those activities that the speaker has also described in present participles, "piping" and "panting"—activities that in fact involve kinds of "breathing." Wasserman puts the case this way: the line "is the syntactical analogue" of a visionary ideal where "breathing human passion" exists in a state "far above," fusing "mortal and immortal, the temporal and the atemporal."[38] We may even be inclined to read "All" as an inclusive noun for the melodist and the lovers, and "breathing" as a verb whose direct object is "human passion."

The comma keeps us reading, however, and as we do, we reject this last syntactic possibility. More important, we find that "far above" is not a place but a value judgment that separates "All breathing human passion" from the conditions of the "happy love" we have been imagining. The value of "breathing" does perplex that judgment with information that will emerge more fully in stanza 5's "Cold Pastoral!"—an obverse evaluation of the same condition. But at this point, "breathing" is realigned only with the "sorrowful" conditions of the immediately ensuing participles, "burning" and "parching," its situation distilled utterly from the possibility of mystical convergence with "for ever panting and for ever young."

What is striking about this line, and the stanza as a whole, is the "phenomenology of reading" it produces.[39] The teetering syntax of "All breathing human passion far above"—first promoting, then subverting, a coordination between the "happy love" on the urn and the highest promise of "human passion"—becomes significant not only for what it would describe, but for the way it behaves. Just as the urn's art resists decisive interpretation, so that one line entangles nearly every reader who has studied Keats's Ode.[40] The question of

---

[37]Some manuscripts have a comma rather than a semicolon after "young." See Robert Gittings, *The Odes of Keats and Their Earliest Known Manuscripts in Facsimile* (Kent, O.: Kent State University Press, 1970), pp. 46–47. There is no holograph, but Gittings supplies George Keats's copy, which has the comma, as does Charles Brown's copy.

[38]Wasserman, *Finer Tone*, p. 40.

[39]Wolfgang Iser ponders the dynamics and theoretical implications of "the actions involved in responding to [a] text" in "The Reading Process: A Phenomenological Approach," *New Literary History* 3 (1972):278–99.

[40]Wasserman wrestles bravely with the syntax, first admiring the way it seems "nicely calculated to express the fusion of the human and the superhuman," but then thinking that its disintegration "into a mere opposition" expresses "a certain degree of bewilderment" on Keats's part. He refuses to think Keats has deliberately "created

narrative legend ("What men or gods are these?") moves, in this stanza, into a question of grammar and syntax: "What nouns or verbs are these?" Ambiguity is now the common property of urn and rhyme, and the dilemma of interpretation, the common situation of Keats's speaker and Keats's reader.

The return of questions in stanza 4 can be only an ironic event after these doublings of dubious surmise. They seem deliberately calculated to demonstrate the futility of certain interpretation:

> Who are these coming to the sacrifice?
> To what green altar, O mysterious priest,
> Lead'st thou that heifer lowing at the skies,
> And all her silken flanks with garlands drest?

This object of address is not the potentially intelligent "Sylvan historian" of stanza 1 but a "mysterious priest," whose knowledge (like his identity) is beyond possible knowing. Nor is there any possibility of discerning a historical context for this "sacrifice": origin and termination can be a matter of surmise only:

> What little town by river or sea shore,
> Or mountain-built with peaceful citadel,
> Is emptied of this folk, this pious morn?

The question of "what little town" echoes the earlier inquiry for "what leaf-fring'd legend," but here the configuration of "or"s concerns one of those "Nothings" that have existence only in the "ardent pursuit" of imagination (I:243). The circumstance is without a representation and, significantly, without a voice:

> And, little town, thy streets for evermore
> Will silent be; and not a soul to tell
> Why thou art desolate, can e'er return.

The connective "And" hardly breaks the flow of the question, for it produces a response that extends interrogative motion into an undoing of its very premises. In stanza 1, the urn as a "bride of quietness" or a "foster-child of silence" suggested a haunting indeter-

---

the confusion" and argues that it is more likely that the instability of the fusion he has envisioned "has bewildered him in the midst of his ecstasy and forced him into a direction that he did not intend or expect" (pp. 40–41). For other perplexed commentaries, see Dickstein, *Keats and His Poetry*, p. 225; Bate; *Keats*, p. 514; Brooks, "Keats's Sylvan Historian," p. 159.

minacy, while the paradox of "unheard melodies" made that "silence" an elusive spiritual extension of sound. Stanza 4 reduces that potential to mere emptiness. Like the landscape in "La Belle Dame" where "no birds sing," here, too, is a tableau of absence: there is finally no "historian," "not a soul to tell / Why," and the voice of bold inquiry, eager to ravish the urn for its "what" and "why," finds itself ironically partnered to her silence. The final stanza completes this movement: all questions are absorbed by the object that had excited them, and the urn relapses to a mere "Attic shape"—the "attitude" of "silent form" that signals the silencing of inquiry.

Yet even as Keats's speaker appears to concede this consequence, Keats's rhyme redeems language by exploiting its multiplicity of interpretive signals. For the profusion of puns and shades of signification that play through the ode's final stanza at once speak of and enact the indeterminacy the ode has dramatized throughout.[41] If the urn's art withholds its spectral legend, flattening illusory possibility to a merely opaque "Fair attitude! with brede / Of marble men and maidens overwrought," Keats takes advantage of the "heard melodies" of poetry to multiply the dimensions of its activity. "Brede," for instance, describes the quality of the urn's figured design, but its punning against "breed" and ironic half-echoes of "bride" and "breathe" subtly reject the "human passion" the speaker had projected onto the urn's fair attitudes. Indeed, "Fair attitude" refers both to the loveliness of the urn's art and to the fairness, or justice, of its silent seeming. "Overwrought" involves similar shadings, for while it refers to the lapidary quality of the urn's design, it also criticizes an eternity where one may never, never kiss. And as a pun on over-"raught" (an archaic or Spenserian version of "reached"),[42] it gently mocks the speaker's previous overreaching to idealize the urn's tableau, as well as implicates his view of the overwrought figures before him with his own overwrought postures of interpretation—that voice given to chanting, "Ah, happy, happy boughs! . . . More happy love! more happy, happy love!" "I found my Brain so overwrought that I had neither Rhyme nor reason in it—so was obliged to give up," Keats reports of one mood of composition in the midst of *Endymion* (I:146).

The transition from the "overwrought" brain to "giving up" is in

---

[41]See Kenneth Burke, "Symbolic Action in a Poem by Keats," *Accent* (1943); reprinted in *Perspectives by Incongruity* (Bloomington: Indiana University Press, 1964), pp. 123–41.
[42]See *Endymion* 2:282 ("he has raught / The goal of consciousness") and 3:856 for instances of this usage.

fact the consequence Keats's final stanza enacts. The resistance of both urn and rhyme to any single pattern of significance is again underscored with the utterance, "Thou, silent form, dost tease us out of thought / As doth eternity: Cold Pastoral!" "Cold Pastoral!" is, of course, the speaker's decisive revision of his previous surmise, "For ever warm": the epithet coolly extinguishes the ardor of that pursuit. More important, however, is the way this phrase not only juxtaposes the beholder's conflicting responses ("Cold" marble, "Pastoral" illusion), but translates that perplexity of signification into a compelling linguistic figure. "Cold Pastoral!" is no reconciliation but rather a tensed collation of opposites: a dynamic, because, unresolvable, oxymoron. The disjunctive effect of reading Coleridge's Marginal Gloss against his Mariner's "Rime" is something Keats's "Cold Pastoral" concentrates into a single phrase. It is Coleridge in fact who provides the most cogent Romantic argument for the imaginative value of oxymorons. To defend Shakespeare's attraction to the figure, he urges allowance for the way oxymoron reveals and perpetuates that

> effort of the mind, when it would describe what it cannot satisfy itself with the description of, to reconcile opposites and qualify contradictions, leaving a middle state of mind more strictly appropriate to the imagination than any other, when it is, as it were, hovering between images. As soon as it is fixed on one image, it becomes understanding; but while it is unfixed and wavering between them, attaching itself permanently to none, it is imagination. . . . a strong working of the mind, still offering what is still repelled, and again creating what is again rejected.[43]

Not only is this a provocative countertext to Coleridge's favored poetics of reconciliation, but it is the best reading of "Cold Pastoral" ever not written about the phrase, for it speaks to the way the voice of judgment Keats produces in stanza 5 keeps the mind of the reader working hard in a dialectic of constructions and deconstructions. However teasingly silent this "Sylvan historian" remains about its informing "legend," it becomes, through the very provocation of its silence, the historian of urn-readers and urn-reading, a historian of the speaker's activity and our own. The urn befriends its beholders the way Keats's rhyme does—by encouraging their imaginative activity. We come to value its artistry not so much by what it yields to

[43]*Shakespearean Criticism*, ed. T. M. Raysor, 2 vols. (London: J. M. Dent, 1960), II:103–4.

thought as by what it does to thought—provoking questions and refusing to confirm any sure points and resting places for our reasonings.

The voice of the urn, were one to imagine it, is a perfect contrast to the voice that declares "Cold Pastoral!": "Beauty is truth, truth beauty" is such a piece of self-enclosed harmony that it merits separation by quotation marks from the rest of the rhyme.[44] Its status is another matter, however. "Beauty is truth, truth beauty" emerges in part as the final, desperate surmise of a beholder not happy with an absent legend, nor with being so teased out of thought, and determined to tease the silent form into oracular utterance. And oracular utterance it seems—a rich, cryptic piece of *sententiae antiquae*. Yet despite the grace of its neatly balanced syntax, its language proves for some a cold comfort; for the ambiguous situation of this voice compromises its high philosophical tone, bringing a special kind of "woe" to "generations" of readers expecting something more accessible to interpretation.[45] The phrase all but requires another

[44]There is of course a well-known controversy over the punctuation of the last two lines of the ode, for which there is no holograph manuscript. Stillinger follows the text of *Lamia, Isabella, the Eve of St. Agnes and Other Poems* (1820), which puts only "Beauty is truth, truth beauty" in quotation marks, and he summarizes his reasons for doing so in Appendix III of *The Hoodwinking of Madeline and Other Essays on Keats's Poems* (Urbana: University of Illinois Press, 1971), "Who Says What to Whom at the End of *Ode on a Grecian Urn?*" (pp. 169–71). Other versions omit the quotation marks, to yield the possibility that the urn "say'st" the whole of the last two lines. Leo Spitzer suggests that the variations themselves ought to be taken as evidence of "hesitations in the poet in regard to the relationship of the aphorism to the rest of the legend" ("The 'Ode on a Grecian Urn,': or Content vs. Metagrammar," *Comparative Literature* 7 [1955]:203–25). The second section of Stillinger's Appendix (pp. 171–73) summarizes critical discussion (before 1968) on the question posed in its title. Whatever we include in the voice of the urn, however, it is still an imagined utterance, "an act of ventriloquism," in Perkins' phrase (p. 242), with the tonal separation of the aphorism explicit in the 1820 printing and implicit otherwise. The commentary ("That is all . . ."), whether it issues directly from the speaker or indirectly though the act of "ventriloquism," is sufficiently ambiguous in tone to be included in the problem of cryptic utterance. Again, the ambiguity is significant in itself.

[45]T. S. Eliot famously declared this "statement of equivalence" to be "meaningless," a "serious blemish on a beautiful poem" ("Note" to "Dante," in *Selected Essays, 1917–1932* [New York: Harcourt, Brace, 1932], p. 231). Brooks struggles with Eliot's dismissal, making a case for the utterance as "a consciously riddling paradox," "in character" with the "paradoxes" that have expressed the urn throughout (p. 154); Burke enhances the case for meaningful ambiguity by associating the cryptic effect of the aphorism with the quality of oracular utterance (p. 134); Barbara Herrnstein Smith, too, finds the aphorism an "oracular motto," but bluntly declares that its relation to the ode's structure has to be judged as a "tenuous and perhaps spurious" one, evidence for her, in fact, of one of poetry's "Failures of Closure," namely Keats's failure to trust his reader's ability to be satisfied "with something far less authoritatively conclusive" (*Poetic Closure: A Study of How Poems End* [Chicago: University of Chicago Press, 1968], p. 232). Closest to my own view, though in a context of

"legend" to help us know what it means. Indeed, the words "Beauty" and "truth" seem so inscrutable as an abstract and brief chronicle of the urn's art that they sound its "ditties of no tone" with a vengeance. As with the marble brede of figures on the urn's surface, one may project whatever significance onto the aphorism one wishes; but as with those figures, this phrase contracts to mere opacity if its mystery is too irritably teased.

The statement "Beauty is truth, truth beauty" is a lofty answer that in effect plays ironically against the rhetoric of answering, for it simultaneously invites and repels the possibility of understanding, shaping a piece of "charactered language" that is partly like the "hieroglyphics" Keats celebrates in Kean's "music of elocution"[46] and partly like the "{hie}rogueglyphics in Moor's almanack" (II:247). The two poles of meaning, "Beauty" and "truth," slide across their marker of equivalence, "is," reverse positions at the comma, and so elude syntactic priority that, despite the elegant symmetry of statement, its logic can only be wondered at, like the urn itself. Urn and aphorism together go round and round, each serenely self-enclosed, endlessly circular, resonating with mysterious promise, but "still unravish'd" at last.

The only consequence is a further mockery of the questioner: "— that is all / Ye know on earth, and all ye need to know." This statement, too, has the sound of stable wisdom, but the more one teases it, the more one discovers a tone that unsettles its terms of resolution. That "all" hints at sufficiency, even at mysterious plenitude, and yet it has a ring of dismissal, as if parodying anyone's effort to "know" "all." The irony against interpretation is as wry as Robert Frost's couplet: "We dance round in a ring and suppose, / But the Secret sits in the middle and knows."[47] For Keats, however, there may be no "Secret"—only the effect of those dancing round and supposing. Whether the speaker imagines "that is all" as the urn's comment on its aphorism, or himself tells us this, the opacity of the

---

discussion quite different, is Dickstein's proposal that "Keats means the sweeping generality of the urn's statement to be self-limiting, a piece of dramatic irony" (p. 228, n. 32). Stuart Sperry offers the fullest and most perceptive analysis of the "problems of interpretation" posed by these lines, arguing that such problems are "a legitimate part of the poem's larger aesthetic and metaphysical effect" (*Keats*, pp. 271–78).

[46]"On Edmund Kean as a Shakespearean Actor" (originally published as "Mr. Kean" in *The Champion*, December 21, 1817), in *The Poetical Works and Other Writings of John Keats*, ed. H. Buxton Forman, rev. Maurice Buxton Forman, 8 vols. (New York: Scribner's, 1939), 5:229.

[47]*The Poetry of Robert Frost*, ed. Edward Connery Lathem (New York: Holt, Rinehart & Winston, 1969), p. 362.

pronoun "that" and the uncertain tone of the whole still leave us wanting to know "*what* is all?" Keats takes us only this far, then to relinquish us to an utterance that, like the contemplation of eternity, absorbs inquiry into silent thought. Here, a negotiation with "uncertainties, Mysteries, doubts" is not merely an act of mind we observe in another (be it Mariner, Marginal Editor, Sea Captain, knight, or poet), but one that the play of Keats's language has produced and sustained in the reader's own experience.

2 /

The Ring of Gyges and the
Coat of Darkness: Reading
Rousseau with Wordsworth

CYNTHIA CHASE

I

At the end of the *Sixième Promenade*, Rousseau closes a complaint about his inability to appear to his contemporaries as he really
is with a fantasy of possessing the power of invisibility:

> If I had been invisible and powerful like God, I should have been good
> and beneficent like him.

> If I had possessed the ring of Gyges, it would have made me indepen-
> dent of men and made them dependent on me. I have often wondered,
> in my castles in the air, how I should have used this ring, for in such a
> case power must indeed be closely followed by the temptation to abuse
> it. Able to satisfy my desires, capable of doing anything without being
> deceived by anyone, what might I have desired at all consistently? One
> thing only: to see every heart contented.

> Always impartially just and unfalteringly good, I should have guarded
> myself equally against blind mistrust and implacable hate, because
> seeing men as they are and reading their inmost thoughts without
> difficulty, I should have found few who were likeable enough to de-
> serve my full affection and few who were odious enough to deserve my
> hate, and also because their very wickedness would have inclined me to
> pity them out of the sure knowledge of the harm they do themselves in
> seeking to harm others.[1]

[1]Jean-Jacques Rousseau, *Les Rêveries du promeneur solitaire, in Oeuvres complètes*, vol.
1: *Les Confessions, autres textes autobiographiques*, ed. Bernard Gagnebin and Marcel
Raymond (Paris: Gallimard, 1962), pp. 1057–58. All page references to the *Rêveries*
and the *Confessions* are to this edition. For translation of the former I have used,
substantially modified, *Reveries of the Solitary Walker*, trans. Peter France (New York:
Penguin, 1979).

Rousseau conceives this fantasy out of the sense of his intolerable dilemma, that "men insist on seeing me as entirely other than I am":

> As for me, let them see me if they can, so much the better; but this is beyond them, instead of me they will never see anyone but the Jean-Jacques they have created and fashioned for themselves so that they can hate me to their heart's content.[2]

Inclined to "follow blindly my penchant for doing good," Rousseau has become convinced that "the greatest concern of those who control my fate having been to keep me entirely surrounded by false and deceptive appearance, any motive for virtuous behaviour is never more than a lure to draw me into the trap where they want to entwine me."[3] The effects of his actions are concealed from him and cut off from his good intention. This dilemma inspires a fantasy in which the inability to see or be seen gets reimagined as the ability to see and act unseen. Instead of "blindly" following his penchant for doing good, Rousseau would now be capable of "seeing men as they are and easily reading at the bottom of their hearts." Blindness, which accompanied the inability to *be* seen, is converted to lucidity. Rousseau's fantasy converts a predicament into a privilege. The invisibility of the link between the motive force and the effects of his actions, first bewailed as the powerlessness to be known for what he is (good), gets reimagined as a form of power.[4]

The power of invisibility, produced by a wishful reversal, appears in a passage of Wordsworth's *Prelude* that seems to differ in nearly every way from Rousseau's *Sixième Promenade*, a passage to which we are guided by the most superficial resemblance: Wordsworth refers to a "coat of darkness" operating like the ring of Gyges, making the wearer invisible. He is describing a performance of "Jack the Giant-Killer" at Sadler's Wells.

---

[2]Rousseau, *Rêveries*, p. 1059.

[3]Ibid., p. 1051.

[4]The immediate context of Rousseau's reference to a ring of Gyges—the question of the character of his actions were he to be protected by the power of invisibility—closely resembles the context in which Glaucon relates the tale of "the ancestor of Gyges, the Lydian" in Book II of *The Republic*. As part of his argument that men act justly only when their power to act unjustly in their own interest is restrained, Glaucon recalls that the possessor of the magic ring used his power to commit adultery with the king's wife, kill the king, and become the new ruler. Rousseau reappropriates the reference to the ring in an argument that is the inverse of Glaucon's: a man (or Rousseau himself, at any rate) acts unjustly only when his power to act is restrained. Rousseau's claim is made all the more emphatic by performing this inversion of the traditional moral of the story. At the end of the passage, however, Rousseau reintroduces the suspicion that the gift of invisibility must induce some kind of disaster.

> Nor was it mean delight
> To watch crude Nature work in untaught minds;
> To note the laws and progress of belief;
> Though obstinate on this way, yet on that
> How willingly we travel, and how far!
> To have, for instance, brought upon the scene
> The champion, Jack the Giant-killer: Lo!
> He dons his coat of darkness; on the stage
> Walks, and achieves his wonders, from the eye
> Of living Mortal covert, 'as the moon
> Hid in her vacant interlunar cave.'
> Delusion bold! and faith must needs be coy;
> How is it wrought? His garb is black, the word
> 'Invisible' flames forth upon his chest.[5]

Wordsworth's tone is satirical, Rousseau's confessional; Rousseau evokes his own lasting dilemma, while Wordsworth apparently describes a momentary distraction; Rousseau's text is claustrophobically self-enclosed, while Wordsworth's giddily appropriates a line from Milton. This line of Milton, however, reveals that the same reversal that stands out in Rousseau's *Promenade* also stands behind this passage of Wordsworth's. For the quoted line comes from Samson's lament for his blindness at the opening of *Samson Agonistes*, "The sun to me is dark . . . ," in which he compares the sun's darkness to the darkness of the waned moon, "Hid in her vacant interlunar cave." Wordsworth's appropriation systematically reverses the context of the line he quotes from Samson. Instead of presenting a captive unable to appear to himself or his contemporaries as what he is (a hero of the Lord), the new context in *The Prelude* summons up an adventurer able to appear invisible and therefore able to be a hero. Instead of a giant *killer* (Samson's original and final identity), the new context refers to a "giant-killer." And like Rousseau's fantasy of possessing the ring of Gyges, Wordsworth's description of Jack's "coat of darkness" converts a prior account of blindness and powerlessness to a depiction of omnipotent invisibility. What can be at issue in the peculiar conjunction of wish fulfillment and invisibility presented by these passages from the *Promenades* and the *Prelude?* If Wordsworth's quotation of Milton alerts us to read his lines as more than a good-tempered smirk at a

---

[5]William Wordsworth, *The Prelude* (1850), in *The Prelude: 1799, 1805, 1850,* ed. Jonathan Wordsworth, M. H. Abrams, and Stephen Gill (New York: Norton, 1980), VII, 279–87.

convention of popular theater, is there any clue that we should read Rousseau's lines as other than intemperate self-justification and wishfulness?

Rousseau's *rêverie* has an argument, in fact, about the relationship between the motives and the effects of actions. He does not simply assert their discontinuity; he laments it. It is easy, and in some measure unavoidable, to practice a psychological reading of the *Promenades,* focused on the confessional nature of Rousseau's discourse. It is also possible to focus on his manifest argument about intentions and conventions. The *Sixième Promenade* appears to offer us an account of natural and naturally good motives caught in the trammels of culturally determined and malevolent interpretations and effects. One could suppose one recognized here as in other more patently philosophical, nonautobiographical writings (such as the First and Second Discourses) a story about nature obscured and degraded by the elaborations of culture. These two ways of reading (psychological and "philosophical") would not have to contradict one another, and they might meet in an account of Rousseau's "ethics of intention." Neither approach, however, enables us to read much in Rousseau's lingering imagination of the power of invisibility. What is at stake in Rousseau's conceiving a situation in which the link between the motive force and the effect of an action is invisible?

A long philosophical tradition, which achieved its classic formulation in Kant's *Critique of Judgement,* identifies the absence of interest or motive as the condition of the existence of an aesthetic object. We might read Rousseau's imagined "invisibility" in this way: as the condition of his writing.

Written marks, to the extent that they are writing, are in some sense invisible—to be read, not seen. We can construe another hint to understand the fantasy of invisibility in this way if we compare Rousseau's description of his motivation in the *Sixième Promenade* and in the *Quatrième.* In the *Sixième Promenade* Rousseau identifies the "penchant for doing good," the wish to make others happy, as his fundamental, primary motivation. In the *Quatrième Promenade,* Rousseau identifies the same "primary and irresistible impulse of [my] temperament" in different terms: as the drive to produce an utterance he explicitly identifies as "fiction." In this context Rousseau's concern is to distinguish fiction from lies: "to lie without profit or prejudice to oneself or others," or to invent "an idle fact, indifferent in all respects," would mean to escape the opprobrium of lying. It may seem perverse to identify Rousseau's fantasy of omnipotent altruism in the *Sixième Promenade* with this scathing description of not-lying in the *Quatrième*, in order to call them both "fiction." Yet the two *Promenades* do move among the same concerns: at issue in them both are truth and falsehood, statement and interpretation, and guilt and innocence; epistemological and ethical issues are combined. More tellingly, both situations (invisibility and not-lying) are ascribed the same intentional status with regard to motive. Rousseau describes how he is driven to talk, to produce nontruths, by a "mechanical effect" quite distinct from the motive to influence or deceive, simply under the pressure of the social situation of conversation, which comes to compound a "primary and irresistible impulse." Thus the originary motivation, itself motiveless, which Rousseau in the *Sixième Promenade* calls his "penchant for doing good," is identified in the *Quatrième* as the impulse to produce fictions.

We will have occasion later to notice an odd similarity in the turn of the argument of the two *Promenades*. At present we are committed to a working hypothesis: that Rousseau's imagination of invisibility is a conception of the condition of his own writing as fiction.

The wishfulness of Rousseau's fantasy does not preclude its interpretive function. We can hazard an account of the significance of the transformation worked by the ring of Gyges before determining the status of that transformation. Let us speculate, then, that in reimagining his predicament as a writer as possession of the ring of Gyges, Rousseau's *rêverie* suggests that the incomprehensibility of the mode of intention animating his writing (his inability to be seen as he is) can be imagined as a radical abstraction of intention (such as characterizes fiction) lending that writing a unique productive and interpretive power. If our reading of the *Sixième Promenade* can proceed along these lines—if the intentional mode of Rousseau's writing is indeed at issue—it will be all the more important, finally, to interpret the nature of the wishfulness involved in his evocation of the ring of Gyges.

The *Sixième Promenade* is about Rousseau's relation to others in the world, which is essentially determined by his status as a writer. Let us suppose, then, that Rousseau is writing about his relation to his readers. This approach may prove more productive than those that first seemed most plausible (attending to the psychological and "philosophical" statements of the text), for it enables us to identify the stakes of Rousseau's fantasy of invisibility. That fantasy has to do with the power to read. Rousseau imagines himself "reading the depths of [men's] hearts" ("lisant au fond des coeurs").

The ability to read is quite literally part of Wordsworth's topic in his lines on the performance at Sadler's Wells. The story of Jack the Giant-Killer can be performed because the audience can read, and willingly accepts an actor's marking with the word "invisible" as a real state of invisibility.

While ethical judgments are conspicuous in Rousseau's *Promenade,* in the *Prelude* passage the implications of the acts of reading and writing as an ethical issue must be inferred from shifts of tone and from the gesture represented by citation. Wordsworth's citation changes the associations of Milton's phrase from failure to success and displaces it from a context of tragic seriousness to one of satire. He stresses the actor's facility in representing the magical power of invisibility with the simplest stage device, a cloak with a labeling word, and he flaunts his own facility in recycling the language of Milton—not only the phrase from *Samson Agonistes* but also the "darkness visible" of *Paradise Lost.* The stage at Sadler's Wells is the scene, then, of a travesty. (That travesty situates the pantomime among the other "London" spectacles, which are all presented as distorted or degraded forms of imaginative energy.) The very effectiveness of the stage prop "coat of darkness"—and the very ease of Wordsworth's deployment of Milton's line—are rather disturbing.

This turns out to be the case for the ring of Gyges, too. Although Rousseau initially pictures the effects of his magical power as wholly good, he ends by qualifying and reversing that judgment:

> There is only one point on which the ability to go everywhere unobserved might have made me seek temptations that I should have found it hard to resist, and once I had strayed into these aberrant ways, where might they not have led me? It would be showing great ignorance of human nature and myself to flatter myself that such easy opportunities [*facilités*] would not have seduced me or that reason would have halted me on this downward path. I could be sure of myself in every other respect, but this would be my ruin. The man whose power sets him above humanity must himself be above all human weaknesses, or this excess of power will only serve to sink him lower than others, and lower than he would himself have been had he remained their equal.
>
> All things considered, I think I will do better to throw away my magic ring before it makes me do something foolish.[6]

The coyness of this passage is unpleasant. Rousseau is evidently following up a claim about the highest, freest privilege of serving the general happiness with an unstated allusion to the advantages of

[6]Rousseau, *Rêveries,* p. 1058.

invisibility for reaping private sexual benefits, requiring him to renounce his aspiration to omnipotence. The well-known story of Gyges—whose first use of his ring was to perform adultery with the queen—allows Rousseau to make us take his meaning without actually spelling it out. The Gyges legend also gives Rousseau's retraction a predictability that makes his initial presumption of altruism seem coy as well, and the entire fantasy a double self-indulgence.

The passage has to be taken as a coy allusion to sexual license, but it cannot be left at that. The break in tone with the previous paragraph does not release us from the text's implicit concern with the power of fiction. Rousseau's determined avoidance of particularizing the anticipated wrongdoing can be taken not only as false *pudeur*, but also as an injunction to read the passage in the abstract terms he provides: "*facilités*" and the inducement to "seek temptations." Invisibility, then, turns out to entail the danger of degradation, and both Wordsworth and Rousseau imagine a certain facility as a threat associated with the power of invisibility. Wordsworth shows this facility distinctive of effects achieved by being read—by using a mere written word to produce belief and construct imaginary events; Rousseau too describes a magical facility of reading ("easily reading the depths of their hearts"). What can it possibly mean that both Wordsworth and Rousseau associate the power of reading with an effect of travesty or degradation? This is the enigma that will animate our reading of Wordsworth's lines on Jack the Giant-Killer and Rousseau's *Sixième Promenade*.

II

The predicament evoked by Rousseau in the *Sixième Promenade* is a state of radical discrepancy between intentions and meanings. Rousseau's desire to exercise generosity, for example, cannot be fulfilled, for the very act of satisfying another's desire retroactively establishes an implicit contract according to which one's action becomes simply the fulfillment of an obligation: "But from these first acts of charity performed with an overflowing heart arose chains of successive obligations which I had not foreseen and which it was now impossible to shake off. My first favours were in the eyes of those who received them no more than an earnest of those that were still to come."[7] Rousseau complains that every intention promptly becomes entangled in a web of conventional meanings

[7]Ibid., pp. 1051–52.

alien to it, since an intended meaning must take the form of an action that stands as a sign, deriving its signification not from an intention but from the other signs that form its context.

Avoidance of such a subversion of his intention is the motive Rousseau claims to discover for the first action of the *Promenade*, his detour past the spot where previously he had often given alms to a lame boy. This anecdote is the warrant for the statement with which the text begins: "We have hardly a mechanical movement whose cause we cannot find in our heart, if we really knew how to look for it." This statement seems to set up a contrast and a hierarchy: there is "our heart," the realm of desires and intentions, and "mechanical movements," which take their meaning from such intentions. As the context is elaborated, however, motive and mechanism turn out to have "another and a finer connection than that of contrast."[8] The anecdote and explanation that follow reveal that the intention motivating Rousseau's "mechanical movement" is nothing other than the impulse to avoid having an intention—to avoid an intention that will be a repeated action in an established context, hence a sign not effectively invested with intention.

> This pleasure become by degrees a habit was somehow transformed into a sort of duty which I soon began to find irksome, particularly on account of the preamble I was obliged to listen to, in which he never failed to address me as Monsieur Rousseau so as to show that he knew me well, thus making it quite clear to me on the contrary that he knew no more of me than those who had taught him. From that time on I felt less inclined to go that way, and in the end I mechanically adopted the habit of making a detour when I approached this shortcut.[9]

The motive for the mechanical movement is simply the negation of motivation—the suppression or elision of the motive to do good.

Not only does the suppression of a generous motive produce a mechanical movement; acting in consistency with that motive produces the same kind of motion: Rousseau refers to his tendency "to follow blindly my penchant for doing good." This penchant, according to Rousseau, is the original motive that defines "my character and my nature." What is the content of this original motivation? It is described as a desire for "public felicity," for general happiness—

---

[8]William Wordsworth, *Essays upon Epitaphs*, in *The Prose Works of William Wordsworth*, ed. W. B. J. Owen and Jane Worthington Smyser (Oxford: Clarendon Press, 1974), II, 53.
[9]Rousseau, *Rêveries*, pp. 1050–51.

described as fundamental generosity. It is a desire to gratify others' desires, a desire for a correlation between desire and gratification and between motive and realization. It is the motive to discover desires and to make them into motives for action. What Rousseau identifies as his originary motive, then, is the motivation to postulate motives.

Such a motivation to find motives is the cause or condition of the very predicament of which Rousseau complains, the subversion of the correlation between intention and meaning. This is the paradox that promptly appears in Rousseau's account of his dilemma: it is the energy for motivating signs, the drive to ascribe motives to actions, that saturates the complex of significations which Rousseau describes as irreparably subverting his intentions. The motive to establish motives is the very condition of their ruin. The beginning of the *Sixième Promenade* thus requires a different reading than its opening sentence seems to invite. The opening, which initially appears to announce an argument in favor of motivation, claiming and hoping to find particular intentions behind the apparently automatic movements of the self, turns out rather to introduce an account of the motivation to *suppress* motivation. The opening anecdote depicts a mechanical reflex that reacts against the mechanical character of motivation itself, motivation as a mere mechanism for the production of motives. What has to be avoided, then, is precisely motivation. Rousseau arrives at this inference: "a motive for virtuous behavior is never more than a *lure* to draw me into the trap where they want to entwine me." Hence the only possible motive, for Rousseau, must be the avoidance of motivation.

This will be the motive for Rousseau's fantasy of possessing the ring of Gyges, of being "invisible," "all-powerful," and "disinterested for myself." This state is conceived to escape the double bind of motivation. It is an escape from a predicament not of bad faith but of error: what matters is not that Rousseau's *own* motivation powers the complex of significations that subverts his intentions, but rather that the meaning of his actions, when apprehended according to a conception of localized motives, must invariably be misinterpreted.[10] The *Sixième Promenade* relates that Rousseau's action—his writing—will be systematically misinterpreted so long as its

---

[10]Like Rousseau's statements about "*le coeur*," his critique of motivation concerns not just desire, in a psychological sense, but the production of meaning, generated by positing motives—or intentions—for signs. Cf. Juliet Flower MacCannell, "Nature and Self-Love: A Reinterpretation of Rousseau's 'Passion primitive,'" *PMLA* 92 (1977):890–902.

meaning is construed as the correlative of particular intentions or motives. Rousseau's writing is "motivated" in a manner invisible in such a perspective: it is motivated only with regard to motivation itself, which it may either posit or negate.

Rousseau's fantasy of possessing the ring of Gyges would then name the truth of the following predicament: inasmuch as his writing is not generated by the particular intention of a particular agent, but rather by a stance in regard to motivation in general, it is indeed—within a system conceiving meaning as intentional or motivated—action generated by an invisible agency. Rousseau's fantasy of invisibility would interpret the intentional structure of his writing, correcting the error inherent in the interpretive process that seeks to visualize the agent and motive for the production of meaning. Possession of the ring of Gyges signifies that condition of language in which no motive can be ascribed as the meaning of an utterance: it is an allegory for the state of fiction. Rousseau's imagination of being invisible is an insight into the fictional status of his own writing.

His evocation of the effects of the ring of Gyges must then be read as an account of the effects of fiction. It is an allegory recounting the consequences of the radical abstraction of intention involved in the production of a fictional text, or, which may amount to the same thing, in the reading of a text as primarily self-referential, the "vision" of a text as "invisible." Rousseau describes an access of power and lucidity: with invisibility comes the power of vision, and more particularly the power of reading ("seeing men as they are and easily reading the depths of their hearts"). Rousseau thus draws a connection between a text's fictional, self-referential status and its power to "read" other texts. Some such connection is suggested by one's own experience reading "fiction" and "criticism": it is often less productive to interpret the fictional text by means of the critical text than to do the reverse.[11] Why should this be so? Rousseau's allegory of altruism suggests that a fiction, free of the intention to impose the communication of its own particular meanings, can refer rather to its conditions of signification. These are the conditions too of the signifying strategies of other texts designed to conceal rather

[11]Paul de Man's *Blindness and Insight: Essays in the Rhetoric of Contemporary Criticism* (New York: Oxford University Press, 1971) theorizes the power of the fictional text to analyze its critical interpretations. Interpreting the critical accounts by means of the fictional text they claim to interpret is a strategy that has informed many highly productive readings, among them Shoshana Felman, "Turning the Screw of Interpretation" (*Yale French Studies* 55/56 [1977]:94–207) and "Woman and Madness: The Critical Phallacy" (*Diacritics* 5 [1975]:2–10) and Barbara Johnson, *The Critical Difference* (Baltimore: Johns Hopkins University Press, 1980).

than display their rhetorical structure, which the fictional text brings
to light. Rousseau's own writing can be shown to have this extraordinary interpretive power.[12] In what sense might fiction be, like invisibility, singularly equipped to produce "public felicity"? Fiction has
the ability to "see all hearts contented" through its power to exemplify virtually any meaning that may be wanted by another text or
reader.

It would seem that Rousseau need have no misgivings in imagining himself invisible—in identifying his writing as fictional. The text
whose status is fictional or self-referential would seem to hold a
powerful position. Yet the next paragraph goes on to describe that
position as intolerably precarious. Being invisible comes to entail,
here, something that closely resembles the power to *lire au fond des
coeurs:* the power to "seek temptations." The danger was already
inherent in the effects of invisibility as described in the first part of
the ring of Gyges fantasy, which itself reinterprets the dilemma we
have already analyzed in one version, in the opening paragraphs of
the *Promenade,* where we discovered the intrication of motivelessness
and motive. Freedom from motive, it appeared, could be the only
motivation for Rousseau; freedom from motive will itself operate as
a motive, and as a motive to posit, not just to negate, motivation. In
Rousseau's fantasy, the power to fulfill others' desires becomes a
drive to produce them—to "seek temptations." At the beginning of
the allegory, freedom from motive went along with omnipotence,
with the power to fulfill the desires, to realize the motives, of others;
now the power to realize motives becomes an impetus to look for
them. What does this mean in relation to Rousseau's writing? Freedom from motive gave Rousseau's self-referential writing the power
to "read" other texts. But that very power of reading is grounded in
a practice of motivation (an ascription of motive to the meaning of
texts) that must inevitably entail, so Rousseau concludes, the re-
motivation of his own text as well, with the lapse into error and the
loss of power that that involves—the liabilities of the first form of
"invisibility" which were Rousseau's complaint in the rest of the
Promenade.

The lucidity of the self-referential text is complete except with
regard to the figural status of lucidity itself. Lucidity as an attribute
of magical invisibility is a figure for the endemic "invisibility" of the

---

[12]*La Nouvelle Héloïse* portrays the complete sequence of interpretive moves that are
possible in reconstruing a figurative system, as Paul de Man argues in "Allegory
(Julie)," in *Allegories of Reading: Figural Language in Rousseau, Nietzsche, Rilke, and
Proust* (New Haven: Yale University Press, 1979).

text whose intentional status is indeterminate, in an indeterminate relationship to motivation. The ability to fulfill desires will have the effect not only of suppressing them but also of producing them; so the power of language (distinct from any intention) to designate meanings will produce intentions toward meaning.

Just as the idea of the invisible is part of a conception of the world as visible, so the idea of fiction, or of an unmotivated text, is solidary with a conception of writing defined by its relationship to motive— of writing motivated, always, in some way, if only by the negation of motives. What Rousseau's text shows us is not only that these conditions (motivated or unmotivated) are part of the same system but that one produces—demands—the other. The insight into the radically fictional nature of language and the error of motivating texts with intentions thus occur close together.

Rousseau's misgivings about fiction have to do with the fact that fiction above all provokes literal reading and a passage into action, as if the very vacuum of motive inevitably drew toward it a very powerful motive indeed. Rousseau describes how the interpretation of a discourse as fictional takes place at the same time as its manipulation in the service of a compelling motive. This strange occurrence characterizes the type of response produced by an action set on stage and read as fictional. The intense yet disengaged response of the spectator is associated, in Rousseau's *Lettre à d'Alembert sur les Spectacles*, with murderous slander:

> Tacitus reports that Valerius-Asiaticus, accused calumniously at the order of Messalina, who wanted to make him perish, defended himself before the emperor in a way that moved that prince extremely and drew tears from Messalina herself. She went into a neighboring room to recover herself, after she had, all the while weeping, in a whisper given notice to Vitellius not to allow the accused man to escape. At a play I never see one of those weepers in the boxes [*pleureuses de loges*] so proud of their tears without thinking of those of Messalina for that poor Valerius-Asiaticus.[13]

In the *Sixième Promenade* Rousseau describes his own stance as that of a spectator at a theatrical performance. Here he adduces as evidence of his intact moral impulses the same imaginative sympathy de-

---

[13]Rousseau, "Lettre à M. d'Alembert sur son article 'Genève' dans le septième volume de l'*Encyclopédie*, et particulièrement sur le projet d'établir un théâtre de comédie en cette ville," in *Du Contrat social et autres oeuvres politiques* (Paris: Garnier, 1962), pp. 140–41.

tached from participation that he attributes to the *"pleureuses de loges"*:

> Even my indifference to them only concerns their relations with me; for in their relations with one another they can still interest me and move me like the characters in a play I might see performed. My moral being would have to be annihilated for me to lose interest in justice. The sight of injustice and wickedness still makes my blood boil with anger; virtuous actions where I see no vainglory or ostentation always make me tremble with joy, and even now they fill my eyes with precious tears. But I must see and judge them for myself, for after what has happened to me I should have to be mad to adopt the judgment of men on any matter or to take anyone's word for anything.[14]

The ability to see everything himself, the position of omniscient spectator, is the privilege of the possessor of the ring of Gyges which Rousseau goes on to imagine. It is accompanied by invisible and absolute power, like the power of Messalina to determine, by a word to the emperor, the death of Valerius-Asiaticus.

In the *Quatrième Promenade* Rousseau refers to an occasion on which he brought about not the death but the dismissal and disgrace of a fellow servant, even while feeling the intensest sympathy for her predicament. The incident is recounted in Book II of the *Confessions*. Accused of stealing a ribbon, Rousseau declares that it has been given to him by Marion, a pretty servant girl employed in the same house: "Never was spitefulness farther from me than in that cruel moment, and when I accused that unlucky girl, it is bizarre but it is true that my friendship for her was the cause of it. She was present to my mind, I excused myself on the first object that offered. ['Elle était présente à ma pensée, je m'excusai sur le premier objet qui s'offrit.']"[15] Like the double gesture of Messalina, Rousseau's action combines two incompatible positions: a speech act promptly effective in protecting the speaker and destroying its object; and a spectator's appreciation of a scene of unmerited suffering. Rousseau not only sees the scene as a spectacle, he speaks his lines as a figurative statement. This is what Rousseau is concerned to explain in the *Confessions*. "I accused her of having done what I wanted to do and of having given me the ribbon because my intention was to give it to her."[16]

---

[14]Rousseau, *Rêveries*, p. 1057.
[15]Rousseau, *Confessions*, p. 86.
[16]Ibid.

In the interest of making his excuse, Rousseau closely identifies the motive for an utterance with the meaning one wishes to communicate by it. Rousseau implies that his judges misunderstood his meaning in misunderstanding his motive, in failing to infer that his liking for Marion was the sense of his mentioning her name in connection with the ribbon. Rousseau claims that the statement "Marion gave me the ribbon" was a figure for "I would have liked to give the ribbon to Marion." And behind the inverted substitute statement produced by Rousseau stands not simply a particular motive—the intention of giving Marion the ribbon—but the wish that such inversions or substitutions should come into play, as they would if Marion reciprocated Rousseau's affection. Behind the figurative statement stands a desire that there be desire in circulation (between himself and Marion)—a desire that there be motives (for taking a ribbon). Rousseau's explanatory account implies that Marion was not the only victim in this episode, that his words, too, fell victim to a hasty literal interpretation by his employers (who failed to infer his wish to give Marion the ribbon). More fundamentally, however, they also failed to understand the order of motivation at work: one consisting not in particular motives, but in an orientation toward motivation itself. Rousseau makes nearly the same claims here about his act of speaking as he does about his writing in the *Sixième Promenade.* Even while accusing himself of slander, he declares his language to have been subjected to misreading.

But in the very midst of his account in the *Confessions,* Rousseau offers another version of how the slander occurred: "I excused myself on the first object that offered." Rousseau declares that his pronunciation of Marion's name was a matter of accident; it was the first sound that came out of his mouth when he was under pressure to open it. Instead of explaining what he said in terms of his motivation toward motivation, this half-sentence adduces no motivation at all for the enunciation "Marion." It was an altogether arbitrary expression: not even figure, a substitute name motivated by the wish to find a resemblance, but fiction in the most radical sense—without referent and without motive. According to this description of Rousseau's utterance, it was not simply misunderstood by his listeners; it was a misunderstanding to seek to understand it at all, for nothing at all stands behind it.

This reading of the passage in the *Confessions* follows the same sequence as the *Sixième Promenade:* a description of the predicament produced by a practice of interpretation based on the inference of motives, followed by an evocation of the state of fiction. The question arises whether Rousseau's two accounts of his utterance of the name "Marion" are related to each other in the same way as his diagnosis of his dilemma in the first part of the *Sixième Promenade* and his imagination of possessing the ring of Gyges in the second part. We saw that the predicament of being perpetually misinterpreted in an interpretive system matching meanings with motives impelled Rousseau to imagine a condition free of motivation. In imagining that condition—the fictional status of his language— Rousseau was at once realizing a certain motive (that of escaping motivation, which was bound to ensure his guilt), *and* actually replacing an erroneous conception of his language with a truer one. It is possible—almost—to read Rousseau's "second" account of his slander (as sheer accident) in much the same way. Thus on the one hand Rousseau's description of his utterance as arbitrary and unmotivated can be interpreted as correctly designating the status of his language (as fictional); and on the other hand, this description functions as an excuse, and thus apparently realizes a motive (that of excusing Rousseau in the reader's eyes for his role in the dismissal of Marion). When one distinguishes between the act of accidentally saying "Marion" and the act of saying that one accidentally did so, it appears that whereas the first is unmotivated, the second is motivated—to escape motivation, in order to deny guilt. The second act and not the first would then be of the same order as Rousseau's fantasy of invisibility in the *Sixième Promenade*.

Rousseau's fiction "Marion" is an instance of the danger of fiction. The danger is not only that a fiction may invite its audience to read into it a particular motive (as Rousseau's employers do), but also that it may write a particular proper name. The most arbitrary fiction can coincide with the most efficient slander, and the account of the production of a fiction (the identification of an utterance as fiction) can function as the most effective denial of guilt.[17] Such an account is therefore powerfully motivated. In this way fiction does enter into the system of interpretation according to motive; the accident, which can be fatal, does enter retroactively into an economy in which the victim's identity is not arbitrary. The capacity to count one's acts as fictions is the power to deny any guilt—but without the power to control those acts or to elude the guilt that attaches to that account itself. Therefore Rousseau finally calls "inexcusable" his practice of producing fictions. This judgment comes in the next to last para-

---

[17]My discussion of this passage in Book II of Rousseau's *Confessions* repeats the reading of de Man in "The Purloined Ribbon," *Glyph* 1 (1977):28–49.

graph of the *Quatrième Promenade* (which begins by reinvoking the episode of the slander of Marion). It comes as a surprise after the preceding paragraphs, which distinguish persuasively between lies and fictions. The same pattern of last-minute retraction occurs near the end of the *Sixième Promenade* where Rousseau renounces his fantasy of possessing the ring of Gyges. We seem to know the reason for this renunciation of fiction: its power arbitrarily to engender guilt which cannot finally be excused. The claim that one's language is fiction has to be retracted because of the way it becomes implicated after all in the order of motivation.

Something in Rousseau's account of the Marion episode resists this reading, however, and resists being read in the same terms as Rousseau's imagination of the ring of Gyges (and this resistance might lead us to suspect that our reading of the latter passage has not gone far enough). If we look again at Rousseau's second account of his slander—the half-sentence positioned between the start and the finish of his confession of his motives—"I excused myself on the first object that offered"—we must conclude that guilt is not the greatest danger to the integrity of the speaker here. It is simply that he has no control over the act of utterance, which is described as if it were an involuntary physical motion. This intimation must alter our estimate of the relationship between uttering a fiction, in this sense, and claiming to have uttered one. To account one's utterance fictional, in this sense, is to evoke a dispersal of the speaking subject too drastic for there further to exist a speaker who would be acquitted, by the alibi of fiction, from the charge of willful slander. The claim that an utterance was fiction may still occur as an excuse, but as an excuse that is merely the material of a fiction, for there is no subject (no agent with a mode of motivation) to be excused.

We were wrong, then, to think that the identification of an utterance as fictional could be adequately accounted for in terms of a motive to deny motivation in order to defend the integrity of the speaker. The loss of control evoked by such a claim can in no way be motivated. Rather, the claim itself repeats the unmotivated gesture of the fiction "Marion." Rousseau's half-sentence "je m'excusai sur le premier objet qui s'offrit" is a repetition of the accident of saying "Marion." It cannot be accounted for, either, as a true estimate of the status of Rousseau's utterance coming to replace an erroneous estimate (as we read Rousseau's fantasy of invisibility). It must be read neither as a motivated, interested negation of motive nor as a motiveless, disinterested, in some sense inevitable disclosure of the truth about Rousseau's language. This is as much as to say that it must not be *read*. The clause on "Marion" interrupts Rousseau's account of the episode rather than follows it. This interruption differs entirely from the articulation of the *Sixième Promenade*—which we must no longer attempt to read in terms of the structure of the passage in the *Confessions*.

We have been led to repeat the gesture of last-minute retraction performed by Rousseau at the conclusion of his celebrations of fiction in the *Quatrième Promenade* and in the passage on the ring of Gyges. Does coming upon his fiction "Marion" have any effect on our reading of his allegory of invisibility? We read that passage in the light of the concept of motivation, taking a cue from the terms proposed by Rousseau in the course of the *Promenade* ("a motive . . . is never more than a *lure*"). We found Rousseau's fantasy of invisibility to be motivated as an escape from the order of motivation, an order that permanently threatened the subject with errors of interpretation. We read the imagination of invisibility as an imagination of the condition of fiction or an order of meaning dissociated from motives. We then interpreted Rousseau's renunciation of this imagined invisibility in terms, once more, of the danger of motivations, for the very negation of motive instituting fiction turned out to take its place in an economy of motivation all the more powerful for being denied. Throughout our reading, the order of motivation appeared as the danger, of error or of guilt, which Rousseau's *Promenade* attempted to circumvent.

But Rousseau's ultimate wariness of his position as invisible spectator led us to passages describing that position in the *Lettre à d'Alembert* and in the *Confessions;* and, in the latter text, fiction appeared in a form that could not be connected, by any means, with the order of motivation but rather occurred as an accident—as the incursion of sheer contingency into the activity of speech, a fatal accident to the idea of a subject in control of his utterance. We must note at once that no such accident takes place in the passage invoking the ring of Gyges in the *Sixième Promenade*. Here Rousseau writes an allegory on fiction as invisibility, an allegory that can be read, and read to designate the order of motivation as a permanent threat to the writing subject, and especially to the writing of fiction. Our perspective on this passage about the danger of motivation must shift once we have encountered, in Rousseau's fiction "Marion," the danger of accident—of a fiction that falls outside the order of motivation altogether. What falls outside such an order is also excluded from the passage of the *Sixième Promenade*. What we discover in that passage is the motivated negation of motive, which belongs to the order of possible motivations, even as the invisibility conferred by the ring of Gyges is a possibility included within the system of visibility in general. What we do not discover in the passage is the accident that does not take place there. But the exclusion of accident leaves a trace: in the peculiar pattern of retraction that ends the fantasy with a repetition of the finish of the *Quatrième Promenade,* and in an image not of guilt but of degradation: "this excess of power will only serve to sink him lower than others." We have as yet no term to identify the excluded accident and differentiate it from the invisibility we have consistently interpreted as the condition of fiction. Invisibility is a sign, however, pointing us to another text where the "invisible" appears, indeed, as a sign—Wordsworth's. His lines on the "coat of darkness" may spell out for us what was occulted by Rousseau's ring.

III

Wordsworth's lines on invisibility raise two issues absent from Rousseau's: the question of how it may be represented and the question of the pertinence of another text, the passage from *Samson Agonistes* which Wordsworth quotes. Wordsworth describes with ironical amusement how easily invisibility is represented on stage, and his irony here also touches Milton:

> How is it wrought? His garb is black, the word
> *Invisible* flames forth upon his chest.[18]

Invisibility can be represented with the greatest of ease abbreviated in language, in a written word. Milton is the master of such an effect: he makes "darkness visible" precisely by means of that formula, which becomes a label as reuseable as "Jack's." Juxtaposing a Sadler's Wells pantomime and the poetry of Milton typifies Wordsworth's imagination of London, where all human inventions appear equalized by their common denominator, the capacity to be displayed as signs:

> The comers and the goers face to face,
> Face after face; the string of dazzling wares,
> Shop after shop, with symbols, blazoned names,
> And all the tradesman's honours overhead:
> Here, fronts of houses, like a title-page
> With letters huge inscribed from top to toe;

[18]Wordsworth, *Prelude* (1805), VII, 308–9.

> Stationed above the door, like guardian saints,
> There, allegoric shapes, female or male,
> Or physiognomies of real men,
> Land-warriors, kings, or admirals of the sea,
> Boyle, Shakespeare, Newton, or the attractive head
> Of some quack-doctor, famous in his day.[19]

Just as Shakespeare's shape can be set beside a quack doctor's, Milton's text can be set beside a quack Jack's. Wordsworth is writing in the tradition of *The House of Fame*, not only Pope's satirical *reprise* but Chaucer's ironical allegory, which places "Omer" and the other immortal poets in Fame's palace along with the horde of rumor-mongers and ambitious fakes. Wordsworth's irony embraces the fact that any work of poetry, including Milton's, depends for its effects on rhetorical devices requiring the complicity of the reader. That reading effect is magically efficient in presenting the idea of invisibility, not so much despite as because of the very paradox that when invisibility is made visible (by becoming readable) its invisibility becomes invisible. Language is the neatest trick. Wordsworth's quote reveals that a quite specific trick is at issue here: producing invisibility from blindness by means of an act of reading. Wordsworth too creates invisibility from blindness, using Samson's lines on blindness to describe the actor's fictive invisibility. As easily as invisibility becomes visible, blindness turns to invisibility by another act of reading, Wordsworth's reading of the phrase from *Samson Agonistes*.

While Rousseau condemns the error of visualizing a particular agent and particular intention behind a text, Wordsworth satirizes the inverse misreading. Jack the Giant-Killer's invisibility makes his deeds seem to his victims to be caused by an impersonal agency such as destiny, and this invisibility is all too easily accepted and appreciated by the audience reading the actor's label. Wordsworth's account of the scenario shows it to be a trick of writing. His text reveals the blindness involved in *not* identifying a particular agency behind what can be read as "invisible"—read as the unmotivated action of language itself, the nonintentional and nonreferential language of fiction. (Wordsworth's poetry characteristically provokes and seems to celebrate such a reading, which occurs, for instance, in critics' and in Wordsworth's own interpretation of his encounter with the blind beggar further in Book VII.) Although Rousseau's passage on the ring of Gyges initially proposes the truth in the invisibility of the

---

[19]Ibid., VII, 156–67.

agency of Rousseau's language, Wordsworth's lines on the "coat of darkness" stress how wishful that conception of language is—one all too easy to write and to read, as Wordsworth indicates in showing the ease with which Jack's invisibility can be *visualized,* thanks to writing. As it happens, Wordsworth's judgment of the collusion between performers and audience—"Delusion bold! and faith must needs be coy"—could serve as an epigraph to Rousseau's fantasy of possessing the ring of Gyges, marking its slide from a "bold" "faith" to a "coy" concession of "delusion." Wordsworth's judgment implies (as the final turn of Rousseau's text also suggests) that the notion of unmotivated nonreferential language falls within the conception of motivation, belongs to the system of visibility, to the specular system conceiving language as the reflection of a subject.

Like the kind of misreading described by Rousseau, such as the error of his employers in taking literally his accusation of Marion, the misreading described by Wordsworth also has violent, if not serious, consequences. One can compare the Sadler's Wells "Giant-Killer" with Odysseus, who escaped unscathed after putting out the eye of the giant cyclops Polyphemus, thanks largely to a similar technique: he introduced himself to Polyphemus by the name of "No Man."[20] When Polyphemus bellowed for help to his fellow cyclopes and they asked him who had injured him he replied, "No Man," whereupon they replied that if no man injured him, then it must be an act of the gods: he must be either sick or mad. Since, therefore, none of the other cyclopes came to take revenge on him, Odysseus was able to pass out of Polyphemus' cave invisibly (eluding Polyphemus' touch as well by hanging beneath the belly of one of his rams going out to pasture). It was Polyphemus' listeners who effectively transformed the name No Man to the meaning "no man." In the same way, it is Jack the Giant-Killer's audience who transform the label "Invisible" into effectual invisibility, enabling the killing—on stage, to be sure—of several more giants blind to their adversary. If reading *in* a particular motive can be a dangerous error of interpretation, so can the reverse: ascribing an action to a disinterested agency, accounting it inevitable, or necessary.

In the case of Odysseus' feat as in the case of Jack's, the establishment of signification (with its prompt consequences) depends on a reading that must pass by way of an audience, a third party, a third

---

[20]See de Man, "Theory of Metaphor in Rousseau's Second Discourse," in *Romanticism: Vistas, Instances, Continuities,* ed. David Thornburn and Geoffrey Hartman (Ithaca: Cornell University Press, 1973), p. 107n.

reader distinct from the reader who is directly concerned (the giant) as well as from the producer of the sign. There is a further dimension, then, to the danger of reading (the enigmatic suggestion that initially induced our reading of these texts). It would seem to lie not only in the destructive action to which it may offer immunity, but in the elision of the speaking (or writing) or the reading (or listening) subject, bypassed for a third instance that functions more or less mechanically.

Wordsworth's evocation of the reading process as producing invisibility concerns not only the effects of language in general but Miltonic effects in particular, as his quotation suggests. The feat of converting blindness to invisibility is originally and peculiarly Milton's. Milton's literal blindness figures as a sign for his blindness to natural continuities, a blindness that operates, in turn, as visionary power. Like Jack the Giant-Killer, Milton becomes the invisible agency of extraordinary feats. "Miltonic blindness to the identity of the self as creator and the self being objectively represented in the process of wavering growth"[21] makes possible the poetry of *Paradise Lost.*

Miltonic blindness and visionary invisibility are so closely identified, and so different from the resources required by the autobiographical poet of *The Prelude,* that it would be wrong to suppose that Wordsworth's passage is designed (like Rousseau's) to fulfill the wish to produce invisibility from blindness. Rather, such blindness itself may appear as the content of a renounced wish:

> These beauteous forms,
> Through a long absence, have not been to me
> As is a landscape to a blind man's eye.[22]

Here Wordsworth's affirmation of his own distinctive gift as a poet takes the form of a denial of Miltonic blindness. The denial that seeks to be an affirmation has the resonance of regret or renunciation. The tone is very different in the lines from the Prospectus to *The Excursion* where Wordsworth deliberately compares his project with Milton's.

[21]Leslie Brisman, *Milton's Poetry of Choice and Its Romantic Heirs* (Ithaca: Cornell University Press, 1973), p. x.
[22]Wordsworth, "Lines composed a few miles above Tintern Abbey," in *The Poetical Works of William Wordsworth* (Oxford: Clarendon Press, 1952), II, 259, ll. 23–25.

The Ring of Gyges and the Coat of Darkness

> Not Chaos, not
> The darkest pit of lowest Erebus,
> Nor aught of blinder vacancy, scooped out
> By help of dreams—can breed such fear and awe
> As fall upon us when we look
> Into our minds, into the Mind of Man—
> My haunt, and the main region of my song.[23]

To write the "more lowly matter" of "Tintern Abbey" and *The Prelude,* an account of "the Mind and Man contemplating," Wordsworth abandons comparison with Milton's project—to engage in a different kind of passage past "blind vacancy."

The structure of such a passage may perhaps be inscribed in the phrase Wordsworth selects to cite in his lines on the Sadler's Wells pantomime.

> He dons his coat of darkness, on the stage
> Walks, and achieves his wonders from the eyes
> Of living mortal safe as is the moon
> 'Hid in her vacant interlunar cave.'[24]

The phrase from Milton is an oxymoron designating two contradictory spatial situations: the moon is "hid in her vacant interlunar cave," yet the cave is nonetheless "vacant." The moon and her cave are a radiant source and the site of its withdrawal, an inner agency and an outer site. The phrase simultaneously negates and affirms the persistence of an inner agency that is absent; absent, it either is, somewhere, or is not. The phrase asserts both these alternatives. In addition, the site of this absence is not in fact spatial but temporal: her "interlunar cave" is that phase of the moon in which the moon is intermitted, left out.

Is there a "hidden" agency, or no agency, rather a "vacant" site? Wordsworth's citation makes the question undecidable. The question and the assertion of both its contradictory answers constitute a gesture that we have traced in the text of Rousseau's fantasy on the ring of Gyges. That gesture is also enacted by the two texts taken together, as we are reading them here: whereas Wordsworth's lines on the "coat of darkness" first of all display the operation of a

---

[23] Wordsworth, *The Excursion,* in *Poetical Works,* V, 4, ll. 35–41.
[24] Wordsworth, *Prelude* (1805), VII, 304–7.

"hidden" agency, Rousseau's account of his ring first of all maintains the vacancy of its site. We can read Wordsworth's citation as an emblem of the issue raised between his text and Rousseau's.

We can also read it as an emblem for the "blinder vacancy," unlike Miltonic blindness, that takes place in *The Prelude*. One place it occurs is in "London," in a passage not far from the scene at Sadler's Wells. Wordsworth here is "smitten" by a spectacle—the spectacle not of imaginary invisibility but of literal blindness.

>   'Twas my chance
> Abruptly to be smitten with the view
> Of a blind beggar, who, with upright face,
> Stood propped against a wall, upon his chest
> Wearing a written paper, to explain
> The story of the man, and who he was.
> My mind did at this spectacle turn round
> As with the might of waters, and it seemed
> To me that in this label was a type
> Or emblem of the utmost that we know
> Both of ourselves and of the universe,
> And on the shape of this/unmoving man,
> His fixed face and sightless eyes, I looked,
> As if admonished from another world.[25]

As at Sadler's Wells, it is a man wearing a label that Wordsworth finds so powerfully diverting ("My mind turned round . . ."). Once again the impact of the scene depends on an act of reading. The blind beggar, like Jack the Giant-Killer, cannot read his own label. In the other passage it was the imaginary magical power of an actor that depended on an audience's participation, which seemed to function according to a guaranteed mechanism. Here it is the man's very identity that depends on the mediation of a third person, a spectator, a passerby who may happen to turn his gaze from the blank face and read the written figures. Or rather, there can be no identity in this composite of "fixed face and sightless eyes" and "written paper." The blind beggar displays the separation between functions as intimately interdependent as writing and reading and shows that the text exists precisely by virtue of this division. In the blind beggar Wordsworth confronts an image of the auto-biographical poet unable to read his own text.

[25]Ibid., VII, 610–23.

The Ring of Gyges and the Coat of Darkness

It appears that Wordsworth's "coat of darkness" is a wishful inversion of blindness after all. Yet the role in both passages of a written label reveals that the crucial inversion at stake is, rather, the conversion of the arbitrariness of mere chance, in the generation of meaning, into the arbitrariness of a mechanism, the mechanics of rhetorical and theatrical tricks. The spectators who guarantee special power to the Giant-Killer of Sadler's Wells are there to supplant the absent or vacant spectator who would confer intelligibility on the beggar with his written paper. In the case of the blind beggar, the connection between text and meaning is intermittent and contingent. But Wordsworth's response to the "spectacle" promptly reaffirms their connection: his mind "turn[s] round," to pass from the vacancy of the accidental encounter between himself and the beggar and the darkness of the fatal juxtaposition of "sightless eyes" and "written paper" to the plenitude of an ulterior sense: "an apt type / This label seemed of the utmost we can know . . . I looked / As if admonished from another world." It is as if the label in its role as "type" had made the literal blind beggar invisible, like the actor playing Jack the Giant-Killer, and enabled him to appear, like Jack, as the operation of a supernatural agency. (It should be noted here that our own acceptance of the composite image of the beggar as an emblem for autobiography performs, inevitably, a similar recuperative gesture. Yet the conjunction of "emblem" and "autobiography"—of the autobiographical and the pictorial or visual— proves, in Wordsworth's text, to resist restorative responses.) That final line, however, can also be read another way. The "other world" from which the poet is (paradoxically) "admonished" might be a world in which reading occurs or fails to occur by accident rather than for cause. This is the world, or the time, in which the condition of the possibility of meaning is "hid in her vacant interlunar cave." Reading occurs by accident: the cave is vacant; but that accident occurs in a reading (such as the reading that it occurs by accident): a condition for meaning *is* there, "hid."

The lines that recount Samson's final action in *Samson Agonistes* share the same narrative perspective as Wordsworth's description of the scene at Sadler's Wells in Book VII of *The Prelude*. The scene at the temple of Dagon is recounted afterward by an eyewitness, the Hebrew messenger. Samson is absent; from blind subject he becomes, in effect, the invisible agent of the closing scene. That is, the same conversion that takes place between Milton's lines and Wordsworth's also takes place within Milton's poem itself. The question arises of what Wordsworth is converting and what he is repeating. The Hebrew messenger tells of a hero's deed requiring self-destruction.

> The building was a spacious theatre
> Half round on two main Pillars vaulted high,
> . . .
> At length for intermission sake they led him
> Between the pillars: . . .
> . . . which when Samson
> Felt in his arms: with head a while enclined
> And eyes fast fixed he stood, as one who prayed
> Or some great matter in his mind revolved,
> At last with head erect thus cried aloud,
> Hitherto, lords, what your commands imposed
> I have performed, as reason was, obeying,
> Not without wonder or delight beheld.
> Now of my own accord such other trial
> I mean to show you of my strength, yet greater;
> As with amaze shall strike all who behold.
> This uttered, straining all his nerves he bowed;
> As with the force of winds and waters pent,
> When mountains tremble, those two massy pillars
> With horrible convulsion to and fro,
> He tugged, he shook, till down they came and drew
> The whole roof after them, with burst of thunder
> Upon the heads of all who sat beneath.
> Lords, ladies, captains, counsellors, or priests,
> Their choice nobility and flower, not only
> Of this but each Philistian city round
> Met from all parts to solemnize this feast.[26]

This is the performance of a giant killer, and one that exploits his rhetorical manipulation of his audience. Jack the Giant-Killer's feat requires that his audience read him literally and referentially (taking the label to mean "This person is invisible"). Samson invites his audience to understand his words in their ordinary figurative sense, to assume that he will "strike them" with amazement, rather than strike them in such a way as to amaze them. At last Samson effectively both destroys and becomes the "Tongue-doughty giant" who had been his antithesis (personified by the giant Philistine Harapha).

[26]John Milton, *Samson Agonistes*, in *Complete Shorter Poems* (London: Longman, 1968), 1605–6, 1629–30, 1635–36.

Samson's alienation from his own language finally takes the form of mastery of a rhetorical device in the service of effective action. Yet this reuniting of language and power produces no *Aufhebung* but spectacular downfall and destruction.

The change from lack of control of one's own language to mastery of a rhetorical device is the transformation at issue in Wordsworth's metamorphosis of Samson and the label-wearing beggar into the label-wearing actor at Sadler's Wells. This transformation is an instance, rather more intricately condensed than usual, of that "discourse . . . sustained *beyond* and in spite of *deprivation*"[27] which characterizes Wordsworth's autobiographical writing in *The Prelude*, which orders, for example, the passage of the Winander Boy from "pauses of deep silence" to "the bosom of the steady lake" and the village churchyard, and the passage of the drowned man's "ghastly face" to "purest Poesy." One could work out the recurrence of this scheme in Book VII: the discourse of autobiography, as a process of self-reading, is interrupted by the shock of "London," by an accident like the blind beggar's deprivation of sight to read his own story; discourse is sustained by the theatrical trick that passes by way of an audience reading and identifying the text with its wearer. The trick also inverts the relation between the two subjects, so that the blinded writer is replaced by a blinded reader, in a reading process that transfers authority to the writing subject.

"Half-rural Sadler's Wells" thus serves, in Wordsworth's "London," to assimilate the compulsion of accident, as it appears for example in the "mill" and the monsters of the "true epitome / Of what the mighty City is herself" (the Fair), to a visible scene revealing a specular structure. Wordsworth's very ability to distinguish himself from the simple spectators at the performance ("nor was it mean delight / To watch crude Nature work in untaught minds") gives him the security of finding himself beyond the confines of the theatrical performance, like the pleasure of self-consciousness he recalls from the "country-playhouse" of his childhood, when "having caught / In summer through the fractured wall a glimpse / Of daylight, at the thought of where I was / I gladdened" (1805, VII, 482–85). This pleasure depends on a stable distinction between the inside of the theater and the space outside it, between sunlight and the artificial lighting that by itself becomes sinister, like the glare of the theater in the scene in which the beautiful baby boy appears to Wordsworth "Of lusty vigour more than infantine . . . a cottage-

---

[27]Paul de Man, "Autobiography as De-facement," *MLN* 94 (1979):919–30.

child," miraculously immune to his position "environed with a ring / Of chance spectators."[28] Wordsworth shares some of Rousseau's mistrust of the theater. Spectacle is associated for him with the tyranny of the eye, "a transport of the outward sense, / Not of the mind."[29] Hence it is unlikely that a theatrical spectacle should serve primarily in Wordsworth's writing to restore a disrupted specular structure, as in the reading we have just suggested—unless, indeed, that specular structure itself were to turn out to share the disturbing qualities of spectacle, rather than serving to stabilize a self-conscious subject.

A "theater" is the scene, a "spectacle" the pretext, of Samson's heroic deed. The very theatricality of Samson's final act could threaten to diminish its tragic effect. Irony encroaches on the drama not only because the hero's action is one of mass destruction that also destroys himself. The more corrosive irony lies in the rhetorical character of Samson's feat. Not that his feat is easily trivialized; a theatrical performance, and an act of language, become the pretext for actual annihilation. Language and power coincide here in an act of destruction. But what is also threatened with destruction, in Milton's text, is the meaningfulness of their momentary convergence. For good reason Samson's play on the word "strike" is not conspicuous in Milton's lines: his feat must not seem to depend on an arbitrary mechanism. Such a reading would deprive the disparity between "eyesight" and "strength" of pathos and make Samson's tragedy an essentially linguistic predicament, a matter of the way language functions or fails to function. That functioning is the very topic of Wordsworth's passage on Jack the Giant-Killer, which deliberately empties of pathos the phrase from *Samson*. Wordsworth's lines repeat and make explicit the depiction of the theatrical and rhetorical devices at work in Samson's plot. Yet the workings of such devices threaten the pathos and meaning not only of Milton's tragedy, but of the discrepancy between "knowledge" and "power" and the impossibility of self-reading that are themes of Wordsworth's autobiographical writing.

A greater threat to self-reading or autobiographical writing emerges in Wordsworth's text by way of what it precisely declines to repeat: the exact wording of the blind Samson's enigmatic opening monologue. Wordsworth's citation of *Samson Agonistes* in fact entails

<hr />

[28]Wordsworth, *Prelude* (1805), VII, 379, 381, 386–87.
[29]Ibid., XI, 187–88. See Mary Jacobus, "Wordsworth and the Language of the Dream," *ELH* 46 (1979):629–30, on how "spectral saves spectacle for the imagination," in Books VII and VIII of *The Prelude*.

a crucial discrepancy. We shall find that Wordsworth's revision reveals the stakes of his reading of Milton, and even more, of the act of reading in general.

The citation designs to turn us away from its source as much as to turn us back to it. Milton writes:

> The sun to me is dark
> And silent as the moon
>
> . . .
>
> Hid in her vacant interlunar cave.

Wordsworth, in the text of 1805, writes,

> safe as is the moon
> 'Hid in her vacant interlunar cave.'[30]

Wordsworth's rewording converts "silent" to "safe"; his revision of Samson's lines follows the affirmative negation composed by Milton in a passage evoking his own blindness:

> Half yet remains unsung, but narrower bound
> Within the visible diurnal sphear;
> Standing on earth, not rapt above the pole,
> More safe I sing with mortal voice, unchanged
> To hoarse or *mute*, though fallen on evil days,
> On evil days though fallen, and evil tongues,
> In darkness, and with dangers compassed round.[31]

Wordsworth might well have wished to appropriate these lines for his own project, and his revisionary citation of Samson's lines might appear consistent with such an attitude. Something else, though, is at stake.

In Milton's text, "silent" interrupts the already contradictory spatial image (further complicated by a temporal description) with a term from a different order, that of sound. It is as though Samson's lament for being blind suddenly shifted to a lament for being deaf. Samson does lose the sense of the meaning of others' utterance. "I hear the sound of words, their sense the air / Dissolves disjointed ere it reach my ear."[32] The true strangeness of these lines, however, lies

[30]Wordsworth, *Prelude* (1805), VII, 306–7.
[31]Milton, *Paradise Lost*, VII, 21–27; my italics.
[32]*Samson Agonistes*, ll. 176–77.

in the fact that the interruptive part of Samson's complaint might truthfully be echoed by anyone: "The sun to me is silent." Just this Wordsworth will not repeat. For what Samson makes a measure of the most terrible deprivation is the condition of anyone who hears and sees. To lament that the sun is silent is to identify the condition of *sense,* the possession of physical senses and the ability to conceive sense or meaning, as a state of deprivation. Samson's disorienting complaint for the very orientation of language is a lament for the unintelligibility of the most fundamental figure, whereby *light* is imagined as intelligibility conceived as *voice.* To refer to the silence of the sun as a catastrophe is to point to how vital is the identification of light with meaning conceived as voicing, and how fatal the strictly figurative, rhetorical status of that identification.

That identification is imposed by "decree." Samson's lament associates the deprivation of sense with the Word that imposes meaning even as it gives light. Here Milton's lines link the issue of "sense" (of figuration and meaning) with the issue of motivation—to suggest that the imposition of sense is *un*motivated, or rather that for the "prime decree," the question of motivation is unmotivated and arbitrary. Since it is without intentional status, its figurative status is also indeterminable, and its truth status undecidable. As the imposition of "sense" through an arbitrary speech act, the "prime decree" is a bereavement. In this passage, the moment in which the system of motivation is exceeded and the moment in which the system of figuration is exceeded come into play together.

If sense is identified as a state of deprivation, the restoration of sense becomes a meaningless project. Lamentation that "the sun . . . is silent" threatens both Milton's tragedy and Wordsworth's autobiography. In particular, it subverts the project of restoring and maintaining the identity of the subject beyond death, which is the theme of *Samson Agonistes'* final lines and of Wordsworth's *Essays upon Epitaphs.* The first essay states that an epitaph is composed in a "belief in immortality" yet designed "to be accomplished in close connection with the bodily remains of the deceased." The mediation between the two ideas depends, in Wordsworth's essay, on an analogy between the "journey" of life (toward death and immortality) and journeys following the sun—"voyage toward the regions where the sun sets," which will ultimately approach the east, and "voyage toward . . . the birthplace of the morning," which will ultimately approach the west.[33] Such "lively and affecting analogies of life as a

---

[33]Wordsworth, *Essays upon Epitaphs,* p. 53.

journey" are meant to give "to the language of the senseless stone a voice."[34] A meaningful epitaph, a text that achieves restoration of meaning, is supposed to have a voice. (Manoa too imagines inscribing "sweet lyric song" on Samson's grave.) Voice is the value threatened by the inalterable silence defined in Samson's complaint about the sun. In describing a lack constituted by sense itself, by the very condition of meaning, that complaint describes language, the condition of intelligibility, as a deprivation. The subject's relation to his own language is lacking; the privation at issue here is muteness, the subject's deprivation of his own voice. This is the silence that Wordsworth censors when he quotes Samson in *The Prelude*.

In concluding the last of the *Essays upon Epitaphs*, Wordsworth quotes himself, and here he designates the inalterable silence mentioned by Samson. The lines Woodsworth cites are a passage from Book VII of *The Excursion* ("The Churchyard among the Mountains") concerning the life, death, and grave of a deaf-mute.

> . . . when stormy winds
> Were working the broad bosom of the lake
> Into a thousand, thousand sparkling waves,
> Rocking the trees, or driving cloud on cloud
> Along the sharp edges of yon lofty crags,
> The agitated scene before his eye
> Was silent as a picture: evermore
> Were all things silent, whereso'er he moved.[35]

One's own muteness is as such inconceivable (just as one cannot conceive oneself incapable of meaning anything). Yet the way the Dalesman's lack is described here suggests, like the interruptive part of Samson's lament, a condition not peculiar to him but inevitable. "Silent as a picture," "the sun is silent"—these lines require us to think the very forms of intelligibility—the visible, the figural—as forms of privation.

Wordsworth's lines on the deaf-mute go on to describe his compensations. Though we have already inferred from the format of Samson's complaint that compensation or restoration must lose their meaning if sense is a deprivation, it is important to be explicit about the forms such compensation takes. Wordsworth's lines on the Dalesman are explicit on the matter, and what we find ourselves reading is a description of reading:

[34]Ibid., p. 54.
[35]Ibid., p. 94.

> ... books
> Were ready comrades whom he could not tire,—
> Of whose society the blameless Man
> Was never satiate. Their familiar voice,
> Even to old age, with unabated charm
> Beguiled his leisure hours; refreshed his thoughts.[36]

Muteness is compensated for, Wordsworth tells us, by means of books. That is, books do not have a voice themselves; they provide a substitute "voice," once they have been personified (as "ready comrades," in the phrase of *The Excursion*). This is a "voice" only according to a rhetorical device—one on which the intelligibility of language depends, for it is impossible (or lunacy) to conceive of language without reference to the idea of voice. Books, however, are precisely a voiceless language, as the very nature of their "voice" indicates, and as Wordsworth's focus on their role as "ready comrades" for a deaf-mute emphasizes. Wordsworth's phrase here stresses simultaneously the personifying figure that lends books a "voice" and the fact of their muteness.

Books themselves, the means of compensation or restoration, install the very deprivation for which they were meant to compensate. When Wordsworth quotes Milton's poem "On Shakespeare" in the first *Essay upon Epitaphs*, he leaves out the following lines:

> For whilst to the shame of slow-endeavoring art,
> Thy easy numbers flow, and that each heart
> Hath from the leaves of thy unvalued book
> Those Delphic lines with deep impression took,
> Then thou our fancy of it self bereaving
> Dost make us marble with too much conceiving.[37]

The "book" makes its reader mute. To *hear* a monument, to hear its "easy numbers flow," is to take on ourselves the mute fixity of a text. By revealing the figurative and fictive nature of its voice, the book exposes the voicelessness of language, which is an unthinkable conception, "bereaving" the reader of his relationship to language.

One's relation to one's own voice is not a specular one. The projection of voice in a text, however, installs a specular structure. Just as "light" must imply intelligibility conceived as voice, as meaning, so

[36] Wordsworth, *Essays upon Epitaphs*, p. 95. The following account of the muteness of language derives from de Man's interpretation in "Autobiography as De-facement."

[37] Milton, "On Shakespeare," in *Complete Shorter Poems*, p. 37.

"voice" must imply meaning conceived as light, as the presentation of an intelligible figure; otherwise the very sense of voice or light is lost. But as voice is projected in a text or a figure, "voice" is substituted for voice; in Milton's account, the reader becomes the mute marble of an epitaph. As the nonspecular relation to voice becomes a specular structure, it becomes a trope.

Specularity does turn out, then, to have the disturbing effect Wordsworth associates with spectacle, "the transport of the outward sense." The very textual structure that was supposed to compensate for or restore the relation to voice definitively subverts it. The epitaph's visual and figural language, and its figural and literal orientation toward the sun, was supposed to ensure its genuine voice. Instead, it effects the "voice" of a silent reading: "The sun looks down upon the stone, and the rains of heaven beat against it." In this sentence, which seems to celebrate the natural condition of the epitaph, "the sun . . . is silent" and the inscription "silent as a picture." The epitaph itself is revealed to install, by the very achievement of the "voice" of legibility, a voicelessness that is a more radical privation than death.

In the context of the citations in the *Essays upon Epitaphs,* it becomes possible to determine the significance of Wordsworth's citation of *Samson Agonistes* in the passage on Jack the Giant-Killer. It becomes evident, in the first place, why Wordsworth changes "silent" to "safe": not because Milton's powerful voice threatens his own with silence, but because this "silent" moment in Milton's text designates Wordsworth's peril from his own writing. This is also the case in the omission of the lines on the "unvalued book" from Milton's poem "On Shakespeare." To identify the "book" as Milton's poetry, making it Milton's presence that threatens Wordsworth with self-"bereaving" through "too much conceiving" so that he censors these lines, is to adopt as a final explanation what is rather an explanatory figure in the poetry itself. Milton's figure is not a reassuring one: "we" readers are portrayed as being turned to stone by reading another's book; yet simply by differentiating the names of writer and readers, it preserves a notion of the individual subject that remains informed with the idea of individual voice. In this sense it is more reassuring, and more explanatory, than the idea of a muteness induced by one's own language.

Wordsworth turns to quote Milton when his own voice is threatened. Wordsworth is then like the Dalesman turning to his "ready comrades," the "books he could not tire," for a compensatory "voice." Yet that very supplement confirms the deprivation, as the instance in the lines on Sadler's Wells makes clear: the cited passage designates the very privation at issue, so that Milton's writing must be censored in turn.

What specifically, in Wordsworth's own writing, in the passage on Jack the Giant-Killer, threatens his voice and impels him to borrow Milton's? It is the spectacle of the voiceless efficacy of writing that has such an impact, the actor's role played out "silent as a picture" through the written label on his coat. It is not simply the effectiveness of theatrical or rhetorical trickery that is involved. The lines on the deaf-mute spell out what was "silent as a picture": "stormy winds . . . working the broad bosom of the lake," "the agitated scene before his eye"—nature. The lines on the quality of his enjoyment at Sadler's Wells spell out that the same order of reality is at issue: "Nor was it mean delight / To watch crude Nature work in untaught minds." "Crude nature" is crude literacy, the ability to read a written sign. Language is nature, and language as such, not simply the rhetorical device, is silent, a deprivation of one's own voice. This deprivation is the very scenario at Sadler's Wells. For the power that is "invisible" ought to be the power of voice. It must take the form, however, of writing. Not invisibility, not blindness, but visibility itself is the predicament, the system of visibility that is the system of literal and figural language. Intelligible language, intelligible nature, is mute—an idea that makes no sense, that mutes the mind that articulates it, and that Wordsworth therefore silences.

To silence it, though, Wordsworth repeats the very gesture that was disturbing: he displays a label, a phrase detached from its context in the speech of Samson, and flaunted, like the actor's label, to produce an image of invisibility. The poet's irreverence toward Milton resembles the actor's irreverence about invisibility. The trivializing of potentially serious themes gets contrastingly stern treatment in *Essays upon Epitaphs,* where Wordsworth recurrently denounces the subversion of taste "by the artifices which have overrun our writings in metre since the days of Dryden and Pope." Wordsworth's satirical writing in "London" has a Popeian resonance in the very lines where he is criticizing this culture of wit and satire, and his gesture in citing *Samson Agonistes* in his lines on Sadler's Wells could be described as he describes the unpardonable fault of writing bad epitaphs.

Energy, stillness, grandeur, tenderness, those feelings which are the pure emanations of nature, those thoughts which have the infinitude of truth, and those expressions which are not what the garb is to the body, but what the body is to the soul, themselves a constituent part and power or function in the thought—all these are abandoned for their purposes,—as if our Countrymen, through successive generations, had lost the sense of solemnity and pensiveness (not to speak of deeper emotions) and resorted to the Tombs of their Forefathers and Contemporaries only to be tickled and surprized.[38]

The practice of citation in this present exercise at times may have seemed to invite the same reproach. The fault finally at stake, though, is the act of reading. Quoting is a would-be reading aloud, an effort to give voice to language. Such an effort is doomed to make sense—sense that is a state of deprivation, as Wordsworth characterizes the sense that resides in language.

Such sense is senseless. Wordsworth writes this out in a passage that must be quoted here, in a conspicuously final position, as if to serve as the telos of a certain trajectory—imitating a gesture that occurs more than once in current writing on Wordsworth and on language.[39]

> Words are too awful an instrument of good and evil to be trifled with: they hold above all other external powers a dominion over thoughts. If words be not (returning to a metaphor before used) an incarnation of the thought but only a clothing for it, then surely will they prove an ill gift; such a one as those poisoned vestments, read of in the stories of superstitious times, which had power to consume and to alienate from his right mind the victim who put them on. Language, if it do not uphold, and feed, and leave in quiet, like the power of gravitation and the air we breathe, is a counter-spirit, unremittingly and noiselessly at work to derange, to subvert, to lay waste, to vitiate, and to dissolve.[40]

At Sadler's Wells, language is "noiselessly at work," as the Giant-Killer achieves his wonders "silent," precisely, "as the moon." This threat to the "body" of The Prelude Wordsworth displaces by citing and censoring Milton—only, indeed, to designate by omission the very effect that threatens him: clothing the gap with a quote only gives it more permanent outline. The "poisoned vestments" Wordsworth mentions refer to the tunic of Nessus, that compensatory garment supposed to ensure the wearer's love for the giver, but

---

[38]Wordsworth, *Essays upon Epitaphs*, p. 84.

[39]See, for example, Frances Ferguson, *Wordsworth: Language as Counterspirit* (New Haven: Yale University Press, 1977), pp. xv–xvii, and de Man, "Autobiography as De-facement," p. 929.

[40]Wordsworth, *Essays upon Epitaphs*, pp. 84–85.

which in fact guarantees its wearer's lunacy.[41] The Giant-Killer's "coat of darkness" is a comparable garment, a compensatory device that installs a still worse deprivation. Samson too, with his "redundant locks," risks the mad death of the other giant-killer, Hercules.[42] Autobiography becomes as mad a gesture as the blind beggar's appears to be when, by wearing his story in written form rather than uttering it, he compounds blindness with muteness. Wordsworth's *Essays* and *The Prelude* are such "poisoned vestments": autobiographical writing does not "leave" a life "in quiet," but through the very process of giving it a "voice" in language, which is voiceless, makes it mute.

Rousseau's possession of the ring of Gyges is another such project. (It was supposed to ensure the mutual love of the giver and his recipients, his dazzled readers.) As in Wordsworth's case it is the silent "voice" of language that exposes its voicelessness, in Rousseau's case it is the system of motivation itself that reveals its lack of motivation. The condition of invisibility imagined by Rousseau is one of unmotivated motivation, unmotivated inference of motives, a gratuitous act of reading "au fond des coeurs" that is mad in the sense that it reinstalls the conception of the motivation of meaning that as "invisible" fictional writing it had begun by renouncing. The very omniscience and omnipotence that should free one of unrealized motives, unsatisfied desires, and temptations becomes a compulsion to "chercher des tentations." The unintentional intending evoked here by Rousseau can also be read in the last word of *Samson Agonistes:*

> Oft he seems to hide his face,
> But unexpectedly returns
>
> . . .
>
> . . . whence Gaza mourns
> And all that band them to resist
> His *uncontrollable intent;*[43]

[41]De Man, "Autobiography as De-facement," p. 930.

[42]Wordsworth has recourse throughout the *Essays* to the metaphors of "garment" and "body," maintained in an opposition to each other which as such is tenuous and breaks down when further specifying terms are added, such as "incarnation" (Wordsworth's word here) or "skeleton." The evocation of the deaf-mute also evokes the vulnerability to accident that is constitutive of the body, an arbitrariness in "the incarnation of the thought." Like Samson's complaint that the sun is silent, the Dalesman's predicament in possessing sight "silent as a picture" entails an ironic generalization about the subversive weakness of sight in its very site—provokes a reflection on what it meant to be "sighted." Being "sighted," for Wordsworth and for Milton, is a privative mode of being blind, a blindness taking the form of silence.

[43]Milton, *Samson Agonistes,* ll. 1749–50, 1752–54; my italics.

Here in the voice of piety, under cover of the idea of necessity, once again we come upon the language of "prime decree" and unreadable motive.

The term we were seeking, for a fiction distinct from fiction as "invisibility," could be *muteness*—fiction as language deprived of voice. The accident that occurs, in Rousseau's lines on "Marion," is an incoherence that interrupts his relation to his own voice. Rousseau's "inexcusable" ceding to "le babil de la conversation," like Samson's, is but the inverse of muteness. The degradation that Rousseau realizes to be the ineluctable effect of using the ring of Gyges is muteness or madness—being a vegetable, as Shelley will put it:

> I turned and knew
> That what I thought was an old root which grew
> To strange distortion out of the hill side
> Was indeed one of that deluded crew,
> And that the grass which methought hung so wide
> And white, was but his thin discolored hair,
> And that the holes it vainly sought to hide
> Were or had been eyes."[44]

Shelley has Rousseau tell us how this degradation came about: because he "joined the dance" of "Life." He joined in motivation; he joined in the process of reading. This joining in occurred through the very lucidity of an "invisibile," unreadable fictional text, capable of reading other texts and finally voicelessly reading its own. Shelley is also evoking another madness, the inevitable misreading of Rousseau's texts that came "in the guise"[45] of the French Revolution. The "Rousseau" at issue here for Shelley is also a certain Wordsworth. For, as the end of *Essays upon Epitaphs* suggests, the effort to give voice to language can give rise only to a voiceless "language unremittingly and noiselessly at work . . . to vitiate and to dissolve" the condition of the possibility of meaning.

---

[44]Shelley, "The Triumph of Life," *Shelley's Poetry and Prose: Authoritative Texts and Criticism*, ed. Donald Reiman and Sharon Powers (New York: Norton, 1977), p. 460.
[45]De Man, "Literary History and Literary Modernity," in *Blindness and Insight*, p. 165.

3 /

Wordsworth's
Rhetorical Theft

TIMOTHY BAHTI

Considered as an autobiography—not in the narrow sense of a chronicle of the life one might have lived, but as a narrative in which the self coheres over time and arrives at the condition of meaningful existence through the power of a retrospective understanding— Wordsworth's *Prelude* locates itself among such works as Augustine's and Rousseau's *Confessions,* Dante's *Commedia,* and Proust's *A la recherche du temps perdu.*[1] In these "conversion narratives," the decisive moment—indeed, the moment of *conversion*—should in principle occur as the persona whose life is being narrated becomes transformed into the author with the authority to read and understand the significance of that life and thus to write the life in the first place. It would be a mistake to think of this moment as a single, unified one, such as Augustine's reading from the Bible in the garden at Milan, for this scene is prefigured and echoed throughout the *Confessions,* most often when Augustine is discussing the exegeses of specific biblical passages or his situation of writing to the two audiences of God and human readers. Likewise, Dante's "conversion" cannot be accounted for by the single scene of his surviving a shipwreck that immediately opens the *Inferno,* but rather is displaced across a number of encounters with authority figures—Ovid, Virgil, Statius, Arnaut Daniel, Brunetto Latini—onto the appearance of "God's book" in the final canto of *Paradiso.* What is determining in the tradition is not the number or even the precise location of the conversion scenes, but

[1]On autobiography as a "narrative of the self," see John Freccero, "Introduction" to *Dante: A Collection of Critical Essays,* ed. John Freccero (Englewood Cliffs, N.J.: Prentice-Hall, 1965), pp. 1–7; on Wordsworth's *Prelude* within this convention, see M. H. Abrams, *Natural Supernaturalism* (New York: Norton, 1971), chap. 2, "Wordsworth's *Prelude* and the Crisis-Autobiography," pp. 71–140.

rather the fact that they inevitably manifest themselves as moments of reading.

The encounter with antecedent texts in these narratives is also always a confrontation with the author's own text, which comes before or appears to him at that moment when in the course of composition he is both writing and reading. Whether this situation obtains in the tradition at large—the suggestion is only that and would have to be refined through specific interpretations of the works in question—it can be shown to be the case with *The Prelude*. It has been persuasively argued that the governing "conversion" moments in this autobiography are the apocalyptic recognition of imagination's power in the face of the natural world at the Simplon Pass in Book VI and then the reestablishment of a bond of reciprocity between imagination and nature on Mount Snowdon in XIII (1805). Such an analysis reached its limits of rigor and comprehension in Geoffrey Hartman's phenomenological study of Wordsworth's consciousness.[2] It remains for Wordsworth critics to read and understand how Wordsworth's autobiography writes its way from its initial projection, a reading of the book of nature[3] as imagination's writing, to a writing of the power of signification and narration as triangularly and "transcendentally" suspended *between* imagination and nature, mind and text ("a mind sustained / By *recognitions* of transcendent power" [1850, XIV, 74–75; my italics).

To the extent that this question is central to an understanding of the textual character and self-interpretive dimensions of *The Prelude*, it is also beyond the scope of this essay. Elsewhere I have discussed the figural problem posed in Hartman's exemplary interpretation of the interrelations of Simplon and Snowdon, a problem complicated not least of all by the fact that the Snowdon passage was written before the crucial middle part of the Simplon passage, although it comes after the Simplon passage in the poem's narrative sequence.[4] Furthermore, the difficulties in understanding Wordsworth's rewriting of biblical and Miltonic texts in these passages—a necessary

[2] Geoffery Hartman, *Wordsworth's Poetry, 1787–1814* (New Haven: Yale University Press, 1964; rev. ed. 1971).

[3] Cf. "the end and written spirit of God's work, / Whether held forth in Nature or in Man," IV, 358–59; and "With such a book / Before our eyes, we could not chuse but read," VI, 473–74. All quotations from *The Prelude*, by book and line numbers only, are from the 1805 text, ed. Ernest de Selincourt; 2d rev. ed., ed. Helen Darbishire (Oxford: Clarendon Press, 1959). Occasional references to the 1850 text will be indicated as such and are from this same edition; references to other manuscripts and editions are documented individually below.

[4] See my "Figures of Interpretation, the Interpretation of Figures: A Reading of Wordsworth's 'Dream of the Arab,'" *Studies in Romanticism* 18 (1979):601–27; 602–7.

TIMOTHY BAHTI

Vorstufe to any serious attempt to understand the text's interaction with its own writing—are immense. But these problems of textuality and autointerpretation can be addressed by another path.

Readers of *The Prelude* know there are other, more accessible passages where the Wordsworth persona encounters written texts and the poem represents "his" (its) reading of them. These passages are less central perhaps to the overarching narrative of the poem than are Simplon and Snowdon, but nonetheless are instrumental in determining that narrative's joints and seams. I am thinking of Book V, the book of "books"—but especially of the drowned man's "unclaimed garments telling a plain Tale" (V, 467)[5]—the Blind Beggar passage of Book VII, and the first "spot of time" in Book XI (1805), which tells of the "monumental writing" of a murderer's name "inscribed" by "some unknown hand" at the scene of his execution by hanging (significantly followed by the second "spot of time," on the death of Wordsworth's father, as if "executed" by Wordsworth's "anxiety of hope"). Rather than discuss such passages directly, I shall analyze the theft scenes of Book I as a sort of prologomenon to further interpretation of the textual character and strategy of Wordsworth's autobiography. Such an approach is not gratuitous. The importance of the theft scenes is less that youthful thefts are a convention in autobiographical writing than the way they function in a narrative of the self. Like Augustine's pear and Rousseau's ribbon, Wordsworth's birds, eggs, and boat are objects whose appropriation serves at once to determine his character and to redetermine the character of the objects themselves. That is, Wordsworth's self is designated as an identifiable agent acting on its desires in the thefts, actions that recharacterize the objects as his own rather than something else or someone else's. As the self begins to become properly itself, or *autos* in these acts of appropriation—a self whose story, including those thefts, it could then tell—the objects tend to become improper to themselves because of both the strange characterizations of their own properties and their questionable status as being proper to someone or some place, of their being *property*. Because the self is "produced" by this act of appropriation, however, it is from the beginning structurally dependent on the rendering of objects as improper. And what renders them improper could be called the act or process of figuration, a movement from proper status and meaning to improper ones. The self is thereby in turn appropriated, so to speak, into this figural structure, itself a structure of allegory

[5]On this passage see Cynthia Chase, "The Accidents of Disfiguration: Limits to Literal and Rhetorical Reading in Book V of *The Prelude*," *Studies in Romanticism* 18 (1979):547–65.

wherein a thing both is itself and also signifies or figures something else, an insubstantial state and meaning. The theft scenes thus display the self engaging its world and itself in a rhetorical economy of the proper and the improper, or literal and figural representations and meanings, the distinctions of which are always at stake when (autobiographical) narrative writes the reading of its own (self's) text.

The theft scenes appear in the earliest drafts of *The Prelude* and are retained largely unaltered throughout all the versions of the poem—even in the 1850 *Prelude,* where many another passage suffers considerable decomposition. If the scenes are thereby at the beginning of the poem compositionally, they also begin Wordsworth's autobiography, in that they are essentially[6] the first acts of his childhood that the poem narrates. But in fact, Book I of the 1805 *Prelude* begins, in its well-known "glad preamble," not with thefts but with a gift: the "blessing in this gentle breeze" that meets the poet as he leaves London has its liberating effects "As by miraculous gift" (l. 22), and it is then said of this meaning that "this hour / Hath brought a gift that consecrates my joy" (ll. 39–40). The opposite of a gift is a payment or a reward, received because it is one's due or even one's property. But a theft may also be the opposite of a gift—the act of *taking* what is not one's property or due. How and why, then, does *The Prelude* move in scarcely more than three hundred lines from the gift scene to its "opposite," the theft scenes?

The first incident is not a simple, unified interaction of giving and receiving. The first gift is divided between the divine "blessing" of the breeze—a "Messenger" or *angelos,* later called "the sweet breath of Heaven" (l. 41)—and the complementary "gift that consecrates my joy" of "a corresponding mild creative breeze" felt "within" the poet. This second breeze, which has been identified as the initial appearance in the poem of the "power" (l. 47) of imagination,[7] immediately becomes entangled in its response: "is become / A tem-

[6]I say "essentially" because as the autobiographical narrative of the poem begins chronologically from the Derwent passage ("Was it for this / That one, the fairest of all Rivers," ll. 271ff.) onward, it admittedly refers first to his "infancy" with his nurse, then to his being "a five years' Child, / A naked Boy" playing beside the river. But these passages can scarcely be considered as autobiographical incidents that are set and narrated with the detail and interpretive power of the theft scenes; the Derwent passage is more an apostrophe to the river than the beginning of the poem's autobiographical narrative. Cf. Richard J. Onorato, *The Character of the Poet: Wordsworth in The Prelude* (Princeton: Princeton University Press, 1971), p. 168.

[7]See M. H. Abrams, "The Correspondent Breeze: A Romantic Metaphor," in *English Romantic Poets: Modern Essays in Criticism,* ed. M. H. Abrams, 2d ed. (New York: Oxford University Press, 1975), pp. 37–54, esp. pp. 39–40.

pest, a redundant energy / Vexing its own creation" (ll. 45–47). In the earliest manuscript, MS. JJ, this first scene of gift and "return gift" does not distinguish between two different givers, but rather presents a negative grammatical and rhetorical structure that nonetheless involves the same entanglement: "Creating *not but* as it may / disturbing things created—" (MS. JJ, leaf Z^v; my italics).[8] "Creating not but," closely akin to Wordsworth's more frequent and crucial "cannot chose but" construction,[9] is perhaps a form of litotes (denying the contrary, or in logic, double negation), and this negativity appears thematically as creativity that is not creating except as it is also "disturbing things created." From the beginning, in other words, the gift's reception and repetitions are complicated and destabilized by what I call the negativity of Wordsworth's language, grammatical and rhetorical forms of negation and qualification that undercut the representation of a single, identifiable meaning— here, that of the giving of a gift and its reception.

In the 1805 *Prelude,* the first gift has the effect of a "miraculous gift" in that

> 'tis shaken off,
> That burthen of my own unnatural self,
> The heavy weight of many a weary day
> Not mine, and such as were not made for me.
> [ll. 22–25]

The shaking off of the "unnatural self" of the city dweller is here still associated with the "gentle breeze / That blows from the green fields and from the clouds / And from the sky" (the 1850 version omits the reference to the "miraculous gift"), but this "natural supernatural" breeze is also clearly associated with an intellectually "transcendental" act, in that the "miraculous gift" is also qualified by the immediately preceding line, "Trances of thought and mountings of the mind" (20). The supernatural or transcendental gift is thus supposed to throw off an unnatural self, which at this point in the poem is the speaker's "own" self ("my own unnatural self"). Yet it is not:

---

[8]All references to MS. JJ and other pre-1805 manuscripts of *The Prelude* are from *The Prelude, 1798–1799,* ed. Stephen Parrish (Ithaca: Cornell University Press, 1977), and are cited in the text either by the original manuscript pagination or by the line numbers established in Parrish's "reading texts."

[9]This connection and its importance were suggested to me in conversation with Neil Hertz. The "not but" construction is essentially a sign of repression that denies a desire (e.g., for choice) by converting it into a compulsion. The recurrence of the construction could thus be understood as a repetition-compulsion.

"my own *un*natural self, . . . Not mine." It is this paradox of negativity, of the speaker being in a negative or privative state that is his own and yet not his, that the first gift presents: a supernatural gift received by an unnatural self is to have the positive effect of yielding a *natural* self, but the self's position is bound in the same negativity as is the "Creating not but . . . disturbing things created," where the effect is one of "vexation." The double negation here is of a self both his own and not his, and therefore neither his own nor not his: the gift is one of subtraction, a giving that takes away. To this extent, the "glad preamble" beginning *The Prelude* yields, in its scene of gift and response, an interplay of opposites in a structure of negation that can be understood tropologically as that of litotes—in other words, as having a rhetorical character. Whether these opposites are the supernatural or transcendental on the one hand and the unnatural on the other, or the outside breeze and the "corresponding breeze within," they issue in a structure of neither/nor, of neither unnatural nor natural, not creating without "disturbing" or "vexing."

It is from this negative situation that Book I continues, and this same "unnatural act" of a poem beginning without either an ontologically stable speaker or an unvexed scene of its own creation impels the following two hundred–odd lines toward the actual beginning of the poem's autobiographical narrative, the young Wordsworth's thefts from nature. That is, the poem seeks to move from the narrator's unnatural situation in order to begin a narration of his autobiography as a "natural history," a story guided by and unfolded through nature's teaching. That autobiographical story nonetheless begins with the thefts and the consequent unnatural appearances of nature. And the way to the theft scenes is not without its further complications, providing images and passages that restate the negativity of the persona's double bind and give it a more explicit characterization as a problem of language and rhetoric. To note only one such image, the scene of the breeze and the poet's response to it recurs, but this time without promise (cf. ll. 50–60) or other positive issue: "nor did [my soul] want Eolian visitations; but the harp / Was soon defrauded, and the banded host / Of harmony dispers'd in straggling sounds / And, lastly, utter silence" (ll. 103–7). Having portrayed himself as an Aeolian harp, inspired by nature's breeze and responding—or at least promising to respond—with "natural" poetic sound, Wordsworth here "defrauds" this image of poetic economy. The would-be sound of "harmony" is "dispersed" in a phrase whose lisping alliteration mimics its semantic content, and the passage ends ("lastly") abruptly in midline with "utter si-

lence." "Utter silence" is the result of the attempts thus far to generate poetry from an interchange of "gifts" with nature, but one can
also hear it as a predicate phrase in its own right: the words of the
poem at this point "utter silence," neither prophecy nor its fulfillment. The image of failed gift giving and countergiving returns yet
again when Wordsworth, in an allusion to the New Testament's
parable of the talents (Matt. 25:14–30), speaks of himself "Like a
false Steward who hath much received / And renders nothing back"
(ll. 270–71). The images of exchanging gifts with nature have been,
respectively, doubly negative, vexing, fraudulent, and false; they
either generate ("utter") "utter silence" or, what may be the same
thing, "render nothing." It is at this point, of course, that Book I
breaks, again in midline and in evident frustration as well, into the
apostrophe to the river Derwent: "Was it for this . . ."

   If these repetitions demonstrate, in the perpetuated instability of
the opening image of the gift, the poem's difficulty in beginning, the
first three hundred lines also provide telling depictions of a poetic
self that would locate itself in a different economy of exchange, one
that would escape sheer circularity through producing the power of
poetic language, or what Wordsworth called "prophecy." When
Wordsworth speaks of his aspirations toward a poetic project, he
writes:

> I had hopes
> Still higher, that with a frame of outward life,
> I might endue, might fix in a visible home
> Some portion of those phantoms of conceit
> That had been floating loose about so long.
> [ll. 127–31][10]

The reader does not need to have in mind Heidegger's well-known
adage "Die Sprache ist das Haus des Seins" ("Language is the house
of being")[11] to appreciate the power of this passage. Having arrived
at his own "home" or "hermitage" (l. 115) at Racedown, Wordsworth would now find or "fix" a "home" for his poetic "hopes" that
otherwise were mere "floating phantoms." But they are "phantoms

---

[10]A. F. Potts, *Wordsworth's Prelude: A Study of Its Literary Form* (Ithaca,: Cornell
University Press, 1953), p. 270, notes echoes of Mark Akenside's *Pleasures of the
Imagination* (1744; rev. 1772) here. I would note that the "hopes" anticipate the Blind
Beggar passage (VII, 592–622), where the phantom-like and rhetorical "second-sight
procession" that floats about then appears as "fixed" in the "view / Of a blind Beg-
gar," "the shape of the unmoving man, / His fixèd face and sightless eyes."

[11]*Brief über den Humanismus* (1947), in Martin Heidegger, *Wegmarken* (Frankfurt: V.
Klostermann, 1967), p. 145.

of conceit," a phrase that suggests both that they are only mental or intellectual abstractions ("conceit" derives from "conceive") until "fixed in a visible home" and, given the baroque sense of "conceit,"[12] that they are somehow already rhetorical. The "outward frame" that would "fix" or anchor and house them may well be a construct of natural images and events to embody Wordsworth's poetic notions, but it also is clearly writing, in the sense of "visible" language that might literally—as letters—frame and fix the figural "phantoms of conceit." But Wordsworth does not begin to write here; rather;

> . . . I have been discouraged; gleams of light
> Flash often from the East, then disappear
> And mock me with a sky that ripens not
> Into a steady morning.
>
> [ll. 134–37]

The experience of such a "false dawn," a conventional topos here given a specific sense in a failed scene of writing,[13] should be no surprise, with the "I" of the lines—the "I" who would write his story—having been repeatedly unsuccessful in its interactions with nature and in portraying itself as a coherent, "natural" self. Seven lines later, the poet's self is described in lines that closely echo the initial depiction of "my own unnatural self . . . not mine," indicating that that "unnatural self" was not so easily "shaken off." Halted in his poetic project, Wordsworth writes of the poet's

> fits when he is *neither* sick *nor* well,
> Though *no* distress be near him *but his own*
> *Un*manageable thoughts.
>
> [ll.147–49; my italics]

The passage repeats and recapitulates the double negativity of the self's neither/nor situation, where what is "his own" is itself negative

---

[12]*The Compact Edition of the Oxford English Dictionary*, 2 vols. (Oxford: Clarendon Press, 1933; reprint 1971), I, 499, "conceit," sense 8 (hereafter cited as *OED*).

[13]Wordsworth is probably alluding to Milton's use of this topos in allusion to his blindness: "thee [Light] I revisit safe, And feel thy sovran vital Lamp; but thou / Revisit'st not these eyes, that roll in vain / To find thy piercing ray, and find no dawn" (*Paradise Lost*, III, 21–24). Thematically, Wordsworth's use of the "false dawn" here also accommodates itself to Milton's principle of accommodation between God and man, grace and labor, as in *Paradise Lost*, VIII, 94–97: "the Sun that barren shines, / Whose virtue on itself works no effect, / But in the fruitful Earth; there first receiv'd / His beams, unactive else, their vigor find"; cf. Geoffrey Hartman, "Adam in the Grass with Balsamum," in *Beyond Formalism* (New Haven: Yale University Press, 1970), pp. 124–50.

or privative ("unmanageable thoughts") and thus not properly his. "Hopes" and "thoughts," then, are issuing from an "I" that is itself in a condition of lack or need. The "I"'s *manque à être* to be filled by language, specifically by the language of an autobiographical poem telling the story of a self having become coherent and stable, is a central feature here. But it may be more important that, at this juncture, the language of the poem not only is precisely recapitulative in its negativity, but also already anticipates the negativity of the first autobiographical acts of the thefts, and especially of the third in the series.

These lines are immediately followed by a further image of Wordsworth's mind:

> The mind itself
> The meditative mind, best pleased, perhaps,
> While she, as duteous as the Mother Dove,
> Sits brooding, lives not always to that end,
> But hath less quiet instincts, goadings on
> That drive her as in trouble through the grooves.
> [ll. 149–54]

Editors of *The Prelude* point out the allusion to Milton's "Spirit," addressed as "Dovelike satst brooding on the vast Abyss" (*Paradise Lost*, I, 21); some also refer to the determining image of Snowdon,

> the emblem of a mind
> That feeds upon infinity, that broods
> Over the dark abyss, intent to hear
> Its voices issuing forth to silent light
> In one continuous stream.
> [1850; XIV, 70–74]

The poem would wish to make its way from the narrative uncertainty of the opening of Book I to this late, overstated image of unified narration (a critical reading of the Snowdon passage and its implications remains to be performed). Here the Mother Dove does not conform to its own proper end, but rather strays and errs; this negative alternative is implicitly, through the allusion, contrasted with the image of sitting "brooding on the vast Abyss." The situation of either erring or finding oneself over an abyss is perhaps a neither/nor situation of its own. In any case, the image of the Mother Dove moving "as in trouble through the grooves," more than merely echoing earlier instances of "disturbing," "vexing," and "distressing," exactly anticipates the language of the first and second thefts, where Wordsworth "seemed a trouble" "among the Cliffs / And the smooth Hollows, where the woodcocks ran" and "was . . . a plunderer" "where'er, among the mountains and the winds, / The Mother Bird had built her lodge." In other words, the first scenes of autobiographical acts repeat and represent this image of the poet's mind: Wordsworth's "mediatative mind," as a dove, first troubles nature, and then Wordsworth tells of his having troubled nature and its birds. A human figure still troubles nature, but the second version, in its verbal reference to the first, exposes its "trouble" as a narrative representation of the poetic mind's "own" "trouble." The image of the mind's own trouble with its proper end—emblematic of the failed attempts toward a poetic desire or teleology already in the opening of the poem—becomes the scenes of Wordsworth's impropriety amid nature and the sense of its corresponding improperness. In those scenes, to anticipate, the self discovers the improper or figural character of natural objects and their names, and thereby writes itself into its "own" allegory, a reflexive representation of its improper self-signification.

Two more early images of Wordsworth's poetic frustrations may be examined before turning to the interpretation of the theft scenes. The first of these images occurs in the midst of Wordsworth's notoriously weak cataloging of his various poetic options (Miltonic epic? Spenserian romance? national history?):

> But deadening admonitions will succeed
> And the whole beauteous Fabric seems to lack
> Foundation, and, withal, appears throughout
> Shadowy and unsubstantial.
>
> [ll. 225–28]

The "shadowy and unsubstantial" appearance of the poetic fantasies echoes the "phantoms of conceit." The "Fabric"—the word meaning any artifice rather than cloth in particular[14]—is apparently without "foundation," the ground or grounding element for the poem. This "foundation" is language itself, written or composed (for the poem is not yet written), but coextensive with the language is the poetic self, depicted several times already as without its self, or in a state of "lack." The self has yet to write its story of itself, its autobiography, which would be the precondition for that same self to have the

[14]Cf. *OED* I, 945, "fabric."

authority to write any poetry or text at all, for the "fabric" to have any "foundation."

The final image appears just before the frustrated simile of the "false Steward," where Book I then breaks from its "beginning" into the apostrophe to Derwent. Here, as Wordsworth pessimistically questions the whole enterprise of poetry ("better far than this, to stray about / Voluptuously through fields and rural walks, / And ask no record of the hours" [ll.252–54]), he offers this image of his mind:

> to live
> Thus baffled by a mind that every hour
> Turns recreant to her task, takes heart again,
> Then feels immediately some hollow thought
> Hang like an interdict upon her hopes.
>
> [ll. 258–62]

Being "baffled by a mind" as it "turns recreant" recalls the earlier images of vexation and disturbance created as Wordsworth tried to "turn recreant" toward the inspiring breeze coming from nature's fields. More significant in this highly recapitulative image is the reference to "hollow thought" that comes between and halts his poetic "hopes": this is the "fabric" still "lacking foundation" that was "shadowy and unsubstantial" and blocked his poetic hopes earlier in the same catalogue. Moreover, as disembodied, "hollow," or "unsubstantial" thought, as a poetic artifice without the "foundation" of a written form, this "shadowy" state of mind recalls "those phantoms of conceit" without "a frame of outward life" or "a visible home." Those unwritten "phantoms of conceit" were already faintly rhetorical in their first mention. Their status can now be more appropriately understood as a meaning, or at least an intention toward meaning, without a written sign, in other words, as a figure—of meaning, of poetic intention—without its literal, textual embodiment. But here the "hollow thought / Hang[s] like an interdict upon her hopes." The figural "hollow thought" prohibits the hope for literal writing, for writing a poetic text. The thought that needs a textual foundation also prohibits this founding or writing from occurring literally, or as written letters, instead of remaining merely a fantasy or hope, a prophecy or promise. But an "interdict" is also an act of language; it not only prohibits language, but also "speaks between" or against language. At this point in Book I, in an image that may be understood as emblematic of the whole course of the opening three hundred lines, Wordsworth's language speaks against and blocks itself as it tries to write its way toward an autobiographical narrative. But it does so hollowly, as it were, ready to give way to narrative. Here a figure that is hollow or unsubstantial without its founding, literal narrative—the "I" of Wordsworth's poetic self—needs this narrative to fill its lack, but also threatens to prohibit such a story through its "own" figural discourse.

How can this bind be understood? A hint may be found in the choice of the word "hang" in the phrase "feels immediately some hollow thought / Hang like an interdict." It is precisely this word that Wordsworth singles out in the "second" Preface to the *Lyrical Ballads* (1815 edition) when he examines its metaphoric usages in passages drawn from Virgil and Shakespeare, while asserting the essentially metaphorical power of imagination as distinct from the faculty of fancy:

> Imagination . . . has no reference to images that are merely a faithful copy, existing in the mind, of absent external objects; but is a word of higher import, denoting operations of the mind upon those objects, and processes of creation or of composition, governed by certain fixed laws. . . . images [are] immediately endowed by the mind with properties that do not inhere in them, upon an incitement from properties and qualities the existence of which is inherent and obvious. These processes of imagination are carried on either by conferring additional properties upon an object, or abstracting from it some of those which it actually possesses.[15]

We need not involve ourselves in the larger questions of Wordsworth and Coleridge on imagination and fancy to understand what is being said here. Images of "imaginative" poetry will not be literal embodiments or "faithful copies" of natural objects, but rather will be figural, or figurations of the mind. "Properties" will be metaphorically transferred to the objects and "hang" upon them, with the proper or literal character of the objects thereby becoming improper or figural. But Wordsworth explicitly notes that this transfer or metaphorization of properties can be *from* those that the object "actually possesses" as well as an "addition" of properties *to* the object. In other words, imagination can commit a theft of properties from natural objects as well as metaphorically supplement their characteristics.

[15]*The Prose Works of William Wordsworth*, ed. W. J. B. Owen and Jane Worthington Smyser, 3 vols. (Oxford: Clarendon Press, 1974), III, 30–32.

TIMOTHY BAHTI

If one hangs these remarks from the Preface onto Wordsworth's predicament in Book I, its character becomes more precise. The embodiment, foundation, or "visible home" for Wordsworth's poetic intentions, which is literally lacking in that it is unwritten and which would function as the literal sign for "shadowy," figural "phantoms of conceit," will itself be figural, or specifically metaphoric, involving the transfer of properties to and from natural objects. It has already been argued that the poetic "I" itself likewise lacks "foundation," or a literal or "natural" location and stance, for it only anticipates the actual beginning of its autobiographical narrative. Thus *The Prelude* tells at once of poetic or rhetorical language being written as such, as figural, and the story of the self, beginning or being constituted in scenes that disembody nature of its property so that the self may become "natural" or proper to itself.

The theft scenes are therefore anything but accidental or "natural": they function as a convention of autobiographical writing,[16] but they are also the predetermined issue of Wordsworth's poetic or imaginative project as it unfolds in the opening of Book I. What the "mind" or self cannot effect in an exchange of "gifts" with nature (when the gift itself already involves a kind of theft), it will steal from nature in acts that metaphorize natural objects but also, ultimately, the self that would have a literal story of its "natural" and proper coexistence with nature.[17] Thus Wordsworth's autobiography begins by writing itself as an allegory of metaphor. Paul de Man has interpreted the significance of the word "hang" in the Boy of Winander passage (V, 389ff.);[18] it remains to see how this same word functions explicitly in the second theft scene and indeed hangs over all three scenes as a sign for the structure and operation of language

[16]Frank D. McConnell, *The Confessional Imagination: A Reading of Wordsworth's Prelude* (Baltimore: Johns Hopkins University Press, 1974), begins by discussing the "theft" in Wordsworth's "Nutting" vis-à-vis Augustine's theft of the pears (pp. 5ff.), but nowhere returns to this convention of conversion autobiography when treating the third theft scene itself (pp. 90ff.).

[17]For an argument that preserves the governing role of nature in this project (anticipating a reading of the Blest Babe passage of Book II), see Hartman, *Wordsworth's Poetry*, pp. 35–37: "The poet's anticipation of autonomy is probably less a matter of pride than of necessity: he will *steal* the initiative from nature so as to freely serve or sustain the natural world should its hold on the affections slacken. His poetic power, though admittedly in nature's *gift*, must perpetuate, like consecration, vital if transitory feeling" (my italics). Thus a page later Hartman can say, "Wordsworth not only cannot, he *need* not steal the initiative from nature."

[18]"Wordsworth und Hölderlin," *Schweizer Monatshefte*, April 1966, 1141–55, esp. 1145–47. On "hang" and imagination, see also Leslie Brisman, *Milton's Poetry of Choice and Its Romantic Heirs* (Ithaca: Cornell University Press, 1973), pp. 5, 6, and Cynthia Chase, "The Accidents of Disfiguration," pp. 550–53.

as metaphor.[19] The product of the scenes becomes a state wherein imaginative or metaphoric language "dispossesses the creature almost of a corporeal existence"[20]—to allude to another passage from the "second" Preface, where Wordsworth is discussing imagination in the context of language that once again specifically figures in the thefts ("dove," "broods," "bird"). The "creature" is of nature or it is Wordsworth's "own" self: in a series of mutually determining interactions, both nature and the self become dispossessed of their properties and of their possible representation as being proper to themselves, as they are rendered improper, or figural, in writing that calls into question the very condition of—or the possibility of knowing and naming—"corporeal existence."

> 'twas my joy
> To wander half the night among the Cliffs
> And the smooth Hollows, where the woodcocks ran
> Along the open turf. In thought and wish
> That time, my shoulder all with springes hung,
> I was a fell destroyer. On the heights
> Scudding away from snare to snare, I plied
> My anxious visitation, hurrying on,
> Still hurrying, hurrying onward; moon and stars
> Were shining o'er my head; I was alone,
> And seem'd to be a trouble to the peace
> That was among them. Sometimes it befel
> In these night-wanderings, that a strong desire
> O'erpower'd my better reason, and the bird
> Which was the captive of another's toils
> Became my prey; and, when the deed was done
> I heard among the solitary hills
> Low breathings coming after me, and sounds
> Of undistinguishable motion, steps
> Almost as silent as the turf they trod.
>
> [ll. 313–32]

[19]I here follow the hints in Hartman's Preface to *Wordsworth's Poetry* that point to Wordsworth's "unique style, in which metaphor (transference) is a generalized structure rather than a special verbal figure" (p. xxiii) and in his later "Retrospect 1971" to that book, in which he postulates "a general theory linking verbal figures and structures of consciousness" (p. xvii). I would argue, however, that such a theory—to the extent that it is implied in this essay—ought not to presuppose a *self* whose consciousness would then be found in some relation to figural language; rather, structures of language would be the condition of possibility—if that—for the self and its faculties of consciousness.

[20]*Prose Works of William Wordsworth,* III, 32.

One way to begin to understand a passage from *The Prelude* is to observe what is added and dropped among the various versions of the text in question, not in the manner of constructing an artificially coherent textual history (*Entstehungsgeschichte*), but more simply to attune oneself to the particulars of Wordsworth's language. In this first theft scene, lines 316–18 are unchanged through the 1805 text, but then "In thought and wish" and "I was a fell destroyer" are dropped from the 1850 version, with the middle line undergoing some alteration. What is at stake here? The "wish" recalls all the proleptic terms of the poem's opening: "promise," "hope," "prophecy," "confidence in things to come" (l. 67), "assurance," "longing," "wish," "aspiration," "trust"—in short, the language of those images that "Are mine in prospect" (l. 29). If those prospective "thoughts and wishes" were repeatedly frustrated, culminating in the image of "some hollow thought / Hang[ing] like an interdict upon her hopes," here too the proleptic language is conjoined with the word "hung." While it is obviously "springes" (traps) that are "hung," one should not allow thematics to deflect attention too quickly from this appearance of the word. For the inversion in Wordsworth's syntax places the word at the line's end, in which position "hung" is left hanging. Its placement recalls the famous "Then sometimes, in that silence, while he hung" of the Boy of Winander passage (V, 406) or the line twenty-five lines below, in the second theft scene, ending "Oh! when I have hung." Hanging implies groundlessness ("lacking Foundation") and threatens a fall: here, once again not thematically but verbally, the "fall" appears in the phrase "I was a fell destroyer." Thematically, the "destruction" here echoes Wordsworth's earlier frustrating of his own desires, from the "disturbing things created" and "Vexing its own creation" to the "interdict upon her hopes."

Such a highlighting of key words, and their association with a larger and apparently different problem, would be gratuitous were it not that this scene goes on to envelop Wordsworth's "wish" to be "a fell destroyer" in much the same problematic as was unfolded in the opening of Book I—which may be why the key words are suppressed in the rewritten 1850 text. As the Wordsworthian persona "plies" his "anxious visitation," he shifts from "stealing" birds from nature (trapping them) to stealing them in the strict sense from others' traps. This shift would seem to remove his actions from the sphere of the self's exchanges with nature, but in fact the language of the text links these acts ever more directly to the familiar problematic of the opening of Book I. Immediately before the shift in thefts, the text reads: "I was alone, / And seem'd to be a trouble to the peace / That was among them [moon and stars]." These lines are absent in the earlier versions: MS. JJ reads "how my bosom beat / With hope & fear." (leaf X^r), and the 1798–99 "two-part" *Prelude* (MSS. U and V) reads "how my bosom beat / With expectation" (ll. 41–42). The persona's "wish"—already complicated, as I have argued, with associations of hanging and falling—becomes the ambivalent "hope & fear" before his state of mind is represented as "a trouble to the peace / That was among them" in lines that recall the earlier representation of his mind displaying the Mother Dove's "less quiet instincts, goadings on / That drive her as in trouble through the grooves." Most striking, however, in this comparison of the different manuscript versions is the MS. V from which today's "reading text" of the 1798–99 *Prelude* is derived. There, above Dorothy Wordsworth's fair copy, Wordsworth is already revising the text toward the 1805 version; on this manuscript page (2^v), the lines in question read: "I was alone / And seem'd to be a trouble to the peace / That was among them; and they troubled me" (ll. 40–42). In other words, the persona's "troubling" of nature's moon and stars— a representation of his "own" troubled "wish" or "hope & fear"—is immediately met by a corresponding "troubling" of himself *by* nature. This symmetrical exchange or "double trouble" between Wordsworth and nature thus introduces the shift in, or exchange of, thefts that closes the passage.

The shift from exchanges of "gifts" to those of "trouble" and theft can be further noted in the lines' resonances as the passage unfolds. "I was a fell . . ." at the beginning of a line is echoed by the rhythm of "I was alone" at a line end. The "fall" of "fell" surfaces in the text as "Sometimes it befel . . ." Specifically, the result of "a strong desire / O'erpower'd my better reason" is that "the captive of another's toils / Became my prey." Rather than receiving something given by another, "desire" here takes something possessed by ("captive of")—or some property of—another. If this exchange corresponds roughly to the metaphorical structure of the operation of the Wordsworthian faculty of "imagination," the transformation also appears in these lines as the product of a specific, however buried, trope. That is, "the bird . . . became my prey" displays the chiasmus whereby the idiomatic "bird of prey"[21] becomes this "prey of bird."

It is following this "deed" that the first theft scene culminates in its famous lines: "I heard among the solitary hills / Low breathings coming after me, and sounds / Of undistinguishable motion, steps /

---

[21]*OED*, II, 2295, s.v. "prey," notes the use of this idiom as early as 1485.

Almost as silent as the turf they trod." What might the lines actually be saying?[22] To begin with, the image is a phantasm: there is no "one" ("I was alone," "among the solitary hills"), but aspects of a personification ("Low breathings," "sounds / Of . . . steps") appear. That this personification, or, more properly, its dismembered aspects, appear as retribution for Wordsworth's theft—perhaps even as the "original" owner/thief returning to lay claim and to punish—is clear, but psychologistic reading (or speculation) is not our concern here.[23] More specifically, the partial personification yields "sounds" or signs "Of undistinguishable motion." This phrase would seem to mean that the "body" that is "moving" or "stepping" is itself "undistinguishable"—it appears nowhere in the image—but more precisely it is the "motion" that is "undistinguishable." In other words, it is less a matter of not being able to move cognitively from the "motion" (the "steps") to the body that is moving or is the agent of the "steps" than of not being able to distinguish the meaning (what "motion"?) of signs ("sounds"). In rhetorical terms, the epistemological problem here is less one of metalepsis or metonymy—moving from effect back to cause or agent—than one of metaphor, of substituting a meaning for its sign(s).[24]

---

[22]Geoffrey Hartman writes that "when a poet approaches the ineffable, a critic is inclined to fall back on the nearest steadying commonplace" (*Wordsworth's Poetry*, p. 66). To call this scene "ineffable"—Hartman does not—would itself be a falling-back upon a steadying commonplace. Indeed, these lines, and especially the phrase "undistinguishable motion," are often collocated immediately with the lines from the end of the third theft scene, "a dim and undetermin'd sense / Of unknown modes of being" (ll. 419–20), an association that is then often followed by some brief statement about Wordsworth's "mysticism" (e.g., R. D. Havens, *The Mind of a Poet* [Baltimore: Johns Hopkins University Press, 1941], pp. 141, 142, 168, 169, 171, 172). It is difficulty enough that two discourses can rarely be expected to share the same understanding of the term "mysticism." In fact, such gestures tend to render an obscure matter only more thoroughly opaque, instead of pursuing the task of critical reading.

[23]Cf. Onorato, *Character of the Poet*, p. 185: "The act of stealing from the traps of others by yielding to a strong desire produces the unmistakable dread of being followed by something large and frightening from his own conscience." The considerably more sophisticated discussion of Leslie Brisman, *Romantic Origins* (Ithaca: Cornell University Press, 1978), pp. 284–85, seeks to expand upon such a psychologistic vocabulary: "The characteristic early spot of time in *The Prelude* figures a ghostly presence in nature, haunting the mind like a bad conscience—or, more precisely, haunting the mind like a reproving *figure of authority not yet internalized, not yet made the self-haunting of conscience*. . . . a shadow moving by itself betokens a mind more than *self*-haunted" [my italics]. Referring to the "measur'd motion, like a ghostly thing" of the third theft, he concludes: "Originally something like a representation of the superego, warning the child that his actions are not independent of antecedent authority, these ghostly motions come to guarantee that the present self will also not be cut off from futurity. Motion guarantees not only the life of the ghost, but life in general against the stasis and discontinuity of death" (p. 285).

[24]For this use of metaphor for the act of substitution implied in any interpretation, see Roman Jakobson, "Two Aspects of Language and Two Types of Aphasic Distur-

Such an introduction of rhetorical categories may be justified by the remainder of the passage, which appears to be an appositive to the "sounds / Of undistinguishable motion," for "steps / Almost as silent as the turf they trod" sharpen the nonmetonymic character of the situation. Causes (steps) and the scene or place of their effects (turf) are scarcely distinguishable, as the "sounds" that themselves did not serve to distinguish or to articulate their meaning become "Almost as silent as the turf" would be without the sounds of the steps. Sounds appearing among and on natural objects ("among the solitary hills," on the "turf") are evidently meaningless and scarcely distinguishable as signs—of a possible or intended meaning—at all against the backdrop or surface of "silent" nature.[25] Most radically, the opposites of sound (of human, or at least of animate, "personified" actions) and silence (of inanimate nature) are becoming "undistinguishable."

If "sounds" yield only "undistinguishable motion" as their meaning and thereby become "almost silent," almost nonsignifying, then the consequence of this first theft is the appearance of signs without apparent meanings, like the appearance of aspects of a personified figure without the appearance of the figure or body itself. But to say that there is a sign is to say that there is signification: these are "sounds of . . . motion," however "undistinguishable." Thus signs and meaning(s) cannot be distinguished here not because there *is* no meaning, but rather because sign and meaning, and the distinction between them, have been collapsed, just as the distinction between the steps and their surface tends to collapse into "silence." If sign and meaning are indistinguishable, then the sign may be said to be *literal,* not in the sense of having a single, determinable, and delimitable denotation or reference, but in its meaning; it is literally only a sign and nothing else. The literal sign here—sounds, steps—has a meaning "Of . . . motion" but does not in turn figure the meaning of this sign beyond its being a sign of some meaning: the motion is "undistinguishable" from one or another sound and step signifying one or another motion, and thus the sign does not figure its meaning in the sense of sounds and steps indicating what is happening or who is enacting the signs.

bances," in Roman Jakobson and Morris Halle, *Fundamentals of Language* (The Hague: Mouton, 1956: 2d rev. ed. 1971), p. 95: "Similarity in meaning connects the symbols of a metalanguage with the symbols of the language referred to. Similarity connects a metaphorical language with the term for which it is substituted."

25On the image of "silent" nature, see the inside back cover of MS. JJ (*The Prelude, 1798–1799,* pp. 118–19), where the line "How often in the silence of the hills" is introduced between "Almost as silent as the turf they" and the apparent word "trod."

The literal sign that signifies only its letter, or literal status as sign, as its meaning is suggestively given its rhetorical due in a line that appears in one of MS. JJ's versions of the first theft scene: "When shape was [?not ?no] figure to be seen" (leaf B^r), inserted before "Low breathings . . ." The editor's transcription is faithful to the unreadable hand of the manuscript, but there is no intent here to make this an instance of "double negation." Rather, in its allusion to *Paradise Lost*'s "If shape it might be called that shape had none / Distinguishable in member, joint, or limb, / Or substance might be called that shadow seemed, / For each seemed either" (II, 667–70), the line suggests two meanings. First, as an anticipatory gloss upon the situation in which minimal, dismembered actions of a person-ified figure appear without the whole body or even the members of the figure likewise appearing, "shape" is synecdochally indicated without the full personification of a "figure to be seen." But with respect to the discussion above of the literal sign, the "shape," like the "sounds" and "steps," signifies itself *as* a shape or sign *of* some-thing ("Of . . . motion," of a "figure") without the meaning of the shape being distinguishable or available to being "seen."

Milton's language anticipates Wordsworth's dilemma: "If shape it might be called that shape had none . . . / Or substance might be called that shadow seemed, / For each seemed either." In this quin-tessential moment of deceptive appearance, shadow seems substance and shape figure, but the former "distinguishes" only itself as ap-pearance, if it distinguishes anything at all. In other words, the shape is literally a shape of a figure, but the figure of the shape, the personification, cannot be understood. The discursive representa-tion of the appearance of the literal sign thus recasts itself as the appearance of a sign which literally means that it is a sign, that is, that a material shape—a letter—has a meaning which is "of" the sign and which the shape figures, without the meaning being distin-guishable as any figure—a personification, a particular motion or step—other than the figure of the sign (sounds, steps). At this point, the literal sign means the figure of the letter; its figuration is of a sign that distinguishes only itself, without distinguishing any mean-ing other than itself as sign. The consequence of Wordsworth's first theft is an encounter with signs amid nature that are of an in-complete figure (a dismembered personification) and that thus fig-ure themselves as signs without any distinguishable meaning beyond that of being literally figural signs.

It is important to bear in mind that the closing lines are repre-sented as the persona's experience following his act of theft, and they represent no guilt or punishment, no feeling or opinions, only the aural experience of signs ("and, when the deed was done I heard . . ."). As the theft of a property—whether the bird is considered as a property or attribute of nature's "Cliffs" and "smooth Hollows" and "open turf" or as the property or "captive of another's toils" makes no difference here—the act yields a sign without distinguishable meaning, and as such, a sign of the sign and of its process of signification: a reflexive representation of signification that has been analyzed, from Walter Benjamin to de Man, as the structure of allegory.[26] The appropriation of the property produces an encounter with a sign that ultimately appears to be a sign of itself *as sign,* or reflexively proper to itself as a literal sign. If this sign were still considered to be *of* its "original" "owner" or possessor—again, whether of the natural order of things or of the "first thief" makes no difference—then, as a severed or dispossessed property, the literal sign would become a simple figure, that is, the specific trope of synecdoche, with a single part signifying a whole from which it is detached but which it nonetheless represents. But the text conveys none of this. Rather, the figural character of the literal sign takes on a dimension larger than that of any particular trope.

For the text speaks of the signs considered from the point of view of (heard by) the "new thief" or "owner": the Wordsworthian persona and also the reader. The appropriation of the property by the persona yields an appearance of an unfamiliar condition—signs heard without their meaning(s) being distinguished, except as the reader who "overhears" the passage may understand the signs as literally signs of or for this figural situation, the apparent absence of identifiable meaning. At this moment in the text's narrative, however, the persona encounters the signs only literally as signs, just as the dispossessed birds, however improper the act of their theft and their subsequent possession, are now "his" "property." This condition may be called that of the "proper improper": improper because signs (and birds) have been dispossessed of their "own," identifiably "proper" meaning(s), but properly so because they reflexively signify their appropriation into a rhetorical structure of signification, a structure of signs signifying other signs. Alternately, this condition is

---

[26]See Walter Benjamin, *Ursprung des deutschen Trauerspiels* (1928; reprint Frankfurt: Suhrkamp, 1963), pp. 174–268 ("Allegorie und Trauerspiel") (published in English as *The Origin of German Tragic Drama,* trans. John Osborne [London: New Left Books, 1977], pp. 159–235, and Paul de Man, "The Rhetoric of Temporality," in *Interpretation: Theory and Practice,* ed. C. S. Singleton (Baltimore: Johns Hopkins University Press, 1969), pp. 173–209, esp. pp. 190–92.

literally figural: figural as without any determinable literal meaning (or as a partial personification without the literal representation of any body), but *literally figural* because this figural character is displayed in material signs, like the *spiritus* of the opening breeze being ironically recalled by the passage's "Low breathings."

It is from this condition that the text, across the next two theft scenes, moves to represent the persona becoming "improperly proper," or figurally "himself." The Wordsworthian persona appropriates himself figurally, or as a figure, as his autobiographical poem represents him attempting to read or understand the signs that here, at the end of the first theft scene, are unreadable as either literal or figural, for—in Milton's words—each seemed either. To the extent that the persona would become the reader of the signs that (in his narration) his acts produce, he becomes "undistinguishable" from Wordsworth the author, who writes his text as this appropriating reading of his own writing. This is a figural appropriation of a literary character, one composed of literal characters, or letters. This (mis)reading—*The Prelude* itself—represents as the story of a self, or as an autobiographical narrative, what is in fact the unfolding of a figural structure: an encounter with or reading of literal signs or characters that misunderstands them as figuring the character of a self with the authority to produce or to write the literal signs, or the text, in the first place. The reciprocal "understanding" that the text—and the persona—can read in(to) its writing, but never write as such, as an explicit reading or self-interpretation, deconstructs the figure of the self, or inscribes it as a product of the text's writing, for what the writing writes is that it will be misread by someone who thereby declares himself a "self." This is Wordsworth's allegory of reading.[27]

[27] I use the phrase "allegory of reading" as it is developed in Paul de Man, *Allegories of Reading* (New Haven: Yale University Press, 1979), esp. pp. 76–78. It is obvious that in reading such an allegory in *The Prelude,* I must reject as naive the distinctions implied in Herbert Lindenberger's assertion, in *On Wordsworth's Prelude* (Princeton: Princeton University Press, 1963), pp. xii–xiii, that "the fact that *The Prelude* generally reveals its 'objective' meaning on the level of direct statement—in contrast to poems such as *The Faerie Queene* or Blake's prophetic books—makes an explicatory reading, in the usual sense of the term, seem unnecessary. Certainly the poem does not reveal a hidden allegory, nor does it convey its central meanings with any of the ambiguities which make works so diverse as *Gulliver's Travels* and *Endymion* difficult to read correctly." But I must also reject Hartman's more modest claim, made in reference to the encounter of Wordsworth with the crowd of French delegates along the Rhone (VI, 391ff.), that "the encounter always keeps below the level of allegory: it is accidental and unpredictable as all incidents in *The Prelude*" (*Wordsworth's Poetry,* p. 55). My essay might be understood as an inquiry into *what is* the "level of allegory" in *The Prelude;* it is surely there, including its power to structure and control the apparently "accidental and unpredictable incidents" of its narrative. See Chase, "Accidents of Disfiguration."

> . . . was I a plunderer then
> In the high places, on the lonesome peaks
> Where'er, among the mountain and the winds,
> The Mother Bird had built her lodge. Though mean
> My object, and inglorious, yet the end
> Was not ignoble. Oh! when I have hung
> Above the raven's nest, by knots of grass
> And half-inch fissures in the slippery rock
> But ill sustain'd, and almost, as it seem'd,
> Suspended by the blast which blew amain,
> Shouldering the naked crag; Oh! at that time,
> While on the perilous ridge I hung alone,
> With what strange utterance did the loud dry wind
> Blow through my ears! the sky seem'd not a sky
> Of earth, and with what motion mov'd the clouds!
>
> [ll. 336–50]

The second theft occurs in the same "lonesome" or solitary setting as the first, starkly foregrounding the structural dimension of another encounter between Wordsworth and nature, each alone. His acts as "plunderer" of the "lodges" of the "Mother Bird"—obviously understandable as stealing nests or their eggs—recall, more closely than did the first theft's lines of "trouble," the earlier image of his mind as the "Mother Dove": one could suggest that Wordsworth here steals as much from himself, or his poetic mind, as he does from nature or mother. The lines "Though mean / My object, and inglorious, yet the end / Was not ignoble," which sound like an interpolation although they are present in the scene in some form from the earliest manuscripts onward, are highly problematic in their attempt to anticipate reassuringly the "end" of this theft. This interpretation, which would distinguish means (or "objects") and ends in the course of privileging the latter, is purely proleptic: the telos of a happy end that could be understood as having guided or governed the narrative of his life from its beginning is not yet there, being the very object of the narrative itself, and it can be posited here only through the grammatical turn of "Though . . . yet . . ." Furthermore, the wording of the noble "end" allows the negativity of its positing to surface in the double negative of the litotes "not ignoble."

It is from this negative position of the prospective narrative that the passage's language attains its greatest power with the final and haltingly sustained single sentence. Once again, Wordsworth is immediately found hanging. In fact, he hangs throughout as the sentence—one of the most beautiful, most effectively seductive in

TIMOTHY BAHTI

Wordsworth's oeuvre—repeats his hanging and sustains itself by leaving the reader hanging to the very end. The sentence's structure is determined by the first "Oh! when I have hung" being repeated by the "Oh! at that time, / While on the perilous ridge I hung alone," thereby displaying the delaying effect of its first half and heightening the anticipatory power of its closure. And these are not the only points on which the sentence hangs and turns. The original JJ manuscript included an extra and immediate repetition of Wordsworth hanging: "Oh when I have hung / Above the ravens nest, have hung alone / By half inch fissures . . . ah then / . . . While on the perilous edge I hung alone" (leaves Y^v, X^v). Moreover, the highly detailed and focused image of Wordsworth's hanging "But ill sustained" (without ground or "Foundation" beneath him) includes within it a paradoxical representation wherein this condition of hanging is, "almost, as it seem'd," a hanging from nothing solid, but one that nonetheless suspends and sustains the persona. We recall that it is the very word *pendere* in Virgil's first *Eclogue* that Wordsworth cites in his "second" Preface when he introduces his discussion of the metaphoric operation of imagination. In *The Prelude* Wordsworth's hanging yields metaphorically to his *seeming* "Suspended by the blast which blew amain," as wind appears to be solid, "endowed . . . with properties that do not inhere in [it]"—the very properties of a sustaining stability that the sentence has ever more asymptotically narrowed toward a virtual vanishing point ("half-inch fissures").[28]

This remarkable sentence, which leaves Wordsworth hanging at the ends of two lines and "Suspended" by the power of metaphor in between, sustains itself through the temporality of what Hartman calls "whiling":[29] the "Oh! when . . ." haltingly prolonged so that a point in time stretches into the duration of "Oh! at that time, / While . . ." The "whiling" having at once conveyed in detail the structural situation of Wordsworth's hanging and kept the reader in heightened suspense throughout, the sentence closes with its powerful final three lines. Once again, the persona encounters a semiotic event after his theft: the "strange utterance" of the "loud dry wind." But the utterance is not simply of the wind: "the loud dry wind

[28]Concerning this image of hanging "But ill sustained," in a state of suspension that implies a threatening fall, cf. the sustaining "accidental gift" of a "fall" in the opening lines of Book II: "the passion yet / Was in its birth, *sustain'd*, as might *befal*, / By nourishment that came *unsought*" (ll. 5–7; my italics).
[29]In "Words, Wish, Worth: Wordsworth," in Harold Bloom et al., *Deconstruction and Criticism* (New York: Seabury, 1979), p. 204.

[blew] through my ears!" That is, the signifying act occurs as an interaction between the natural wind and Wordsworth in an image that echoes the earlier "Aeolian harp" images of the opening of Book I. And here, after Wordsworth has been thieving from nature, the product of this "Aeolian" exchange between nature and the persona is an "utterance" that is proper to neither wind nor ear—or, quite literally, "strange" in its original sense of "foreign," as that which is without or outside the realm or dominion of either agent.[30]

But if the signs—the "utterance"—at the end of the narrative of the second theft are represented as "strange" or improper, the following line displays the improperness and even the impossibility of any such representation: "The sky seem'd not a sky / Of earth." The enjambement halts the line so as to have it read: "The sky seem'd not a sky," with the "Of earth" following all the more strangely. What, after all, is "a sky / Of earth"? The conflation of the two dimensions is typical enough for Wordsworth—be it in the form of the "uncertain heaven" received into the "steady lake" in the Boy of Winander passage or the confusions of mist and sky with sea and shore on Mount Snowdon—but our examination here must guard against premature generalization. "A sky / Of earth" would be a sky that had been appropriated to or by precisely that which it is not: earth. This impropriety or figure would then take on the character of the proper state of affairs: the sky is *of*, or the property of, earth, and together they make up nature or a natural condition. If this is the condition already described as the "proper improper," then the issue of the second theft has been to disrupt it: "The sky seem'd not a sky / Of earth." Richard Onorato writes: "The effect was one of reality seeming unreal."[31] As a paraphrase, this tells one rather little, but Onorato's formulation nonetheless focuses on the problem that it itself avoids. What does it mean for reality to *seem?* And what does it mean for reality, in this mode of semblance, to have *unreal* properties? The sky is "distinguished" from itself as such a "properly improper" property of earth. To say that "the sky seem'd not a sky" is to say that it does not appear as itself, in other words, that it is not its "own" one, self-same thing or literal "identity" (not "the same" as itself). This sky neither is nor is not: its identity can no more be denied that it can be posited or indicated. In this condition of double negation, it can only appear, not be. The "properly improper" "sky /

---

[30]Cf. ibid., p. 192: "Sense, itself, the direct referential meaning, is 'almost suspended.'"

[31]Onorato, *Character of the Poet*, p. 187.

Of earth," taken as the literal or natural sky, is disappropriated of its proper identity and becomes improper to itself, or quite simply improper—figural, in the realm of appearance rather than of being or identity. This is why the line must read "The sky seem'd not a sky."[32] The sky has no identity that it could be said to be or not to be; it has only a figural or improper semblance—"seem'd."

Thus the second theft scene ends with the "proper improper"—the literally figural sign, the sky as "a sky / Of earth"—appearing as the sheerly improper, which is to say, appearing as or being only its improper appearance or semblance: "the sky seem'd not a sky." This articulation is a representation not of something that is or was but rather of what it did not seem to be. In other words, the text here articulates not a representation but the impossibility of a representation: nothing was; something only seemed not to be. It is this inarticulateness or blockage of narrative representation that is also implied in the exclamatory phrases "With what strange utterance did the loud dry wind / Blow through my ears!" and "with what motion mov'd the clouds!" This "motion" cannot be said to be; it is "undistinguishable motion" in that signs cannot represent it. To the extent that it is purely figural, and not at all literal, it is unsayable. Likewise, the "strange utterance" can be uttered only as unutterable, as "strange" or outside what *is*—that is, as improper or figural. At this point, after the first two theft scenes—the first acts "recounted," or represented, in Wordsworth's autobiographical narrative—the text's language cannot be indicative, but only exclamatory; and it might as well be interrogative ("with what strange utterance?" "with what motion?") for it questions the improper or figural character of nature but cannot articulate it. This is *The Prelude*'s "own" "strange utterance"—its "own" "proper improper"—not as the language of representation, but as the representation of language.

> One evening (surely I was led by her)
> I went alone into a Shepherd's Boat,
> A Skiff that to a Willow tree was tied
> Within a rocky Cave, its usual home.
> 'Twas by the shores of Patterdale, a Vale
> Wherein I was a Stranger, thither come
> A School-boy Traveller, at the Holidays.
> Forth rambled from the Village Inn alone

[32]MS. JJ has, evidently as its first start, "The sky was then no sky / Of earth" (X^v), then rewritten immediately below on the same page, "the sky seemd not a sky / Of earth."

No sooner had I sight of this small Skiff,   [380]
Discover'd thus by unexpected chance,
Than I unloos'd her tether and embark'd.
The moon was up, the Lake was shining clear
Among the hoary mountains; from the Shore
I push'd, and struck the oars and struck again
In cadence, and my little Boat mov'd on
Even like a Man who walks with stately step
Though bent on speed. It was an act of stealth
And troubled pleasure; not without the voice
Of mountain-echoes did my Boat move on,   [390]
Leaving behind her still on either side
Small circles glittering idly in the moon,
Until they melted all into one track
Of sparkling light. A rocky Steep uprose
Above the Cavern of the Willow tree
And now, as suited one who proudly row'd
With his best skill, I fix'd a steady view
Upon the top of that same craggy ridge,
The bound of the horizon, for behind
Was nothing but the stars and the grey sky.   [400]
She was an elfin Pinnace; lustily
I dipp'd my oars into the silent Lake,
And, as I rose upon the stroke, my Boat
Went heaving through the water, like a Swan;
When from behind that craggy Steep, till then
The bound of the horizon, a huge Cliff,
As if with voluntary power instinct,
Uprear'd its head. I struck, and struck again,
And, growing still in stature, the huge Cliff
Rose up between me and the stars, and still,   [410]
With measur'd motion, like a living thing,
Strode after me. With trembling hands I turn'd,
And through the silent water stole my way
Back to the Cavern of the Willow tree.
There, in her mooring-place, I left my Bark,
And, through the meadows homeward went, with grave
And serious thoughts; and after I had seen
That spectacle, for many days, my brain
Work'd with a dim and undetermin'd sense
Of unknown modes of being; in my thoughts   [420]
There was a darkness, call it solitude,
Or blank desertion, no familiar shapes
Of hourly objects, images of trees,
Of sea or sky, no colours of green fields;

But huge and mighty Forms that do not live
Like living men mov'd slowly through my mind
By day and were the trouble of my dreams.

The third theft scene is preceded by twenty lines of reassuring teleology: talk of "harmony" and the "reconciling" of "discordant elements," summed up in the exclamation "Praise to the end!" Just how problematic this reassuring pause between theft scenes actually is—how tenuous its propositions, how qualified its self-conviction— another exegesis would have to show. But the pause does account for the parenthetic "surely I was led by her [nature]," which introduces the scene of Wordsworth's stealing the boat. This opening line thereby qualifies this theft, too, as an engagement of the persona with nature, even though the specific object of the theft is a boat rather than birds or eggs.

This most extended theft scene is also the most complex, and only some of its complications can be accounted for here. The first striking feature is that the boat is in "its usual home" while Wordsworth—again "alone"—"was a Stranger." The boat is the property of a shepherd, but more important, it is proper to its location or home; this state of affairs is "usual," like the "usual" character of "a sky / Of earth." The persona, on the other hand, introduces an *unheimliches* element: he is strange, or *improper*. Far beyond the homey character of the thematics of this introduction to the theft—a boy traveling on a school holiday—it is as if Wordsworth had incorporated the strangeness of the previous theft's "strange utterance" into his very persona: "I was a Stranger." Such an incorporation would mean that he is, to himself, properly improper, echoing the opening's "my own unnatural self." Finally, this first feature inverts another image from the opening of Book I: if there Wordsworth would have "fix[ed] in a visible home" the uncanny "phantoms of conceit," here he is the uncanny agent stealing or literally "unfixing" (untying: "I unloos'd her tether") something from "its usual home" and appropriating it as "his" property.

The third theft scene varies remarkably little from MS. JJ through the 1805 *Prelude,* but this introduction, wherein "I was a Stranger" is included, is one such alteration. Lines 376–82 seem to be designed primarily to provide the physical and chronological detail that the more complete autobiographical poem might have demanded at this point in its composition, but they include the line about the boat, "Discover'd thus by unexpected chance," which either undercuts the teleological claim of "surely I was led by her" or else raises "chance" to an allegorical function, as in a Spenserian romance. Allegory does seem to be at issue here, for as Wordsworth sets out with the boat, the directness of his language—"from the Shore / I push'd"—evokes the typology of the epic voyage—Odysseus departing from and returning to Ithaca; Aeneas's voyage to Latium; Dante's journey on his *barca*—finally rendered nonepic in the images of sailing and shipwreck in Petrarch's *Canzoniere*. But the voyage is immediately given its full resonance as autobiographical, as a would-be voyage of self-discovery and self-appropriation (as the image is treated already in Augustine). The boat is now immediately "his," "my little Boat," repeated later as "my Boat" and (in a proleptic allusion to Dante—proleptic because Wordsworth had not yet read him) "my Bark." Along with this theft of someone else's property and its appropriation as "mine," the boat is explicitly depicted as the vehicle—or metaphor—of Wordsworth's self: "my little Boat mov'd on / Even like a Man who walks with stately step." At the moment the boat becomes "his," it assumes the appearance of being *him,* that is, the vehicle whereby—in this dispossession, transfer, and appropriation of property which is the very structure of Wordsworth's metaphoric imagination—the child would become "a Man." That such a self is the product of a metaphorical operation, and as such exists as rhetorical appearance, is displayed not only in the explicit image of the boat or vehicle, but also in the attention called to the functioning simile or substitution *"Even* like."

The metaphoric character of Wordsworth's appropriation is immediately highlighted, and in a way that anticipates the scene's later developments. The text reads: "not without the voice / Of mountain-echoes did my Boat move on." The boat—"his" and, "like a Man," like *him*—moves, via the subtly deflating effect of the litotes "not without," with not its own voice but the voice of an echo. As a vehicle, it has no voice of its "own," for it metaphorically carries or transfers another's voice or tenor; here the autobiographical vehicle retains and carries another voice, that of the "hoary mountains." Stolen from "its usual home" within nature ("a Willow tree," "a rocky Cave") and appropriated as "his," the boat stands for Wordsworth and nonetheless is still a property of nature, echoing its natural signification as such. If Wordsworth steals or appropriates property to become "himself," his "poetic self" here—in the simile of the boat—only echoes the voice he would make "his own" nature or natural voice.

This double or split character of the metaphoric appropriation of voice would then appear unified in the following lines: "Small circles melted all into one track / Of sparkling light."[33] This unified "track" is the trace of his autobiographical act—stealing the boat—and his autobiographical voyage, already constituting, as a delicate pre-figuration, the unified narrative that would lead to the authoritative self who could write that narrative in the first place. But the image of unification in "sparkling light" is made of "Small circles glittering idly in the moon," that is, of reflections. And as the phrase "in the moon" lightly but clearly indicates, these reflections are double re-flections: the moon, itself a reflection (of the sun's light or power), is in turn reflected upon the lake's water, where Wordsworth and "his" boat—also reflected in the water—would authoritatively trace their act of appropriation. Their unity—of appropriation, in that they enact the structure of metaphor as the dispossession, transfer and appropriation of properties—highlighted itself as a strong simile, in fact, as substitution or metaphor ("my little Boat mov'd on / Even like a Man"). Here it retraces itself as an instance of the appropria-tion of power through rhetorical reflection, that is, reflecting its "own" unified narrative "voice" and "track" as the product of meta-phoric echoes and reflections that in their doubled character carry and carry over (transfer) an other power (of the mountains, the moon, the sun, nature).

At this juncture the theft scene becomes a more complex matter than a mere stealing of the boat and rowing into the lake. The development of the theft and its consequences also presents, through the introduction of a telling word, this scene of the rhe-torical appropriation of a self as one that would be available to a psychoanalytic understanding as that of the child's appropriation of of his primal signifier, that is, his phallus.[34] But to the extent that such a psychosexual understanding is implied in the narrative, the psychosexual dimension operates as an allegorical representation of a possible meaning. The text itself will at once represent this mean-ing and undo the terms of its understanding, in a development that undermines the drama of self-appropriation and self-representation through narrative.

A shift in dimensions is introduced representationally as Words-worth and "his" boat, who together had assumed their "voice" from

---

[33]J. C. Maxwell, in *The Prelude: A Parallel Text*, ed. J. C. Maxwell (Harmondsworth: Penguin, 1971), p. 541, notes a possible allusion here to Coleridge's *Rime of the Ancient Mariner*, l. 274: "tracks of shining white."

[34]I owe to Neil Hertz the suggestion to pursue this line of interpretation. To the skepticism of another friend, Reeve Parker, I owe whatever circumspection the in-terpretation may claim.

the "mountain echoes," now navigate the flight of their theft against the backdrop of the mountain. This "rocky Steep" above the "home" of the boat appears as if for the first time and with a word that will be increasingly accented: "A rocky Steep uprose."[35] Wordsworth "fixes" his vision and attention on the "top" (or head) of the ridge, which constitutes, in an aptly phenomenological formulation, "The bound of the horizon, for behind / Was nothing but the stars and the grey sky." That is, the mountain constitutes the horizon within which Wordsworth's theft—with its adherent play between the subject stealing away and the fixed locus that still provides the "voice" through its "echo"—can have its sense or meaning; beyond, there is "nothing but the stars."

It is in the lines immediately following that the act takes on its overtly phallic character. After the mountain "uprose," the boat is identified as "an elfin Pinnace," and immediately thereafter the line continues: "lustily . . . as I rose upon the stroke, my Boat / Went heaving through the water, like a Swan." The crucial, telling sign here is the near homophony between the "elfin Pinnace" and a little penis.[36] Once this homophony is recognized, the logic of the following lines is clear in the implied near-pun between the boat as "Pinnace" and the ridge as a "pinnacle": stealing away from, but still "echoing," this one mount that was already there and now appears erect ("uprose"), the persona would appropriate and erect his "own" phallus. The associations of "heaving through the water, like a Swan" alleged by psychoanalysis—that penetrating the water is the penetration of a female element, that the swan represents a particularly male or phallic image—are of less concern here than the explicit response of the persona's "lust" in the clearly masturbatory, self-erecting image of "as I rose upon the stroke," where the phallus is appropriated as a sign signifying the "I" or self itself; it is worth remembering that the single real change in this scene from MS. V to the 1805 version was the alteration of "twenty times I dipp'd my oars" to "lustily I dipp'd my oars." One last reference to an early

---

[35]Jonathan Bishop, "Wordsworth and the 'Spots of Time,'" *ELH* 26 (1959):50, usefully collocates the appearances of a similar term in the "spots of time" when, as he puts it, "the other world is literally beyond the limits of this": *upright*, for the discharged soldier (IV, 407), the drowned man (V, 471), and the blind beggar (VII, 611).

[36]The sexual crossing in the line "She was an elfin Pinnace" is already evident in the initial, nongenital depiction of the feminine boat as moving "Even like a Man." My interpretation leaves this sex change unaccounted for, beyond remarking upon the general crossings over from proper to improper (as here, already, in the boat curiously belonging to a landed "Shepherd").

manuscript version serves to confirm this interpretation of the theft as an appropriation and erection of the self via the phallus: when, a dozen lines later, the chastised persona returns "With trembling hands" the "Bark"—which had been identified as "Even like a Man"—one leaf of MS. JJ (R^v) shows "my little bark" altered to "my little pinnace."

At this very moment of Wordsworth's self-erection or erection of a self against the backdrop of the erect ridge, a third "erection" appears that overpowers them both. The "huge Cliff" that appears "from behind that craggy Steep" does so in language that echoes the "uprising" of the first mountain and the "rising" of Wordsworth "upon the stroke": it "Uprear'd its head . . . / And, growing still in stature, the huge Cliff / Rose up between me and the stars." This cliff constitutes a new horizon, eliminating the previous, lesser one that is recalled as "till then / The bound of the horizon." It also, of course, causes Wordsworth to "turn" and to reverse or undo his theft ("I . . . stole my way / Back") by returning "his" boat. The third "erection" could be thematically understood—for these suggestions toward a psychoanalytic interpretation remain only thematic—as the retributive reappearance of the father's phallus into this oedipal struggle, undoing the child's premature attempt to appropriate "his" phallus or "pinnace" from the diminutive image of the smaller "uprisen" mountain.[37] But such a psychoanalytic reading, however penned by however more competent a hand, necessarily gives way here to further aspects of the appearance of this "huge Cliff," aspects that unfold the rhetorical structure of the theft scene and undo its thematic representations, psychosexual or otherwise.

If the persona was to appropriate himself through stealing the boat from its "usual home" and having it take on an appearance "Even like a Man," as well as through his "rising" against the backdrop of the "uprisen" mountain, he is here "replaced" by this larger appearance of nature, an appearance whose language increasingly displays its rhetorical structure and predicament. Whether the cliff that "Uprear'd its head" "As if with voluntary power instinct" is understood as being a personification of a man or only of one significant and signifying part of a man (the phallus)—"its head" serving both interpretations—it nonetheless is a personification. As it continues to rise, it assumes the character of a full personification in that it "Strode after" Wordsworth. But the intervening line describes this striding as "With measured motion, like a living thing." As a person-

---

[37]Cf. Onorato, *Character of the Poet*, pp. 271–73.

ification, the cliff is like a man, menacing Wordsworth's attempt to become "Even like a man," but more precisely, a *figure* of man—the personification—is menacing Wordsworth as a figure of or for himself (Wordsworth as "Even like a man"). The personification is then rhetorically described as "like a living thing," which is to say that representationally it is like a man-mountain or mountain-man (a "living thing"). But within this representation, given both the preceding attention called to the similic trope ("Even like") and the abstract character of the word "thing," especially in Wordsworth's usage, there is the semantic meaning that it is *like* a personification that functions representationally: a "thing"—the trope of nature personified—taken, in the personification, as "living." Only from this position, the figure identified rhetorically ("like") as a figure, does the "motion" of the theft scenes appear as "measur'd." That is, the motion of the steps in the first theft was "undistinguishable" in that the signs of the steps were literally figural or "properly improper"; and the motion of the clouds in the second theft was unutterable ("with what motion"?) in that the signs were purely figural or sheerly improper. Here, when the sign is *figurally figural* ("like a living thing," a simile of a personification), the "motion" can be said to be "measur'd"—that is, identified and known as what it was in each case: rhetorical motion.

It is from this moment of discursive self-knowledge, where Wordsworth's language writes itself rhetorically as rhetoric and states this to be its "measur'd motion," that the persona "turns" and undoes his theft. Returning "homeward," however, Wordsworth does not find himself at home in nature; rather, it is more *unheimlich* than ever. That this return homeward is said to have been "with grave / And serious thoughts," where the line's end accents the word "grave," is significant, for the famous ten lines that close the scene indicate an experience of death, the death of a certain illusion and representation of the self, indeed, of the illusion *of* the representation of self.

Several versions precede that of the 1805 *Prelude*'s "after I had seen / That spectacle," and these earlier formulations can help to unfold the precise choice and valence of the term "spectacle." MS. JJ (leaf T^r) has "unusual was the power / Of that strange spectaccle [*sic*]" before leaf R^v alters "spectaccle" to "sight." In either case, the experience of the mountain-man or the "living thing" is "strange" in the same sense that Wordsworth initially was a "Stranger" within the "usual home" of nature. In having been appropriated as a property figuring in a metaphoric dispossession and transfer, nature has become improper or "strange" to itself. But after Wordsworth has returned "homeward," the power of the experience remains "unusual" for him. In other words, Wordsworth is suspended between an experience of the improperly improper—"like a living thing"—and a "present" rendered "unusual" or improper. Hence the situation can be reduced to "see[ing] / That spectacle": not merely because "seeing that sight" would be flat and even tautological, but because the relationship is *specular* in the sense that the self is suspended between a past experience and a present consciousness that codetermine or mirror each other as rhetorical—the rhetorical structure of "like a living thing" in relationship with a rhetorical or "unusual power." This may also be why, in a crucial alteration between the 1805 and 1850 *Preludes*, the word "hung" is reintroduced: "O'er my thoughts / There hung a darkness" (1805, ll. 393–94). "Hung," almost always in Wordsworth a sign of metaphoric or rhetorical dispossession and appropriation, here hangs over the persona and the scene: "thought," and its articulation, are suspended specularly; or, more precisely, a "darkness" of nonliteral, improper knowledge "hangs over" the persona and "his" discourse.

There follows, then, the famous formulation of "my brain / Work'd with a dim and undetermin'd sense / Of unknown modes of being." The persona's experience and "his" discourse have a "sense" or meaning, but it is "dim," dark, or obscure, which is to say that it is allegorical or, more specifically, enigmatic (an enigma being, technically, a "dark or obscure allegory"), and to that extent "undetermin'd" and undeterminable in any proper or literal sense.[38] This is an allegorical understanding "Of unknown modes of being," that is, of a state of being that is "unknown" and unknowable as literal or proper knowledge or understanding. The allegorical understanding alleged here is this discourse's own interpretation—as unfolded in these very lines—of the rhetorical representation of rhetoric that appeared at the end of the theft itself: "the huge Cliff . . . like a living thing, /

---

[38]Lindenberger (*On Wordsworth's Prelude*, p. 5) dissolves the significance of this formulation by ignoring the structure and belittling it as mere "subjectivity," thus missing the point of the William Empson essay that he rightly admires. Empson ("Sense in the *Prelude*," in *The Structure of Complex Words* [London: Chatto & Windus, 1951], p. 290) observed that the issue here is not subjective "feeling" but a particular interpretive or comprehending power: "There is a suggestion here from the pause at the end of the line that he had not merely 'a feeling of' these unknown modes, but something like a new 'sense' which was partly able to apprehend them—a new *kind* of sensing had appeared in his mind." He nonetheless notes only one aspect of the term "sense"—as a power—ignoring its other aspect as the result or *meaning* arrived at through this power of understanding.

Strode after me." The "undetermin'd sense / Of [the] unknown" reveals its enigmatic power, finally, as a specular or self-reflexive construction more powerful than ordinary grammar would allow. The genitive "of" in "undetermin'd sense / Of unknown modes" has each phrase determining the other: the allegorical understanding "senses" something, or is actively "of" the "unknown modes"; and yet the "undetermin'd sense" is "of," belonging to or appropriated by, the very rhetorical structure that it would but cannot "know"—the "unknown mode."

This "co-privative" discourse, in which a mode of knowing and an object of knowledge—a reading or interpretation embodied in lines 417–20 and in the preceding lines of the theft scene that it would understand—reciprocally negate the terms of any literal or proper knowledge,[39] continues through the remainder of the passage, in language that is as negative as any in Wordsworth. The "darkness" hanging over or lodging in the persona's consciousness, which was understood as enigma, is called "solitude"—the persona alone, without any proper knowledge or understanding of literal things—"Or blank desertion." This latter phrase supplants MS. JJ's initial "strange desertion" (R^v), but its added evocative power does not alter its basic meaning: in either case, the persona and his understanding are "deserted" by the very objects he would steal, leaving an effect of "strangeness" or "blankness," of the absence of literal objects in the sense of his being dispossessed of them after he would have dispossessed them of their proper character through his act of theft or appropriation. Corresponding to this reading, MS. JJ (T^r) first had "no show / Of usual objects" at this point, indicating that it is not nature "itself" that has "deserted" the persona, but rather its usual appearance as literal things, "showing" itself now only as improper. The lines are recast in the 1805 version as "no familiar shapes / Of hourly objects." The "shapes" of the objects are unfamiliar or "unusual"—"undetermin'd" or "unknown"—in that the objects do not embody their literal or proper shapes, but rather are figural, like the "shape" of "a living thing," neither properly alive nor properly a thing. There follows a specific privative listing of missing shapes—"no . . . images of trees, / Of sea or sky, / no colours of green fields"—the last of which reposes the rhetorical and verbal dilemma: "no colours of green fields" here means that al-

---

[39]Given this deeply embedded rhetorical structure of a "sense of [the] unknown," Robert Langbaum (*The Poetry of Experience* [New York: Oxford University Press, 1957], p. 42) is wrong, I think, to speak here of "revelation."

though the fields can still be called "green," their color is no longer literally determinable since it is not "of color" and therefore not "green."

This theft scene closes with its most powerful lines, describing what remains to this allegorical or enigmatic understanding in the absence of literal or proper things and appearances: "But huge and mighty Forms that do not live / Like living men mov'd slowly through my mind."[40] Like "the sky [that] seem'd not a sky," recalled in this context by the conspicuous noting of the absence of the sky ("no . . . sky"), these "Forms" seem not to live like usual or familiar forms, like "Forms of life" or like the earlier "sky / Of earth." But one should not conflate the two lines so easily. Here, as with "sky / Of earth," the enjambement of the lines invites one to pause and to consider the first part in its "own" right.

These forms are said *not* to live. But then, in one conventional understanding of the following line, they are said to "move" "Like living men" (this phrase modifying "mov'd" rather than the preceding line). This construction appears as a paradox, but it signifies a representational personification nonetheless: the forms, not literally "alive," nonetheless can be represented as moving "like living men." If the continuation of the phrase in the following line is read, in an alternate interpretation of the grammar, as qualifying the first part's utterance in the sense of making it less absolute, then these forms are said not to "live like living men" rather than not to live at all. This construction too can be readily understood as personification, in that the "huge . . . Forms" allude to the "huge Cliff," and they "do not live like living men" because they *are not* "living men," but rather, like the cliff, personified "living things." These two readings seem to be mutually exclusive: either the forms move "Like living men" or they "do not live / Like living men." But this double bind of understanding—my discourse of personification at this point, of two interpretations that contradict one another under the common rubric of personification—finds itself in its contradictory situation because it seeks a representational interpretation that suppresses, forgets, and misunderstands the text's figural discourse and its negation of literal understanding.

---

[40]Darbishire (*Prelude*, 2d rev. ed., pp. 517–18) confirms that MSS. A, B, and C show no commas in the two lines; more recently, Parrish, *Prelude, 1798–1799*, pp. 84–85 (JJ, Rᵛ), 90–91 (JJ, Tʳ), and 134, 137 (Dorothy Wordsworth to Coleridge, December 1798) confirms as much for earlier manuscript versions. MS. V alone has commas after "forms" and "men," and they were evidently added later (Darbishire, p. 518; Parrish, pp. 240–41).

For the forms neither *are* nor *are not* some literal thing, but, like the cliff again, only appear like or unlike something else. They are not living men or living things, but rather, like the earlier "like a living thing," they appear rhetorically ("like")—in a negative mode in the second alternative ("not . . . like")—as being rhetorical. That is, if the earlier "like a living thing" was a simile of a personification (a trope or thing that represents itself as living), the "Forms that do not live / Like living men mov[ing]" are paradoxes of personification that hinge on a simile, representing either a "not living" that nonetheless appears "like living men" or a "not like living men" that nonetheless is represented as "living" (because moving). What might this reading mean?

If the representational understanding of the "Forms" is maintained—that is, that they are not living but nonetheless move like men *or* that they live and move, but not like men—then the contradiction effectively dissolves, because both readings yield an equivalent rhetorical representation, however paradoxical it may be. But this interpretation takes the "Forms" as representing any one thing in a literal or proper sense, even if this one meaning is understood as rhetorically motivated by the simile, by the play of the signifier "like." That is, they are taken as forms moving "like men" or as being "like" the earlier personification of the "huge Cliff . . . like a living thing"—which also moved "like" a man. But such a literal or representational understanding via the simile necessarily forgets that Wordsworth's discourse denies any literal or "determin'd" sense of any properly "known mode of being." This reading reduces Wordsworth's language to a thematic understanding—even if the thematics here are the thematics of rhetoric—similar to a thematic reading of the personification of the "huge Cliff" as the father or the father's phallus.

Rather, just as the personification of the "huge Cliff" was not represented *to be* a personification, but instead *appeared as* (was a simile of) a personification ("like a living thing"), so here, too, the "Forms" are not said to live like anything else any more than "Like living men." Here a third alternate reading emerges. The line pauses with its enjambement, having said that the "Forms" are not alive, and the following simile is an elaboration of "do not live," meaning that these "Forms" are not alive as living men are, an addendum that does not qualify or temper the first absolute claim but only gives it a precise signification. There is, then, neither the "life" or "motion" of living men here, nor the "life" or "motion" of living things (personifications functioning in a representational narrative) but only "Forms that do not live" "moving." Which means that when the "Forms"—no longer either representational similes ("Like living men mov'd") or representational personifications (like "living things")—are said not to live, their only motion, in the persona's "mind" or in Wordsworth's discourse, can be rhetorical: the movement of tropes or, here, specifically, the movement of the simile "Like living men" within the paradox and chiasmus ("not live / Like living") of the phrase. This is a discursive re-presentation of the earlier rhetorical representation of rhetoric—the personification of the "huge Cliff" appearing as a simile ("like") of a personification (a "thing" or trope taken as "living"). As such a re-presentation of the representation of rhetoric, it signifies the text's "own" deconstruction of the possibility of literal or representational understanding— be it such understanding of this passage or of the text's earlier deconstruction of literal representation, when the cliff moved rhetorically as rhetoric, "like a living thing."

Thus the third theft scene arrives at a deconstructive "formalism" that, as it "rereads" the scene's earlier writing of the personification of the "huge Cliff," denies both thematic or representational narrative and any thematic or representational understanding of this formalism that would appropriate a literal or proper interpretation of it, even on its "own" terms of a formally operative rhetoric. To understand the rhetorical crux exemplified in the phrase "Forms that do not live / Like living men mov'd" as an instance of representation through rhetoric (i.e., through personification) would be to attempt to appropriate an allegorical rhetorical structure literally. It would repeat, in the mode of a blind reading, Wordsworth's narrative of the thefts that sought to dispossess, transfer, and appropriate properties from nature for the sake of a stable and coherent image of one's self. This critical repetition would occur insofar as it would appropriate a rhetorical structure and operation—Wordsworth's discourse—for the critic's "own" desired understanding and self-image (as a "proper critic") within an allegory of criticism. In the very repetition, the reading would misread Wordsworth's text, wherein the "Forms that do not live / Like living men" only appear to and "move" in "a dim and undetermin'd sense," and remain "Of unknown modes of being," belonging to an allegorical discourse of nonunderstanding rather than to any understanding that could articulate or represent itself as literal or proper knowledge. This misreading is the personification of discourse: to move from "forms" and "things" to "Forms . . . mov[ing]" and "things living" with some life or motion other than what the text writes, namely, that they "do not live," that they have only the "measur'd motion" of rhetoric presented rhetorically. Fundamentally, the misreading performs in an interpretive mode what Wordsworth's *Prelude* attempted—but did not achieve—here in a representational mode: to write a narrative that would move from the beginnings of writing a text—also a "Form that does not live"—to the construction of an auto-biographical persona or self adequate to the writing and reading of that text. As sufficiently close readings of *The Prelude* always show, that Wordsworthian self misreads the literal signs or characters of his figural text as figuring himself, as their meaning (their *character*) and therefore as their author, with the authority to produce and interpret them—a procedure whereby he moves from a "Form that does not live / Like living men" to misunderstanding himself as "Even like a man," rhetorically fulfilling in this reversal the trajectory of the third theft. When the critic anticipates—or repeats—Wordsworth's narrative, he enters into the allegory of criticism as Wordsworth's *Prelude* enters into the allegory of autobiography.

Wordsworth's autobiographical thefts, conventionally taken as resulting in encounters with "Forms . . . like living men" or "like . . . living thing[s]," would be the exchange of gifts that the opening of Book I could not perform: the persona would be granted an auto-biographical self in his appropriation of nature's property, and nature would be personified as "like man," with an intention and a meaning. But this personification—in the literal sense, a persona-fication or a persona-fiction, Wordsworth's "own" project here—is never literal, but always figural, both as the self metaphorically appropriated and as nature rhetorically represented and then allegorically "understood," or at least written as allegory. Wordsworth's text thus performs a rhetorical writing of rhetoric that represents the process of persona-fiction as yielding neither the representation of the object personified (nature as *of* human meaning) nor the appropriation of the self to be "persona-fied" ("Wordsworth" as *of* human nature), nor even a literal understanding of the first two consequences. This rhetorical structure, which is not mere (or conventional) personification, is the text's allegory of theft—of the attempt to get from properties to *the proper* (self or understanding) by way of dispossession, transfer, and appropriation. Most fundamentally, it is the attempt to get from the rhetorical "properties" of language (its structure and operation) to a language of proper meaning and literal representation: the story of European romanticism, in its idealist or speculative philosophy and theories of language as well as in its poetry. As such, it is an allegory of metaphor:

TIMOTHY BAHTI

in Wordsworth's terms, an allegory of "imagination" and of his "own" imaginative discourse. In a more structural understanding, it is an allegory of allegory "itself," of allegory as that which Walter Benjamin described as "signifying precisely the non-being of what it presents."[41]

[41] Benjamin, *Ursprung des deutschen Trauerspiels*, p. 266 (*Origin of German Tragic Drama*, p. 233).

4 /

"Oh Could You Hear His Voice!": Wordsworth, Coleridge, and Ventriloquism

REEVE PARKER

Given the affective situations generally so prized by drama-tists in the Romantic period in England, one might expect to find in that drama a congruence of interest in the powerful presence of voice and in the representation of character. Nor is it surprising, in crit-icism of Romantic drama, to find the text regarded as a transparency, providing as it were a lantern image of the author, whose figure and "self" are discernible in the dramatic persons. But Wordsworth's *Borderers*, arguably the most neglected play of the period (now pub-lished in its fine early version), when read in the context of his succeeding works and of aspects we can reconstruct of his and Col-eridge's relationship, prompts considerations of the relation of work to author, of the shaping influence of dramatic representation, and of the role tale-telling voices play in art and life—considerations that call into question the adequacy of situational premises and familiar bio-graphical analysis as critical and interpretive instruments. Recent initiatives in criticism of the novel offer a helpful analogy. Influenced in part by Walter Benjamin's reading of Goethe's *Elective Affinities*, J. Hillis Miller has contended that in reading novels it is probably a mistake to think of the "self" of the writer as the "explanatory origin of the work. That origin, or rather the apparent origin, metaleptically reversing cause and effect, is another more genuine self. This self is made by the work. The self exists only in the work and in the work's detachment from the 'real life' of the author"[1] *The Borderers* brings

[1]J. Hillis Miller, *Fiction and Repetition: Seven English Novels* (Cambridge: Harvard University Press, 1982), pp. 11–12.

these issues to focus in the context of drama rather than narrative fiction, but by means of an unprecedented generic contamination that makes narrative itself an element of crucial dramatic moment.

Wordsworth recalled in 1842 that his care in composing *The Borderers* had been "almost exclusively given to the passions and the characters, and the position in which the persons in the Drama stood relatively to each other."[2] He chose ultimately not to publish his preface to the play, but in this century its extensive hypothetical psychobiography of the villain Rivers has doubtless helped to distract readers' attention from "the passions and the characters" of the other persons in the play, especially as they stand "relatively to each other."[3] *The Borderers* is much more than a vehicle for Wordsworth's dramatization of the Rivers hypothesis. Its intricate tragic structure develops through his elaboration of three interrelated premises: that character is engendered and shaped in passionate response to affecting narrative; that the person whose character is so engendered in effect reenacts the material of the narrative and at the same time becomes an image of the teller; and that through their passions in such reenactment and repetition the persons of the drama become bound to the purposes that embody their characters and in that bondage become tragically vulnerable.

Almost without exception in *The Borderers,* the characters of the persons in the drama develop or come into play through the tales they hear, and the relations of these characters, according to the premises defined above, form a ventriloquistic network. The stripling hero Mortimer becomes what the villain Rivers calls "a shadow of myself, made by myself" (p. 256) through the treacherous tales Rivers inflicts upon him, so that Mortimer reenacts Rivers' own crime when he abandons Herbert on the heath. (Before that deed, the gulled Mortimer echoes Rivers' own tales when he spins narratives about Herbert to his fellow borderers, manipulating their passions to the point of righteous, vengeful frenzy.) Herbert likewise is a tale-teller, and his daughter Matilda is crucially the creature,

---

[2]William Wordsworth, *The Borderers,* ed. Robert Osborn (Ithaca: Cornell University Press, 1982), p. 814. All subsequent quotations from *The Borderers,* unless otherwise noted, are from the "reading text" derived from the fair copy of the "early version" made in 1799 by Dorothy Wordsworth and published for the first time as such in this edition.

[3]*"The Borderers:* Wordsworth on the Moral Frontier," *Durham University Journal* n.s. 25 (1963–64): 175–76. See also R. F. Storch, "Wordsworth's *The Borderers:* The Poet as Anthropologist," *ELH* 36 (1969):340–60; and David V. Erdman, "Wordsworth as Heartsworth; or, Was Regicide the Prophetic Ground of Those 'Moral Questions'?" in *The Evidence of the Imagination,* ed. Donald Reiman et al. (New York: New York University Press, 1978), pp. 12–41.

from childhood on, of hearing his tale-telling voice. As she says feelingly in the first scene,

> . . . think not, think not, father, I forget
> The history of that lamentable night
> When, Antioch blazing to her topmost towers,
> You rushed into the murderous flames, returned
> Blind as the grave, but, as you oft have told me
> You clasped your infant daughter to your heart.
>
> [P. 86]

Herbert reenacts his threshold clasp each time he repeats the story to Matilda, for his tale binds her by rousing her passions to a ruling gratitude: her character is so defined by the embrace of his passionately affecting narrative voice that she can live only for the consuming, pitying purpose of saving him, repeating his original act just as, ventriloquistically, she repeats his tales. Further, the trust she places from infancy in her father's saving voice—act and voice indistinguishable in her ears—is generalized in her character to a trust in the saving power of all voices, a trust that renders her blind and vulnerable in a world unworthy of that trust. She is thus a shadow of Herbert, made by Herbert. It is Rivers' diabolic genius to play upon both Herbert's clasping and Matilda's embrace, persuading Matilda to forswear her lover Mortimer in order to devote herself to protecting him in the infirmity of his aged blindness, a sacrifice that in the passionate blindness of her own devotion she is tragically bound to enact. What might on a casual reading seem like innocent filial gratitude in Matilda becomes in this context the (over)determined response to a tragically suffocating clasp: there is more than a shadow of truth in Rivers' insidious allegations to Mortimer that Herbert has made of his daughter's virtues the very instruments with which to torture her: "to see him thus provoke her tenderness / With tales of symptoms and infirmities." In a fine touch early on in the play, Wordsworth dramatizes the pathos of Matilda's predicament by the cry she twice utters in her futile attempt to persuade her father of Mortimer's heroic virtue: "Oh could you hear his voice!" (pp. 86 and 88).

From childhood on, moreover, Matilda herself is also a tale-teller, repeating her father's stories in innocent ventriloquism. So affecting are *her* tales that she reenacts in her audience the genesis-by-narrative of her own saving character. Hearing her voice, the child Mortimer and his playmates form a band whose common bond is pitying tears for the narrated plight of the infant Matilda and her

exiled father. As Mortimer recalls, initially in part resisting Rivers'
troubling allegations,

> Nay, be gentle with him;
> Though I have never seen his face, methinks
> There cannot be a time when I shall cease
> To love him.—I remember, when a Boy
> Of six years' growth or younger, by the thorn
> Which starts from the old church-yard wall of Lorton,
> It was my joy to sit and hear Matilda
> Repeat her father's terrible adventures
> Till all the band of play-mates wept together,
> And that was the beginning of my love.
> And afterwards, when we conversed together
> This old man's image still was present: chiefly
> When I had been most happy.
>
> [Pp. 78–80]

"This old man's image" has then a double reference: both to the
figure of the old man depicted in Matilda's tales and to the figure of
Matilda herself as she, in her father's voice, repeats those tales. Mortimer's childhood bondage in pity in turn generates his character
and prefigures his passionate career as captain of the borderers
whose banded character expresses itself in acts to save and protect
the wretched. (Operating on the borders, they reenact Herbert's
doorway rescue of his infant from the flames of his burning Antioch
home.) By a nice irony of the plot, one of the early "victims" of
Mortimer's saving passion is Rivers himself, who is preserved by the
borderers' captain from violent death at their hands before the
play's opening scene; later, perversely repeating this saving act,
Rivers triumphantly justifies his tale-telling treachery against Mortimer as a character-building intellectual rescue:

> Enough is done to save you from the curse
> Of living without knowledge that you live.
> You will be taught to think—and step by step
> Led on from truth to truth, you soon will link
> Pleasure with greatness, and may thus become
> The most magnificent of characters.
>
> [P. 244]

Compounding the irony, Matilda in the final scene rushes onstage
from a vigil over her dead father's body, crying in vain as the bor-

derers this time drag Rivers off to death, "Oh, save him, save him—"
(p. 292), her character so bound in the passion of saving innocence
that she includes in her pity even the monster whose treachery has
killed her father.

Though there are many other instances in *The Borderers* of tale-
telling repetition, involving all of the major and minor characters,
including the cottager couple, Robert and Margaret, and even the
beggar woman Rivers suborns as a false witness against Herbert, one
moment in particular warrants special consideration here, focusing
all the relations of passion and character in the play's most powerfully tragic moment of repetition and reenactment. Echoing words
Rivers used earlier when he unveiled his treachery to Mortimer ("I
am a murderer" [p. 288]) and professing to Matilda in "most unusual fondness" his wish that she be "wise as I am," Mortimer enacts
his deranged intent to protect her from further misery by inflicting
upon her what he hopes will be a fatally wounding confessional tale:
"I am thy father's murderer" (p. 276n). If narrativity earlier in the
play is associated with generation, with the birth of character, passion works here to transform tale-telling into a death-dealing act:
crazed by remorse at Herbert's fate, Mortimer exchanges roles with
Matilda by "repeating her father's terrible adventures" to her. Originally the very creature of Matilda's tales, Mortimer is now transformed into the "monster" who tortures her. His succinct tale is thus
an act of double ventriloquism: from the perspective of Matilda's
narrative agency, she has created in the blindness of her tale-telling
childhood passion the very instrument of her undoing. In Mortimer's murderous tale we hear the stabbing fulfillment of her earlier cry, "Oh could you hear his voice!"

According to many readers, Wordsworth wrote autobiograph-
ically in *The Borderers,* projecting aspects of his subjective experience
into the characters of Rivers and Mortimer. In Roger Sharrock's
words, Rivers and Mortimer are the two aspects of Wordsworth's
divided mind. His "partial sympathy" with his villain "is shown by
the intimate touch with which he picks out the warp and woof of
[Rivers'] psychological development; this was a stage he himself
could have taken." That comment chimes with Wordsworth's own
remark to Isabella Fenwick that the Pedlar was "chiefly an idea of
what I fancied my own character might have become in his circumstances." Relevant are the comments Wordsworth made in 1842 and
1843 about composing *The Borderers* as a means of preserving processes of change witnessed during the early years of the French
Revolution:

The study of human nature suggests this awful truth, that, as in the trials to which life subjects us, sin and crime are apt to start from their very opposite qualities, so are there no limits to the hardening of the heart, and the perversion of the understanding to which they may carry their slaves. During my long residence in France, while the Revolution was rapidly advancing to its extreme of wickedness, I had frequent opportunities of being an eye-witness of this process, and it was while that knowledge was fresh upon my memory, that the Tragedy of "The Borderers" was composed.[4]

These comments have encouraged attempts to recover Wordsworth's state of mind in 1792–93 and in 1796–97, the most suggestive being David Erdman's reading of *The Borderers* as a work Wordsworth wrote to purge the warlike spirit that had impelled his soul to feed on vengeance, exulting in the violent deaths of both Louis XVI and Robespierre (the Robespierre whose corruption in power may have doubled in Wordsworth's mind with the reckless career in France of the radical idealist John Oswald). *The Prelude* likewise was "undertaken to cure the poison at the heart of man by establishing a faith to overcome despair about France."[5] Such readings interpret the work as part of a purgative process, a sort of psychological cathartic, the reader seeking to discern the malaise or poison that occasioned the curing enterprise. The premise of such criticism is that the product reveals the author, whose figure thus recovered it tends to privilege over the work. In that tendency it is perhaps congruent with the impulse in Coleridge's sharp decrying of the ventriloquism he heard marring the poetry occasionally of Wordsworth and typically of less gifted dramatic writers. Regarded thus negatively, ventriloquism leads us from the dummy back to the animator; and in his impatience with the perceived fault, Coleridge could even wish away the dummy altogether. As he said in *Table Talk*, "I am always vexed that the authors do not say what they have to say at once in their own persons. . . . I have no admiration for the practice of ventriloquizing through another man's mouth."[6]

There may be some use, nevertheless, in a contrary but complementary criticism that, admiring ventriloquism, reinforces the popu-

---

[4]*Borderers*, p. 813.
[5]Erdman, "Wordsworth as Heartsworth," p. 33.
[6]*Specimens of the Table Talk of the Late Samuel Taylor Coleridge*, ed. H. N. Coleridge, 2d ed. (London: John Murray, 1836), July 21, 1832, p. 174. See also *Coleridge's Shakespeare Criticism*, ed. T. M. Raysor, 2 vols. (Cambridge: Harvard University Press, I, 73; II, 124, 196; and *Coleridge's Miscellaneous Criticism*, ed. T. M. Raysor (London: Constable, 1936), pp. 54, 90, 394, 411.

lar tendency to be fascinated by the puppet as much as by the animator's art. In one sense this reading would see "Wordsworth" as the creator of "Rivers" rather than Rivers as the product of Wordsworth. A slight—or sleight—difference; perhaps, as with Escher's art, the chief pleasure derives from the interplay of one criticism with another. In any case, a ventriloquism focusing on the puppet can yield some pleasing fictions. Twice in the early version of *The Borderers* Rivers claims that his tales will make Mortimer into "the most magnificent of characters," and in his words we can hear how much he resembles the playwright at work.[7] The character Matilda and Rivers created prompted Wordsworth to submit to the *Morning Post* in December 1797 a poem called "The Convict" over the name we perhaps inaccurately think of as a pseudonym, "Mortimer."[8] Was Rivers then in some significant sense the author of Wordsworth? If we think of the figure of Rivers who emerges in the play and in the psychobiographical prefatory essay as the result of a heuristic ventriloquism that leads Wordsworth on to imagine the Pedlar in the various stages of the *Ruined Cottage* complex, we can then think of Rivers' tales about himself and others as fathering not only "Mortimer" but the Wordsworth who grew out of the Pedlar, "sounding his dim and perilous way" through the lines of his next major work, *The Prelude*. Adapting from *The Excursion* the resounding words the Solitary uses to describe his experience of the French Revolution, I mean to gather that figure also into the cast of Rivers' progeny, for it is in Rivers' mouth originally that we first hear of distress spent in "sounding on / Through words and things a dim and perilous way" (p. 236).[9]

The lineage is not so tenuous as it might seem: at the end of *The Borderers*, repeating with a difference Rivers' originating sin, Mortimer "abandons" himself to just such a solitude as Wordsworth created for the darkly despondent hero of *The Excursion*. Rather than charge his survivors with the burden of drawing narrative breath in pain, he calls instead for a mute epitaph:

> Raise on this lonely heath a monument
> That may record my story for warning—
> [P. 294]

---

[7]See also p. 128 and, for a similar usage by Rivers about himself, p. 238.

[8]*Essays on His Times in the "Morning Post" and "The Courier,"* ed. David V. Erdman, 3 vols. (Princeton: Princeton University Press, 1978), III, 286.

[9]See also *The Excursion*, III, 700–701.

And in his closing speech embracing suicidal exile, he repudiates the banded clamor of his borderers' voices ("Captain!" they cry), thereby performing a final rejection of faith in the power of voice to set things right:

No prayers, no tears, but hear my doom in silence!
I will go forth a wanderer on the earth,
A shadowy thing, and as I wander on
No human ear shall ever hear my voice,
No human dwelling ever give me food
Or sleep or rest, and all the uncertain way
Shall be as darkness to me, as a waste
Unnamed by man! and I will wander on
Living by mere intensity of thought,
By pain and thought compelled to live,
Yet loathing life, till heaven in mercy strike me
With blank forgetfulness—that I may die.

[P. 294]

Biographical interpretations read *The Borderers* itself as a monument to Wordsworth's experience in the French Revolution, veiled (however wittingly or unwittingly) as a dramatic representation of betrayal and suffering. Read another way, however, the play is a monument to a process of literary "self"-creation, whose story reverberates in other, subsequent works. Mortimer's muteness prefigures the reticence, for example, of the "Wordsworth" who so oddly narrates the degeneration into imbecile muteness of Vaudracour in the tale that concludes Book IX of the 1805 *Prelude*. If Vaudracour is, as Erdman brilliantly argues, "Heartsworth," he, like Mortimer, lapses, and it is the voice of Rivers that instead survives in the "self" we hear narrating that poem and *The Excursion,* and, as we shall see, in the "Wordsworth" whose words so thoroughly struck Coleridge. Recalling Hillis Miller's rendering of Walter Benjamin's metaleptic notion of the more genuine "self" made by the work, we may find it useful to think provisionally of the self we associate with Wordsworth as being a product of the characters we ordinarily think of as "his." The Wordsworthian Solitary and the Wordsworthian narrator of *The Prelude* are in a sense repetitions of earlier figures, Rivers and the Pedlar, at least in that each emerges in part through language initially used to represent the earlier figure. In "Michael," Wordsworth's narrator proclaims the agency of his tale, in collaboration with natural objects, in leading him to feel for passions that were not his own; he intends to relate the same tale, "for the sake / Of youthful Poets, who among these Hills / Will be my second self when I am gone." The words recall Rivers' boast that Mortimer will be "a shadow of myself, made by myself." One hardly needs to add that Matthew Arnold was not the last of the line of poetic readers whose image of Wordsworth's self derives from the (spell)binding force of narrative: "And never lifted up a single stone."

II

The telltale structure informing the dramatic action at virtually every significant juncture of *The Borderers* must have had much to do with the strong impression that hearing Wordsworth read his tragedy made on Coleridge. Perhaps even more than *Adventures on Salisbury Plain* or *The Ruined Cottage,* the play stirred Coleridge's admiring affection for the genius of his new friend. The character of his response emerges suggestively in the phrasing of a letter to Joseph Cottle:

> Wordsworth admires my Tragedy—which gives me great hopes. Wordsworth has written a Tragedy himself. I speak with heart-felt sincerity & (I think) unblinded judgment, when I tell you, that I feel myself a *little man by his* side; & yet do not think myself the less man, than I formerly thought myself.—His Drama is absolutely wonderful. You know, I do not commonly speak in such abrupt & unmingled phrases.[10]

The heartfelt response to Wordsworth's dramatic tale, the context of blindness and judgment, that ventriloquistic *"little man by his* side" and the concern with what makes a "man" (in the final scene, Mortimer's "I am a man again" resolves a major theme in *The Borderers* [p. 286]), all resonate so tantalizingly with the language of "the greatest Man, he ever knew" that it is tempting to imagine some genial, half-knowing imitation in Coleridge's tribute, a far cry as it were from the stodgy lament he voiced when, later, he had come to deplore Wordsworth's ventriloquism.

Just how far Wordsworth's voice as he read *The Borderers* influenced Coleridge in 1797 and 1798 may be suggested by the real-life drama with Charles Lloyd, Charles Lamb, and Robert Southey in which he soon found himself embroiled, a tale-ridden tangle of calumny, imitation, and gossip. *Edmund Oliver* itself seems to have

[10]*Collected Letters of Samuel Taylor Coleridge,* ed. Earl Leslie Griggs, 6 vols. (Oxford: Clarendon Press, 1956–71), I, 325.

been Lloyd's dummy-like fictionalizing of Southey's malicious gossip about Coleridge. (In the wake of their 1795 quarrel, Southey himself had planned a novel by that title in 1796, and Coleridge, for his part, not only published the Higginbottom parody sonnets but built aspects of Southey's personality into the character of Osorio, whose name Kathleen Coburn suggests is an anagram [Ro-So-io] of Robert Southey).[11] However his quarrel with Lloyd started, Coleridge was acutely distressed by the treachery he saw in *Edmund Oliver*. When he heard that Lamb, under the influence of Lloyd's tales, intended to break off their correspondence, Coleridge wrote his friend, attempting to forestall what he saw as an abandonment, his Herbert perhaps, Lamb's Mortimer. Absolving Lamb of malicious intent ("You are performing what you deem a duty"), he instead blamed Lloyd's treachery. His self-justifying rehearsal of his own part in generating Lloyd's affections for Lamb resembles Mortimer's account of the ventriloquistic origin, in hearing Matilda's affecting tales, of his love for her father. Lamb's "performance" of a duty was, Coleridge wrote,

> painful, for you could not without some struggles abandon me in behalf of a man who wholly ignorant of all but your name became attached to you in consequence of my attachment, caught *his* from *my* enthusiasm, & learnt to love you at my fire-side, when often while I have been sitting & talking of your sorrows & afflictions, I have stopped my conversations & lifted up wet eyes & prayed for you.[12]

Professing even to have risen by "thinking" above the passion of resentment against Lloyd, he takes the high ground of the *Osorio*-author's prescription for Lloyd's character: "The best & kindest wish which as a christian I can offer in return is that he may feel remorse."[13] An apt gloss of his own account of the fireside conversations with Lloyd might be Coleridge's observation, two months earlier, to Joseph Wicksteed: "People in general are not sufficiently aware how often the imagination creeps in and counterfeits the memory—perhaps to a certain degree it does always blend with our supposed recollections."[14]

Coleridge's response to *The Borderers* suggests the appropriateness

---

[11]*The Notebooks of Samuel Taylor Coleridge*, ed. Kathleen Coburn, 3 vols. to date (Princeton: Princeton University Press, 1962–), I, 2928n.

[12]*Collected Letters*, I, 404.

[13]Ibid.

[14]Ibid., I, 394.

of ventriloquism as a metaphor generally for Wordsworth's influence. (The later scenes of *Osorio* show that influence most directly, even imitating elements of Wordsworth's tale-telling dramatic structures.) When he recalls in letters, in the *Biographia,* in notebooks, and, most significantly, in "To William Wordsworth" his most powerfully revelatory experiences of Wordsworth's genius, the moments recalled are those when he was moved, often to tears, by a voice reciting tales: *Adventures on Salisbury Plain,* those tales *The Borderers* itself comprises, "Michael," and the "long sustained" narrative song of *The Prelude.* The final lines of "To William Wordsworth" depict his soul, Matilda- or Mortimer-like, "in silence listening, like a devout child / . . . by thy various strain / Driven as in surges now beneath the stars, / With momentary stars of my own birth." And when "thy deep voice had ceased—yet thou thyself / Wert still before my eyes, and round us both / That happy vision of belovéd faces," the blending of the poet's being resonates with Mortimer's account of hearing, among his band of weeping playmates, Matilda repeat her father's tales:

> And afterwards, when we conversed together
> This old man's image still was present: chiefly
> When I had been most happy.
>
> [P. 80]

But however he could with such "momentary stars" achieve a ventriloquistic transcendence in verse, Coleridge also thought about such listening experiences as those in which he came to realize he had no major poetic gift. To Godwin in 1801: "If I die, and the Booksellers will give you any thing for my Life, be sure to say— 'Wordsworth descended on him like a Γνῶθι σεαυτόν [Know thyself] from Heaven; by shewing him what true Poetry was, he made him know, that he himself was no Poet."[15] Played out in Coleridge's self-pitying image here is a deferential parody of inspiration by the muse, a demonic influence quite contrary to that celebrated at the end of "To William Wordsworth," prefiguring rather Wordsworth's whelming tide. Instead of generating in him the passion and character of a poet—in the "Michael" narrator's terms, Wordsworth's second self—the voice he heard in Wordsworth's tales saved him by destroying him. Enlightenment as the saving destruction of illusion resembles Rivers' agency in *The Borderers* ("strong to destroy—

---

[15]Ibid., II, 714.

strong also to build up" [p. 286; see also p. 76]), an influence that works to shatter Mortimer's Matilda-bred illusions, illuminating the stripling hero into a being of nothingness. Ruthlessly unveiling his treachery, Rivers offers Mortimer this grim shadow of justification: "I felt for your delusion . . . / I would have made you equal with myself, / But that was a vain hope . . . / Therein for ever you must yield to me." (pp. 242–43) His devastating descent, like that which Coleridge ventriloquized for Wordsworth, "saves" his victim from the curse of living without knowledge that he lives.

The proleptic bookseller's "Life" that Coleridge the ghost writer proposed to Godwin sounds more like a death; it has the elegiac ring of an epitaph, in this respect not unlike the lines in the verses he sent to various correspondents in 1833: "Beneath this sod / A poet lies: or that which once seem'd He."[16] It would not perhaps be excessive in this context to think of some of his meditative poems as looking beyond the grave of the death-in-life of dejection and despair to imagine the agency of blessed and blessing survivors (Lamb, his infant Hartley, Sara, Wordsworth himself) in saving him from the sepulchre of himself. Wordsworth, in the first of his "Essays on Epitaphs" (published in Coleridge's periodical The Friend, which died in 1810), analyzed the "tender fiction" of prosopopoeia by which, in epitaphs that personate the deceased speaker from beyond the grave, "survivors bind themselves to a sedater sorrow, and employ the intervention of the imagination in order that the reason may speak her own language earlier than she would otherwise have been enabled to do."[17] By a less tender fiction, Coleridge's brief "Life" reverses the process that Wordsworth called "shadowy interposition," personating Godwin's voice relating the role of Wordsworth's voice in the tale of his own demise. It is a symptomatic gesture on Coleridge's part, like what W. J. Bate has called the "usher" tendency in his relations to others: celebrating Wordsworth's genius entails the denial of self.

III

If Coleridge's "Life" attests to the destructive power of Wordsworth's art, we cannot doubt, from the profuse admiration he

---

[16]Ibid., VI, 973; see also pp. 963, 969–70.

[17]The Prose Works of William Wordsworth, ed. W. J. B. Owen and Jane Worthington Smyser, 3 vols. (Oxford: Clarendon Press, 1974), II, 60. See also The Friend, ed. Barbara Rooke, 2 vols. (Princeton: Princeton University Press, 1969), II, 345.

expressed at the time for his new friend's dramatic genius (which he implied exceeded in some respects not only Schiller's but even Shakespeare's), that it was *The Borderers* as much as any other work that brought home the sense of the "Giant" poet's power. We sense a notable irony, then, when, turning to the most palpably destructive enactment of that power, the so-called quarrel of 1810–12 that meant curtains for their friendship, we find there, in the passions and the characters and the position in which the persons of that dispiriting drama stood relative to each other, resemblances to those represented in *The Borderers*. Whatever Wordsworth actually said to Basil Montagu when he told him tales about Coleridge's unseemly and insupportable habits we can never know, although Coleridge's notebook entries suggest strongly that Montagu at least reported these notorious, devastating words: "No Hope of me! absol. Nuisance!"[18] In a letter to J. J. Morgan, Coleridge later recalled Montagu saying, "Nay, but Wordsworth *has commissioned* me to tell you, first, that he has no Hope of you."[19] Whatever the "truth" here, Coleridge believed Wordsworth had poisoned Montagu's ear, and he spent many wretched days going about London telling his friends, the Beaumonts and Crabb Robinson among them, the tale of Wordsworth's perfidious tales. To Richard Sharp he branded Wordsworth his "bitterest calumniator."[20] To Robinson he complained that Wordsworth had described him as a "rotten drunkard" who had been "rotting out his entrails by intemperance."[21] Coleridge's own intemperate self-pity—at least as it can be heard between the lines of Robinson's scarcely sympathetic diary—underscores how thoroughly capable he was of ventriloquizing Wordsworth's voice at its imagined worst. Bate has observed that "if the breach with Wordsworth was so long drawn out (in a sense almost permanent), it was because the indictment was really a self-indictment."[22] We may add that it took Wordsworth's imagined voice to make the indictment so fatal. Coleridge, as reported by Robinson: "I should have not been almost killed by this affair if it had not been that I had loved Wordsworth as a great and good man."[23] If this

[18]*Notebooks*, III, 3991, 3997.

[19]*Collected Letters*, III, 382.

[20]Ibid., III, 389. Wordsworth himself saw the letter, written to Richard Sharp. See *The Love Letters of William and Mary Wordsworth*, ed. Beth Darlington (Ithaca: Cornell University Press, 1981), pp. 121, 123.

[21]*Henry Crabb Robinson On Books and Their Writers*, ed. Edith J. Morley (London: J. M. Dent, 1938), I, 74–75.

[22]Walter Jackson Bate, *Coleridge* (New York: Macmillan, 1968), p. 125.

[23]*Henry Crabb Robinson on Books and Their Writers*, p. 71.

sounds excessively morbid, there were answering thoughts from the other side. So exasperating was Coleridge's conduct in blaming Wordsworth that even their mutual friends were driven to *parti-pris* bursts of passion. When Coleridge disappeared from view for a month in March and April and it turned out that he had been to Keswick and Penrith without so much as a word to Grasmere, Catherine Clarkson waxed vehement to Robinson, reenacting Wordsworth's alleged betrayal:

> So there is an end of the Friend & the articles for the Eclectic Review & most likely of his Lectures also—Will Wordsworth's unkindness serve this turn I wonder? Heaven forgive my hard-heartedness but I think he had better follow poor Jebb Loffts example & put a pistol to his brains—Now I have written the sentence I turn sick at the thought—If you hear any more of the stories about W. & C. I wish you would express your belief that Wordsworth never could have used the vulgar expressions attributed to him.[24]

Clarkson's comment, like a smoking gun, corroborates Coleridge's worst fears.

In November 1810, under the immediate shock of Wordsworth's treachery, Coleridge dredged up for his notebook a turbulent "Elucidation" of the quarrel with Lloyd thirteen years before, including a resentful anecdote about the Wordsworths' shortly thereafter preferring Lloyd's company to his own.[25] If to Coleridge 1810 seemed like a rerun of 1797, the scenario we can recover from the new quarrel has some aspects also of a revival of *The Borderers*. Lloyd's betrayal and Lamb's abandonment pale before the present atrocity: "Wordsworth, Wordsworth has given me up," he moaned to Mary Lamb, who perhaps there played Matilda to his Herbert.[26] On Wordsworth's side, evidence in *The Love Letters of William and Mary Wordsworth* leaves little doubt that, resenting the nuisance Coleridge's "scandalous conduct" was causing in London, Wordsworth in effect *had* abandoned him. Wordsworth went to London in the spring of 1812 to heal the breach, but the mission was grudgingly undertaken and brought him no pleasure. His letters to Mary reflect his distaste, even when a resolution was in sight: "This ugly affair of Coleridge which I hope may now be considered as settled, has ham-

[24]*Correspondence of Henry Crabb Robinson with the Wordsworth Circle, 1808–1866*, ed. Edith J. Morley (Oxford: Clarendon Press, 1927), I, 68.
[25]*Notebooks*, III, 4006.
[26]Quoted in Bate, *Coleridge*, p. 125.

pered me grievously; & defrauded me of many days & hours of days."[27] He complained indignantly that a series of lectures Coleridge had advertised was "a most odious way of picking up money, and scattering about his own & his friend's thoughts. Lady B[eaumont] has taken 30 tickets, which she will have to force upon her friends and where she cannot succeed must abide by the Loss."[28] The subject of the lectures—significantly enough—was the drama, about which he and Coleridge had had intense conversation and correspondence in 1796–97, during the composition of *The Borderers* and *Osorio*. On the eve of the first lecture, Wordsworth again predicted failure. "He has a world of bitter enemies, and is deplorably unpopular."

In the same letter (May 18, 1812) Wordsworth wrote Mary disappointedly about missing another, quite different public performance, a ticket for which he had put himself to some trouble to get:

> The Assassin has not been executed in Palace Yard as was first proposed; had that been the place I should this morning have been a Spectator in safety, from the top of Westminster Abbey: but he suffered before Newgate; and I did not think myself justified, for the sake of curiosity in running any risk.—I should have been miserable if I had brought my life or limbs into any hazard upon such an occasion.—We have not yet heard what passed at the Execution.[29]

The assassin was John Bellingham, a deranged Liverpool tradesman who on May 11 had put a pistol to the heart of the prime minister, Spencer Perceval, at the entrance to the House of Commons. (May 16 to Mary: "The Country is in a most awful state. The Monster is to be executed on Monday Morning I hope to procure, by means of the Poet Bowles a stand upon The top of Westminster Abbey whence I may see the Execution without risk or danger. It takes place on Monday Morning. I long to be with you for this London life does not agree with me because If I am ever thrown out I cannot find leisure to recover.")[30]

[27]*Love Letters*, pp. 148.
[28]Ibid., p. 125.
[29]Ibid., pp. 161–63.
[30]Ibid., p. 158. We can, of course, only speculate about what fueled Wordsworth's interest in the execution, and the range of considerations would have to include the sorts of cultural contexts Michel Foucault brings to bear on the Enlightenment's attitude toward crime and punishment in *Discipline and Punish*. One way to chart the inherent paradoxes and contradictions, and at the same time to indicate how far Coleridge could go to idealize the monstrous, is to ponder the juxtaposition of Wordsworth's phrase "Spectator in safety" and Coleridge's contention in *Table Talk* (July 21,

One wonders whether, during that week of feverish summary justice and efforts through Bowles for a ticket to the execution, Wordsworth recalled the lines from the last stanza of *Adventures on Salisbury Plain,* a poem written (he said in 1795) "partly to expose the vices of the penal law and the calamities of war as they affect individuals":[31]

> They left him hung on high in iron case,
> And dissolute men, unthinking and untaught,
> Planted their festive booths beneath his face;
> And to that spot, which idle thousands sought,
> Women and children were by fathers brought.

Coleridge's lectures were postponed a week because of the assassination, but his pen was not idle. The *Courier* for Thursday, May 14, carried his obituary for Perceval. (David Erdman notes that Coleridge was that paper's "mainstay for important obituaries.") "Perplexed and confused by the crowd of thoughts and painful feelings which succeed the first stupor impressed by the awful event," he wrote, echoing the language of Wordsworth's essay, "the mind almost of necessity seeks a resting place for itself." We should not be surprised, given the turbulence of his own painful feelings as the victim of Wordsworth's alleged character assassination, that

---

1832) that Wordsworth "ought never to have abandoned the contemplative position which is peculiarly—perhaps I might say exclusively—fitted for him. His proper title is *Spectator ab extra.*" The irony is compounded when one realizes that, at least as early as the composition of the *Biographia* in 1815, Coleridge was celebrating the spectator in Wordsworth as comprising an essential identity of self and work, character and action. Here is his account of the fifth of the "characteristic excellences" of Wordsworth's poetry:

> . . . a meditative pathos, a union of deep and subtle thought with sensibility; a sympathy with man as man; the sympathy indeed of a contemplator, rather than a fellow-sufferer or co-mate, (spectator, haud particeps) but of a contemplator, from whose view no difference of rank conceals the sameness of the nature; no injuries of wind or weather, of toil, or even of ignorance, wholly disguise the human face divine. The superscription and the image of the Creator still remain legible to *him* under the dark lines, with which guilt or calamity had cancelled or cross-barred it. Here the man and the poet lose and find themselves in each other, the one as glorified, the latter as substantiated. In this mild and philosophic pathos, Wordsworth appears to me without a compeer. Such he *is:* so he *writes.* [*Biographia Literaria, or Biographical Sketches of My Literary Life and Opinions,* ed. James Engell and W. Jackson Bate, 2 vols. (Princeton: Princeton University Press, 1983), II, 150]

[31]*The Letters of William and Dorothy Wordsworth: The Early Years 1787–1805,* ed. Ernest de Selincourt; 2d ed., rev. Chester L. Shaver (Oxford: Clarendon Press, 1967), p. 159.

Coleridge found his resting place in self-portraiture, by a familiar displacement writing his own death notice. His tribute to "this great and good man" rings with the intense, even paranoid idealizings of his own public and private life we know from notebooks and letters:

> A man . . . whose sweetness of disposition disarmed, at times, his most inveterate and acrimonious opponents . . . a man, to whom his bitterest enemies can attribute no other defect than that which his numerous and at least equally enlightened supporters honoured in him, as his appropriate excellence, a firm attachment to those principles and institutions religious and political, under which Great Britain has become the proudest name of history—This man, pierced to the heart, in the very manhood and harvest of his talents and labours by the pistol of a malcontent . . .[32]

His nature "vibrating to the inmost heart," Coleridge's obituary closes with a telling vignette, imagining Perceval's glorified spirit "already perhaps pleading before the Throne of his Maker for his murderer, and his slanderers, in the words of his Saviour—'Father! forgive them! they know not what they have done.'"[33] It is a transcending gesture we may recognize. (Paired antithetically with Perceval in Coleridge's *Courier* essay is Napoleon, a figure of treachery who "destroyed the very hope of liberty for the nation which had trusted him," leaving "thousands pining with broken hearts, amid the relatives of myriads, whose lives have been sacrificed to the grim idol of his remorseless ambition."[34] Is it too much to hear, in that last phrase, a submerged *j'accuse* against Wordsworth, whose consuming passion Coleridge decried openly only in the notebooks of 1808 and after?) With Wordsworth, however, transcendence was out of the question. His disappointment at missing the execution soon gives way in the letter to Mary to a long argument rejecting the notion that the monster's madness might have exempted him from public justice. For Wordsworth, Bellingham was a detestable fanatic who had lurked at Parliament more than a fortnight "to perpetrate the execrable Deed."

> Would it not be a horrible thing, that the extreme of a Man's guilt, should be pleaded as a reason, why he should be exempted from punishment; because, forsooth, his crime was so atrocious that no Man in his senses could have committed it? All guilt is a deviation from

[32]*Essays on His Times*, II, 347–48.
[33]Ibid., II, 349.
[34]Ibid., pp. 347–48.

reason. And had such an Assassin as this been acquitted upon the ground of insanity, the verdict would have held out an encouragement to all wicked Men, to transcend the known bounds of Wickedness, with a hope of finding security from law in the very enormity of their crimes.[35]

Wordsworth's language here seethes with the diction and tone of *The Borderers'* villain. Pursuing his malicious plot against Mortimer and the monster of his poisonous tales, Herbert, Rivers had argued against the baby-spirited impulse of mercy:

> The wiles of Women
> And craft of age, seducing reason first
> Made weakness a protection, and obscured
> The moral shape of things. His tender cries
> And helpless innocence, do they protect
> The infant lamb? and shall the infirmities
> Which have enabled this enormous culprit
> To perpetrate his crimes serve as a sanctuary
> To cover him from punishment? . . .
> —We recognize in this old man a victim
> Prepared already for the sacrifice—
>
> [P. 178]

For all their erotic suggestiveness, scarcely glimpsed before in Wordsworth, the love letters make disquieting reading; they remind us too often of the man who in Robinson's hearing one evening, deploring a Commons speech that might have inflamed Bellingham to act, answered a young radical who resentfully asked what the starving were to do. "Not murder people," said Wordsworth, "unless they mean to eat their hearts."[36] Coleridge in 1808, brooding neurotically on the quarrel with Lloyd and the many friends who had treated him cruelly over the years and recalling how he had urged Wordsworth to marry Mary Hutchinson, diagnosed his friend's sclerosis: "A blessed Marriage for him & for her it has been! But O! wedded Happiness is the intensest sort of Prosperity, & all Prosperity, I find, hardens the Heart."[37] In the letter to Mary just quoted, the Rivers voice gives way, momentarily, to a softer muse: "And now my darling let me turn to thee, and to my longing to be

---

[35]*Love Letters*, p. 162.

[36]*The Diary, Reminiscences, and Correspondence of Henry Crabb Robinson*, ed. Thomas Sadler, 2 vols. in 1 (New York: Hurd & Houghton, 1877), II, 247.

[37]*Notebooks*, III, 3305.

with thee. Last night, and this morning in particular I had dream after dream concerning thee; from which I woke and slipped again immediately into the same course." But the nuptial dreams are themselves interrupted by what, borrowing a Hollywood term, we might call a "voice-over" by the remorselessly derogative Rivers:

> Coleridge begins his Lectures to morrow, which I shall not be sorry to hear. I do not think, they will bring him much profit. He has a world of bitter enemies, and is deplorably unpopular. . . . You cannot form a notion to what degree Coleridge is disliked or despised notwithstanding his great talents, his genius & vast attainments. He rises every day between 8 & 9 or earlier, this I think a great conquest. But his actions in other respects seem as little under his own power as at any period of his life.[38]

Mary surely kept her husband's confidence, but we cannot doubt—so sensitive were Coleridge's ears—that Wordsworth's voice found its devouring way to his heart. Little wonder, then, with the wounds of the quarrel barely patched and the poison certainly not purged and with Wordsworth back home with Mary at Grasmere, that Coleridge soon found in himself the voice to revise *Osorio* for the dramatic performances that brought him—however briefly—his greatest public success, *Remorse*.

Strong passion, repetition, and ventriloquism mark the relationship of Wordsworth and Coleridge at many turns. More than has been generally recognized, *The Borderers* gives form to their passions and their characters and the ways in which these persons stood relatively to each other. It was Wordsworth's innovative genius, so admiringly argued by Coleridge, to see that in tales might be found the life of drama. It was Coleridge's confused genius to realize, under Wordsworth's influence, how much tales provoked the drama of life. From our vantage, their relationship has telling implications for the inevitably persistent notion that authors authorize their works and lives.

[38]*Love Letters*, p. 163.

5 /

The Mind at Ocean:
The Impropriety of
Coleridge's Literary Life

JEROME CHRISTENSEN

> But the stranger has appeared, the forgiving friend has come, even
> the Son of God from heaven: and to as many as have faith in his
> name, I say—the debt is paid for you;—the satisfaction has been
> made.
>
> —Samuel Taylor Coleridge, *Aids to Reflection*

I

When, during his defense of genius from the abuse of anonymous critics, Coleridge asks in the *Biographia Literaria*, "Has the
poet no property in his works?"[1] he wishes his question to be rhetorical. And it can uncritically be taken so. But if rhetoric succeeds
when it turns wishes into acts, criticism works when it reacts, when it
returns the wish in a different, if not finer, tone. One reaction to the
Biographia is to suspect that the poet's title to his works is not wholly
secure—and if the poet's property in *his* works, so the man of letters'
property in his literary life. Far from closing an argument, Coleridge's rhetorical question wishes open room for more, critical
questions.

What is property? is so nearly the same question as what is propriety? that for Coleridge the answer to one is involved in the solution of the other. The solution of both involves the question of
meaning itself. Coleridge raises that question and proposes a partial

A portion of this essay appeared in slightly different form in chapter 4 of Jerome
Christensen, *Coleridge's Blessed Machine of Language*. Copyright © 1981 by Cornell
University Press. Used by permission of the publisher.
[1]Samuel Taylor Coleridge, *Biographia Literaria*, ed. John Shawcross, 2 vols. (1907;
reprint ed., Oxford: Oxford University Press, 1967), I:29. Subsequent references to
the *Biographia* (*BL*) are given by volume and page in the text.

answer when he offers as preliminary justification of his distinction between imagination and fancy the observation that "in all societies there exists an instinct of growth, a certain collective, unconscious good sense working progressively to desynonymize those words originally of the same meaning" (I:61). The history of language is the elaboration—creative, discriminating—of meanings. That process is progressive, indeed meaningful, however, only because it is the expression of a "certain . . . unconscious good sense," the active aspect of what Coleridge calls "the reversionary wealth of the mother tongue" (I:63n). The mother tongue is the matrix of nativeness, an abiding source of essential propriety which ordains that the elaboration of senses never strays from the good sense with which the language has been originally endowed and by which its history is silently nourished. And, though unconscious, the mother tongue is no spendthrift. Desynonymization is not a blind largesse but a canny outlay: *reversionary* wealth. Perpetually owned by its source, language is a property whose history is a disbursement of wealth under the terms of an estate that reserves the right of the future possession of all profit. The discrimination of words, the multiplication of senses, always contributes in inevitable recourse to the increase of aboriginal sense; history refills the plenum. Hence it is that as the historical process of discrimination is ideally a reunification, so the conscious desynonymization of certain words such as *imagination* and *fancy* is complemented by the meaningful resynonymization of others: particularly and crucially, *property* and *propriety*, words that were, we are informed, incorporated under the single spelling *propriety* in the seventeenth century, the last age of true sovereignty in nation and self. By resynonymizing property and propriety, Coleridge hopes to restore that lapsed sovereignty, the absolute synonym of self-possession, and to secure thereby what he calls the "sacred distinction between things and persons" (I:137). The synonymity of *propriety* and *property* disciplines the dissolution of synonyms within history and the *Biographia* to a benign, unifying, self-confirming teleology.[2]

When Coleridge writes of Gray's "imitation" in "The Bard" of a passage in Shakespeare's *Merchant of Venice* that "all the propriety was lost in the transfer" (I:12), his remark both suggests the impropriety of tampering with a great poet's property and epitomizes

[2]See Joel Weinsheimer's essay "Coleridge on Synonymity and the Reorigination of Truth," *Papers on Literature and Language* 14 (1978):269–83, for a closely argued interpretation of Coleridge's theory of synonymity that differs significantly in its method and its conclusions from mine.

the *Biographia* as a whole, which attempts to return all propriety lost in various deplorable transfers to where it belongs. One explanation for the eccentric method of the philosophical criticism of the *Biographia* is that propriety cannot, without hazard, be neatly abstracted for analysis because propriety belongs to the man; to transfer propriety from the person to the arid discourse of the understanding would be to assist in the dispossession that reason and imagination would reverse. As for the critic, so for the critic's critic: what is at stake for Coleridge in the issue of propriety can be most decorously engaged by examining, if not the man himself, at least that place where the man clearly perceives the liability of poetic transfer, in Gray's "imitation" of Shakespeare.

In Chapter I of the *Biographia* Coleridge contrasts the inspiriting meditative verse of William Lisle Bowles with the dessicated Augustan poetry of "point," wherein "matter and diction seemed . . . characterized not so much by poetic thoughts as by thoughts *translated* into the language of poetry" (I:10). As another example of the defect of poetic translation or transfer, Coleridge juxtaposes Shakespeare and Gray. The Shakespeare:

> How like a younker or a prodigal
> The scarfed bark puts from her native bay,
> Hugg'd and embraced by the strumpet wind!
> How like the prodigal doth she return,
> With over-weather'd ribs and ragged sails,
> Lean, rent and beggar'd by the strumpet wind!
>   [*Merchant of Venice*, II.vi.14–19]

The Gray:

> Fair laughs the morn, and soft the zephyr blows
> While proudly riding o'er the azure realm
> In gallant trim the gilded vessel goes,
> YOUTH at the prow and PLEASURE at the helm;
> Regardless of the sweeping whirlwind's sway,
> That hush'd in grim repose, expects its evening prey.
>   ["The Bard," II.2.71–76][3]

---

[3]The capitalization of the Gray passage is that of the Shawcross edition of the *BL*. In George Watson's edition (1965; reprint ed., London: Everyman's Library, 1971), the first letter of all nouns is capitalized and only "YOUTH" is printed entirely in uppercase (Watson, *BL*, p. 10). Shawcross's edition is a reprint of the original 1817 edition, which, however, "contains many peculiarities of spelling" and numerous misprints. Shawcross admits that "it has been difficult to discriminate between the printer's errors and Coleridge's idiosyncracies" (I:xcvii), a comment echoed by Roger Lonsdale with regard to Gray (*The Poems of Gray, Collins and Goldsmith*, ed. Roger Lonsdale [1969; reprint ed., London: Longman, 1976], p. xiv).

Certainly Shakespeare's diction is both concrete and perspicuous: not only is it appropriate to the station of Gratiano, the character who speaks the lines, but the words are uniformly strict in their reference, and, taken together, enrich the rhetorical structure of the passage. The basic trope is metonymy, here doubled: the ship stands metonymically for the tenor of the lover's (Lorenzo's) mind, and the ship in turn becomes the tenor for the metonym of the younker, or errant youth. Metonymy, a figure of incapable imagination, here directly tropes that incapacity as an overreaching desire, but a desire subdued by decorous diction and by the disciplined symmetry of the twin "how like's," which enforce by repetition a powerful statement of a coherent moral economy. From its glad venture out in the bedizened pride of its youthful passion to its sad return, "lean, rent, and beggar'd," the ship of desire follows an ordained course. Desire may be satisfied—enjoyed in the margin, as it were—but it is represented only in the moral symmetry of its fond aspiration and its inevitable ruin. The repetition of "the strumpet wind" at the end of each rhetorical unit reinforces desire's essentially ironic structure. Nevertheless, though passion dies, death is endowed with a life-giving meaning through its subsumption in a larger pattern that both maintains and ultimately transfigures the ironic economy of the figure itself. Although the voyage outward, the metonymic thrust onto strange seas, may end in catastrophe, the ship does, reassuringly, return to shore—as a "prodigal." That repeated reference to "prodigal" signals that this necessary pattern is not merely circular but typically circular, charting in small the great romantic myth of the ill-starred journey out and the redemptive voyage back.

The synechdochal relations of this passage to the play as a whole seem at first sight to reinforce the sense of its complete, even ultimate, propriety and attest to Coleridge's canny advertence in the selection. Although the ships are figurative in the immediate context (the speculative byplay of Gratiano and Salarino as they await the tardy Lorenzo beneath Jessica's window), the figure is literalized in the central action of the play, only to be troped once again. The pattern that Gratiano finds in love's ardent venture imitates the fate of Antonio's actual argosy, the merchant ships that he has pledged as surety for his loan from Shylock. Antonio's gilded frigates in turn represent both the passion for Bassiano that motivated the loan and his proud self-sufficiency in the exercise of that passion. Passion and pride are chastened in the report of the destruction of Antonio's ships and by his consequent inability to redeem his loan. The penalty to be inflicted with evident justice by Shylock, though horrible, would nonetheless be the logical result and concrete manifestation of a loss of self in reckless and unacknowledged desire that has already occurred. On this level of the play, the transcendent economy that subsumes the figure of the ship is especially evident, for it is the catastrophe suffered by Antonio that makes possible Portia's famous redemptive speech in which the economy of desire and the economy of justice are (optatively) canceled under the dispensation of mercy. That the literal catastrophe of Antonio's ships has actually the emblematic function of heralding this theophany becomes evident when, in the final scene, Antonio receives the news from Portia that the real ships, the ones that are the pretexts for the figurative transactions of the play, have survived the storms after all—a providential reward granted to the prodigal Antonio now safe within the enchanted grounds of Belmont.

Gray seems to exploit the same metonymy as Shakespeare. Not only is his figure structured by desire, but the metonymy also represents desire and its inevitable fate. Though it is clearer in Gray than in Shakespeare that the speaker is not talking about actual ships, it is less clear exactly what he is talking about. The context supplies the grim prophecy of an eventual humbling of pride and a general tone of doom, but it is difficult to understand what the figure adds in either specificity or intensity to effects already amply elaborated. The problem lies in the vagueness of the tenor. The "gilded vessel" evidently stands for something like a man's falsely proud aspiration, but beyond that point glossing becomes guessing. I would suggest, however, that the obscurity of the referent enhances rather than diminishes the effect of the figure: the lack that articulates the tenor reinforces the lack that structurally afflicts desire—the apparent subject of the figure as a whole. The plot of Gray's passage also differs strikingly from Shakespeare's: in Gray the ship does not and will not return to shore. Instead of desire being judged according to a stable economy that is, in turn, subsumed by a transcendent value, in Gray the frigate of passion fares toward an inevitable and total loss. The ship has certainly been lost to the whirlwind from the moment it left the harbor, doomed, perhaps, even at its gilding. As it breasts the waves in the laughing morn it is as though evening were already falling, as though the whirlwind were attracting not only space but time within its deadly sway. The figure divulges death at every turn. Coleridge's most specific stricture against the impropriety of Gray's diction, that he "preferred the original on the ground that in the imitation it depended wholly in the compositor's putting, or not putting, a *small Capital* both in this and in many other passages of the same poet whether the words should be personifications or mere abstracts" (I:12), marks the peculiar fatality of the figure. His objection seems to refer to the impossibility of keeping "youth" and "pleasure" in line 4 on the same level of abstraction or concreteness at the same time, a problem indicated rather than solved by Coleridge's own capitalization (or was it only his compositor's?). If "YOUTH" is read as the personification of the abstraction "youth," then the personification necessarily evokes the person himself, a youthful body on the prow. To personify pleasure in the same degree might give it dramatic attributes but would leave it vitally short of embodied form. Although "youth" and "pleasure" ship out on the same "gilded vessel," they cannot both occupy the same figurative space, an incompatibility owed to the poet's failure to assign either signifier a place of its own. The factitious stability imposed by the compositor cannot, as Coleridge testifies, efface a slippage between personification and abstraction that, read morally, violates "the sacred distinction between things and persons" that the *Biographia* aims to indemnify and that, read phenomenologically, imitates the deadly circulation of the whirlwind that holds the passage in its sway. The confusion of person with thing into "an amphibious something, made up, half of image, and half of abstract meaning" (I:15) is the very vertiginous fatality of desire that Gray figures. His imitation of Shakespeare loses all propriety in the transfer, in part because it figures the ease with which propriety *can* be transferred. In Gray propriety acts as if it had no place of its own in language. Its vagrancy undermines the autonomy of the subject that Coleridge would have it ground.

Although I have identified what are, I think, the standards Coleridge applies in his judgment of Gray's impropriety, to understand Coleridge's hypopoetics[4] we must go further and examine the process of judgment as well. In this case we need to pursue the problem of imitation past the criteria of good and bad, to ask in what way Gray's passage is an imitation of Shakespeare at all. The two passages do not notably resemble each other; indeed, according to Gray's most recent editor, no one except Coleridge ever proposed a homology between the two figures.[5] Given Coleridge's thorough

[4]In a notebook entry Coleridge contrasts hypopoesis with hypothesis: "Hypothesis: the placing of one known fact under others as their *ground* or foundation. Not the fact itself but only its position in a certain relation is imagined, it is Hypopoesis not Hypothesis, subfiction not supposition" (*The Notebooks of Samuel Taylor Coleridge* [hereafter *CN*], ed. Kathleen Coburn, 3 vols. to date [Princeton: Princeton University Press, 1973], III:3587).
[5]Lonsdale, *Poems of Gray, Collins, and Goldsmith*, p. 191n.

disapproval of the Gray, it is peculiar that he would elevate it with the term "imitation," which in the *Biographia* he invariably opposes to mechanical copying as an honorific of Platonic lineage.[6] Imitation, he says, "consists either in the interfusion of the SAME throughout the radically DIFFERENT, or of the different throughout a base radically the same" (II:56). By calling the Gray an imitation, Coleridge invites us to examine the way in which same and different convene in the relations of the two passages. In the absence of any evident verbal or structural correspondence we must join with the idealist and ask in what way Gray "Shakespearanizes" the Shakespeare, in what way the latter passage does "master the essence" (II:257)[7] of the former. I will not pretend that that question is innocent; it queries the *Biographia* into a predicament because for Coleridge the essence of the Shakespeare *is* its propriety, which is just what he misses in Gray. To retrieve the *Biographia* from the predicament of implicit contradiction means that we have to turn against the text in order to make sense of, if not master, it. To turn against Coleridge is to follow Coleridge, however, for the charm of Gray's "imitation" is that it encourages what Coleridge calls "the too exclusive attention" to certain truths which tempts the reader "to carry those truths beyond their proper limits" (II:95). What makes the Gray both an imitation and the model of a bad imitation in the *Biographia* is that its association with the Shakespeare provokes an exclusive attention that discovers in the source a previously imperceptible and unsuspected impropriety that subverts the idea of the proper limits of truth.

Attention to the Shakespeare with an eye to its genetic powers

---

[6]Coleridge did not require a systematic theory of imitation because his distinction between imitation and copy did not vary significantly from the Platonic distinction between copy and simulacrum, summarized by Gilles Deleuze in *Logique du sens* (Paris: Minuit, 1969):

> We can, then, better define the range of the platonic motivation: it is a question of selecting the pretenders, by distinguishing good and bad copies, or rather the always well founded and the simulacra, always abysmal in their dissemblance. It is a question of assuring the triumph of copies over simulacra, of repressing the simulcra, of keeping them chained down to the bottom, of preventing them from appearing at the surface and insinuating themselves everywhere. [p. 296]

[7]Coleridge uses "Shakespearianize" as a synonym for "imitate" in this extract from *Anima Poetae:* "Surely on this universal fact of words and images depends, by more or less mediations, the imitation, instead of the *copy*, which is illustrated, in very nature Shakespearianized—that Proteus essence which could assume the very form, but yet known and felt not to be the thing by that difference of the substance which made every atom of the form another thing, that likeness not identity" (quoted in II:273, editor's note). The phrase "master the essence" occurs in a discussion of imitation in "On Poesy or Art."

brings within ken the genealogy of the figure within the play. The progenitor is a comment by Salarino to Antonio in the first scene. He replies to the merchant's puzzled confession of sadness by observing, "Your mind is tossing on the ocean" (I.i.8). Salarino and Salanio account for Antonio's dejection by characterizing what they conceive to be his proper concern for his fleet. Salarino fancies that, were he in Antonio's place, in his anxiety he would convert all actions and objects into signs of commercial success or failure, and he justifies his diagnosis of Antonio's mood by the demonstrated power of his fancy to transfigure all things into versions of one obsessive concern: "Shall I have the thought / To think on this, and shall I lack the thought / That such a thing bechanced would make me sad?" (I.i.36–38). The physical lack is supplemented by thought, which is, however, motivated by a desire constituted by a lack that lets sadness in. Antonio does not directly dispute that his mind is tossing on the ocean; he only demurs that his cargo is safe because his "ventures are not in one bottom trusted" (I.i.42) and therefore his merchandise does not make him sad. In reply, Salarino not only maintains his analysis, he extends it by exploiting the substitutive dynamics implicit in the initial trope: "Why, then you are in love" (I.i.46). Salarino good-naturedly accepts Antonio's denial only to reduce it wittily to the absurd and thereby to sharpen his original point: if there is any explanation for Antonio's sadness, it is that his mind is tossing on the ocean, abroad in the bottom of a ship or a lover or both. As Salarino elaborates it, the mind tossing on the ocean is a figure for the abstraction of a person into its objects, a symptom of what might be called a metonymic moodiness in which the mind is vulnerable to the fever of substitution. One impropriety will beget another: the impropriety of a self abstracted into its aspects produces the impropriety of one aspect substituting for another: lover for self, ships for self, lover for ships, ships for lover. Not only one's chattel but the soundness of one's soul is submitted to the caprice of ocean squalls.

The mental association developed between Bassanio and ships, between ships and life, is fully staged in the courtroom scene of Act IV, in which Antonio's resigned acceptance of death presumes an interchangeability among loss of merchandise, loss of Bassanio, and loss of life. Antonio's inability to distinguish between things and persons makes him the perfect match for Shylock and a fit subject both for Portia's virtuosic movement through the scales of passion and power in the courtroom and her later pointed play with the ring that Bassanio, abetted by Antonio, has simultaneously overvalued and underesteemed. Portia's every action from Act IV on works to cut Bassanio away from his imaginative possession by Antonio—bloodless cuts that reduce Antonio as thoroughly as ever would have Shylock's crude, murderous violence. Portia reduces Antonio both by cutting him off from Bassanio, for whose sake he claims to love the world, and by restoring him to his ships, which she implicitly gives as sufficient compensation for the loss of his lover. Indeed, Antonio confirms the adequacy of the compensation when he gratefully exclaims, "Sweet lady, you have given me life and living" (V.i.286). Although the play has plotted the restoration of life before living, Antonio's conjunction of the two is true to their identification in his imagination. Returning the ships is returning Antonio to his life less than before, not because Bassanio has been cut loose but because the loss of Bassanio makes no essential difference. That Antonio's life and living must be returned to him by another character seals Antonio's impropriety. Portia's surgery confirms Salarino's diagnosis: Antonio less than before is Antonio the same as before: the merchant's mind still finds its life only in its movable property and tosses abroad in a confusion of persons and things.

That a mind can be constantly at sea is the concealed impropriety of a figure that may return the prodigal ship and depict Antonio's recovery from sadness but can efface neither the liability to prodigality nor the metonymic impulse that constitutes and disables Antonio's imagination. Nor, finally, can the return of the prodigal ships and the retreat into Belmont cancel the impropriety of Shakespeare's substitution of the figure for the man, which makes Antonio's attitudes and actions not only congruent with the figure of the ships' venture and return but apparently a function of the figure—a mechanism of transfer whose power implies a loss of the person's autonomy to something neither person nor thing. Gray's imitation is vicious because it accurately imitates the transfer of propriety that motivates the machine of Shakespeare's play.

II

For the philosophical critic, literary imitation mirrors verbal derivation. Like an etymologist he tracks what has been desynonymized back through unfolding synonyms to the source where a pregnant identity obtains. The desynonymization of propriety and property in Gray into an amphibian something may be an exception to the general rule of progressive good sense: nonetheless, by referring the epigone to its great original, the analyst can hope to redress deviance and restore the true and healthy line of succession. But derivation also mirrors imitation. The loss of all propriety, supposedly consequent upon a transfer in which a later poet derives his vertiginous language from the property of another, actually imitates an equivocation, a transfer of propriety, in the original. Because the impropriety of Gray is derived from a source already improper to itself, the etymologist traces a path undetermined by any clear-cut synonymity, which cannot be subjected to either rule or exception, and which, therefore, validates the procedures of etymology at the expense of its premise of an aboriginal fullness of meaning, "the reversionary wealth of the mother tongue."

I cannot prove that Coleridge had such an etymology in mind when he juxtaposed the Shakespeare and the Gray, but that is because what Coleridge or Gray, or Shakespeare, or YOUTH, or PLEASURE, or Antonio has or can have in mind is problematic here and, indeed, throughout Coleridge's writings. The problem can be clarified by examining one of Coleridge's explicit etymologies, this one in the third of his series of four philosophical letters to Josiah Wedgwood attacking Lockean empiricism. Here Coleridge challenges the language that Locke uses to specify mental agencies and entities. "In Mr Locke," he comments, "there is a complete Whirl-dance of Confusion with the words *we, Soul, Mind, Consciousness, & Ideas.*" In the *Biographia* Coleridge attempts to calm Gray's whirlwind by citing the authority of its source; here he replies to Locke's "Whirl-dance" with the diagnostic question, "What is the *etymology* of the Word *Mind?*"[8]

Coleridge's answer conveys him into the German language and the word *Meinen* ("to think"), which in its "old signification," he says,

> *exactly corresponds* with the provincial use of the verb "To mind" in England. . . . Hence it appears to be no other than provincial Differences of Pronunciation between the words Meinen, & Mahnen ["to remind, admonish"]. . . . But the insertion of the *n* in the middle of a German verb is admitted on all hands to be *intensive* or *reduplicative.* . . . In reality it is no more than repeating the last syllable as people are apt to when speaking hastily or vehemently. Mahnen therefore is Mahenen, which is Mähen spoken hastily or vehemently. But the oldest meaning of the word mähen is to move forward & backward, yet still progressively—thence applied to the motion of a Scythe in mowing— from what particular motion the word was first abstracted, is of course in this as in all other instances, lost in antiquity. . . . To mow is the same as the Latin movere which was pronounced mow-ere—& monere in

[8]*Collected Letters of Samuel Taylor Coleridge [CL]*, ed. Earl Leslie Griggs, 6 vols. (Oxford: Oxford University Press, 1956–71), II:696.

like manner is only the reduplicative of mow-ere—mow-en—mow-enen—mow-nen, or monen.[9]

The etymology of the word *mind* may be said to quiet Locke's "Whirl-dance" for several reasons. First, for Coleridge the actual history of the word has greater authority than any signification arbitrarily assigned by any particular philosopher or philosophical convention. Second, the development of *meinen* from *mähen* makes the mind a concept rather than a mere notion because it affixes the mind to a substantive, even sensible word. Third, the etymology synthesizes the quality of mind as the union of intellective essence with physical activity. The property that Coleridge would have of the mind—a progressive, protodialectical movement—is validated by etymology as the propriety in the mind. Coleridge's etymology enables him and his reader to conceive of the mind, in which *meinen* is synonymous with *mähen,* as the identity of property and propriety: the mind mows in its own field.

But (and here I rely on an authority greater than Coleridge in these matters, his editor, Kathleen Coburn) Coleridge's etymology is, contrary to his profession, secondhand, borrowed without acknowledgment from Adelung's Dictionary. Moreover, it is inaccurate: Coburn judges that "the connexion of *meinen* with *mähen* is unlikely. Its Latin counterpart is *meto; moveo* does not belong here." To counter Locke's confusion and to identify the mind as what it surely is, Coleridge relies on a series of "etymological fancies," some his own, some the "property" of Adelung, to import into the mind that which surely does not belong there. The authentic property of the mind is deeded to it by a double impropriety. Coburn's interpretation of Coleridge's relation to Adelung anticipates my "etymology" of Gray and Shakespeare. According to Coburn Coleridge did not borrow or steal from Adelung; he "derived" his false information. And because Coleridge's wishful supplement to the Adelung etymology (the assertion that *Min* was once pronounced as *Mein*), like Gray's imitation of Shakespeare, only makes legible an impropriety already there in the original derivation of mind, Adelung, like Shakespeare, "must bear the blame for some" of his successor's "fancies."[10] Such a distribution of blame involves the conclusion that what Coleridge has in mind belongs to Adelung as much as to himself—and, always, vice versa. More concretely, the synonymity of movement and thought that Coleridge wishes for the mind is

[9]*CL* II:696–97.
[10]*CN* I:378n.

154

attained only by the wittily improper transfer of the letter *n* (hardly a letter, a mere "intensive" or "reduplicative") between *mähen* and *meinen*, a transfer supervised by the almost providential appearance and mediation of *mahnen*, vehicle of continuity and agent of economy. The mind moves only as a consequence of the manipulation of the *n*, an instance of etymological inventiveness that at once contrives and relinquishes all propriety. Coleridge answers Locke's "Whirl-dance" with an etymology in which the historically progressive movement of the word *mind* and the epistemologically progressive movement in the mind are both indeterminate functions of a wholly textual process: an oscillation back and forth along a line of type (*mähen—mahnen—meinen*) tracking a wayward letter (*n*) whose place is subject not to unconscious good sense but to the etymologist's, or perhaps the compositor's, whim.

When, in the following letter to Wedgwood, Coleridge summarizes his objections to Locke's supposed merit as a philosopher, he comments that his "arrangement" is so "defective that I at least seem always in an *eddy* when I read him / round & round, & never a step forward."[11] The philosopher's "Whirl-dance" is the reader's eddy—a reading experience phenomenologically akin to but gentler than the vertiginous confusion between things and persons provoked by Gray. Like the invocation of Shakespeare, the etymological leap across the "Whirl-dance" of Locke to the primal stuff of language (not coincidentally German[12]) represents a return to the supposed source in order that the stream may be unblocked and the progressive movement of desynonymization may flow onward within an horizon of ultimate synonymity. But instead of divulging synonymity, Coleridge reproduces and refines an eddying indeterminacy, demonstrating that what might to the casual eye seem an adventitious confusion reads to the armed vision as the very praxis of the mind's variably improper encounter with language.[13] It is the

[11]*CL* II:700.

[12]Coleridge's tactical use of the German binds together a Kantian conception of mind with an older German tradition, represented by both Böhme and the Nuremberg school, of "assimilating all oral manifestations to a primeval linguistic state" and explicating the "peculiar analogy" that was fancied to obtain between the German language and nature (see Walter Benjamin, *The Origins of German Tragic Drama*, trans. John Osborne [London: NLB, 1977], pp. 203–5).

[13]In his *The Study of Language in England, 1780–1860* (Princeton: Princeton University Press, 1967), Hans Aarsleff notes that "mind" was not "etymologically transparent" at the end of the eighteenth century and that even "Tooke never attempted an etymology of that word" (p. 109). Coleridge's eccentric improvisation may be taken as vindication of Tooke and the other etymologists who avoided scrutinizing the history of a word that was the elastic premise for their entire enterprise. For Coleridge, however, the "mind" unexamined was not worth thinking, even if such examination might carry thinking beyond its proper limits.

character of the mind, its quality, to have characters (Shakespeare's Antonio, Antonio's ships, *mahnen*'s *n*) in which it appears and by which it ineluctably transfers its propriety.

Has the poet no property in his works? No more, it would seem, than the mind has property over its character or the man has property over his letters. Poet, etymologist, and critic are of imagination all compact: each is the indefinitely repeatable figure of the transfer of propriety. Reading Coleridge's reading of Gray's imitation of Shakespeare isolates a hermeneutical plot and (what amounts to the same thing for the Romantic) a story of the self. We read Coleridge reading to characterize who he is. This plot leads us to Antonio, the concealed subject of Coleridge's criticism of Gray, and returns Coleridge as a version of that subject, imprudent merchant and mental mariner. Imprudent merchant applies not only because Coleridge's earlier commercial ventures as itinerant propagandist and book vendor receive burlesque treatment in the *Biographia* but also because the disarray of the book itself attests to Coleridge's adverse experiences with the trade.[14] Mental mariner is all but a cliché in Coleridge criticism: Coleridge's intellectual voyage is the explicit subject of much of his text and has, since John Livingston Lowes, distinguished his Romanticism for most readers. Of especial interest to me, however, is the mind's navigation of strange seas of *print:* quotations, theses, italics, footnotes, and so forth. The salient difference between Antonio and Coleridge is that the career of the latter is not and cannot be staged as an action but is and must be written and read as a text. Hence the language about language, which may seem tendentiously allegorical when applied to Antonio, is perfectly apt when referred to Coleridge, who by writing a literary life takes on language as his essential property. The phrase that captures the variety of the commerce (moral, intellectual, and financial) in the *Biographia* and that also specifies the difference between Coleridge and Antonio is "man of letters"—the type from which all the figures of transfer in the *Biographia* are set. When, in Chapter XI, Coleridge admonishes the aspiring author that he "be not *merely* a man of letters (I:158), he marks the unsettling equivocation of propriety and property, person and thing, with a warning that has the distilled power of a slogan. The *Biographia* is that text in the English tradition wherein the possibility of becoming "*merely* a man of letters" is taken literally and feared.

[14]See *BL* I:110–21 for Coleridge's account of the vicissitudes of *The Friend* and *The Watchman*. On the *Biographia*, see Daniel Mark Fogel, "A Compositional History of the *Biographia Literaria*," *Studies in Bibliography* 30 (1977):219–34.

In part the possibility is to be attributed to the "multitude of books and the general diffusion of literature, [which] have produced . . . lamentable effects in the world of letters." In part it can be explained by "the labours of successive poets and in part by the more artificial state of society and social intercourse, [in which] language, mechanized as it were into a barrel-organ, supplies at once both instrument and tune" (I:25). In part it results from the "*narcotic*" effect of "the *necessity* of acquiring" not learning but "money, and immediate reputation" (I:151, 152). In part the mind's own curious and frightening susceptibilities, as exemplified by the narrator of "The Thorn" (II, 36ff.) and the glossalalic maid (I:78–79) are responsible. Whatever lamentable social, cultural, and psychological tendencies contribute to it, however, the preposterous fate of becoming merely a man of letters haunts the *Biographia*.[15] In its most explicit description, that fate is imagined not as the result of accident or deviance but as the apparently inevitable consequence of authorship itself. At the end of Chapter XI Coleridge quotes the advice of another man of letters, Herder:

> With the greatest possible solicitude avoid authorship. Too early or immoderately employed, it makes the head *waste* and the heart empty; even were there no other worse consequences. A person, who reads only to print, in all probability reads amiss; and he, who sends away through the pen and the press every thought, the moment it occurs to him, will in a short time have sent all away, and will become a mere journeyman of the printing-office, a *compositor*. [I:159n–60n; Coleridge's translation]

By sending away his every thought through the pen and the press, the author spends his capital of head and heart with a prodigality that ends with the loss of all his authority as he finally materializes into a compositor. Having signed away his property and transferred his propriety to the instrument of his dissipation, the typical writer is all too ready to settle into a routine vagrancy on the face of the page. Forgetful of home, the writer's soul has only the significance of type capable of being retyped. A man of letters, he is subject to endless transformations and indefinite reproductions—echo upon echo of an altogether superfluous voice.

[15]Examples of the type are the student (identified by Charles Lamb as Coleridge himself) who incurred the wrath of the Reverend Bowyer for his prodigious rhetorical inventiveness (*BL* I:5), the pseudonymous Nehemiah Higginbottom (*BL* I:17), and Coleridge's persistent antagonists in the *Biographia*, the anonymous critics of the reviews.

Herder's fatalism is not the final word in the *Biographia,* of course. Superintending Coleridge's text, like the representative of the reversionary wealth of the mother culture, is the motto he has adopted from Goethe:

> Little call as he may have to instruct others, he wishes nevertheless to open out his heart to such as he either knows or hopes to be of like mind with himself, but who are widely scattered in the world: he wishes to knit anew his connections with his oldest friends among the rising generation for the course of his life. He wishes to spare the young those circuitous paths on which he had lost his way.   [I, title page, verso]

The motto affixed to the margin of his book is a figure for Coleridge's own marginal life. Both centripetal promise and binding filament, it supplies the literary life with a structure and the author with a vantage ground from which he can benignly and safely offer heartfelt advice to like-minded youth, who, in turn, can credit the promise to knit anew because the promise itself is a knitting. Not merely another souvenir picked up by the man of letters on his wanderings, the Goethean motto is a harbinger of home. Coleridge hearkens to it when, in the crucial Chapter XI, he offers himself as the monitory example of the man who had deviated "into a labyrinth where when he had wandered till his head was giddy, his best good fortune was finally to have found his way out again, too late for prudence though not too late for conscience or for truth!" (*BL* I:159).

All of Coleridge's figures—the circuitous paths, the ships at sea, the labyrinth, the printing press—project error and loss; all except Gray's imitation and Herder's dour vision of the typesetting of the mind predicate a redemptive return. As he did with Gray, Coleridge attempts to turn Herder to his own teleology, this time by exploiting both the marginal opportunity for choice implied in Herder's warning and the margin of his page to rescue his literary life from the bleak forecast of mechanization. In a note supplementing the translation of Herder, he prescribes an alternative economy in which what is sent away never entirely departs. "To which I may add from myself," he comments, "that what medical physiologists affirm of certain secretions applies equally to our thoughts; they too must be taken up again into the circulation, and be again and again re-secreted in order to ensure a healthful vigor, both to the mind and to its intellectual offspring" (I:160n). Coleridge invents an escape from the fate of the journeyman ever faring forth in the simulacrum of print by inventing an organism that runs on itself, that has its sole extension in the slight, hardly perceptible turn from secretion to resecretion—a biological machine prudently cogitating its own integrity, a body of language in solitary conjugation.

What Coleridge adds to Herder in Chapter XI he instaurates in Chapter XIII as the secondary imagination, which "dissolves, diffuses, dissipates, in order to recreate" (I:202). Each circulative model has the function of both identifying and indemnifying a processive space insulated from the labyrinth of letters in which a person first loses his way then loses his memory that there is a way to lose. Both models, physiological and epistemological, promise to protect the author from dispersion because both processes are conceived as operating without letters; they secure the author in his proper place by the hypopoesis of an authoring independent of script. The physiological model secures the autonomy of the author because under its dispensation the thoughts he circulates testify to the authority of him who thinks in the compliant witness of their faithful return. The objects of the imagination are, crucially, not specified in Coleridge's definition because imagination's object is imagination itself, its aim the smooth operation of its own restorative processes. The organism's monotonously recursive pattern of affecting itself is justified by the economic principle of homeostasis, the need to conserve its health, vigor, and life. The imagination is similarly the defense of the self; it legislates a processive space of economical venture and return that circumscribes and cancels all possible losses. As the physiological process is under control of that which thinks, so the circulation of the imagination derives its purposiveness from the presumption of a power within, something reserved from dissolution and recreation, which can send out and retrieve. One can afford to send one's thoughts abroad because both the sending and the abroad are wholly imaginative. The imagination is both goal and guarantee of Coleridge's return from the circuitous paths of the *Biographia*.

Although the imagination is proposed as a constant epistemological and moral alternative to the tyranny of the association of ideas, the definition of the imagination emerges at the end of a labyrinthine philosophical argument that exhibits the most objectionable features of Coleridge's desultory prose: an apparent progression that goes nowhere, a dispersion of the author's moral and ontological integrity through the erratic, unacknowledged use of others' ideas and words. Although the argument is offered as a methodical ascent to the imagination, the further it proceeds, the more it recedes from any evidence that the imagination is at work. Logical progress is countered by a rhetorical regress. The reader does not observe a genius objectively disclosing the source of his subjective power; he tracks the writer's entanglement in the intricacies of his composition, as if the man of letters had no defense against the lettering of his text(s). That suspicion is only partially quelled by the revelation of the imagination in Chapter XIII, because the transition from lettering to imagination is executed not by the author alone but in collaboration with one of the best known men of letters in English literature, the fictive correspondent who admonishes Coleridge to cut short the philosophical deduction of the imagination and come, finally, to the point.

Coleridge's correspondent is a man of letters in the conventional sense. Well-read, he alludes to the classical topos of "the dark cave of Trophonius" (I:200) as well as to Milton, Bishop Berkeley, and Coleridge himself. He has the man of letter's taste, or perhaps appetite, for the anecdotal, possesses a capable, relaxed style, and cultivates the literary in diverse aspects. He admits with cheerful candor to a limited patience with abstruse works that demand sustained effort at strenuous reasoning—an impatience aggravated when the reasoning is, like Coleridge's, disjunctive and dense. He suspects that his impatience would be shared, and probably to a greater degree, by most of the readers who would purchase the *Biographia Literaria*. Hence, although this man of letters sympathizes with Coleridge's speculative ambitions, he politely dishes out hardheaded advice: give the reader what he pays for.

Those conventional lineaments of the man of letters—his bookish cultivation and worldly prudence—are a species of figurative extavagance, however, for Coleridge's correspondent is a man of letters not merely in the ordinary, metaphorical sense but in the most literal. The man of the letter is strictly a man of letters because he has no existence apart from the words that Coleridge attributes to him, no life outside the text in which those words appear. The metaphor of man of letters is brought home to its literal sense by the appearance of a man who has no home, no property at all, besides "his" letters, which are his personification.

The structural function of the intervention of the letter has been examined by Gayatri Spivak, who gingerly brings a Lacanian model to bear on the relation between the "cut" the letter makes in the philosophical argument and the immediate emergence of the full-fledged statement of the imagination. The pressure of contradiction which, I have argued, can be discerned in the tension between argument and rhetoric[16] afflicts the argument itself, according to Spivak, who contends that Coleridge's philosophical theses in Chapter XII, which begin with the problem of the priority between subject and object, inexorably gravitate toward a gap between knowing and being that is logically irreducible yet metaphysically inconceivable. "And it is this gap," Spivak urges, "between knowing and being that the episode of the imaginary letter occludes." That occlusion is "the eruption of the Other onto the text of the subject. Read this way, what is otherwise seen as merely an interruption of the development of the *argument* about the imagination may not only be seen as a keeping alive, by unfulfillment, of the desire that moves the argument, but also as the ruse that makes possible the establishment of the *Law* of the imagination."[17] By cutting off the argument, the letter liberates the author from his writing and enables the Law, which is the law of the sovereign self, to emerge and dictate according to its God-given prerogative.

It is a characteristic of the text and a problem for the imagination that even if we were benevolently to ignore the contradictions of chapters XII and XIII, confident in the constant supervision of the imagination despite a temporary occlusion, there would remain the condition on the imagination's appearance as theory that it must manifest itself at a certain point in the text. That engagement with the physical, the material moment, is not only a logical inevitability but also an analogical necessity, whether we consider the imagination under the rubric of the law, where the manifestation of the divinity on Mount Sinai is the corroborative type, or under redemption, where the crucifixion of Christ is the paradigm. But let not this necessity of engaging the text be considered as a degradation of imagination's power. It is far otherwise. It is an opportunity for the imagination to manifest itself not as just another theoretical approximation of an ineffable metaphysical gravity but as guarantee, agent, and sign of the return to the constant center, as the resynonymizing economist of desire. Certainly the manifestation of the imagination in Chapter XIII is meant to be the return of the writer of the *Biographia* to a self where property and propriety are synonymous: it returns him after years of doubt and disagreement to the original vision of creative possibility he experienced in the dawning of Wordsworth's genius; it returns the intellectual and emotional in-

[16]"Coleridge's Marginal Method in the *Biographia Literaria*," *PMLA* 92 (October 1977):928–40.
[17]Gayatri Chakrovorty Spivak, "The Letter as Cutting Edge," *Yale French Studies* 55/56 (1977):218.

vestment he has made in disputing associationism; it recovers a self that had been lost both to journalistic ephemera and the vicious nominalism of anonymous reviewers. Even more immediately, the imagination returns the author from and even gives teleological sanction to the tortuous deviations and plagiarisms of chapters V–XIII. It is in those chapters that the Coleridgean path turns most circuitous; there Coleridge's letters begin to letter him in his very defense against becoming a mere man of letters; his voice is almost reduced to just another inflection in the eloquent ventriloquism of the text. But the imagination redeems all losses; it "dissolves, diffuses, dissipates, *in order* to recreate." Part of the master plan, plagiarism invokes the truth it cannot tell and takes its place as the designed propaedeutic of the manifestation of purposiveness that is the return of the imagination.

The imagination does return. But that return happens on a letter. The redemptive appearance of the imagination is preceded and prepared by the providential apparition of the man of the letter, with the consequence that whatever good faith the reader espouses, he or she cannot read the imagination as its own deliverer. It is the man of the letter who manages the sublime transition from Schellingian ventriloquism to the true Coleridgean voice. That generous act is of equivocal virtue. Although the letter makes possible the establishment of the law of the imagination, its appearance interrupts teleological continuity and disrupts, perhaps subverts, the analogical network that endows the imagination with conceptual plausibility and moral power. Leslie Brisman, another recent commentator on the passage, has confronted and attempted to overcome this consequence by situating the letter within an alternative analogical frame that would recuperate its subversive discontinuity. Brisman ascribes the interrupter to a figurative category he identifies as the "Porlock" in Coleridge, that is, the "natural man." He calls "his Porlock a serpent in the garden . . . because the relaxation of the will that lets the 'natural man' take over is to some extent a fall."[18] The "some extent" allows Brisman to allegorize Chapter XIII as the story of Eden, fall, and Paradise regained. Allegory upon allegory: the plausibility of lost groves elysian wholly depends on the initial figurative move, the christening of the fictional correspondent as Porlock, natural man. If we were to adopt the metaphysical perspective Coleridge prescribes, however, the intervention of the letter would resemble less the intrusion of nature as a result of relaxed authorial will (it would be difficult to identify the will in Chap-

18Leslie Brisman, *Romantic Origins* (Ithaca: Cornell University Press, 1978), p. 34.

ter XII) than the interruption of the will on the nature of the book. "Nature," according to the authoritative Coleridge of *Aids to Reflection,* "is a line in constant and continuous evolution. . . . But where there is no discontinuity there can be no origination, and every appearance of origination in nature is but a shadow of our own casting. It is a reflection of our own will or spirit."[19] The fictional correspondent, both a discontinuity in the evolution of Coleridge's dialectic and a shadow of Coleridge's own casting, would have to be allied with the will in any Coleridgean metaphysical allegory. But the characteristic of this "appearance of origination" that enfeebles any metaphysical allegory is that from the very beginning the man of the letter is a simulacrum; though it disrupts the book *like* the will, it does not have the ontological gravity *of* the will. The discontinuity of the letter equivocates the will with a willfulness that is its duplicitous semblance. Regardless of metaphysics, however, the rendering of the letter as Porlock *"in propria persona"*[20] addresses it mistakenly because what distinguishes this interruption is that the man of the letter does not hail from Porlock, nature, or anywhere else; he has no home but his assigned, marginal resting place. Brisman's imaginative misreading has the virtue of allowing us to see that among the various interruptions in Coleridge's writings this one has a priority of sorts because it is without any genealogy whatsoever. The man of the letter is a man of the text he interrupts. Allegorical redundancy and displacement are functions of the attempt to characterize a correspondent who is already a personification of the interruption that he is. He exists only in the character of the letters that mark his appearance in the argument of Coleridge's literary life.

To profit fully from this passage in the *Biographia* the critic must try to *think* the interruption. But to attempt that thought is to be impressed by the mutual implication of critical profit with critical loss, for thinking the interruption slips, ineluctably and almost indifferently, into a thinking *of* the interruption. Deprived of angelic intuition, criticism must discourse, and to think of the interruption is to characterize it discursively. Man of (the) letter(s) is, I think, the least possible characterization that will transfer the interruption into discourse. Angus Fletcher has commented, "Formally, we can say that personification is the figurative emergent of the liminal scene."[21] That my characterization is the most appropriate for the personifica-

---

[19]*Aids to Reflection,* ed. Henry Nelson Coleridge (5th ed.; London: William Pickering, 1843), p. 202n.

[20]Brisman, *Romantic Origins,* p. 33.

[21]"Positive Negation," in *New Perspectives on Coleridge and Wordsworth,* ed. Geoffrey Hartman (New York: Columbia University Press, 1972), p. 158.

tion of this liminal interruption is indicated by its analytic instability, an instance of what Coleridge elsewhere calls a "practical pun."[22] Any accurate characterization of the way the interruption figures in the text will pun on *letter*, just as the man of the letter, neither fully synonymous nor desynonymous with Coleridge or himself, is a practical pun on *author*. Its punmanship represents the embarrassing impropriety of the interruption, and that impropriety is its power, the power that Coleridge names "impropriation": the taking of metaphors literally.[23] Here in Chapter XIII of the *Biographia* we read an impropriation so insatiably comprehensive that the literal, gorged by its aggrandizement of the figurative, spills forth new metaphors, as if to feed its own appetite. The existence of an actual man of letters who corresponds with Coleridge is a metaphor of and for the writer who has drafted the letter. But the metaphorical man of letters becomes literal through the impropriation of the text. And the writer who has sent himself abroad finds himself returned in the literal correspondent of a mere man of letters, who, neither self nor other, is a man at once wholly abroad and entirely at home in language, a person who leads a completely literary life.

Although the discourse of this interruption may dance on the head of a pun, the letter *does* discourse, and the dance *does* figure. Reflecting on the effect of reading the *"Chapter on the Imagination,"* including, evidently, the section as yet (and ever) untranscribed for the press, Coleridge's correspondent concludes by epitomizing Coleridge's rhetorical power: *"In short, what I had supposed substances were thinned away into shadows, while everywhere shadows were deepened into substances"* (I:199). Substances to shadows, shadows to substances. In characterizing Coleridge's prose, the correspondent characterizes himself—the shadow line between man and letters—and the action of the interruption, a chiasmic crossing between man and letters, letters and man. Marvelously economical, the elliptical chiasmus tropes the imagination's grand project of desynonymization within an horizon of synonymity. It figures the disclosure of meaning as a polarization and reversal that is circumscribed by the reversionary unity of the figure as a whole.[24] Moreover, the specific chiasmus that the man of (the) letter(s) employs to give substance to the shadowy

---

[22]*The Friend* (1818), ed. Barbara Rooke, 2 vols. (Princeton: Princeton University Press, 1969), I:273.

[23]*Aids to Reflection*, p. 248.

[24]For an example of the chiasmus as "vicious circle," see Arden Reed's "Coleridge, the Sot, and the Prostitute: A Reading of *The Friend*, Essay XIV," in *Studies in Romanticism* 19 (1980):113.

chapter on the imagination not only prepares for but prefigures what is to follow by troping the imagination proper, which presumably begins with some sort of substance that it then dissolves into shadows in order to recreate substance. The telling difference between the trope and the faculty is that the chiasmus lacks the imagination's "in order to," its progressive good sense. The apparent order of thinning then deepening is strictly a function of the semantic inclination of this particular utterance and decisively subordinate to the formal antithetical balance and material equivalence of the interrupted halves of the figure. The ostensible dissolution or desynonymization in the chiasmus (*a* to *b*, *b* to *a*) is executed by the arbitrary transposition of signifiers, or, to put it in Coleridgean terms, by the fanciful manipulation of "counters." Though formulaic and manipulative, the fancy has its charms nonetheless. If not good sense, the fanciful arrangement of "fixities and definites" (I:202) into a chiamsus is the next best (or perhaps next better) thing: its counterfeit. Having pledged that his theses would deduce the imagination, Coleridge attempts to cancel the unpaid debt by forging a friend, who tells him that what he has done (thinning, deepening) is sufficient and *proves* it to both Coleridge and his readers by counterfeiting Coleridge's imagination in the chiasmus. The counterfeit works: the imagination follows. But success spoils. The plausibility of the counterfeit, its aptitude for success, derives from its unconscionable ability to impropriate the essential distinction of the imagination, its property to recreate. Hence, though the debt be paid and the goal attained, all the propriety of the imagination is lost in the transfer. For what could be more truly recreative and yet more blatantly fanciful than to thin a man away into letters while deepening letters into a man?

To recapitulate the episode of the interruption: Between the dialectical mowing (*mähen*) and the ontological faculty (*meinen*) emerges an admonition (*mahnen*) which makes ends meet. The letter (*n*) literalizes the origination of the imagination and the sovereign self of which the imagination is the guarantee. By its articulate textual transactions, the letter typifies the shifts of a writer who is a practiced, ingeniously ambivalent man of letters. Or, to describe the interruption another way, it is as if a man had sent himself abroad, his living borne in fragile ships, had lost those vessels, and in that loss his life had fallen due. It is as if circumstances had then come to a pass where no hope remained, where the course of justice could not be stalled, when suddenly a sympathetic, powerful man of letters appeared and, astonishingly, both saved the victim's bodily integrity and restored his property. But it is also as if the man of letters were not really a man and the law he represents were not really the law; as if salvation were actually a sleight of the savior's hand, which sealed an unredeemable impropriety.

No doubt the interruption could be put in other ways. One might, for example, exploit the man of the letter's allusion to "Christabel" (" *'Now in glimmer, and now in gloom'* " [I:199]) as the pretext for an investigation of the way letter and poem interpret the thresholds, passages, and correspondence in each. Or one might take the connection between digressions and physical torture that Coleridge establishes earlier in the *Biographia* (I:110), compound it with his insight, recorded in the notebooks, "That *Interruption* of itself is painful because & as far as it acts as Disruption,"[25] and make the argument that the digressive interruption of the man of the letter epitomizes the perdurable pain in Coleridge's literary life that the imagination cannot sublimate or resecrete. The multiplication of plausible hypotheses, analogies, and arguments attests to the impossibility of thinking the interruption without characterizing it, without transferring it to an always inappropriate critical discourse. Such criticism is, I would admit, fanciful. But the fancy is our only guide to an accurate, if not true or final, reading of an interruption that once read can never convey us wholly to the haven of the imagination. No matter how many readings the interruption may provoke, the tally will never rival the number devoted to the theory of the imagination itself, readings equally as fanciful and generally more bemused in their futile enterprise to render unto Coleridge or God what is not the property of either.

I would not call the prospect of indefinite readings of the interruption vertiginous. At least it does not feel vertiginous to me. If we seek an image for the chiasmic rhetoric of the interruption, we do not find it in the whirlwind of Gray, which is, after all, a dreadful exaggeration of mere poetic license, nor in the tempest that sadly weathers Antonio. But we might be satisfied with the eddy that involves Coleridge when he tries to make sense of Locke. To read the interruption in Chapter XIII of the *Biographia* is similarly to "go round and round with never a step forward" in an eddy of the text. The eddy, one of Coleridge's favorite images, illustrates various moods of head and heart in his writings,[26] and devil or angel can

[25]*CN* I:1834.

[26]On the image of the eddy in Coleridge, see John Beer, *Coleridge's Poetic Intelligence* (New York: Barnes & Noble, 1977), pp. 41–69, and Edward Kessler, *Coleridge's Metaphors of Being* (Princeton: Princeton University Press, 1979), pp. 15–37.

quote examples to suit his purpose. To cite just one: "Our mortal existence a stoppage in the blood of Life—a brief eddy in the over-flowing Ocean of pure Activity, from wind or concourse of currents."[27] I will not try to perfect the analogy, just note that our mortal existence is not Life but, like the interruption of the letter, a stoppage in the flow, an eddy that figures in the stream much as the chiasmus exquisitely clots the bloodline of the book. Coleridge's mortal existence, the eddying text that survives him, is an interruption of rare device, the literary life of a man of letters.

[27]*CN* I:3151.

6 /

The Mariner Rimed

ARDEN REED

I

La rime—loi générale de l'effet textuel—plie l'une à l'autre une
identité et une différence.

—Jacques Derrida[1]

Criticism of the *Ancient Mariner* has never been long arrested
by the orthography of the title, not surprisingly, since the topic
suggests a frigid pedantry more likely to kill a reader's interest than
to quicken it. But "extremes meet" in Coleridge, as he argued repeatedly, and answering a narrow question such as why he chose the
spelling "Rime" may lead us on to strange seas of thought.

It is generally agreed that Coleridge used the archaic spelling to
help antique his poem, to make it seem more remote or "ancient" to
the reader first encountering the text, or at least to invite his suspension of disbelief. But the history of the title reveals this explanation
to be inadequate. When the poem initially appeared, introducing
the first edition of *Lyrical Ballads* (1798), the title read *The Rime of the
Ancyent Marinere*. For the second edition (1800) Coleridge changed
the title to *The Ancient Mariner. A Poet's Reverie*, apparently at Wordsworth's urging. Finally, when Coleridge himself first published the
poem, in the collection of his own lyrics called *Sibylline Leaves* (1817),
he settled on *The Rime of the Ancient Mariner*, and so the title has
remained in all subsequent editions. Why then in 1817, long after he
had modernized the spelling of "Ancient" and "Mariner," did Coleridge revert to the old-fashioned and now disjunctive orthography
of "Rime"?

[1]Jacques Derrida, "La double séance," *La dissémination* (Paris: Seuil, 1977), p. 309.
Barbara Johnson translates the line as follows: "Rhyme—which is the general law of
textual effects—is the folding-together of an identity and a difference." *Dissemination*
(Chicago: University of Chicago Press, 1981), p. 277.

We may find a hint in a piece of marginalia he left in a volume of Milton. In his note, Coleridge expresses agreement with Bishop Pearce (and against Warton) that when Milton wrote "rhime" he meant something different from "rime." Coleridge's reasoning on this point follows from the general principle that all languages tend to take advantage of accidental differences in spelling "to make a word multiply upon itself."[2] Generating puns is thus one of the structural characteristics of language; in fact, Coleridge asserts that "language itself is formed upon associations of this kind."[3]

The prestige he attributes to puns helps explain Coleridge's continuing interest in them and in the often-mentioned project to write an "Essay in Defense of Puns."[4] In typical fashion, he never completed it, but those passages in the 1811–12 lectures that defend Shakespeare's "wit" against the strictures of the neoclassic critics constitute a fragmentary form of this essay. To Dr. Johnson and his school, who had complained of artificiality and contrivance, Coleridge responded that puns exemplify language in its natural and original condition. Certain puns in Shakespeare "appear almost as if the first openings of the mouth of nature."[5] Furthermore, puns and conceits have a legitimate function as linguistic forms of the sublime, because they are the only fit expressions for overwhelming or excessive states of passion: "passion . . . carries off its excess by play on words, as naturally . . . as by gesticulations, looks, or tones" (II:135). The only time a pun should be censured, then, is when it is dissociated from such "exuberant activity of mind" (I:20), as in Voltaire, for instance, where wit serves only to display the author's cleverness (II:90).[6]

Coleridge's speculation on puns suggests an answer to the question of orthography: he fails to modernize "Rime" along with the rest of the title because only the archaic spelling creates a pun, meaning both verse with like endings, and also hoarfrost, frozen

[2]*Coleridge's Miscellaneous Criticism*, ed. Thomas M. Raysor (London: Constable, 1936), p. 173.

[3]*The Notebooks of Samuel Taylor Coleridge*, ed. Kathleen Coburn (Princeton: Princeton University Press, 1957–), n. 3762; hereafter *CN*.

[4]See, for example, *Letters of Samuel Taylor Coleridge*, ed. Earl L. Griggs (Oxford: Oxford University Press, 1956–71), letter 522 (hereafter *CL*), *CN* 3762, and *CN* 4444. At one point he even speaks of "an Essay, I have written called an 'Apology for Puns'" (*Miscellaneous Criticism*, p. 144).

[5]*Shakespearean Criticism*, ed. Thomas M. Raysor, 2 vols. (New York: Dutton, 1960), II, 89. Further references will be found in the text.

[6]For further remarks on puns in the Shakespeare lectures, see I:35, 70, 71, 135–36, and II:73, 88–91, 103–5, 143–45, 231.

mist, or a chill mist or fog (*OED*).[7] What hoarfrost and the like have to do with the *Ancient Mariner* will soon become clear, but first it should be remarked that the pun on "rime" is inscribed in a series of doublings that pervades the poem, as well as standing outside that series, as its point of origin. Among other instances of doubling that come immediately to mind are the sun and the moon ("The bloody Sun, at noon, / Right above the mast did stand, / No bigger than the Moon" [ll. 112–14]), the death ship and its passengers ("Like vessel, like crew!" [gloss to l. 190]), or the death ship and the Mariner's skeletal ship as it returns to home port. All of these doublings are themselves redoubled time and again, because the Mariner keeps repeating the story that has articulated them; indeed, his tale itself and the frame story of the wedding form another pair in the series.

To be more precise, the process of doublings in the *Ancient Mariner* operates in two directions. One is the creation of resemblance or identity out of difference, when the poem demonstrates how two things that seem unrelated or even opposites can come to mirror each other. Although sailing without wind or crew across a desolate ocean, for example, the Mariner nonetheless hears in the sails "A noise like of a hidden brook / In the leafy month of June, / That to the sleeping woods all night / Singeth a quiet tune" (ll. 369–72). But beginning with the title itself, the poem is also engaged in splitting identity (the presence of a word to itself, for instance) into differences, in turning the singular "rime" into two meanings that are not necessarily commensurate. This second process may be related to a more general fragmentation that marks the entire poem. Both of these operations—the making and the unmaking of congruence—occur throughout the text and are woven together, although they do not form any regular, much less dialectical pattern.

The great majority of essays on the *Ancient Mariner*, whatever their local disagreements may be, share the presupposition that the critic's task is to uncover or to recover the poem's creation of resemblance. Such a task necessitates the suppression of puns, or dissonant doublings, which frustrate the critical demonstration of "organic unity."

---

[7]"From 16th century chiefly *Sc.* and *north*, but revived in literary use at the end of the 18th century" (*OED*). The word "rime" (originally indistinguishable from "rhythm") splits into a noun and a verb, and the verb is likewise double, meaning both to give up or vacate and to take for oneself; to withdraw, depart, retire and to extend, increase, enlarge; to widen out and to pry into. Through the seventeenth century "rime" in fact signified a sense of fragmentation, for its meanings included "chap, chink, or cleft." Coleridge subtly points to this meaning in describing the "snowy clifts," for as John Livingston Lowes explained, "clift" is a double of "cleft." See *The Road to Xanadu* (1927; reprint ed., Boston: Houghton Mifflin, 1955), p. 453.

The first of these critics was Coleridge himself, on those occasions when he stressed the "synthetic and magical power to which we have exclusively appropriated the name of imagination" to reveal "unity in multeity."[8] Among modern critics the most distinguished representative of this position has been Robert Penn Warren, whose essay continues, despite a number of legitimate objections, to influence critical readings of the *Ancient Mariner* and exemplifies a powerful style of interpreting Romantic literature. According to Warren, the poem offers a "sacramental vision" of the interrelatedness of nature, man, and God, the "one Life within us and abroad."[9] It would be inaccurate to say that he simply ignores the working of difference because late in his essay he acknowledges that "the imagination does not only bless, for even as it blesses, it lays on a curse" (p. 44). This observation names a process of doubling that works much like a pun, splitting imaginative wholeness, or the wholeness of imagination, into irreconcilable difference. But his argument demands that Warren give this insight short shrift because if the imagination is at once positive and negative and if, as he says, the theme of imagination "fuses" with that of the "one Life," then the celebrated sacramental visions may bifurcate into something more ambiguous than he would allow. What happens to Warren's reading and those it typifies, then, if we lift the critical censure and give free play to the generalized process of punning?

II

If every atom of a dead man's flesh
Should move, each one with a particular life,
Yet all as cold as ever—'twas just so!
Or if it drizzled needle-points of frost
Upon a feverish head made suddenly bald

Osorio IV:32–36, completed a month before
Coleridge began the *Ancient Mariner*

---

[8]*Biographia Literaria,* ed. John Shawcross, 2 vols. (Oxford: Oxford University Press, 1907), II, 12. Further references will be included in the text.

[9]Robert Penn Warren, "A Poem of Pure Imagination: An Experiment in Reading," abridged edition included in *Twentieth Century Interpretations of "The Rime of the Ancient Mariner,"* ed. James D. Boulger (Englewood Cliffs, N.J.: Prentice-Hall, 1969), pp. 21–22. Further references to this article will be included in the text. For other critiques of Warren's reading, see Homer Obed Brown, "The Art of Theology and the Theology of Art: Robert Penn Warren's Reading of Coleridge's *The Rime of the Ancient Mariner*" and the response to that essay by Jonathan Arac, "Repetition and Exclusion: Coleridge and New Criticism Reconsidered," in *boundary 2,* 8 (1979):237–72.

To return to the question suspended above, what has hoarfrost to do with the *Ancient Mariner?* What is the reason for this rime? One answer may be suggested by Coleridge's early design for the poem, which was to compose a series of "Hymns to the Sun, the Moon, and the Elements—six hymns" (*CN* 174). John Livingston Lowes convincingly demonstrated how much of that project survives in the poem Coleridge eventually wrote. " 'The Rime of the Ancient Mariner' is to a remarkable degree a poem of the elements. Its real protagonists are Earth, Air, Fire, and Water, in their multiform balefulness and beauty."[10] In the years and months preceding the composition of the *Ancient Mariner,* the search for material often sent Coleridge to travelers' descriptions of the elements, where the word "rime" frequently appears, especially in accounts of sea voyages. One book on which he took copious notes, Frederick Martens's *Voyage to Spitzbergen,* even devotes a chapter to describing rime. And it is this very chapter that figures most prominently in the *Ancient Mariner.*

As a form of the element Water, rime naturally enough leaves its traces in the poem. Although Coleridge uses the word only in the title, he includes more than a dozen instances of that "meteor" in the text; for example, the moonlight "Like April hoar-frost spread" (l. 268).[11] Indeed, the repetition would bear out Wordsworth's charge that the "imagery [is] somewhat too laboriously accumulated,"[12] except that the rime functions as more than redundant window dressing. Consider the case of the albatross, which always appears in the poem shrouded in "snow-fog" (gloss to l. 63). The metonymy of the albatross with the rime is not coincidental because the frozen mist renders the bird an object of superstition. According to an eighteenth-century topos, objects appear enlarged when seen through a mist, and Coleridge took this physical magnification as a metaphor for the psychological enlargement that occurs when man imparts a surplus value of significance to objects of consciousness. The connection is made explicit in the "Verses to Tooke" (1796): "Mists in which Superstition's *pigmy* band / Seem'd Giant Forms . . ." (ll. 15–

[10]Lowes, *Road to Xanadu,* p. 69. Further references to this work will be found in the text. For a contrasting view to Lowes's on Coleridge's interest in these hymns see E. S. Shaffer, *"Kubla Khan" and The Fall of Jerusalem: The Mythological School in Biblical Criticism and Secular Literature 1770–1880* (Cambridge: Cambridge University Press, 1975), pp. 122–23, 129.

[11]See also ll. 75, 77, 85, 100, 102, 134, 150, 153, 276, 378, 403, 619, and the gloss to l. 63.

[12]Wordsworth's note, to which I will refer again, may be found in *Lyrical Ballads,* ed. R. L. Brett and A. R. Jones (London: Methuen, 1963), pp. 270–71.

16, Coleridge's italics). Thus the sighting and interpretation (or reading and writing) of the albatross reenact the process of superstition, as the crew traces a human figure ("a Christian soul") in the frozen mist—a gesture the Mariner will shortly repeat.

The most important role of rime begins in part 3 (though "begins" is somewhat misleading in that it refers only to a sequence of events concluded long before the Wedding-Guest ever encounters the Mariner), when Life-in-Death wins the dice game. She then "begins her work on the Ancient Mariner" (gloss to l. 220), a task she performs by literally freezing him. We know just how she "works" thanks to the Mariner's having identified her a moment before as "she / Who thicks Man's blood with cold" (l. 194). To thick or congeal someone's blood in this poem means to still that person's life, for the Mariner here refers to his "life-blood" (l. 205), invoking the Biblical tradition of "living waters" to make blood the sign of life itself. The Mariner's metamorphosis from life to life-in-death is perfectly figured by petrifying "the life, whose fountains are within" ("Dejection"). In other words, Life-in-Death rimes the Ancient Mariner.[13]

The *Ancient Mariner* is not the first poem in which Coleridge links life-in-death with rime. Two years earlier in *The Destiny of Nations,* to mention but one example, Joan of Arc sees an unattended team of horses trapped in a blizzard. These horses are covered with rime, and as such they represent life-in-death: save for the lead animal they are "yet alive / But stiff and cold, they stood motionless, their

---

[13]Far from being aberrant, freezing or riming the Mariner conforms to the general pattern of romance, at least as Northrop Frye describes it: "In descent narratives the central image is that of metamorphosis, the freezing of something human and conscious into an animal or plant or inanimate object." *The Secular Scripture: A Study of the Structure of Romance* (Cambridge: Harvard University Press, 1976), p. 100. As will become clear, however, the *Ancient Mariner* breaks the pattern because it depicts no unambiguous balancing ascent, characterized by "snow maidens thawed out" or "the conclusion of a masque, where . . . the actors come out of their dramatic frame and revert to the people they actually are" (p. 155). Such actions are precisely what the Mariner cannot in any simple sense perform.

Lowes came uncannily close to seeing the relationship between the Mariner and the climate in an incidental remark on old maps Coleridge might have seen: "One word and only one stretches in dim capitals across the whole southern hemisphere on a fifteenth century chart. It is BRUMAE: fogs—the dense and chilling mists, which, like the flesh of the spectre-woman on the skeleton-ship, 'thick man's blood with cold'" (p. 107).

Cf. in Book I of the *Faerie Queene* the chilling of the Red Cross Knight's blood (which appears as a fever—vii, 6.6–9), his ensuing *acedia*, which similarly parallels the Mariner's, and his condition of Life-in-Death (I. vii. 26.9). Cf. also Polixenes' description of his son in *The Winter's Tale:* "He makes a July's day short as December, / And with his varying childness, cures in me / Thoughts that would thick my blood" (I.ii.169–71)—i.e., make me melancholy.

manes / Hoar with the frozen night-dews" (ll. 198–200). (Compare the Mariner "Whose beard with age is hoar" [l. 619].) Near the team she sees another rimed figure. "A miserable man crept forth: his limbs / The silent frost had eat" (ll. 207–8), yet neither is he dead, but a storyteller like the Mariner.[14]

The strange reactions of the Mariner's interlocutors point to his rimed state, for everyone who encounters him thereafter doubts that he is a living man. When the Mariner tells how Life-in-Death won him, the Wedding-Guest concludes that he must be a ghost (ll. 224–29). The sight of the Mariner on his homecoming provokes the Pilot to fall into a fit, the Hermit to pray frantically, and the Pilot's boy to go crazy. When the Hermit demands "What manner of man art thou?" (l. 577), the Mariner proceeds to rhyme the story of his own riming. His condition further explains the peculiar beginning of the poem—"*It* is an ancient Mariner" (my italics). That "it" should be taken almost literally here, for the Mariner is more an "it" than a "he," more rime than person.

Riming the Mariner is something very different from killing him, however, because that paradoxical transformation—as befits a pun—at once curses and saves him. One reason that Life-in-Death freezes the Mariner is to preserve him in a sort of suspended animation, for like Coleridge and Wordsworth she knows that ice or frost arrests decay in living matter.[15] When the Wedding-Guest encounters him, therefore, the Mariner is not simply old but "ancient," or "hoar[y]" as the Guest puts it (l. 619), having endured far beyond the limits of human or organic life. His state of limbo is reflected in the curious present tense with which the poem opens—"It *is* an

[14]It would seem that this "meteor" was in the air, for in a 1797 review of M. G. Lewis's *The Monk* Coleridge displayed special interest in the "bleeding nun," whose approach prompted the narrator to say, "I felt a sudden chillness spread itself over my body. . . . My blood was frozen in my veins" (cited by Lowes, p. 255). Coleridge was thus well familiar with the figure of a rimed narrator before he wrote the *Ancient Mariner,* which makes it odd that he does not openly allude to this part of the Mariner's fate before the 1817 revision. Only then does he insert the phrases "thicks man's blood with cold," "life-blood," and the specter-woman's name, Life-in-Death.

[15]In "Peter Bell" Wordsworth observed how "the weakest things, if frost / Have stiffened them, maintain their place" (ll. 848–49). Several years before, Mrs. Barbauld had addressed herself to the preservative quality of freezing in her "Inscription for an Ice-House" (cited by John Beer, "Ice and Spring: Coleridge's Imaginative Education," *Coleridge's Variety,* ed. John Beer [Pittsburgh: University of Pittsburgh Press, 1974], p. 70). These texts contrast with such characteristic eighteenth-century poems as Erasmus Darwin's *Economy of Vegetation,* in which a freezing similar to the Mariner's simply kills the character Tremella (see canto 1, ll. 453–70, and the note to canto 1, l. 462). Aristotle, however, already remarks how "what is frozen does not putrefy" (*Meteorologica,* 397b).

ancient Mariner" (my italics)—which continues for four and a half stanzas before slipping into the past. In a curious way, then, the Mariner was not entirely deluded in identifying the specter bark as the ship that would save him.

A different precedent for freezing the Mariner may be found in Dante. The Mariner's voyage to the South Pole is a version of the Fall ("Merrily did we *drop* / *Below* the kirk, *below* the hill, / *Below* the lighthouse top . . ." [ll. 22–24, my italics]), and as Irene Chayes observes, the imagery of Coleridge's polar region owes something to the ice in the ninth circle of the *Inferno*.[16] Turning to canto 32, one finds the Coleridgean seascape of "A lake which though frost had the semblance of glass and not of water" (ll. 23–24),[17] and in this ice (which is probably blood-colored)[18] the frozen sinners of the ninth circle are imbedded. Although they remain stationary and tell their tales to a passing stranger (so reversing the Mariner's situation), they have an important kinship with him because each of them has murdered a guest or a friend. The story of Fra Alberigo is particularly interesting in the present context, for when Dante asks "Are you then dead already?" (33, l. 121), Alberigo responds by describing the condition of life-in-death, and in terms of rime: "that you may more willingly scrape the glazen tears from my face, know that as soon as the soul betrays as I did, its body is taken from it by a devil who thereafter rules it until its time has all revolved. The soul falls headlong into this cistern, and perhaps the body of the shade that is wintering here behind me still appears above on earth" (ll. 127–35). It comes as no surprise to find a notebook entry in which Coleridge refers to this passage (*CN* 4211).

III

> Though birds have no Epiglottis, yet can they so contract the rime or chink of their Larinx [etc.].
> —Sir Thomas Browne, cited in the *OED* entry on "rime"

Until now I have sought, in Coleridgean fashion, to establish a resemblance between the two disparate senses of his pun by showing how the rhymer is composed of rime, or frozen mist. But it is equally

[16]Irene Chayes, "A Coleridgean Reading of 'The Ancient Mariner,'" *Studies in Romanticism* 5 (1965):88.

[17]*Inferno*, trans. Charles S. Singleton (Princeton: Princeton University Press, 1970), pt. 1, p. 341.

[18]*Ibid.*, pt. 2, p. 584, n. 23.

possible to reverse the argument (or to double it): first, the source of language is figured here as rime, or as a Mariner rimed, but second, rime itself (in the strict sense of hoarfrost and independent of the pun) is *already* a name for language. The plot of the poem alludes to this linguistic meaning of rime because the moment Life-in-Death freezes the Ancient Mariner is likewise the moment she condemns him to wander the earth and repeat his tale. Indeed, she freezes or rimes him precisely so that he can go on rhyming indefinitely. To rime the Mariner, therefore, is to turn him into a "blessed machine of language" in two ways: (1) he becomes the mouthpiece of the poem, the means of keeping it in circulation, and (2) transformed into frozen language, he himself turns literally into a "man of letters."[19]

The argument may be demonstrated by a short excursus into some of Coleridge's other texts. About 1795, he began to figure language in terms of mist. The most striking example of that year, although not the only one, occurs in the "Allegoric Vision," in which language precipitates out of the mist: "the mist gradually formed itself into letters and words."[20] Similarly, in "Dejection" (1802) Coleridge says that the poet's soul "must issue forth / A light, a glory, a fair luminous cloud" (ll. 53–54, repeated as "this fair luminous mist" [l. 62], and paralleling the poet's sending forth "a sweet and potent voice" [l. 57]). Finally, in the *Biographia Literaria* (1815) he refers to Wordsworth's supreme poetic gift of "spreading the *atmosphere* [etymologically, ring of vapors] . . . of the ideal world" (p. 48, Coleridge's italics). There is also an oblique reference to the linguistic character of rime within the *Ancient Mariner*. It is no accident that when heard through the snow-mist, the ice itself has a speaking voice: "It cracked and growled, and roared and howled, / Like noises in a swound!" (ll. 61–62). The internal rhyme, richer here

---

[19]Coleridge's phrases as interpreted by Jerome Christensen, in *Coleridge's Blessed Machine of Language* (Ithaca: Cornell University Press, 1981), pp. 161–74, or in his essay in the present volume.

[20]In his lecture this year "On the Present War" Coleridge said of the prejudices of the aristocrat "some unmeaning Term generally becomes the Watchword, and acquires almost a mechanical power over his frame. The indistinctness of the Ideas associated with it increases its effect, as "objects look gigantic thro' a mist!" (*Lectures 1795 on Politics and Religion,* ed. Lewis Patton and Peter Mann [Princeton: Princeton University Press, 1971], p. 52). Under certain conditions, it seems, words carry a shroud of mist that expands their power beyond that of normal, referential usage—conditions even more likely to occur in poetical than in political discourse—if the two can indeed be kept apart.

than anywhere else in the poem, calls the reader's attention to the obvious but startling fact that the rime rhymes.[21]

To equate the frozen mist in the *Ancient Mariner* with the luminous mist in "Dejection" or the "*atmosphere*" of imagination in the *Biographia* may seem to elide a crucial difference. This difference can be understood as an effect of logocentrism, however, and as such precisely confirms the relationship among the texts I seek to establish. In "Dejection" and the *Biographia,* mist betokens poetic production under ideal circumstances, making language flow naturally. By contrast, the Mariner is damned to an endless, mechanical repetition of his tale, thus making it appropriate that the mist should congeal into rime. It is as though the winter wind of "Dejection" had invaded the earlier stanzas to petrify the fountains and the clouds. Thus, if the Mariner has already been turned to hoarfrost when he begins speaking to the Wedding-Guest, his metamorphosis is fitting, because hoarfrost is itself a kind of language, a form of rhyme, and the image of hoarfrost in the text becomes a figure for the text itself. We may now see that the role of "rime" in the poem exemplifies Coleridge's idea that we take pleasure in puns because "words have a tendency to confound themselves and co-adunate with the things" (*CN* 3542), for the words of the poem confound themselves with the hoarfrost they signify.

In a related but ironic way, the connection between the Mariner and the frozen mist or hoarfrost dramatizes the coalescence of subject and object, or consciousness and nature. Conforming to Coleridge's own value system, critics have generally considered such unions to be a central goal of Romantic poetry and so praise the vision in the *Ancient Mariner* as a corrective to what James D. Boulger calls "usual perceptions and modes of thought (in which we distinguish ourselves from the object perceived, and perceive each object as a separate entity)."[22] In this case, however, the poem reads the critics, for the coalescence of rimer and rime subverts the critics'

---

[21]In *Romantic Origins* (Ithaca: Cornell University Press, 1978), Leslie Brisman calls the sounds of the ice "the meaningless sounds of matter chafing against matter" (p. 38). Yet Brisman goes on in his next sentence to invest the following verse ("At length did cross an Albatross") with great significance—based precisely on its relatively poorer internal rhyme. To Brisman, as to the Mariner before his conversion by Life-in-Death, the ice sounds "like noises in a swound." But its language seems to be meaningless only because it has not yet been interpreted by one who learns through his own petrification what such sounds can mean.

[22]James D. Boulger, "'The Rime of the Ancient Mariner'—Introduction," *Twentieth Century Interpretations*, p. 10.

own ideology of organic unity and sacramental visions. But it would be more accurate to say that the categories of subject and object are themselves derivative in this poem, each one appearing in the text only as a differing configuration of the rime.[23]

IV

The troublesome and modern bondage of Rhyming.
—Milton, Preface to *Paradise Lost*

To explore another facet of the rime, indeed its most obvious one, we might ask what difference it makes that the Mariner speaks in rhyme rather than in prose. By definition, rhyme involves a doubling of sound and rhythm; therefore, it creates another layer, or multiple layers, of repetition within the pattern of repetitions I have been tracing. (Alternatively, one could say that rhyme is the layer containing within it all the other strata of repetitions.) Furthermore, like the other repetitions in the poem, rhyme depends for its effect on difference, or on an interplay of difference and identity. Rhyme also resembles puns in joining words that have no association by sense but only by sound.

In the poem's conventional ballad stanza (which varies just enough to remind us that it is the norm) not every line rhymes; in fact, we do not know that the stanza will rhyme at all until its last word: *a b c b*. The key to this scheme is the third line. By that point in the stanza we may anticipate a recurrence of either *a* or *b*, rather than the introduction

[23]In a well-known letter written two years after the last major revision of the *Ancient Mariner*, Coleridge imaged himself encased in rime, and he did so in the context of representing himself as a writer:

I would *allegorize* myself, as a Rock with it's summit just raised above the surface of some Bay or Straight in the Arctic Sea,

While yet the stern and solitary Night
Brook'd no alternate Sway—

all around me fixed and firm, methought as my own Substance, and near me lofty Masses, that might have seemed to 'hold the Moon and Stars in fee' and often in such wild play with meteoric lights, or with the quiet Shine from above which they made rebound in sparkles or dispand in off-shoots and splinters and iridescent Needle-shafts of keenest Glitter. [*CL* 1215]

Although the *Ancient Mariner* is usually taken to be a "symbolic" poem, my reading situates it as an allegory in the precise Hegelian sense of the word (especially in light of Paul de Man's interpretation of the *Aesthetics*): "It is therefore rightly said of allegory that it is frosty and cold [*frostig und kahl*]" (G. W. F. Hegel, *Aesthetics*, trans. T. M. Knox, 2 vols. [Oxford: Clarendon Press, 1975], I, 399).

of a third new sound in the sequence, *c*. But it often happens that the third line rhymes internally, so that we get the double rhyme we expected the stanza to produce, except that one of the rhymes is condensed within a single line rather than spread over two. For example,

The Bridegroom's doors are opened wide,	*a*
And I am next of kin;	*b*
The guests are met, the feast is set	*c, c*
May'st hear the merry din.	*b*

[ll. 5–9]

Might this condensation bear any relation to the controlling theme of freezing in the poem? In any case, ten of the twenty stanzas in part 1 rhyme internally in their third lines, and some add a second internal rhyme (cf. ll. 25–29, for example). Conversely, a single rhyme may stretch out over several lines, adding to the sense of mechanical repetition that the poem associates with freezing. The twelfth stanza (the first to extend beyond four lines) combines both techniques of expansion and condensation:

With sloping masts and dipping prow,	*a*
As who pursued with yell and blow	*a*
Still treads the shadow of his foe,	*a*
And forward bends his head,	*b*
The ship drove fast, loud roared the blast	*c, c*
And southward aye we fled.	*b*

[ll. 45–50]

This essay is not the place to undertake a full analysis of the poem's rhyme, but I shall point out some of the more significant instances. Consider stanza three (my italics):

He holds *him* with *his* skinny hand,	*a*
"There was a ship," quoth *he*.	*b*
"Hold off! unhand *me*, grey-beard loon!"	*b, c*
Eftsoons *his* hand dropt *he*.	*c, b*

This stanza begins and ends on the same word, which is also—and uncharacteristically—rhymed with itself. Adding to the effect of the compacted "he" are the repeated possessive pronouns and the alliterating "h" sounds. It is not difficult to sort out the referents of the pronouns, but as one reads straight through the stanza, the diction

tends to confuse the interlocutors' separate identities, an effect redoubled thematically over the course of the poem. Indeed, one cannot say with absolute assurance to whom the final "he" refers: it is
fair to assume that the Mariner drops his own hand, but there is no
way to know for certain that the Wedding-Guest did not remove it.
Increasing this blending effect is the chiasmatic arrangement of
"me," "loon," "Eftsoons," and "he" in the last two lines. (Cf. the
similar chiasmi in ll. 107–10, which include the word "dropt," and l.
250.) However, it is equally plausible to argue that rhyming and
repetition differentiate the speaker from himself, splinter his identity. This argument confirms that the Mariner is composed of the
rhyme he composes, leaving him necessarily fragmented, at odds
and evens with himself.

The identity of the Mariner and his verse (an identity in difference) is also at play in a rhyme toward the end of the poem:

> Since then, at an uncertain hour,
> That agony returns:
> And till my ghastly tale is told,
> This heart within me burns.
>
> [ll. 582–85]

Having turned around the world, the Mariner returns to his starting
point for a time to tell his tale. The tale itself includes the returns of
sound and rhythm in rhyme, as well as figurative language—tropes
or "turns," which in this context are always re-"turns," inasmuch as
any particular telling is a repetition of the tale already told. Finally,
returns / burns is an exact rhyme in several senses: technically—the
sounds following the vowel are the same; thematically—the sound
of "returns" returns in "burns;" and syntactically—just as the rhyme
is suspended and then resolved at the end of the stanza, so the
Mariner is suspended in a state of "agony" resolved momentarily at
the end of the "Rime."

The preceding stanza rhymes "agony" and "left me free" (ll. 579
and 581) in a yoking of antithetical words that recurs throughout the
poem and that may be read either as a reconciliation of opposites or
as a splitting of sameness. It is best understood, though, as the rhyming equivalent of the figure of Life-in-Death. Examples include
"flute" / "mute" (ll. 364 and 366), "noon" / "moon" (ll. 112 and 114),
"sun uprist" / "fog and mist" (ll. 98 and 100). This last instance
merits reading in context:

Nor dim, nor red, like God's own head,	*a, a*
The glorious Sun uprist:	*b*
Then all averred, I had killed the bird	*c, c*
That brought the fog and mist.	*b*
'Twas right, said they, such birds to slay	*d, c*
That bring the fog and mist.	*b*

[ll. 97–102]

Rhyme *b* ironically equates the rising sun with the spreading mist, and I suggest that the sun's first reappearance, narrated here, is undermined by the rhyming that flanks the sunrise. "Fog and mist" is another name for "rime," so the rime rhymes itself (mechanically) in this stanza, while "Sun" appears but once and appropriately has no rhyme. The rhyme scheme here accords with the story, because, as I will explain, sunrise offers no illumination to the crew. And the figure of a darkening light is picked up by the rhyme "night" / "white," which appears three times (ll. 77; 128, 130; and 206, 207); taken together, these three rhymes also equate fire and fog.

There are also rhymes that perform their secret ministry by intruding between other rhymes:

Her beams bemocked the sultry main	*a*
Like April hoar-frost spread;	*b*
But where the ship's huge shadow lay,	*c*
The charmèd water burnt alway	*c*
A still and awful red.	*b*

[ll. 267–71]

"April hoar-frost" is itself rime, but the rhyme (*b*) of the line in which it occurs is interrupted by that of the ship's shadow (*c*)—the visual intrusion perfectly matched by an aural one. The syntax shows how the hoarfrost rhyme (*b*) englobes or inscribes the burning-water rhyme (*c*). In part 5, lightning intrudes both imagistically and syntactically, "cleaving" the stanza in the same way that the shadow does in part 4:

The thick black cloud was cleft, and still	*a*
The Moon was at its side:	*b*
Like waters shot from some high crag,	*c*
The lightning fell with never a jag,	*c*
A river steep and wide.	*b*

[ll. 322–26]

Here, too, the cloud contains or encircles the fire. Similarly, in ll. 174–85, the sun peers through the ribs of the specter ship, and the word "sun" keeps appearing between rhymes.

V

The ice was here, the ice was there,
The ice was all around . . .

   The frozen mist on which I have dwelled does not appear to spread over all the climates of the *Ancient Mariner*. In a meteorological reading such as the present one, other influences on the weather (both external and the weather of the mind) must be accounted for, primarily the sun, because it is the antithesis of hoarfrost. Will the sun never melt the rime? Because the imagery itself articulates the central moral issues of the poem, the question about melting becomes a question about the Mariner's salvation. If Coleridge here makes rime the image of damnation, he also follows a venerable tradition and makes the sun a figure for God. What comes of transporting the Mariner from the pole to the line, then? We would expect the sun's divine influence to dissolve the hoarfrost and release the Mariner from the linguistic prison of rime, returning to him his right of free speech. That is, the poem ought to end in the same way "Religious Musings" does:

As the great Sun, when he his influence
Sheds on the frost-bound waters—The glad stream
Flows to the ray and warbles as it flows.
                                        [ll. 417–19][24]

Unlike the mechanical or obsessive repetition of frozen language, the voice is thought of as living, spontaneous, original, and in tune with the organic interconnectedness of all life. Voice, in other words, is a form of the *logos*, the divine word, reason, or ratio that could restore the balance or harmony disrupted by shooting the albatross in the land of rime. Indeed, the blessing pronounced at the line is usually interpreted in this ideological way.

   But the sun never does melt the rime of the *Ancient Mariner*, and

---

[24]It is not coincidental that this process should engender a kind of poetry—the stream does not "flow" simply but, echoing Milton, "warbles as it flows," and one could say that what it warbles are Coleridge's first lyrics, his "Effusions."

as the title already suggests, it never can. What role the sun does play may be established by turning to three solar scenes in the poem, moments that contrast sharply with the reconciliation of opposites in "Religious Musings." In the polar region, the sun lacks sufficient heat to melt the hoarfrost: "through the drifts the snowy clifts / Did send a dismal sheen" (ll. 55–56). The climate is the same as that depicted in *The Destiny of Nations*, where "The Laplander beholds the far-off Sun / Dart his slant rays on unobeying snows" (ll. 65–66). But Coleridge would not have considered the sun of light-without-warmth to be an adequate emblem for God, for only when the sun "unites light and warmth" (*CN* 467) may it legitimately symbolize God.[25] The *Ancient Mariner* in fact describes just such a sun a few stanzas later, but the equatorial sun turns out to be no improvement. Rather than saving the Mariner, it is the *daemonio meridiei*, the noon-tide demon, which inflicts one of the great hardships of the voyage.

Even if there is no moral resolution at the line, there should still be a meteorological one; the sun ought at least to evaporate the hoar-frost. But the rime endures because, through a series of very charac-teristic transpositions, Coleridge collapses the distance between the pole and the line, turning their antipodal climates into another set of doubles. The tropical setting is shot through with Antarctic refer-ences: above the ship hangs the moon, whose beams spread the blanket of "April hoar-frost" around the ship; at the other extreme, beneath the ship, lurks the "polar spirit," still controlling its move-ments; and at the center is the Mariner, whose blood is "thicked with cold." Even the sun turns lunar at the line: "The bloody sun, at noon, / Right above the mast did stand, / No bigger than the Moon" (ll. 112–14). (This passage demonstrates that the establishment of identity in difference can be as destructive to the Mariner as the reverse process.) As Lowes puts it, "With that calm indifference to locality which was a distinctive trait of Coleridge's imaginative syn-theses, the slimy things that crawled on slime had been swept down into the tropics from Martens . . . where they disport themselves at large in Arctic seas" (p. 81). This synthesis is one-sided, however, for Coleridge transports only the line to the pole; he never introduces equatorial elements in the Antarctic region. The reason the tropical

---

[25]See *The Friend*, ed. Barbara E. Rooke, 2 vols. (Princeton: Princeton University Press, 1969), I, 105, for the fullest expression of this symbolism, and for a reading of this passage, see my "Coleridge, the Sot, and the Prostitute," *Studies in Romanticism* 19 (1980):109–28. Further references to *The Friend* are cited in the text.

sun never melts the rime, then, is that here as in *Paradise Lost* "the parching Air / Burns frore."[26]

There seems to remain one felicitous appearance of the sun in the *Ancient Mariner*. In part 2, as the ship heads northward from the pole, it reaches a point at which the sun's heat is palpable but not yet unbearable. This moment apparently forms a sort of golden mean or synthesis between cold and heat, and its privileged status is signaled by the fact that the Mariner associates the appearance of the sun there with God (the only such comparison in the poem): "Nor dim, nor red, like God's own head / The glorious Sun uprist:" (ll. 97–98).[27] Here at last, it seems, is the sun that can turn the rime of life-in-death back into living waters.

My reading of these two lines is incomplete, however, for I have ignored the colon at the end of the simile. That colon acts as a grammatical arrow, directing the reader ahead and insisting that the passage be read in the context of the remainder of the stanza: "Then all averred, I had killed the bird / That brought the fog and mist. / 'Twas right, said they, such birds to slay, / That bring the fog and mist." The word "then" functions in part as a logical connective, strengthening the colon by suggesting a cause-and-effect situation. Because the fog and mist dissipate, his shipmates applaud the Mariner's act, and as the gloss says, "thus make themselves accomplices in the crime." It is essential to remark that the crew's interpretation is governed solely by the presence or absence of rime. When the "snow-fog" clouds the sailors' sight, they damn the Mariner; when it lifts, they praise him. The sea breeze, which should be the determining factor according to the crew's own opportunistic set of values, never varies, for even after the Mariner shoots the albatross "the good south wind still blew behind" (l. 87). But the sailors are blinded by the lifting of the mist, so that in the very next stanza they condemn the Mariner twice over for having killed "the bird / That made the breeze to blow" (ll. 93–94)—all the evidence notwithstand-

[26]Coleridge cited this line (misquoted from III:380–81) as the first example of his proverb "extremes meet" (*CN* 1725). In the *Ancient Mariner* Coleridge seems to accomplish what Milton feared was impossible—to write the poetry of the "frozen North." In *Mansus*, for example, he speaks about the "Muse . . . reared under hard conditions in the frozen North" (cited in Z. S. Fink, "Milton and the Theory of Climatic Influence," *Modern Language Quarterly* 2 [1941]:71).

[27]The reviewer for the *British Critic* called this line "a simile which makes the reader shudder . . . with religious disapprobation," so leading Coleridge to alter it to "Angel's head" in 1800. By 1817, however, he reverted to the original. See also *CN* 327.

ing. The glorious appearance of the sun thus emerges among the darkest moments in the poem.[28]

The fact that the sun fails to melt the rime is the imagistic way of saying that the poem offers no redemption for the Mariner. And because there is no redemption, he must go on rhyming and "existing" in a state of rime. Were the sun ever to melt the rime, in fact, the poem would cease to exist, because the narrator—who is preserved in hoarfrost—would die, and simultaneously the linguistic hoarfrost would evaporate. Thus the poem and the protagonist's salvation neatly exclude one another. The *Ancient Mariner* always suggests the possibility of the Mariner's redemption, but it can never do anything more, for the very being of the text depends on the Mariner's never being saved.[29]

VI

My own Shadow too on the wall not far from Mr D's Chair—the White Paper, the Sheet of Harbour Reports lying spread out on the Table, on the other side of the Bottles / — / Influence of mere Color—influence of Shape—wonderful coalescence of scattered Colors, at distances, & then all going to some one Shape / & the modification. Likewise I am now convinced by repeated Observation, that perhaps *always* in a very minute degree, but assuredly in *certain* states (& postures) of the Eye, as in Drowsiness, the state of

[28]In *Coleridge the Visionary* (London: Chatto & Windus, 1959) John Beer calls the flight of angelic melodies to and from the sun (ll. 354–66) the climax of the poem and the strongest sign of the Mariner's redemption (pp. 161–65). But the Mariner himself can take no active part in this scene, and so it heightens his isolation even as it comforts him. The contrast is underscored by his return to a human society immediately afterward, for he gets a decidedly frigid reception. See Raimonda Modiano's critique of Beer in "Words and 'Languageless' Meanings: Limits of Expression in *The Rime of the Ancient Mariner*," *Modern Language Quarterly* 38 (1977):50. The whole article is of interest, and her remarks on the Mariner's point of view are relevant to my present concerns, although she draws different conclusions.

[29]Space does not permit a corresponding discussion of the moon, but analysis would show it to be a double of the hoarfrost. The resemblance is made possible by Coleridge's classifying the moon as light-without-warmth, whence its beams appear "like April hoar-frost." (He similarly associates moonlight with ice in "Christabel" [ll. 17–22] and *CN* 240.) The moonlight / hoarfrost double seems to be undercut because the moon is a perpetual wanderer, whereas frozen mist is stationary. The gloss uses the paradoxical word "still," however (twice over, in fact), to describe the journeying moon, and if the moon is always in its "natural home" there is a sense in which it never moves. Conversely, the hoarfrost is present everywhere, even at the line, and the "natural home" may be read allegorically for the ubiquity of the rime in the poem. A further connection is made in the Wedding-Guest's epithet for the Mariner—"greybeard *loon*."

the Brain & Nerves after Distress and Agitation, especially if it had been accompanied by weeping, & in many others, we see our own faces, and project them, according to the distance given them by the degree of indistinctness—that this may occasion in the highest degree the Wraith, (vide a hundred Scotch Stories, but better than all Wordsworth's most wonderful as well as admirable Poem, Peter Bell, where he seems his own Figure—& still oftener that it facilitates the formation of a human Face out of some really present Object, and from the alteration of the distance, among other causes, never suspected on the occasion, and *substratum.*

S.T.C.

N.B. This is a valuable note / re-read by me Tuesday morning, 14 May. [*CN* 2583]

My assertion that the text dooms the Mariner appears to be contradicted by the text itself. After all, when he blesses the watersnakes "the spell begins to break" (gloss to l. 288), and his winter of life-in-death now turns to "spring" (adumbrated by the "*April* hoarfrost") as his blood begins to flow again: "A spring of love gushed from my heart, / And I blessed them unaware" (ll. 284–85). The gushing spring relieves his *ariditas,* just as the dew and rain quench his physical thirst. Because the Mariner here learns the lesson that "we are all one Life," most critics agree with Warren that the blessing scene is "the very turning point of the poem" (p. 42)—however early a climax that might be. But this interpretation, which forms the center of most critical readings, applies only if one makes the crucial assumption that the Mariner's narrative can be taken at face value, that his point of view is the reliable one, and that there is no need to evaluate it or to set it in a different context.

The credibility of the Mariner's perceptions has been made suspect, however, just before the blessing scene by his misidentifying the specter bark. In fact, the whole journey from the familiar to the foreign, or natural to supernatural, repeatedly shows his understanding to lag behind his experiences. Furthermore, Coleridge's description of the genesis of *Lyrical Ballads* in the *Biographia* indicates that objective and detached portrayal was never his intention. He was rather intending to represent "the dramatic truth of such emotions, as would naturally accompany such [supernatural] situations, supposing them real. And real in this sense they have been to every human being who, from whatever source of delusion, has at any time beheld himself under supernatural agency" (p. 168). Frederick A. Pottle was hardly too blunt in reminding readers that Coleridge had "presented the story dramatically through the lips of a medieval, superstitious, and possibly deranged old man."[30] To accept the Mariner's version of the blessing scene also raises questions of motive and moral in the subsequent parts of the poem. If his story were reliable, why should the polar spirit continue to "requir[e] vengeance" (gloss to l. 377) for the albatross? And why if the Mariner has an authentic perception of the "one Life," must he go on paying servitude to Life-in-Death in a purgatory without end?

Unfortunately, Coleridge does little to situate the Mariner's point of view.[31] The principal comment is the gloss, which he may have added to confirm the Mariner's salvation, since the text itself could not do so, or alternatively, to add another doubling division. The other well-known statement is his remark to Mrs. Barbauld that moral sentiments intruded too much into his poem of "pure imagination"—a comment that by taking the opposite point of view from the gloss suggests that the glossator's perspective is likewise limited or superfluous.[32] If these remarks tend to cancel each other out, they also fail to illuminate directly the scene in question. There is, however, one other text of Coleridge's that does specifically relate to the blessing, the (presumably) late poem "Constancy to an Ideal Object."

In "Constancy" Coleridge makes one of his rare interpoetic references, for its speaker compares himself to the Mariner by virtue of their common loneliness. Separated from his beloved, he shares the Mariner's *acedia* and *ariditas,* feeling his home to be "but a becalméd bark / Whose Helmsman on an ocean waste and wide / Sits mute and pale his mouldering helm beside" (ll. 22–24). Having established the resemblance, he goes on to repeat with some precision the blessing scene:

> The Woodman winding westward up the glen
> At wintry dawn . . . o'er the sheep-track's maze
> Sees full before him, gliding without tread,
> An image with a glory round its head;
> The enamoured rustic worships its fair hues,
> Nor knows he makes the shadow, he pursues!

---

[30]Frederick A. Pottle, "View Point," in Boulger, ed., *Twentieth Century Interpretations,* p. 113.

[31]Many of the direct and indirect references are discussed by Irene Chayes in the article cited above.

[32]Frances Ferguson interprets Coleridge's response to Mrs. Barbauld in "Coleridge and the Deluded Reader: *The Rime of the Ancient Mariner,*" *Georgia Review* 31 (1977):617–35.

Compare the scene in the *Ancient Mariner* where the moon's beams

> . . . bemocked the sultry main,
> Like April hoar-frost spread;
> But where the ship's huge shadow lay,
> The charméd water burnt alway
> A still and awful red.
>
> Beyond the shadow of the ship,
> I watched the water-snakes;
> They moved in tracks of shining white,
> And when they reared, the elfish light
> Fell off in hoary flakes.
>
> Within the shadow of the ship
> I watched their rich attire:
> Blue, glossy green, and velvet black,
> They coiled and swam; and every track
> Was a flash of golden fire.
>
> O happy living things! no tongue
> Their beauty might declare:
> A spring of love gushed from my heart,
> And I blessed them unaware.
>
> [ll. 267–78]

The obvious seasonal disparity between these two scenes is resolved by Coleridge's transforming the equatorial into a polar region,[33] and the difference between the woodman wandering through a rustic glen and the Mariner becalmed in mid-ocean has been collapsed earlier in "Constancy," for the rustic appears as a repetition of the "helmsman." The poems thus parallel each other in three ways. First, they both present a solitary wanderer caught in a web of rime, the "viewless snow-mist" corresponding to the "April hoar-frost."[34] Second, the Mariner casts a shadow onto the rime just

[33]The "burning" water and the "fire" of the water-snakes are actually phophorescent effects given off sometimes by decaying matter. Phosphorescent fire is cold and can occur in any latitude.

[34]In the 1798 version of the *Ancient Mariner* the hoarfrost is likewise a weaver, for the sun rises in pt. 2 "broad as a weft." This became "Still hid in mist" in 1800 and thereafter—once again equating mist and language.

The image of "April hoar-frost" as well as a hint for Coleridge's title came from Frederick Martens' *Voyage to Spitzbergen*. In a chapter called "Of the *air*" Martens writes, "Concerning the meteors generated in the air, I observed the *rime* fell down, in the shape of small needles of snow, into the sea, and covered it as if it was sprinkled all over with a dust. These small needles increased more and more, and lay as they fell,

as the woodman does: if the ship throws a shadow on the ocean, the Mariner, being likewise positioned between the moon and the water, must do the same. In fact, the Mariner and his ship become inseparable, because, as I have noted, the poem makes them the doubles of the death ship and its passengers ("Like vessel, like crew!").[35] Finally, each wanderer mistakes his shadow for an "ideal object" that he blesses, and as the poem says, blesses "unaware" (l. 287).

There are, however, key differences between these blessings. For one, the woodman sees only his own image, whereas the Mariner sees other living creatures. More important, the conceit in the later poem turns on an illusory "glory," but neither a real nor a phantom glory seems to appear in the *Ancient Mariner,* which explains why the woodman's blessing is a curse while the Mariner's leads to salvation.

Beginning with the more crucial disparity, where is the glory in the *Ancient Mariner?* Coleridge offers a clue in a note he appended to "Constancy," where he attempts to ground the woodman's image in "scientific" evidence by referring the reader to an article on glories by one John Haygarth printed in the *Manchester Transactions.* The article is important because Coleridge was already familiar with it when he wrote the *Ancient Mariner,* and in taking notes for that poem he even copied part of Haygarth's description.[36] By using Haygarth's article Lowes was able to demonstrate the presence of a glory in the *Ancient Mariner* (although he did not pause to consider the implications). Coleridge's note paraphrases Haygarth as follows: "The beautiful colors of the hoar frost on snow in sun shine—red, green, and blue, in various angles" (*CN* 258). These same colors resurface in the shadow of the ship as the "still and awful red" of the water and the "blue, glossy green" of the water-snakes (with "hoary flakes" appropriately interspersed). In "Constancy" the halo surrounds the shadow, whereas in the *Ancient Mariner* it is explicitly

---

cross one over the other, and look'd very like a cobweb" (in *A Collection of Documents on Spitzbergen and Greenland,* ed. Adam White [London: Hakluyt Society, 1855], pp. 40–41; Martens'—or his translator's—italics).

[35]Just as the death vessel is called a "skeleton ship" with visible "ribs," so the Hermit compares the Mariner's ship to "Brown skeletons of leaves." (See also the description of the Mariner: "long, and lank and *brown* as is the *ribbed* sea-sand" [my italics].) Moreover, the shadow of the ship could be read as a magnification of the Mariner's shadow, since according to the topos "objects look gigantic thro' a mist." Like the specter ship, the Mariner's moves without wind in pt. 5, and the Mariner tellingly says, "we were a ghastly crew." The increasing parallels between the two ships is matched by the Mariner's coming more and more to resemble Life-in-Death.

[36]See *CN* 258 for some of Coleridge's transcription from Haygarth. See also Lowes for Coleridge's marginalia to *Aids to Reflection* in which he claims to have seen this "curious phenomenon" twice (p. 189).

situated "within" the shadow. The reason (aside from the fact that the glory is an internal or psychological creation) is that the passage in the *Ancient Mariner* is a night scene, and Coleridge knew that colors in phosphorescent water become more vivid as darkness increases.[37] Thus, when the Mariner looks over the side of the ship, he sees the reflection of his own image with a glory round its head, and he "blesses [this image] unaware"—not simply in a moment of Romantic anti-self-consciousness, but because he thinks he is blessing only water-snakes. The linguistic doubling in the pun "rime" is visually represented here by the rhymer who sees his own figure on the rime.

The Mariner's mirroring himself in the water-snakes is prepared several stanzas before the blessing when he associates himself with the sea creatures: "And a thousand thousand slimy things / Lived on; and so did I" (ll. 238–39). Neither one is exactly alive, of course, for the Mariner belongs to Life-in-Death, and the phosphorescence of the water-snakes figures decay in the midst of life. In fact, the snakes appear to be composed of the same matter as the Mariner, for their movements shake off "hoary flakes" of rime (l. 276).

It is not that he fails to see the water-snakes, however. Rather, the two images are superimposed; one comes from below and the other from above, to join at the surface. The Mariner could hardly ignore the snakes, for the light they throw off forms his halo.[38] His perception of the glory already exemplifies what Coleridge was later to call "the great law of the imagination," namely "that a likeness in part

---

[37]Coleridge found the same figure of a glory inscribed on the rime in at least three other texts he read before writing the *Ancient Mariner*: (1) Martens' *Voyage* ("I must not forget," says he, "that we see in these falling needles a bow like a rainbow" [p. 17].) For further passages from Martens that get woven into the *Ancient Mariner*, see the description of the "sea-bow" that follows, and pp. 17, 19, 32, and 65–66. (2) David Crantz's *History of Greenland* (see Lowes, pp. 136–37); and (3) Henry Boyd's translation of Dante: "Antarctic glories deck'd the burning zone / Of night" (canto 26 [on Ulysses], cited by Lowes, p. 236).

About a year after composing the *Ancient Mariner*, Coleridge recorded a sort of repetition of the blessing scene, in a letter to his wife that reappeared in revised version in *The Friend* (I:367). The original text reads, in part, "the water, that ran up between the great islands of Ice, shown of a yellow green (it was at sunset) and all the scattered islands of *smooth* ice were *blood;* intensely bright *Blood:* on some of the largest Islands the Fishermen were pulling out their immense nets thro' the Holes made in the Ice for this purpose, & the Fishermen, the net-poles, & the huge nets made a part of the Glory!" (*CL* 270, Coleridge's italics). See Jerome Christensen's reading of this passage and its revisions in "The Symbol's Errant Allegory: Coleridge and His Critics," *ELH* 45 (1978):645–54.

[38]The image of snakes encircling a face is, of course, suggestive of the Gorgon's head—with the implication that the Mariner's petrification is repeated just when his "life-blood" resumes its flow.

tends to become a likeness of the whole," that "mere *hints* of likeness from some real external object [in this case the water-snakes], especially if the shapes ["they *coiled*"] be aided by colour [the red, blue and green of Haygarth's glory] will suffice."[39] The whole process is further encouraged, as the epigraph to this section of the present essay explains, when the likeness is a human face. Were the likeness not partial and rendered somewhat indistinct by the moonlight and the hoarfrost, the "imagination" would have no space in which to complete the resemblance—whether for good or for ill.[40]

Thomas De Quincey's recollection concerning the *Ancient Mariner* brings together all of the elements I have discussed. According to De Quincey, Coleridge "had meditated a poem on delirium, confounding its own dream-scenery with external things, and connected with the imagery of high latitudes."[41] Just as Coleridge had conceived of it, so in the poem the Mariner confuses internal and external states, and his "delirium" is necessarily linked to Arctic (or Antarctic) imagery for, as Haygarth (and others Coleridge read at the time) demonstrates, the glory exists only as a reflection on the rime.

Whatever ironies the Mariner's self-reflection generates, the image is nonetheless in line with Coleridge's typical poetic practice and his critical statements on poetry and imagination. To see himself in the water-snakes exemplifies the habit of seeing the familiar in the strange, or of naturalizing the supernatural. The Mariner's blessing therefore duplicates Coleridge's own assignment in writing the *Lyrical Ballads:* "to transfer from our inward nature a human context and a semblance of truth sufficient to procure for these shadows [n.b.] of imagination that willing suspension of disbelief for the moment, which constitutes poetic faith" (*Biographia*, II,6). The Mariner lends human interest to the shadows around the ship by transferring

<hr />

[39]*The Friend*, I:145–46, Coleridge's italics.

[40]The albatross seems to function in the same way as the water-snakes. It is obvious from their praising and damning that the sailors read their own hopes and fears in the rime that enshrouds the bird. Furthermore, the crew may see its own image reflected off the "snow-fog": in a scene utterly devoid of human life they hail it as a "Christian soul" (ll. 65–66).

"Peter Bell," written as a reply to the *Ancient Mariner*, suggests that Wordsworth read the blessing scene similarly, because when Peter looks into a moonlit lake he sees his own reflection, although he does not recognize it as such and goes into a trance (ll. 501–20). (See also "The Brothers," in which the "mariner" Leonard gazes over the side of his ship and sees an image of himself in his former life as a shepherd [ll. 53–65].) To be trapped by one's own image is, of course, a typical Romantic dilemma.

[41]Thomas De Quincey, "Samuel Taylor Coleridge," in *The Collected Writings of Thomas De Quincey*, ed. David Masson, 14 vols. (London: A. and C. Black, 1896), II, 145.

his image to the water-snakes and demonstrates his poetic faith by blessing the act.[42]

VII

Pindar's fine remark respecting the different effects of Music, on different characters, holds equally true of Genius—as many as are not delighted by it are disturbed, perplexed, irritated. The beholder either recognizes it as a projected form of his own Being, that moves before him with a Glory round its head, or recoils from it as a Spectre.

—*Aids to Reflection,* cited by Coleridge
in a note to "Constancy"

The structural similarities between the blessing scenes in the *Ancient Mariner* and "Constancy" suggest the possibility of a resemblance between the moral visions of the two poems. Because the Mariner's blessing is founded on the error of mistaking a reflection of the self for a glorified other, one could argue that he fails to make contact with the life of nature, or with any greater "Life," and sanctions only his own delusion and his state of limbo. This interpretation would turn the "blessing" into an act of self-idolatry and therefore a repetition (or a doubling) of the very willfulness that characterized the Mariner's "original sin" in shooting the albatross. A sentence Warren quotes from *The Statesman's Manual* to explain the

[42]See also "On Poesy or Art": art is "the power of humanizing nature, of infusing the thoughts and passions of man in every thing which is the object of his contemplation" (*Biographia* II:253). As Walter Jackson Bate points out, Coleridge did not have in mind the projection of personal sentiment but rather the rendering of nature "realizable to human feelings" in general ("Coleridge on Art," in *Perspectives of Criticism,* ed. Harry Levin [Cambridge: Harvard University Press, 1950], p. 129). Nature may be humanized in a general sense, however, only in and through the individual artist. ("Nothing *lives* or is *real,* but as definite and individual" [*Biographia* II:187].) Shakespeare was the exceptional artist because he possessed a supremely eclectic soul; therefore, to fashion any one of his characters he "had only to imitate certain parts of his own character, or to exaggerate such as existed in possibility, and they were at once true to nature" (*Shakespearean Criticism* II:117). For this reason, Shakespeare may have been "a nature humanized," but when other artists attempt to humanize nature they risk the fate of the speaker in "Frost at Midnight," whose spirit "everywhere / Echo or mirror seek[s] of itself, / And makes a toy of Thought" (ll. 21–23).

To see what the Mariner saw on the water may have been easier before the mass of criticism spread around the poem as it has in our time. In one of the earliest articles on the *Ancient Mariner,* the American Unitarian minister R. C. Waterson observed that the Mariner's mind "fuses and moulds everything into its own likeness—till whatever it looks at it gazes upon itself." Cited by Richard Haven, "The Ancient Mariner in the 19th Century," *Studies in Romanticism* 11 (1972):361.

Mariner's condition *prior* to the blessing would then apply with equal or greater force thereafter: "In its utmost abstraction and consequent state of reprobation, the will becomes Satanic pride and rebellious self-idolatry in the relations of the spirit to itself, and remorseless despotism relatively to others" (p. 26). (Cf. "The Mariner hath his will" [l. 15].) This reading could explain why the polar spirit continues to demand vegeance and why the Mariner has to go on rhyming.

Such a reading suggests one way to counter Warren's interpretation of the *Ancient Mariner,* and a number of critics have made similar cases against him. The most noteworthy is Edward Bostetter, who sees the world of the poem not as sacramental but as a nightmare with arbitrary and inexplicable laws (why should "four times fifty men" drop dead for the shooting of a single bird? he asks). But I have purposely sketched out the "nightmare" reading in conditional terms because it seems to me important to maintain some distance from it, and on two counts. First, the interpretation I have outlined depends on equating the Mariner's vision with the woodman's; however, the implications of the woodman's vision do not all necessarily apply to the Mariner—even if he sees the same thing as the woodman. The halo does not traditionally carry the significance Coleridge gives it in "Constancy," of course, and he himself uses it in a wide variety of contexts. The most significant with respect to the *Ancient Mariner* occurs in the 1811–12 lectures on Shakespeare:

> In the plays of Shakespeare every man sees himself, without knowing that he does so: as in some of the phenomena of nature, in the mist of the mountain, the traveller beholds his own figure, but the glory round the head distinguishes it from a mere vulgar copy. . . . So in Shakespeare: every form is true, everything has reality for its foundation; we can all recognize the truth, but we see it decorated with such hues of beauty, and magnified to such proportions of grandeur, that, while we know the figure, we know also how much it has been refined and exalted by the poet.[43]

In this instance the glorified self-image appears not as the deluded vision of a lovelorn rustic but as an authentic and universal perception ("every man sees himself"): to read Shakespeare is to become

---

[43]*Shakespearean Criticism* II, 125. T. S. Eliot, interestingly enough, interpreted Coleridge's Shakespearean criticism in terms of "Constancy." According to Eliot, Coleridge "made of Hamlet a Coleridge" ("Hamlet," *Selected Essays* [London: Faber and Faber, 1951], p. 141).

enlightened, to progress from ignorance ("without knowing that he does so") to self-knowledge. Completing the contradiction, education is effected by the same "refining" agent, the mist or rime that damns the Ancient Mariner.

Second and more generally, interpretations such as Bostetter's tend to accept the terms of Warren's reading. Therefore, even though Bostetter is convincing (if somewhat less rigorous than Warren), he ends up for all his disagreements reproducing the structure of Warren's interpretation; he simply inverts the contents: a moral and uplifting poem turns into an immoral and depressing one. The appearance of Bostetter's essay was predictable, and perhaps even necessitated by the publication of Warren's, and one could say that the process of spectral doubling within the poem repeats itself in readings of it. This critical state of affairs produces an Uncle Remus land, where a Bostetter chases a Warren round and around the poem until they both start turning to butter. (Once again, the poem prefigures the history of its readings, in the epigraph from Thomas Burnet which asserts that the human mind has always circled round mysteries without being able to penetrate them.)

How are we to respond to these two, mutually exclusive schools of interpretation? The simplest response would be to decide which version is correct. It would be more accurate to maintain that the *Ancient Mariner* creates what Jacques Derrida has called "undecidability," a condition in which the reader is forced to oscillate between the alternatives in a perpetual either/or. (Coleridge himself, in fact, offers an aesthetic version of "undecidability" in *Shakespearean Criticism* when he describes the "effort of the mind . . . when it is hovering between images. As soon as it is fixed on one image, it becomes understanding; but while it is unfixed and wavering between them, attaching itself permanently to none, it is imagination" [II:103].) Neither of these interpretations will suffice, however, because the blessing scene, like so much else in the poem, is a single phenomenon that has a double aspect. Not either/or, but both/and. It is not only legitimate but imperative to supplement the "Constancy" interpretation with the Shakespeare one, for only the two texts taken together can account for both sides of the Mariner's rimed image: "Constancy" evokes the image of hoarfrost and recalls the Mariner's suffering a decomposition of the self, whereas the lecture evokes a "rhymed" image in the sense of a linguistic figure composed with consummate artistry. Although it is necessary to distinguish these two meanings of "rime," it is as impossible to divide them as it would be to divide life from death in this poem. Just as the

Mariner's frigid penance implies the glorification of art, so the creation of art—in keeping with the Romantics' typical self-image—
involves suffering. Like the rime at its center, the entire blessing
scene functions as an extended pun signifying both the "Constancy"
and the Shakespeare texts.

Readers who have felt that the poem creates a sacramental vision
are not misperceiving the text. It does portray the poet as someone
who can see beauty in the slimy water-snakes, much as Burns found
beauty in a louse or in a mouse. Like the poet, the Mariner when he
blesses the creatures of the calm "emancipates his eyes / From the
black shapeless accidents of size" ("Apologia Pro Vita Sua"). If anything, as Coleridge says, "moral sentiment" obtrudes quite openly in
the *Ancient Mariner*. But these readers have not seen far enough, for
they have not observed that the poem is so structured that any
expression of "moral sentiment" will inevitably provoke the reverse
expression. Although the Ancient Mariner is undeniably blessed by
his kind saint, we must think through the insight Warren shied away
from, that his blessing is inseparable from his curse. The Mariner
does experience a moment of spring, but it is likewise a moment of
winter. His vision is at once demystified and mystified, insightful
and blind, and as a result he is simultaneously saved and damned.

This realization should perhaps lead us to abandon the terms of
the argument. Such a renunciation is unlikely to occur, however,
because the ethical vocabulary we would eschew is part of our inheritance from the poem: with a glittering eye the Mariner holds the
critic, and the critic sees things the Mariner's way. Perhaps the best
we can manage is to remain alert to the radically metaphorical or
figurative nature of this shared poetic and critical diction, and to ask
ourselves what, under the circumstances I have outlined, it can
mean to bless or to be blessed. The duplicity of these terms effectively unhinges them from their referents and reveals them to be rhetorical figures deployed by the rime. (The word "rime," it is worth
recalling, is itself duplicitous; see the examples of its split identity in
footnote 7.) Just as the critics have maintained all along, the blessing
scene is indeed the center of the *Ancient Mariner*. What they have
been less quick to recognize, however, is the illogical nature of that
center, composed not of one point but of two—the center turned
aporia.[44] This poetical structure makes it illigitimate or nonsensical

[44] The Mariner's self-reflection is an instance of what John Irwin has called the
"White Shadow." In *American Hieroglyphics* (New Haven: Yale University Press, 1980)
he traces this figure through Romantic literature and certain of its antecedents.
Although (or perhaps because) he nowhere mentions the *Ancient Mariner*, Irwin of-

(however tempting it will always remain) to continue applying the ordinary sense of words such as blessing and curse to the poem. Mrs. Barbauld, it seems, was right after all: the *Ancient Mariner* is a poem that "has no moral."

VIII

marriage, or the knitting together of society by the tenderest, yet firmest ties . . .
—*Shakespearean Criticism* (II:107)

It remains to consider the ending of the poem. According to the gloss (which although part of the poem is also the first Warrenesque reading of it), the conclusion celebrates unity. The sympathetic relationship that the Mariner has formed by blessing the water-snakes expands into an integration of man with nature, with his fellow man, and with God. In asking how far the poem supports the gloss, we might recall that the *Ancient Mariner* begins by excluding the Wedding-Guest from the marriage of his next of kin. In a poem that proceeds from the pole to the line, around the world, and then beyond the natural world, the only threshold never crossed is that closest to hand, the bridegroom's door. The Warrenesque interpretation would assert that his exclusion from this particular wedding makes the next of kin witness to a far greater one. But such is the duplicity of the poem that one could use the same evidence to argue that the Wedding-Guest reads a darker aspect in the Mariner's rime—thus pointing once more to the impasse and futility of arguing either side.

Barring the Wedding-Guest from the wedding is another double

---

fers striking confirmation of two key facets of the rimed image—its status as a figure for writing, and its fundamental duplicity:

> For both Wordsworth [Irwin refers to the shepherd with sheep like Greenland bears] and Paul [in 2 Cor. 3:3–18], man's being is inscribed. It is a writing that can be read according to either the dead letter or the living spirit, a figure that can be interpreted either as the dark shadow of the mortal body (an inanimate "block / Or waxen image,") the "ministration of death, written and engraven in stones") or as a bright reflection in a glass ("the glory of the Lord," a shining image that reverses the usual relationship between the body and its mirror double in that the beholder becomes a reflection of the image). (The word "glory," besides its general meaning of "radiance" or "splendor," has as well the specific meaning of "halo." What occurs at Christ's transfiguration, when the splendor of divinity shining through his body makes his face radiant as the sun and his garments white as snow, is known in theology as 'the clarity of glory.') [pp. 215–16; cf. pp. 205–23]

gesture that at once undermines and furthers the "one Life" theme. More than simply one social event among others, marriage for Coleridge is the act that brings society itself into being and then perpetuates it. To be excluded from a wedding, according to the counterargument, is to be shut out from the life and wellspring of the community. This isolation is made manifest at the end when the Mariner and the Wedding-Guest each heads off on his own path. Despite the Mariner's monotonous insistence on the importance of going "together" to pray, no one gets to the church, and although there are supposedly prayers at the wedding, it remains forever off-limits. The ending, then, would effect no union with God, any more than with the Mariner's fellow men.[45] What of man and nature? In "Dejection" Coleridge asserts that "In our life alone does Nature live / Ours is her wedding garment, ours her shroud" (ll. 48–49). The blessing scene suggests that the double formula (Coleridge does not say "*or* ours her shroud") is inevitable, an articulation of the same pun that has been operative all through the *Ancient Mariner*. To wed nature by language or imagination means simultaneously to kill her. Thus, what is generally regarded as a triple integration of the Mariner with man, God, and nature may equally well be read as a triple alienation—but neither conclusion can ever be conclusive.

If, as Warren says, the theme of imagination is inseparable from the "one Life" theme, it should be possible to show that the working of the imagination in the poem is similarly doubled. Warren refers only to the synthesizing function of the imagination, which has been manifest all along in the process of turning dissimilar things into doubles. (That synthesis may sometimes be unsettling, however, and one wonders what Warren would make of the Mariner's statement that the sun [Warren's figure of evil] appeared at the line "no bigger than the Moon" [his figure of imagination].) But the imagination also decomposes resemblances or identities. Consider, for example, the atmospheric effects, since Warren singles them out as figures for the imagination in the poem (p. 29). The sun is either too cold or too hot, always "burning" but never managing to melt the rime. Another sign of fragmentation is the conspicuous absence in the poem of twilight ("The Sun's rim dips; the stars rush out: / At one stride comes the dark" [ll. 199–200]), a standard figure for mediation. In place of the expected crepuscule, the specter ship arrives, and with it the riming of the Mariner. The poem's geography repeats its mete-

[45]For a biblical comparison of human and divine weddings, see Matt. 22.

orology, as the temperate mean gives way to the extremes of line and pole, while the center—"my own countree"—will not hold.

The narrative itself exemplifies a lack of fusion, as Wordsworth was perhaps the first to remark, when he complained that "the events having no necessary connection do not produce one another." The actions of the poem's plot do not follow from one another in "organic" fashion, and as a result the reader often is tempted to supply connections where none exist. Chayes, for example, explains that "when the ship is becalmed, doubt gives way to condemnation and the Mariner is its object, charged by the rest of the crew with the whole guilt for the common plight."[46] Although logical enough, and helpful in guiding the reader through the poem, her reading contradicts the text. As I have noted, the crew damns the Mariner not when the ship is becalmed but while "the good south wind still blew behind." Chayes's error, which is hardly uncommon (Warren and John Beer make exactly the same mistake),[47] attests to the reader's desire to fill in the gaps in the narrative.

IX

He [the Mariner] does not act, but is continually acted upon.
—Wordsworth, enumerating the
"great defects" of the poem

My concern is this essay has mainly been to establish connections between the two senses of "rime," somewhat at the expense of exploring the disparity between them—which must logically precede any reconciliations. It remains, therefore, to remark on the difference between the Mariner congealed into rime and the rhyme he articulates. One way to get at this difference is to recall the phrase from Coleridge that Warren selected as the title for his essay, "A Poem of Pure Imagination." That title is problematic because Coleridge speaks of the secondary or poetic imagination as "co-existing with the conscious will" (*Biographia*, I, 202), and one would hardly say that his narrative is a product of the Mariner's will. He never

---

[46]Chayes, "A Coleridgean Reading," p. 90.

[47]Beer says, "When bad luck follows the Mariner's actions they obey their superstition and blame him" (*Coleridge the Visionary*, p. 149). In fact, nothing about their situation has changed when the crew condemns the Mariner. Warren says that the shipmates "first condemn the act, when they think the bird has brought the favorable breeze; then applaud the act when the fog clears and the breeze springs back up" ("A Poem of Pure Imagination," p. 28).

chooses to recount the story but is always compelled to do so. If the Mariner can hold the Wedding-Guest spellbound against the latter's will, that power is predicated on the Mariner's already having been ensnared by the sight of the Wedding-Guest, "Which forced me to begin my tale . . . And till my ghastly tale is told, / This heart within me burns" (ll. 580–85).[48]

But the sight of the Wedding-Guest is only the efficient cause of the Mariner's rhyming; finally, it is the tale itself that forces him to articulate it against his will. Indeed, the Mariner's sole *raison d'être* is to act as a rhymer, and he continues to "exist" only as the by-product of a text that wills its own repetition, forcing the Mariner into a continuous action that we may still read in the opening line, "It *is* an ancient Mariner" (my italics). He is thus more the effect of the "Rime" than its cause, the "Rime's Mariner" more than the "Mariner's Rime." (The title allows for either reading, but already displaces the Mariner: not the *Ancient Mariner* simply but *The Rime of the Ancient Mariner*." Wordsworth's objection that the Mariner "does not act, but is continually acted upon" is therefore legitimate, although Wordsworth never names language as the actor. And insofar as the Wedding-Guest serves as an emblem for him, the reader is similarly "acted upon" by the rime.

The plot of the poem likewise reveals that language precedes and constitutes the Ancient Mariner's selfhood. Long before he ever begins to articulate the poem, Life-in-Death has turned him from a unified, intentional self into rime. That is, he is a source of language only insofar as he has already been rhymed. The reader habitually attempts to treat the Ancient Mariner as a subject or character (making the Mariner into his double), but the text never quite grants that illusion and keeps reminding the reader that whatever impression of selfhood remains is only the afterimage of the rime. In this way the text displaces the traditional epistemological reading that would make the blessing scene into a subject/object dialectic in which the subject incorporates or is incorporated by the object. There is in fact neither subject nor object here, but a play of endless linguistic mirrorings between the hoary Mariner and the hoary flakes of light.

In the final image of the poem, the narrator echoes the Wedding-Guest's initial description of the Mariner as a "grey-beard loon" by likewise calling attention to his beard. But the narrator's words reflect the difference that rime has made, for he puts it this way: "The

---

[48]The line "This heart within me burns" does not contradict the Mariner's temper, because he is speaking in the Miltonic sense, as above.

Mariner . . . whose beard with age is hoar / Is gone" (ll. 618–20). The inverted syntax allows one to read "hoar" as a noun rather than an adjective—a beard composed of hoar (frost). Using the word in this strategic position, the narrator underscores the Mariner's status with respect to the tale: by synecdoche the beard describes the Mariner's entire condition as rimed. The *Ancient Mariner* ends by turning the Mariner into a figure in the landscape, which is the imagistic equivalent of collapsing him into the narrator's point of view in the final stanzas of the poem. This merging is a sign for the text's mastery over the Ancient Mariner, its inscription of the rimer in the rime.

"Rime" does not simply signify language in general, however. As I have already implied, it is specifically a figure for written language, because the rime repeats itself endlessly, and this characteristic has distinguished writing from speech at least since the dialogues of Plato. What Socrates says of written language in the *Phaedrus* applies as well to the Ancient Mariner, who "go[es] on telling you just the same thing forever" (275d). And what at first appears to be the Mariner's "speech" to the Wedding-Guest bears all the marks of written language—not the other way around, as is usually supposed. The poem itself therefore upsets the classic model in which writing always comes after and imitates speech. If the Mariner has "strange power of speech," it is first of all because his form of speech is itself strange and estranged. Hence we can read the *Ancient Mariner* in the most general sense as an allegory wherein writing and speech perpetually displace one another.

What opens up the space for my own reading and governs its movement at every point is no more than the difference between "rhyme" and "rime"—a distinction that (as Derrida remarks of the word *différance*) "remains purely graphic: it is written or read, but it is not heard. It cannot be heard [*entendu*], and . . . it is also beyond the order of understanding [*l'entendement*]."[49] It would have come as no surprise to Coleridge that there is a striking resemblance in the difference inscribed by the "rime" of his text and the "différance" of Derrida's essay by that name. Like the *a* of "différance," the *i* of "rime" "remains silent, secret, and discreet, like a tomb." And it hardly seems accidental that what is entombed in the word "rime" is precisely the *i*, or the *I:* the word itself already tells, in its silent and

[49]"La différance," trans. David B. Allison, in *Speech and Phenomena and Other Essays on Husserl's Theory of Signs* (Evanston, Ill.: Northwestern University Press, 1973), p. 132.

discreet way, the tale of metamorphosing the *I* into an *i*, the inscription of the subject or narrative voice as a graphic mark in a text. The I / i in Coleridge's poem is introduced only to be rimed, to have its identity perpetually deferred in an endless journey through time and space. As in Nietzsche, what returns eternally in the *Ancient Mariner* is the very process of differing (be it of identity, redemption, narrative closure, whatever).[50] But the nature of its rime leaves Coleridge's poem in a highly paradoxical position. The *Ancient Mariner* seems to swim against the current of Romantic literature, since it is the recurring pattern of that literature to privilege speech (associated with the presence of a lyrical subject and manifesting itself in "conversation" poems or warbling streams of "living waters") over the dead letter of a written text, or the life-in-death of rime. The *Ancient Mariner* thus subverts the ideology of the very movement it is always taken to exemplify—which may be what makes it a genuinely Romantic poem.

[50]Later in "Différance" Derrida remarks, "It is out of the unfolding of this 'same' as différance that the sameness of difference and of repetition is presented in the eternal return" (p. 149).

Shelley's *Mont Blanc:*
What the Mountain Said

FRANCES FERGUSON

Critics seem to have agreed on one thing about *Mont Blanc*—
that it is a poem about the relationship between the human mind
and the external world. After that, the debates begin—over whether
the mind or the world has primacy, over whether "The veil of life
and death" of line 54 has been "upfurled" or "unfurled" in line 53,
over whether "but for such faith" in line 79 means "only through
such faith" or "except through such faith," and so on.[1] It is not
surprising that debates should have arisen, because the poem moves
through a variety of different ways of imagining the mountain and
the power of which it is symbolic (or synecdochic); and although the
poet may do the mountain in different voices, the variety of conceptions and the rapidity with which they succeed one another are
possible largely because the mountain is like the tarbaby in Uncle
Remus and says nothing.

The question that arises, of course, is, How is the mountain's
silence any different from the silence of the subjects of any other
poem? Grecian urns are likewise silent; and nightingales may sing,
but they do not talk. In the case of *Mont Blanc*, the interest lies,
curiously enough, in the palpable improbability of looking for anything but silence from the mountain, which is repeatedly seen as the
ultimate example of materiality, of the "thingness" of things, so that
its symbolic significance is quite explicitly treated as something added to that materiality.

At moments Shelley seems to be almost defiantly trying to think of

---

[1]The best brief survey of the various debates about the poem appears in the notes
to the poem in *Shelley's Poetry and Prose*, ed. Donald H. Reiman and Sharon B. Powers
(New York: Norton, 1977), pp. 89–93.

the mountain (and the entire landscape connected with it) as a brute physical existence. Such an effort would have to be at least somewhat defiant, both because of the inevitable difficulty of trying to imagine anything completely without history and context (and thus associations) and because of the multiplicity of associations that had accrued to the idea of this mountain. Whereas it is crucial to the mountain's force as an example of pure materiality that it can never know that it is the highest mountain in Europe, it—and the vale of Chamonix generally—had, as Richard Holmes nicely observes, developed a reputation among the "travelling English" of the time "as a natural temple of the Lord and a proof of the Deity by design."[2] The famous story of Shelley's traveling through the region, entering his name in the hotel registers in Chamonix and Montavert, and listing his occupations as "Democrat, Philanthropist and Atheist" serves to indicate the level of his indignation at the way in which religion attributes spiritual qualities to a brute material object when it assimilates such an object to a proof of the deity by design.[3] It serves as well to suggest how difficult it is to think of the mountain as a merely physical object. For in his efforts to counter the myth of natural religion that is attached to Mont Blanc, Shelley does not destroy the mountain's symbolic value but merely inverts it.

To say that Shelley attempts to conceive Mont Blanc in terms of sheer physical force may sound like a movement toward recognizing a gap between signifier and signified and toward trying to accept the mountain not just as pure physicality but also of necessity as pure nonreferentiality. The mountain would function, in such an account, as a linguistic signifier that would reveal the ironic distance between its material presence and any possible signified. Yet I would argue that the poem insists, most importantly, on the inability of one's resting in such irony as it exhibits its own repeated failures to let Mont Blanc be merely a blank, merely a mass of stone: *Mont Blanc* leads to attempts to think of the mountain as physical and without metaphysical attributes, and fails; it attempts to imagine a gap between the mountain and the significances that people attach to it, and fails. But if one way of talking about the poem is to suggest that Shelley is here restricted because of the inadequacy of language, or the way in which language blocks one from saying certain things or certain kinds of things, the other side of that image of blockage—of the inability to break through—is a contrary movement made man-

---

[2]Richard Holmes, *Shelley: The Pursuit* (London: Quartet Books, 1976), p. 342.
[3]See Holmes's account, pp. 339–43.

ifest by the way in which the relationships that are sketched out in the poem are not merely adequate but so abundant and well-fitting as almost to inspire claustrophobia. In this respect, the poem is more nearly akin to Wordsworth's lines about how exquisitely the human mind and the world are fitted to one another than even those lines that Harold Bloom and others have seen echoed in the opening section of *Mont Blanc*—the lines from "Tintern Abbey" in which Wordsworth speaks of having "felt / A presence that disturbs [him] with the joy / Of elevated thoughts . . . / A Motion and a spirit, that . . . / . . . rolls through all things" (ll. 93–102).[4]

Thus, although the motive behind the poem appears to be conceiving of Mont Blanc not just as the white mountain but also as a massive version of blankness—or "solitude / Or blank desertion" (*The Prelude*, I:394–95), the poem has already in its first few lines become a poem about the impossibility of seeing the mountain as alien. As Earl Wasserman observes, the "everlasting universe of things" is like the Arve flowing through the Ravine that is like the "universal mind," and the Ravine of "universal mind" and the Channel in which the brook of the individual mind flows merge with one another.[5] In the midst of all the convergence and congruence of the schema, however, Wasserman very convincingly notes a sensory overload in the image of the brook: "The simile, which has no significant function except to transform the mode of vision, by its very tautology opens the door to an abundance of supposedly external objects that exceed the requirements of the comparison, as though the tendency to conceive of images as external were too great for the poet to resist."[6]

Wasserman's central point here is that the poet conceives of metaphors in which he then finds "a remarkably consistent objective correlative for his metaphor for a total universe that is indifferently things or thoughts and that is located in the One Mind."[7] It is not, of course, particularly surprising that Shelley should see the scene, when he finally looks at it, in the terms in which he thought about it before he looked at it; what is, however, remarkable is not just that the interpretation and the perception are aligned with one another

---

[4]Harold Bloom, *Shelley's Mythmaking* (Ithaca: Cornell University Press, 1969), p. 20. See also Bloom, *The Visionary Company* (Ithaca: Cornell University Press, 1971), p. 293.

[5]Earl R. Wasserman, *Shelley: A Critical Reading* (Baltimore: Johns Hopkins University Press, 1971), pp. 221–38. Wasserman's reading remains, to my mind, the most impressive account of the poem.

[6]Ibid., p. 224.

[7]Ibid.

but that the various portions of the imagery are as well. The river, of necessity, fits the ravine perfectly—and in a way that makes it impossible to say which has priority and determines the other. Whereas a glass of water may be said to be prior to the water in it, in that its shape is one that any water in it must conform to, the course and shape of a riverbed may be said to be determined by the waters that flow through it just as much as the riverbed may be said to determine the course of the river. Yet it is not merely the river and the riverbed that are interdependent and mutually creative, for the height of the mountain and the depth of the ravine have an analogous relation to one another: there is a ravine—and a ravine this deep—because there is a mountain—and a mountain this high— and vice versa.

An additional complication appears, however, in the image of the brook that Wasserman describes as exceeding "the requirements of the comparison."[8]

> The source of human thought its tribute brings
> Of waters,—with a sound but half its own,
> Such as a feeble brook will oft assume
> In the wild woods, among the mountains lone,
> Where waterfalls around it leap for ever,
> Where woods and winds contend, and a vast river
> Over its rocks ceaselessly bursts and raves.
>
> [ll. 5–11]

The "feeble brook" is not described simply as a tributary to the "vast river"; instead, the river is said to "burst and rave" over its—the brook's—rocks, thus introducing the question of whether a brook is still a brook when a river runs in its channel. Although the question itself seems like a bad riddle, it forcibly demonstrates Shelley's procedure throughout the poem of insisting on the changeableness of the identity of any individual entity. For the brook, in becoming a part of the river, both loses its identity as a brook and transcends itself, gaining access to a forcefulness it never had as a "feeble brook."

We have here, in the cluster of images that are continually put into relation with one another, an elaborate schema of reciprocity. The universe of things exists to be perceived by the universal mind, so that the mind does not create things in its acts of perception but rather keeps the things of the world from going to waste. The river

[8]Ibid.

that courses along the channel of the brook enables the individual mind to participate in thought and sensation without ever having to originate them for itself. As we do not make up the world of things as we go along, so we do not discover all of human thought on our own. The relationship between the river and the brook may be seen not only as analogous to that between all of human knowledge and an individual knowing subject but also as similar to all human language in relation to an individual speaker.

It is, however, when the terms that are put into relationship with one another get proper names that the poem begins to flirt with relational punning. Bloom has stressed the importance of Shelley's addressing the ravine and the mountain as "Thou" and has seen it as emblematic of the poem's conjecturing "the possibility of a Thou as a kind of universal mind in nature."[9] Although there are no proper names in the first section of the poem, the second section offers not just the pronoun "Thou" but also the names "Ravine of Arve" and "Arve." The appearance of the names registers the shift from Shelley's imagining a schematic relationship for the ravine and the river to his seeing this particular ravine and this particular river. But the address to the ravine is repeated enough for it to become, as Wasserman might have said, "excessive." For when Shelley turns to look at and speak to the ravine, he calls it "thou, Ravine of Arve—dark, deep Ravine," and in the nomenclature "Ravine of Arve" is another way of suggesting the interdependence of the ravine and the river. There is also, however, a linguistic *tour de force*—or cheap trick—at work here: the river that has been imagined in the first section to "burst and rave" ceaselessly is identified as the Arve, so that the "Arve raves." And it of course turns out that the "Arve raves in the Ravine" (If you drop the article "the" from the previous clause, you have four words that are all contained in the letters of the word "ravine," and it might, with a bit of work, be made into another song for *My Fair Lady*.)

This species of relational punning underscores the symbiosis of things and mind, of river and ravine, that Shelley has earlier been sketching. Further, it raises some interesting questions about the status of language in the poem. Although the punning is a kind of technological trick with language, it is hard to see how this language can really be described as duplicitous, for all it does is reiterate the earlier message: thought takes the world of things to be inextricable

---

[9]Bloom, *Shelley's Mythmaking*, p. 23.

from the mind; the actual perception of the scene confirms this message, in taking the river to be inextricable from the ravine, and at this point in the poem the language itself rather glaringly insists that the Arve exists because it is in the Ravine of Arve. The importance of the language trick lies not, however, in the fact that this language is human and might thus reveal the primacy of the human and the priority of the human mind. Rather, the anagram suggests the inevitability of any human's seeing things in terms of relationship.

The significance of this love language, moreover, goes beyond the familiarity built into a poet's addresses to the personifications that he creates. For the questions about epistemology that Wasserman has very convincingly seen to dominate the poem appear very different if epistemology is correlated wth ontology on the one hand or, alternatively, with love. In the one account—that which continually seeks to align epistemology with ontology so that one's knowing always struggles to coincide with the real existence of what one knows—the adequacy of one's ability to know is always suspect. In the other account—that which aligns epistemology with love—emotional profligacy that continually postulates and assumes the existence of an interlocutor supplants any notion of matching one's knowledge with things as they really are.

In the remarkable fragment "On Love," Shelley approvingly remarks that "Sterne says that if he were in a desert, he would love some cypress."[10] In *Mont Blanc* Shelley falls in love with a ravine, a river, and a mountain not because of the nature of those objects but because of his own, his human, mind, which cannot imagine itself as a genuinely independent, isolated existence. Love is, he says,

> that powerful attraction towards all that we conceive, or fear, or hope beyond ourselves, when we find within our own thoughts the chasm of an insufficient void and seek to awaken in all things that are a community with what we experience within ourselves. If we reason, we would be understood; if we imagine, we would that the airy children of our brain were born anew within another's; if we feel, we would that another's nerves should vibrate to our own, that lips of motionless ice should not reply to lips quivering and burning with the heart's best blood. This is Love. This is the bond and the sanction which connects not only man with man but with everything which exists.[11]

[10]*Shelley's Prose, or The Trumpet of a Prophecy,* ed. David Lee Clark (Albuquerque: University of New Mexico Press, 1954), p. 171.
[11]Ibid., p. 170.

When Shelley views the natural landscape, he immediately begins to speak familiarly to it, not just because poets traditionally personify natural objects and address them with terms of endearment, but because he cannot imagine himself without imagining an anti-type that will enable him to be assured of his own existence. For "the invisible and unattainable point to which Love tends," he says, is "the discovery of its anti-type; the meeting with an understanding capable of clearly estimating our own."[12]

Edmund Burke had identified as sublime not only the experience of contemplating enormous heights and depths but also, and most particularly, the experience of being isolated from other humans.[13] From one perspective, Shelley seems to provide a textbook example of how to experience the sublimity of Mont Blanc as he registers his consciousness of the mountain's force while appearing to speak from a condition of isolation (where no human aid can intervene between him and the mountain's power). It is from this perspective unremarkable that Shelley's account of the mountain continually recurs to the subject of its wildness, of its being a wilderness remote from all that civilization involves. By a peculiar twist, however, Shelley converts the isolation of the mountain from a threat into an opportunity—as if he were not so much alone with the mountain as "alone at last" with it. For the act of imagination or intellection by which he moves from the description of the portion of the mountain that remains hidden to him is an act of sympathy; although he speaks merely of the portion of the mountain that really exists, he in effect woos the mountain with an "imagination which . . . enters into and seizes upon the subtle and delicate peculiarities" that the mountain (if it were human) would have "delighted to cherish and unfold in secret."[14]

Thus Shelley's addressing the ravine and the mountain as "Thou" is only one aspect of the poet's effort to convert epistemological language into love language. For although *Mont Blanc* is a sublime poem upon a sublime subject, it projects an air of sociability. As soon as the poet depicts the "Dark, deep ravine," he provides it with companionship in the persons of "Thy giant brood of pines," those "Children of elder time" (ll. 920–21). Even when he imagines Mont Blanc as a fierce and ravening force, he cannot imagine it as a real desert; it is "A desert peopled by the storms" and a place where the

---

[12]Ibid.

[13]Edmund Burke, *A Philosophical Enquiry into the Origin of Our Ideas of the Sublime and Beautiful,* ed. J. T. Boulton (Notre Dame: University of Notre Dame Press, 1958), pp. 43 and 71.

[14]*Shelley's Poetry and Prose,* p. 170.

poet immediately starts constituting a domestic circle as he asks, "Is this the scene / Where the old Earthquake-daemon taught her young / Ruin? Were these their toys?" (ll. 71–73).

Yet Shelley's famous letter to Thomas Love Peacock describing his first viewing of Mont Blanc makes the poem's love-longing for the mountain seem particularly one-sided, not just unrequited but positively scorned:

> I will not pursue Buffon's sublime but gloomy theory, that this earth which we inhabit will at some future period be changed into a mass of frost. Do you who assert the supremacy of Ahriman imagine him throned among these desolating snows, among these palaces of death and frost, sculptured in this their terrible magnificence by the unsparing hand of necessity, and that he casts around him as the first essays of his final usurpation avalanches, torrents, rocks and thunders—and above all, these deadly glaciers at once the proofs and symbols of his reign.—Add to this the degradation of the human species, who in these regions are half deformed or idiotic and all of whom are deprived of anything that can excite interest or admiration. This is a part of the subject more mournful and less sublime;—but such as neither the poet nor the philosopher should disdain.[15]

The logic by which Shelley regards the degradation of the humans in the vicinity as "more mournful and less sublime" than Buffon's theory that the entire earth will become "a mass of frost" may not be self-evident. But his central point here is that the deformity and idiocy of the inhabitants of the area are, quite literally, not sublime because such deformity and idiocy merely provide, in human form, a repetition of the mountain's role as pure materiality. Thus, although the mountain has the power to make these people less than human, that very power of oppression sets a limit to itself because it annihilates everything in the human that can understand the mountain's material aspect—with an understanding that Shelley speaks of in the fragment "On Love." Throughout *Mont Blanc*, Shelley's attention always moves from images of destructiveness to images of complementarity. In this sense, the poem appears to be almost an endorsement of Kant's remark that nothing in nature is sublime: "All we can say is that the object is fit for the presentation of a sublimity which can be found in the mind, for no sensible form can contain the sublime properly so-called."[16]

---

[15]*Letters of Shelley*, ed. F. L. Jones, 2 vols. (Oxford: Oxford University Press, 1964), I, 499. Quoted in Bloom, *Shelley's Mythmaking*, p. 19, and in Holmes, *Shelley*, p. 340.
[16]Immanuel Kant, *Critique of Judgment*, trans. J. H. Bernard (New York: Hafner, 1966), pp. 83–84.

Shelley here focuses on a central paradox of the sublime—that we should take pleasure in the contemplation of anything that presents a threat to our tendency toward self-preservation. By falling in love with strenuous death, however, Shelley demonstrates the way in which nature's destructiveness is never centrally at issue in the experience of the sublime. Rather, because the human mind can attribute destructiveness to nature, nature needs us for it to be perceived as destructive and to continue to be destructive in any significant way. Thus *Mont Blanc* creates an image of sublimity that continually hypostatizes an eternity of human consciousness. Because even the ideas of the destructiveness of nature and the annihilation of mankind require human consciousness to give them their force, they thus are testimony to the necessity of the continuation of the human.

In the poem's first section, "woods and winds contend" (l. 10); in the second, "The chainless winds" (l. 22) come to hear the "old and solemn harmony" (l. 24) that they make with the "giant brood of pines" (l. 20). The perspective of the mountain, presented in the third section, is the perspective of eternity where "None can reply—all seems eternal now" (l. 75); and the fourth section offers the inverse of that eternal view—the perspective of mutability and mortality that sees that "The race / Of man, flies far in dread; his work and dwelling / Vanish . . ." (ll. 117–19).

These different sections, although obviously similar, do not offer merely different versions of the same message. If the struggle between "woods and winds" of the first section does not negate the possibility of seeing these same woods and winds creating a harmony between them, the relationship between the terms of eternity and mutability is even stronger. For it is not just that mutability and eternity are two different ways of conceiving time, but also that it becomes impossible for the poet to imagine eternity except in terms of mutability—the terms of generation in which earthquakes create epochs and broods of little earthquakes—or to image mutability except in the terms of eternity, in the form of a Power that "dwells apart in its tranquillity" (l. 96).

The poet begins the fifth and final section with a magnificent feat of calculated vagueness and understatement:

> Mont Blanc yet gleams on high:—the power is there,
> The still and solemn power of many sights,
> And many sounds, and much of life and death.
>
> [ll. 127–29]

The understatement registers, among other things, the poet's awareness that his thoughts about the mountain have not changed the universe—or even the mountain. He seems almost to struggle to see the mountain's continued existence as a reason for him to return to his struggle to see it in its materiality. Yet this final section of the poem recapitulates the earlier movement into a language that inexorably begins to treat the mountain landscape as *someone* to be understood not merely through the understanding but through an understanding that operates to complete and magnify its object through an aggrandizement Shelley calls love.

The mountain has "a voice" to "repeal / Large codes of fraud and woe" (ll. 80–81) not because "The secret strength of things / Which governs thought" inhabits it but because the poet is its voice as he finds himself in the process of recognizing the impossibility of taking the material as merely material. Just as one can see the letters that go together to make up "Arve" and "Ravine of Arve" as an example of the material aspects of language but cannot see them as language wthout seeing them as implying something more than matter, so one can see the mountain as an example of materiality but cannot see it even as a mountain without seeing it as involving more than matter. The mountain can repeal "Large codes of fraud and woe" by making it clear that a love of humanity is easy if one can love a mountain that is physically inimical to man. And yet the final irony of the poem is that Shelley can conclude by asking the mountain his most famous question:

> And what were thou, and earth, and stars, and sea,
> If to the human mind's imaginings
> Silence and solitude were vacancy?
>
> [ll. 142–44]

With this question, he reminds the mountain that it needs him. The relationship between man and world has been painted in such a way as to make it clear that complementarity rather than direct communication is at issue in his version of language. But although he reminds the mountain of its need for him, his questions also have all the poignancy of a speech by a lover who still needs to argue his case. He may be a fit anti-type to the mountain, but he is still looking for a mountain who will understand him.

Even though the poem ends with a question directed to the mountain, Shelley's interest in Mont Blanc is, of course, predicated upon the impossibility of the mountain's ever taking any interest in him and answering. The mountain is matter, and its power resides to a very considerable extent in that fact; just as Milton's Eve was once "stupidly good," so matter is, in Shelley's account, "stupidly power-

ful," and powerful more because of its stupidity than in spite of it.
That is, its power depends upon its never being able to move out of
the world of death. Because it can never be alive, it can never be
subject to death; because it can never be conscious, it can never
experience fear (or love or any other emotion, anticipatory or
otherwise).

In light of the poem's final account of the mountain, the first four
verse paragraphs might seem to represent a massive epistemological
error and a mistake in love as well. For the first two verse paragraphs argue for resemblance between the human and the natural
worlds in claiming that the same model can be used for both (the
Arve is to the ravine as the "everlasting universe of things" is to the
individual human mind) and in presenting the similarity between
the two with a lover's air of pleasure in the discovery of himself in
another. In this manner, Shelley addresses the ravine as if it were a
version of himself:

> Dizzy Ravine, and when I gaze on thee
> I seem as in a trance sublime and strange
> To muse on my own separate phantasy,
> My own, my human mind. . . .
>
> [ll. 34–37]

The reversion from thoughts of the ravine to thoughts of his own
mind does not betoken any inappropriate narcissism but indicates,
rather, the translation of the material to the human that is involved
in any effort at making the scene intelligible. As both the formal
analogy and the poet's familiar address to the scene argue for the
equivalence between the material and the human, Shelley pursues
this thinking by analogy down its fallacious course as he attributes
sublimity to the mountain in making it appear to transcend itself.
Thus he speaks of the "Power in likeness of the Arve" as not like
water but more than water as it comes "Bursting through these dark
mountains like the flame / Of lightning through the tempest" (ll.
16–19) and of those "earthly rainbows stretched across the sweep /
Of the etherial waterfall" (ll. 25–26) that refuse to occupy any single
element or place; the transfer of attributes from one element to
another lends each an all-inclusiveness that none would have
individually.

Of course, the phenomena that are presented as more than themselves because of the transfer of attributes *are* palpably more than
themselves, in that the rainbow, while being an interaction of water
and air, is made "earthly" whereas the waterfall produced by the

passage of the water over the rocky earth is made "etherial." The distinct limit to the self-transcendence of these physical elements is, however, implicit in the conspicuous omission (for the moment) of the fire that emblemizes the animation of the elements. Although the water and the air, like the water and the earth, act together to produce a mutual self-transcendence of each, the crucial difference between these mutual magnifications and any real instance of sublime self-transcendence lies in the fact that these elements provide instances of action without representing agency.

If the apparent threat involved in any landscape that might be provocative of a sublime experience is that man (and mind) might be reduced to mere matter, the correspondent activity that occurs is that the poet's sublime account of Mont Blanc and the entire scene around it never allows matter to remain material but rather co-opts it or transmogrifies it by continually mistaking the activity of the material world for agency, by taking it to be as intentional as any human activity might be. Shelley insists virtually throughout the poem upon this confusion between activity and agency as he continually treats the mountain as a person (albeit a particularly large and powerful one). This programmatic confusion discloses a fundamental insight into the nature of sublime experience: in treating natural objects as occasions for sublime experience, one imputes agency (and therefore a moving spirit) to them. Although such imputation would, in other hands, perhaps be the basis for seeing the designedness of nature as an argument for the existence of God, for Shelley it instead identifies the sublime as the aesthetic operation through which one makes an implicit argument for the transcendent existence of man—not because man is able to survive the threat posed by the power of the material world but because he is able to domesticate the material world for the purposes of aesthetics by converting such a massive example of the power of the material world as Mont Blanc from an object into a found object. For what the sublime does for nature is to annex all that is material to the human by appropriating it for aesthetics. In this sense, Shelley in *Mont Blanc* discovers the same assertion of human power that Kant did when he distinguished between the sublime and the beautiful on the grounds that "we must seek a ground external to ourselves for the beautiful of nature, but seek it for the sublime merely in ourselves and in our attitude of thought, which introduces sublimity into the representation of nature."[17] At Mont Blanc, in the assertion

[17]Ibid., p. 84.

of human power that any sublime experience represents, Shelley thus revamps the argument from design to redound to the credit of the human observer who converts the object into a found object, not merely matter but matter designed by its perceiver.

Moreover, in treating the sublime experience of Mont Blanc as not merely adapting the material to the purposes of the human and the supersensible (or spiritual) but as a discovery of the human in nature, Shelley collapses Kant's account of the "purposiveness without purpose" that we discover in aesthetic objects as he speaks of Mont Blanc as if it had purposes in relation to humans. Thus it is that the language of the poem continally moves from epistemological questions, questions of the poet's understanding, to love language in which all the questions are of his being understood.

8 /

The Art of Managing Books:
Romantic Prose and the
Writing of the Past

MARY JACOBUS

I

The butt of Wordsworth's satire in Book V of *The Prelude*, his book on books, is an infant prodigy—"a Child, no Child, / But a dwarf Man" (V, 294–95). This stunted and preprogrammed mini-adult is the product of educational management by "mighty work-men of our late age,"

>   they who have the art
> To manage books, and things, and make them work
> Gently on infant minds, as does the sun
> Upon a flower; the Tutors of our Youth . . .
>   .   .   .
> Sages, who in their prescience would controul
> All accidents, and to the very road
> Which they have fashion'd would confine us down,
> Like engines . . .
>   [V, 373–83]

Nature's education acts otherwise on the Boy of Winander, allowing the unforeseen to enter "unawares" into his mind through the accident of self-forgetfulness. The Wordsworthian curriculum includes truancy, "act[s] of stealth / And troubled pleasure" (I, 388–89), tutelary spirits of beauty and fear (especially fear), and even, in the case of Lucy and the Winander Boy, premature death. Though Wordsworth's own education at Hawkshead Grammar School was traditionally bookish,[1] his out-of-school activities were those he chiefly chose to recall, and when *The Prelude* does mention childhood reading it is to claim that the sight of a drowned man, "a spectre shape / Of Terror" (V, 472–73), could be assimilated without trauma by a boy used to fairy tales and romances. Book learning, then, gets short shrift from an educational point of view, and the whole drift of Book V is toward subsuming literature under the heading of Nature—toward naturalizing it as "only less, / For what we may become . . . Than Nature's self" (V, 220–22).

Wordsworth's satire in "Books" is predictably antiutilitarian, aimed as it is at the educational forerunners of the Gradgrind system in *Hard Times*.[2] But his attack on regimentation and conditioning—rote learning designed to turn children into "engines"—discloses the unease that underlies much Romantic writing about literacy. Though Wordsworth sets out to commemorate "all books which lay / Their sure foundations in the heart of Man" (V, 199–200), he is anxious lest they cut the ground from under Nature as she works through "external accidents" (in his own words about the Winander Boy) "to plant, for immortality, images of sound and sight, in the celestial soil of the Imagination."[3] The fear covertly expressed in Book V is that it is not we that write, but writing that writes us; that the writing of the past, rather than "the spirit of the past" (XI, 342), determines "what we may become"; and that the language of books is "unremittingly and noiselessly at work" (in Wordsworth's memorably obsessed phrases) to derange and to subvert the language of incarnated thought on which Romantic theorists pin their hope of linguistic salvation.[4] The temporal threat contained in the passage from Book V, the control of books over

[1] Wordsworth claimed that "no man in England had been more regularly educated" (see *The Prelude*, ed. Ernest de Selincourt, rev. Helen Darbishire [Oxford: Clarendon Press, 1959], p. 543). For his "nine years from nine to nineteen . . . at Hawkshead, then a celebrated school," see T. W. Thompson, *Wordsworth's Hawkshead*, ed. Robert Woof (London: Oxford University Press, 1970).

[2] See David V. Erdman, "Coleridge, Wordsworth, and the Wedgewood Fund," *BNYPL* 60 (1956):425–43, 487–507, esp. 493–95, for an account of the educational schemes of the 1790s and their impact on Wordsworth in Book V of *The Prelude*. For the earlier and fuller version of *The Prelude* lines in MS. 18A, see *The Poetical Works of William Wordsworth*, ed. Ernest de Selincourt and Helen Darbishire, 5 vols. (Oxford: Clarendon Press, 1940–49), V, 345–46.

[3] 1815 Preface, on "There was a Boy; see *Prelude*, p. 547.

[4] "Language, if it do not uphold, and feed, and leave in quiet, like the power of gravitation or the air we breathe, is a counter-spirit, unremittingly and noiselessly at work to derange, to subvert, to lay waste, to vitiate, and to dissolve" (*Essays on Epitaphs, III: The Prose Works of William Wordsworth*, ed. W. J. B. Owen and Jane Worthington Smyser, 3 vols. [Oxford: Clarendon Press, 1974], II, 85).

infant minds, is amplified in the 1850 version of *The Prelude,* where "Tutors of our Youth" become "keepers of our time"—picking up the Satanic suggestions in Wordsworth's glossing of the "mighty workmen of our later age" as those "Who with a broad highway have overbridged / The froward chaos of futurity' (V, 371–72), bringing death into God's timeless world. Management of books, or rather by books, means management of time too; these "sages" seek to control the future as well as the untoward. Perhaps this is why Wordsworth goes on almost at once in Book V to introduce the Winander Boy, whose attempts to manage owls with his mimic hootings are baffled by Nature's "external accidents" and whose formal education is cut short by the unforeseeable accident of death. "Slumbering" (Wordsworth's euphemism for "dead"), he is released both from writing out a hundred lines and, like Wordsworth himself, from being written out by tens of hundreds of them—laid asleep in nature so that the wordy, university-educated poet can attain to the art of book management. Preserving and laying to rest in one move the fantasy of a self that can neither write nor be written, the dead child is father to the *Prelude* man.

The episode of the Winander Boy, then, bears obliquely on what one might call the oral fallacy of Romantic theories of language— the pervasive notion that "the voice / Of mountain torrents" (V, 408–9) speaks a language more profound than that of books and is carried farther into the heart. Wordsworth's naturalization of "voice" here serves to avert the threat of anarchy that voices bring with them. The Winander Boy, blowing "mimic hootings to the silent owls," has reverted to an innocently prelinguistic phase of repeated sounds (difference without meaning, or babble); but his "feverish and restless anxiety" also initiates a riotous Babel that is "mock'd" in turn by nature's silence ("pauses of deep silence mock'd his skill" [V, 405]):

> —And they would shout
> Across the watry Vale, and shout again
> Responsive to his call, with quivering peals
> And long halloos, and screams, and echoes loud
> Redoubled and redoubled; concourse wild
> Of mirth and jocund din![5]
>
> [V, 399–404]

[5]"The Boy . . . is listening, with something of a feverish and restless anxiety, for the recurrence of the riotous sounds which he had previously excited" (*Prelude,* p. 547). For a reading of this episode, see Cynthia Chase, "The Accidents of Disfiguration: Limits to Literal and Rhetorical Reading in Book V of *The Prelude,*" *Studies in Romanticism* 18 (1979):547–66.

The distinction between parroting and echoing (who is mimicking whom—the owls the boy or the boy the owls?) is lost in the doubling and redoubling of "concourse wild." "Din," though jocund here, brings to mind the confusion of another concourse altogether, Wordsworth's uproarious London in Book VII of *The Prelude*. *Paradise Lost*, too, provides not only a series of usages connected with martial strife, but an archetypal usage that must surely have been in Wordsworth's mind, however subliminally—the most confused din of all, the building of the tower of Babel:

> 'each to other calls
> Not understood, till hoarse, and all in rage,
> As mocked they storm; great laughter was in heaven
> And looking down, to see the hubbub strange
> And hear the din; thus was the building left
> Ridiculous, and the work Confusion named.'
> [*Paradise Lost*, XII, 57–62]

"Oh, blank *confusion!* and a type not false / Of what the mighty City is itself" (VII, 695–96; my italics):[6] Wordsworth's verdict on Bartholomew Fair, the epitome of London's "Babel din," links urban anarchy and uproar with Nimrod's vainglorious architecture. Glimpsed behind the Winander Boy's jubilant dialogue with the owls is a wishful revision of Milton's elegiac motif in Book XII of *Paradise Lost*, the loss of a unified originary language brought about by Nimrod's attempt to rival heaven's towers with his own.

In *The Prelude*, the boy's skill is mocked not by laughter but by silence—saving him, despite himself, from the fall he has initiated. But for the poet there can be no salvation *avant la lettre*. George Eliot, imagining the roar of unlimited sensibility that lies on the other side of silence, wads it thankfully with stupidity.[7] Wordsworth, imagining silence on the other side of uproar, uses his own writing to still the din that threatens when "voice" becomes plural (voices) and to confine proliferation when singleness splits into uncontrolled redoubling. In this sense writing, though subordinated by Romantic theory to "the voice of the living Speaker,"[8] limits as well as inscribes

---

[6]"Babel" is marginally glossed as "Confusion" by the Authorized Version of the Bible; Wordsworth presumably knew this popular etymology.

[7]"If we had a keen vision and feeling of all ordinary human life . . . we should die of that roar which lies on the other side of silence. As it is, the quickest of us walk about well wadded with stupidity" (*Middlemarch*, chap. 20).

[8]"Spoken Language has a great superiority over written Language in point of energy or force. The voice of the living Speaker, makes an impression on the mind, much stronger than can be made by the perusal of any Writing" (Hugh Blair, *Lectures on Rhetoric and Belles Lettres* [1783], ed. H. F. Harding, 2 vols. [Carbondale, Ill.: University of Southern Illinois Press, 1965], I, 136).

an original fall, like Los attempting to bind Urizen's fallen universe lest it get yet further out of hand. Ordering the chaotic multiplicity of the self, writing not only defends against incoherence, but, because it is always of and from the past, it defends against presence— and against the future too; only a hair's breadth separates the characteristic Romantic attempt to "enshrine the spirit of the past / For future restoration" (XI, 342–43) from that overbridging of "The froward chaos of futurity" denounced in Book V of *The Prelude*. What De Quincey calls "the language of books" troubles Romantic writers in much the same way that writing troubles them—because it uncovers aspects of their practice which their theories attempt (even exist) to repress.

I want to explore these hidden contradictions by looking closely at what three major prose writers of the Romantic period have to say about language. Thomas De Quincey's essays on style and rhetoric, William Hazlitt's "On Familiar Style," and Charles Lamb's "Genteel Style in Writing" develop some of the questions that I have tried to introduce by way of *The Prelude*. These questions are ultimately bound up with the writing of Romantic autobiography. That what emerges looks at first sight disconcertingly like a poetics of quotation rather than of prose uncovers my central concerns—not with prose style as such, but with the part played by previous writing in constituting it; not with literary influence in any simple sense, but with the relation between the language of books and the inscribing of temporality.[9] In other words, I argue that the language of books *is* the writing of the past, and the writing of the past is the language of books.

II

Writing in the 1840s, De Quincey identified as a prevalent cultural malaise the "contagion of bookishness" that had infected the urban populace through the rise of journalism. A diverting anecdote in his essay on style brings the book-learned author (De Quincey prided himself on his own classical erudition)[10] face to face

[9]Two essays that have played a part in shaping these concerns are Jacques Ehrmann, "The Death of Literature," *New Literary History* 3 (1971):31–47, and Paul de Man, "The Rhetoric of Temporality," in *Interpretation: Theory and Practice*, ed. Charles Singleton (Baltimore: Johns Hopkins University Press, 1969), pp. 173–209. For a relevant structural analysis of quotation in the European novel, see Herman Meyer, *The Poetics of Quotation* (Princeton: Princeton University Press, 1968).

[10]Ironically, De Quincey attributes his fluency in ancient Greek "to the practice of daily reading off the newspapers into the best Greek I could furnish *extempore*" (*Thomas De Quincy: Confessions of an English Opium Eater and Other Writings*, ed. Aileen Ward [New York: New American Library, 1966], p. 28).

with an egregious example of lodging-house literacy—a landlady "in regular training, it appeared, as a student of newspapers." These are the words that "she—this semi-barbarian—poured from her cornucopia":

> First, "category"; secondly, "predicament" (where, by the way, from the twofold iteration of the idea—Greek and Roman—it appears that the old lady was "twice armed"); thirdly, "individuality"; fourthly, "procrastination"; fifthly, "speaking diplomatically, would not wish to *commit* herself," who knew but that "inadvertently she might even *compromise* both herself and her husband"? Sixthly, "would spontaneously adapt the several modes of domestication to the reciprocal interests," &c.; and finally—(which word it was that settled us: we heard it as we reached the topmost stair on the second floor; and, without further struggle against our instincts, round we wheeled, rushed down forty-five stairs, and exploded from the house with a fury causing us to impinge against an obese or protuberant gentleman, and calling for mutual explanations; a result which nothing *could* account for, but a steel bow, or mustachios on the lip of an elderly woman; meantime the fatal word was), seventhly, "anteriorly". Concerning which word we solemnly depose and make affidavit that neither from man, woman, nor book, had we ever heard it before this unique rencontre with this abominable woman on the staircase.[11]

Belonging as she does to a long line of comic pedants stretching back to Dogberry and beyond, De Quincey's landlady talks quite as much like a court of law as a book—the difference being (in De Quincey's words) "the total absence of all *malaprop* picturesqueness." One could read the encounter as a piece of covert grumbling about the loss of a rich source of linguistic comedy, the pleasure of the educated in the misappropriation of language by their social inferiors, or as a stroke of Juvenalian satire against the talking woman to whom grammarians yield and rhetoricians succumb.[12] In any case, one doesn't have to be a particularly shrewd reader to notice that De Quincey's facetiousness ("impinge against an obese or protuberant gentleman, and calling for mutual explanations") depends, like his rhetorical *suspensio,* on the lodging-house mistress's logorrhea—just as the would-be lodger ends by mimicking her courtroom mumbo-

---

[11]John Jordan, ed., *De Quincy as Critic* (London: Routledge & Kegan Paul, 1973), pp. 71–72. De Quincey's essays on style and rhetoric were originally published in *Blackwood's Edinburgh Magazine* between July 1840 and February 1841 and in December 1828, respectively.

[12]See George Steiner, *After Babel* (London: Oxford University Press, 1975), p. 41, and Juvenal's sixth satire.

jumbo with his "solemnly depose and make affidavit." But there is more going on here than the theft of comic thunder. Outrage focuses on a single word, and one that (deferred by a ballooning parenthesis) could scarcely be more explosive for De Quincey himself: "anteriorly." He is literally put to flight by the past, colliding with the quotidian in the form of obesity. The language of books at once resurrects the past and murders it; as Latin is a defunct language, so "the fatal word," "anteriorly," speaks the language of death intoned by the funereal leitmotifs of De Quincey's writing: "*all is lost*"; "everlasting farewells! And again, and yet again reverberated—everlasting farewells!"[13]

The cryptic narrative contained in the landlady's "anteriorly" ("formerly")[14] returns us to that false point of origin, at once ultimate and penultimate, the long-ago death of De Quincey's sister, on which both his infant sufferings and his writings are posited. But the accident on the topmost stair is doubly fatal in that it not only rifles the tomb of the past but defeminizes language; the landlady becomes a mustachioed Amazon ("twice armed")—a bad mother, pouring words instead of plenty from her maternal cornucopia. Shortly before relating his anecdote, De Quincey had identified the "mother tongue" or "old mother idiom" as surviving particularly among women—"not, Heaven knows, amongst our women who write books . . . but amongst well-educated women not professionally given to literature"; "The pure racy idiom of colloquial or household English," he insists, "must be looked for in the circles of well-educated women not too closely connected with books."[15] (Dorothy Wordsworth, in De Quincey's *Recollections of the Lake Poets,* is just such a woman—the Boy of Winander, as it were, to the prodigiously learned landlady.)[16] Instead of looking to Wordsworth's low and rustic life for the language of passion, De Quincey looks to the sister and to the home. Like his anti-blue-stocking prejudice, De Quincey's representation of women as the site of nature, feeling, and purity is a common Romantic phallacy. But women in his writing are especially accident-prone; if not dead (like his sister), nearly drowned (like his mother), or lost (like the prostitute Ann), they risk being run over by an English mail coach. The young woman threat-

---

[13]Ward, *De Quincey,* pp. 117, 99.

[14]For defunct language, anasemia, and "the exquisite corpse," see Jacques Derrida, "Fors," *Georgia Review* 31 (1977):64–116.

[15]Jordan, *De Quincey as Critic,* pp. 64, 67, 69.

[16]See *The Collected Writings of Thomas De Quincey,* ed. David Masson, 14 vols. (Edinburgh: Adam & Charles Black, 1889–90), II, 295–99.

ened with the accident of sudden death is a favorite and vivid fantasy of De Quincey's, and the language of headlong disaster is apt to spill over from *The English Mail-Coach* into what he has to say about style. Of contemporary writing, he complains: "Whatever words *tumble out* under the blindest *accidents* of the moment, those are the words retained; whatever *sweep* is impressed by chance upon the *motion* of a period, that is the arrangement ratified"; elsewhere he speaks of modern speed reading as "this Parthian habit of aiming at full gallop," while his own subjection to "the mighty Juggernaut of social life"—forcing his brain to "work like a steam-engine" to meet the demands of periodical publication—implicates him in the "hurry and inevitable precipitancy" threatening the young lady of *The English Mail-Coach*.[17]

De Quincey's references to a "monster model of sentence" and "dire monotony of bookish idiom . . . like some scaly leprosy or elephantiasis" infect the monstrous runaway machine and crocodilian driver of *The English Mail-Coach* with the disease of book language. The famous distinction between an *"organology"* and a *"mechanology"* of style is an attempt to free writing—his writing—from the death-dealing machine and to sublimate it in funereal organ music, as the dying children of his childhood visions are borne up to God or the woman of *The English Mail-Coach* is snatched to heaven in his dreams. "Style," he insists,

> may be viewed as an *organic* thing and as a *mechanic* thing . . . Now, the use of words is an organic thing, in so far as language is connected with thoughts, and modified by thoughts. It is a mechanic thing, in so far as words in combination determine or modify each other. The science of style as an organ of thought, of style in relation to the ideas and feelings, might be called the *organology* of style. The science of style, considered as a machine, in which words act upon words, and through a particular grammar, might be called the *mechanology* of style . . . it is of great importance not to confound the functions; that function by which style maintains a commerce with thought, and that by which it chiefly communicates with grammar and with words.[18]

What De Quincey is worried about is that the two functions might indeed be confounded—that the mechanology of style, gaining mo-

---

[17]Jordan, *De Quincey as Critic*, pp. 64–82 (my italics); *Collected Writings of Thomas De Quincey*, XII, 159; V, 304, 307. For the relation between opium and eloquence in De Quincey's writing, see Michael G. Cooke, "De Quincey, Coleridge, and the Formal Uses of Intoxication," *Yale French Studies* 50 (1974):26–40.
[18]Jordan, *De Quincey as Critic*, pp. 70, 82–83.

mentum of its own, might overrun thought and cause a fatal accident in which the feminine (the language of feeling) is the casualty. The fiction that language can retain a saving commerce with thought, independent of linguistic machinery, is not, of course, confined to De Quincey; but an anxiety that Wordsworth figures as fear of fatal poisoning by borrowed robes (the secondhand language of the previous century)[19] takes a distinctively catastrophic form in his writing. De Quincey—willy-nilly—is a helpless passenger on an out-of-control vehicle that threatens death to what he holds dear. Drugged and powerless, barely able to shout his warning, he is at once the agent of disaster, its herald, and its witness. What is figured in *The English Mail-Coach*, in other words, is the untenability of De Quincey's attempt to distinguish between an organology and a mechanology of style. As his facetiousness about lodging-house literacy disguises an inevitable stake in literacy itself, so the melodramatic scenario of *The English Mail-Coach* is generated partly by guilt. Not only does he share the landlady's "contagion of bookishness," but, like the sleeping coachman, he must commit (wo)manslaughter if he is to write at all.

Hence De Quincey's persistence in attempting to sublimate prose to the condition of funereal music. The sublime means Milton ("In Milton only, first and last, is the power of the sublime revealed),[20] and so when De Quincey turns to the prose of an admired and influential predecessor in his essay on rhetoric, music and Milton set the tone: "Where, but in Sir T[homas] B[rowne], shall one hope to find music so Miltonic, an intonation of such solemn chords as are struck in the following opening bar of a passage in the *Urne-Buriall*—'Now, since these bones have rested quietly in the grave under the drums and tramplings of three conquests,' &c."[21] In De Quincey's writing, too, death sounds solemn chords (the "hollow, solemn, Memnonian, but saintly swell" breathed in the bedchamber of his sister's corpse, and "the blare of the tumultuous organ" that sublimates the deaths of infants in *Suspiria de Profundis*).[22] *Urne-Buriall*'s breathings from the depths prefigure the most profound motifs of De Quincey's writing (death, time, the past—an "eternity

---

[19]"If words be not . . . an incarnation of the thought but only a clothing for it, then surely will they prove an ill gift; such a one as those poisoned vestments, read of in the stories of superstitious times, which had power to consume and to alienate from his right mind the victim who put them on" (*Essays on Epitaphs, III: Prose Works*, II, 84–85).

[20]Jordan, *De Quincey as Critic*, p. 255.

[21]Ibid., p. 114.

[22]Ward, *De Quincey*, pp. 131, 138.

not coming, but past and irrevocable").[23] But they also produce echoes of a different kind—the doubling and redoubling of the Winander Boy's mimic hootings. When De Quincey embarks on his own redoubling of *Urne-Buriall* (itself already an echo chamber for Sir Thomas Browne's meditations on mortality), is he echoing or merely parroting, revising or merely belated?

> What a melodious ascent of a prelude to some impassioned requiem breathing from the pomps of earth, and from the sanctities of the grave! What a *fluctus decumanus* of rhetoric! Time expounded, not by generations or centuries, but by the vast periods of conquests and dynasties; by cycles of Pharoahs and Ptolemies, Antiochi and Arsacides! And these vast successions of time distinguished and figured by the uproars which revolve at their inaugurations; by the drums and tramplings rolling overhead upon the chambers of forgotten dead—the trepidations of time and mortality vexing, at secular intervals, the everlasting sabbaths of the grave![24]

"Language," it has been said, "always comes to us from elsewhere (whence its character of echo, of quotation . . .)."[25] De Quincey vexes the sabbaths of the grave with trepidations that are both echoes and quotations; with language that comes from elsewhere— from the past. But (one might claim) his variation on the famous "organ peal" of *Urne-Buriall*'s final and most sonorous chapter displaces, as echo does, the rhetoric of Browne's seventeenth-century original:

> NOW since these dead bones have already out-lasted the living ones of *Methuselah,* and in a yard under ground, and thin walls of clay, outworn all the strong and specious buildings above it; and quietly rested under the drums and trampling of three conquests; What Prince can promise such diuturnity unto his Reliques, or might not gladly say,
> > *Sic ego componi versus in ossa velim.*
> Time which antiquates Antiquities, and hath an art to make dust of all things, hath yet spared these *minor* Monuments.[26]

[23]See H. A. Page [A. H. Japp], *Thomas de Quincey: His Life and Writings,* 2 vols. (London: J. Hogg, 1877), I, 340.

[24]Jordan, *De Quincey as Critic,* p. 114.

[25]Jacques Ehrmann, "The Death of Literature," *New Literary History* 3 (1971):39. For a different approach to De Quincey and literary influence, see Arden Reed, "Abysmal Influence: Baudelaire, Coleridge, De Quincey, Piranesi, Wordsworth," *Glyph* 4 (1978):189–206.

[26]Sir Thomas Browne, *Religio Medici and Other Works,* ed. L. C. Martin (Oxford: Clarendon Press, 1964), p. 118.

Browne's urns are both tombs and wombs, "making our last bed like our first";[27] their buried story is an originating death. Exhuming Browne's language, De Quincey sets going a perpetual-motion machine—recycling words whose meaning, like that of "anteriorly," is always former, always buried, and always a repetition of the past, while achieving a paradoxical priority: his is the melodious prelude.

In 1821, the Tory *Quarterly Review* accused Hazlitt of being a "SLANG-WHANGER"—that is, "'One who makes use of political or other gabble, vulgarly called slang, that serves to amuse the rabble.'"[28] In the politics of style, "gabble" invokes the presumptuous anarchy of Babel while "slang" denounces radicalism as rabble-rousing. As Hazlitt wrote scathingly in *A Letter to William Gifford, Esq.* (1819), the most furious outburst in his sustained political war with the Tory reviewers, "When you say that an author cannot write common sense or English, you mean that he does not believe in the doctrine of divine right."[29] His 1821 essay "On Familiar Style" is thus both a rear-guard action against the *Quarterly*—"I have been (I know) loudly accused of revelling in vulgarisms and broken English"—and an attempt to redefine style in terms of the Bourgeois Revolution. What starts as self-defense turns into an economics of language. Familiar style is not vulgarity, but common use; devaluing pedantry at one extreme and slanguage at the other, the essay sets out to legitimize a different currency, that of the marketplace. Hazlitt as honest broker uses only legal tender, coin made current by "the stamp of custom." His distinction between slang and common usage turns on an example both incisive (as he wished his prose to be) and socially paranoid (as he was himself), salted with a grain of popular learning ("*cum grano salis*"):

> I should say that the phrase *To cut with a knife*, or *To cut a piece of wood*, is perfectly free from vulgarity, because it is perfectly common: but to *cut an acquaintance* is not quite unexceptionable, because it is not perfectly common or intelligible, and has hardly yet escaped out of the limits of slang phraseology. I should hardly therefore use the word in this sense

[27] Ibid., p. 102.

[28] *Quarterly Review* 26 (October 1821):108; the reviewer was John Matthews. For Hazlitt's dealings with the *Quarterly* and the *Quarterly*'s dealings with Hazitt, see R. B. Clark, *William Gifford: Tory Satirist and Editor* (New York: Columbia University Press, 1930), pp. 213–20, and Ralph M. Wardle, *Hazlitt* (Lincoln: University of Nebraska Press, 1971), pp. 242–47, 286–87.

[29] *The Complete Works of William Hazlitt*, ed. P. P. Howe, 21 vols. (London: J. M. Dent, 1930–34), IX, 14.

without putting it in italics as a licence of expression, to be received *cum grano salis*. . . . I conceive that words are like money, not the worse for being common, but that it is the stamp of custom alone that gives them respect, and would almost as soon coin the currency of the realm as counterfeit the king's English. . . . As an author, I endeavour to employ plain words and popular modes of construction, as, were I a chapman and dealer, I should common weights and measures.[30]

The spectacle of Hazlitt the republican invoking the king's English might at first sight seem an odd one; but for him the bloodless revolution of 1688 had meant the introduction of a Bill of Rights by which the king derived his authority not from God but from the people—from the Lords and Commons, the guarantors of constitutional rights. Hazlitt, in fact, answers the *Quarterly Review* by putting himself firmly on the side of New-Whig commerce ("common weights and measures") rather than Tory "Legitimacy," which he elsewhere calls "this foul Blatant Beast . . . breathing flame and blood"—a monstrous Error, regurgitating such books as Burke's *Reflections on the Revolution in France* (1790).[31]

For Hazlitt, "the want of ideas" means inflation. Plagiarizing Hamlet's irritable "words, words, words," he attacks the "florid style" that is the reverse of the familiar: "'What do you read?'— 'Words, words, words.'—'What is the matter?'—'Nothing,' it might be answered." Polonius as windbag provokes a Hamlet-like railing against the flowers of rhetoric—"When there is nothing to be set down but words, it costs little to have them fine. Look through the dictionary, and cull out a *florilegium,* rival the *tulippomania. Rouge* high enough, and never mind the natural complexion." Painted ladies and rouged tulips figure the strumpetry of language that Hazlitt, like Marvell's Puritan mower against gardens, denounces less because art has meddled with nature than because nature has learned to counterfeit rather than cultivate plainness ("The Tulip, white, did for complexion seek; / And learn'd to interline its cheek" ("The Mower against Gardens," 11. 13–14). Or—to exchange one

---

[30]Ibid., VIII, 243–44. See also Jacques Derrida, "White Mythology," *New Literary History* 6 (1974):5–74, esp. 6–17, for coins and metaphors; and Marc Shell, *The Economy of Literature* (Baltimore: Johns Hopkins University Press, 1978), for the relation between literary exchanges and exchanges that constitute the political economy.

[31]Howe, *Works of Hazlitt,* VII, 10. Spenser's Blatant Beast, interestingly, is full of tongues that "Ne Kesars spared . . . nor Kings" (*The Faerie Queene,* VI, xii, 28). For Hazlitt's changing political stance and his alignment with the Hanoverian loyalties and constitutional Whigism of the dissenting tradition, see John Kinnaird, *William Hazlitt: Critic of Power* (New York: Columbia University Press, 1978), pp. 101–28.

metaphor for another—the "merely verbal imagination" becomes a social dragonfly, spawning in Hazlitt's own prose a further proliferation of empty, iridescent, deflationary images:

> Such writers have merely *verbal* imaginations, that retain nothing but words. Or their puny thoughts have dragon-wings, all green and gold. They soar far above the vulgar failings of the *Sormo humi obrepens*— their most ordinary speech is never short of an hyperbole, splendid, imposing, vague, incomprehensible, magniloquent, a cento of sounding commonplaces.[32]

Horace's "words creeping along the ground" (his modestly termed satiric "conversations") are momentarily overreached by glittering hyperboles before they thud to earth as "sounding common-places." This is Hazlitt's equivalent to De Quincey's distinction between "mechanology" and "organology;" but in Hazlitt's case, the "merely verbal imagination" is floated by the fiction of reference—of a saving commerce, less with thought than with things. "Imaginations, that retain nothing but words" have lost their purchase on reality. For Hazlitt this unreality is akin to possession, or madness: "Such persons are in fact besotted with words, and their brains are turned with the glittering, but empty and sterile phantoms of things." They are "the poorest of all plagiarists, the plagiarists of words," inhabiting the world of writing instead of things—"Personifications, capital letters, seas of sunbeams, visions of glory, shining inscriptions, the figures of a transparency, Britannia with her shield, or Hope leaning on an anchor, make up their stock of trade."[33] This is the same text of signs, inscriptions, and allegoric shapes that makes up Wordsworth's London, where the city as book is given over entirely to advertising:

> Shop after shop, with Symbols, blazon'd Names,
> And all the Tradesman's honours overhead;
> Here, fronts of houses, like a title-page
> With letters huge inscribed from top to toe;
> Station'd above the door, like guardian Saints,
> There, allegoric shapes, female or male . . .
>
> [VII, 174–79]

Rejecting "personifications of abstract ideas" in the 1800 Preface to *Lyrical Ballads*, Wordsworth writes: "I wish to keep the Reader in the company of flesh and blood."[34] Ghostliness enters where represen-

---

[32]Howe, *Works of Hazlitt* VIII, 244, 246.
[33]Ibid., VIII, 246–47.
[34]*Prose Works of William Wordsworth*, I, 130.

tation becomes merely apparent, exposing appearances as apparitions, not flesh and blood. When "objects are not linked to feelings, words to things, but . . . words represent themselves," the spectral text of language undoes what Hazlitt calls "the web and texture of the universe"—revealing language as a weapon that cannot "cut with a knife," but can only make feints and passes. Here the literal becomes a phantasm haunting the dematerialized text, as metaphor alternately effaces itself and returns to the surface.

"His words are the most like things" was how Hazlitt chose to praise Burke.[35] Fittingly, what he calls "the true worth and hidden structure both of words and things" are underwritten by the most conservative as well as the most eloquent defender of the status quo. That Hazlitt's political obverse should be the prose writer he admired above all others epitomizes the ambidextrousness not only of literary inheritance but of language itself. Ironically, it was Burke's most self-interested (and ironic) defense of hereditary privilege that had made Hazlitt his ephebe in the 1790s: "We first met with some extracts from Mr. Burke's *Letter to a Noble Lord* in the year 1796, and on the instant became converts to his familiar, inimitable, powerful prose-style."[36] Burke at the top of his form, warding off the Duke of Bedford's attack on his pension with the weapons he had earlier used to defend the hereditary rights of kings, becomes the hero of Hazlitt's leveling essay "On the Prose Style of Poets" (1822). The centerpiece of both essays is Burke's most authoritative celebration of the constitution, of privilege, and of legitimacy. This, for Hazlitt, is prose with its feet on the ground—useful, energetic, and pedestrian (as the prose style of poets is not); above all, prose in which a "vague and complicated idea" is grounded on the bedrock of things:

> As long as the well-compacted structure of our church and state, the sanctuary, the holy of holies of that ancient law, defended by reverence, defended by power—a fortress at once and a temple—shall stand inviolate on the brow of the British Sion; as long as the British Monarchy—not more limited than fenced by the orders of the State shall, like the proud Keep of Windsor, rising in the majesty of proportion, and girt with the double belt of its kindred and coeval towers; as long as this awful structure shall oversee and guard the subjected land, so long the mounds and dykes of the low, fat, Bedford level will have nothing to fear from all the pickaxes of all the levellers of France. As long as our Sovereign Lord the King, and his faithful subjects, the Lords and Com-

[35] Howe, *Works of Hazlitt*, VII, 309.
[36] Ibid., XVI, 222. The irony was not lost on Hazlitt; see ibid., VII, 186.

mons of this realm—the triple cord which no man can break; the solemn, sworn, constitutional-frank pledge of this nation; the firm guarantees of each other's being, and each other's rights; the joint and
several securities, each in its place and order, for every kind, and every
quality of property and of dignity—As long as these endure we are all
safe together—the high from the blights of envy and the spoliations of
rapacity; the low from the iron hand of oppression and the insolent
spurn of contempt. Amen! and so be it: and so it will be,

> Dum domus Æneae Capitoli immobile saxum
> Accolet; imperiumque pater Romanus habebit.[37]

Burke is invoking the authority of the *Aeneid* and Anchises' prophecy from Book IX ("so long as the house of Aeneas shall dwell on the
capitol's unshaken rock, and the Father of Rome hold sovereign
sway") in order to base his defense of property rights on the foundations of Rome. Burke cites Virgil: Hazlitt quotes Burke. The appropriation of authority (in Burke's case to support his view of the
Constitution, in Hazlitt's to support his view of prose style) involves a
form of quotation that not only displaces meaning but reinvests it—
since for Hazlitt the emphasis is not simply on defending the rights
of men against the divine right of kings, but the right of prose
writers to vie with poets, and ultimately his own right to vie with
Burke.

For Burke, who (in the words of the 1850 *Prelude*) "the majesty
proclaims / Of Institutes and Laws, hallowed by time" (VII, 525–
56), the language of books—here, of the *Aeneid*—is the language of
Legitimacy; 'Legitimacy, the very tomb of freedom," Hazlitt called
it.[38] Legitimacy must be deposed if liberty is to flourish. Hazlitt's
writing about Burke is doubly subversive, first displacing "the vague
and complicated idea" of the English Constitution with the figure of
Burke himself, then appropriating his powers. The proud Keep of
Windsor is only a pawn in the battle of words; Burke (according to
Hazlitt) "seized on some stronghold in the argument, and held it fast
with a convulsive grasp . . . He entered the lists like a gladiator."
Burke as gladiator becomes Hazlitt the prose pugilist—"Every word
should be a blow: every thought should instantly grapple with its
fellow."[39] Hazlitt's temperamental pugnacity makes his the pugilistic
style as well as the familiar style (it's no accident that his favorite

---

[37]Ibid., XII, 11–12; cf. *The Works of Edmund Burke*, 5 vols. (London: H. G. Bohn,
1855–64), V, 137–38.
[38]Howe, *Works of Hazlitt*, VII, 10.
[39]Ibid., XII, 269, 11.

among Lamb's essays was the miniature mock epic, "Mrs. Battle's Opinions on Whist"). The fight is ostensibly political—against what Hazlitt on a different occasion called "the 'old proud keep' of intolerance and privilege, fenced by 'its double belt of kindred,' ignorance and pride," subverting the conservative imagery of Burke's *Letter to a Noble Lord* to make a radical point;[40] but it is also "familiar" in another sense, that is, familial. Burke had defended hereditary privilege in order to parry attacks on the pension he had earned: Hazlitt's misreading of Burke contends with an admired predecessor and political adversary in order to wrest from him not his pension but his "power"—a key term, of course, in the aesthetics of both. Burke (in Wordsworth's *Prelude* lines) "Exploding upstart Theory, insists / Upon the allegiance to which men are born' (1850; VII, 529–30): Hazlitt embarks on an oedipal struggle. For Wordsworth too, the elder Burke was a patriarchal figure—

> I see him,—old, but vigorous in age,—
> Stand like an oak whose stag-horn branches start
> Out of its leafy brow, the more to awe
> The younger brethren of the grove.
>
> [1850; VII, 519–22]

—and it is all the more surprising that Hazlitt's essay should cast him as the rebel of the prose sublime: "Burke's style is airy, flighty, adventurous. . . . It may be said to pass yawning gulfs 'on the unsteadfast footing of a spear.'"[41] The allusion here is (bizarrely) to Hotspur's incitement to rebellion by Worcester in *Henry IV, Part I.*

> I'll read you matter deep and dangerous,
> As full of peril and adventurous spirit
> As to o'er walk a current roaring loud
> On the unsteadfast footing of a spear.
>
> [I.iii.188–90]

Why did Hazlitt apply to Burke, of all people, the language of insurrection when it was not Burke but himself that was in revolt against "*pater Romanus*"? Is it because the son, in attempting to appropriate the authority of the father, must identify him as the same, while usurping him as other (conservative, repressive, and authoritarian)?

---

[40]Ibid., XVII, 324.

[41]Ibid., XII, 10. For a recent discussion of Wordsworth's relationship to Burke, see James Chandler, "Wordsworth and Burke," *ELH* 47 (1980):741–71.

Or, to put it another way, isn't Hazlitt himself both the good and the bad son, both Hal and Hotspur, desiring at once to inherit and to contest Burke's proprietary rights over language (while presumably recognizing him to be as much a self-made man as Bolingbroke)? But the ambivalence is not simply that of influence; it is also that of a writer who sees his inheritance guaranteed by the very Legitimacy he challenges. The writing of Hazlitt the radical is constituted, so to speak, by Burke's conservative style. "Always a usurper, meaning is never legitimate," writes Jacques Ehrmann; "meaning," he goes on, "*commands* subversion (as one says of a geographical point that it commands a strategic place; that it both forbids and gives access at the same time)."[42] The proud old Keep of Windsor—at once the Constitution and its chief defender—forbids and gives access in the same way. Hazlitt needs Legitimacy in order to free Liberty from her tomb.

"On Familiar Style" exempts Lamb from Hazlitt's general dislike of antiquarianism, recognizing him to be "so thoroughly imbued with the spirit of his authors, that the idea of imitation is almost done away.... The matter is completely his own, though the manner is assumed." Lamb's antiquarianism is a mask—like the fictional Elia, a means not simply of disguising eccentricity, but of shielding his identity; as Hazlitt puts it, "The old English authors . . . are a kind of mediator between us and the more eccentric and whimsical modern, reconciling us to his peculiarities."[43] The assumed manner mediates as much between past and present as between Elia and his readers; "the film of the past hovers forever before him" to create a temporal interspace where what "touches [Elia] most nearly . . . is withdrawn to a certain distance, which verges on the border of oblivion." Lamb, in fact, is a marginal writer only in the sense of a liminal one, imaginatively haunting the borders of life and death, ideas and reality:

Death has in this sense the spirit of life in it; and the shadowy has to our author something substantial in it. Ideas savour most of reality in his mind; or rather his imagination loiters on the edge of each, and a page of his writing recalls to our fancy the *stranger* on the grate, fluttering in its dusky tenuity, with its idle superstition and hospitable welcome.[44]

[42]Jacques Ehrmann, "The Death of Literature," *New Literary History* 3 (1971):44.
[43]Howe, *Works of Hazlitt*, VIII, 245.
[44]Ibid., XI, 178–80.

If the written page is the *"stranger* on the grate" that in Cowper's
Task (as in Coleridge's "Frost at Midnight") "play[s] upon the bars,"

in the view

Of superstition, prophecying still,
Though still deceiv'd, some stranger's near approach.

[The Task, IV, 292–95]

the stranger hospitably summoned to inhabit it is Elia, that estranged and ghostly version of self brought to life in the hinterland
of writing. This margin is a play space. The "stranger," or the self
doubled and fictionalized, is freed from the trials of empirical existence and in turn frees strangeness—eccentricity and whimsicality—
for the uses of the imagination. The hovering specter here is that of
duplicity, paradoxically animated by writing that De Quincey contrasted with his own "Rhythmus, or pomp of cadence" as "the natural, the simple, the genuine."[45] Lamb uses a different term in his
essay "The Genteel Style of Writing" (1826), which needs Shaftes-
bury's definition from the previous century to bring to light its
veiled subject, the disguise of artifice as nature: "The natural and
simple manner which conceals and covers Art, is the most truly
artful, and of the genteelest, truest, and best study'd Taste" (*OED*).
Naturalness conceals art, taste is studied. Dissembling and study—
the art of counterfeiting and of managing books—underwrite the
"truth" of the genteel style, which is really that of fiction.

Lamb is of all writers the most self-confessedly bookish ("Books
think for me," he confides in his essay "On Books and Reading")
and the most at home in that retreat of the antiquarian imagination,
a library. In "Oxford in the Vacation," the Bodleian combines "the
mystery of retroversion" ("the past is everything, being nothing"),
books, and—gardens. Why should ghostliness and books, antiquity
and libraries, tend to evoke gardens in Lamb's writing? Is it so that
knowledge can regain its innocence and the language of books lose
its duplicity in the unfallen world of Eden? The library of "Oxford
in the Vacation" is a "dormitory" for dead writers, a "middle state"
where they are not dead but sleeping, waiting to be restored to that
"happy orchard" into which death has not yet entered:

> What a place to be in is an old library! It seems as though all the souls of
> all the writers, that have bequeathed their labours to these Bodleians,
> were reposing here, as in some dormitory, or middle state. I do not

[45]Jordan, *De Quincey as Critic*, pp. 448–49.

want to handle, to profane the leaves, their winding-sheets. I could as soon dislodge a shade. I seem to inhale learning, walking amid their foliage; and the odour of their old moth-scented coverings is fragrant as the first bloom of those sciential apples which grew amid the happy orchard.[46]

This kind of reading is called browsing (the apples of knowledge not picked, but enjoyed on the bough; learning inhaled, not as dust, but as paradisal fragrance). Dead knowledge is kept fresh by being embalmed in books as the Boy of Winander is embalmed in nature, a silent surrogate for the unnatural poet. Lamb's surrogate or alter ego in "The Genteel Style in Writing" is Sir William Temple, a retired statesman whose "plain natural chit-chat" and garden retreat give writing its gentility, naturalize the language of books, and restore Elian duplicity to original innocence. Though the manner is assumed, Lamb makes another's matter his own by an innocent form of plagiarism—quotation—which allows him to appropriate Temple's "sweet garden essay" (*Upon the Gardens of Epicurus; or, Of Gardening, in the Year 1685*), turning rank to simplicity and learning to what he calls "garden pedantry." "The rank of the writer is never more innocently disclosed, than where he takes for granted the compliments paid by foreigners to his fruit-trees," reports Elia, drifting into indirect chitchat:

> For the taste and perfection of what we esteem the best, he can truly say, that the French, who have eaten his peaches and grapes at Shene in no very ill year, have generally concluded that the last are as good as any they have eaten in France on this side of Fontainbleau; and the first as good as they have eaten in Gascony. Italians have agreed his white figs to be as good as any of that sort in Italy, which is the earlier kind of white fig there . . . His orange-trees too, are as large as any he saw when he was young in France . . . Of grapes he had the honour of bringing over four sorts into England, which he enumerates . . .

And so on and so on, with the gentle tedium by which the genteel style makes pride harmless and purifies international politics as gardening. Temple's is a Horatian garden ("'May I have books enough; and one year's store . . .'") designed as much to pastoralize learning as to make horticulture erudite. Invoking Temple's role in the Battle of the Books ("the controversy about the ancient and the modern

---

[46]*The Works of Charles and Mary Lamb,* ed. E. V. Lucas, 7 vols, (London: Methuen, 1903–5), II, 172, 9, 10.

learning"), Lamb looks back to a lost classical tradition; " 'Certain it is,' " he quotes Temple as saying, " 'that . . . the great heights and excellency both of poetry and music fell with the Roman learning and empire.' "[47] For Temple (fancifully or not), such learning can be found in courts and cottages; but for Lamb, it has taken refuge in libraries. A tradition that Temple could still pretend was alive in the latter part of the seventeenth century inscribes for Lamb the site of a *hortus conclusus* where, in Temple's phrase, the mind can be protected from "the violent passions and perturbations" of the world. Learning for Lamb, in other words, has passed from being ancient to being antique, becoming an aspect of Temple's antiquarian appeal. The language of books, in refusing modernity, not only mediates between past and present, but guarantees the radical alterity or strangeness of the self that generates the fiction of Elia. Lamb's version of Romantic irony is bound up with his antiquarianism. The language of (old) books makes the self both safe and other, at once protecting and estranging it; if threatened, he can "retire, impenetrable to ridicule, under the phantom cloud of Elia."[48] Calling Temple's style a "humour of plainness," he uses the same word in the context of the fictional alias who bears the letter of his name (L-ia) when he signs off in the Preface to *Last Essays* (1833): "The humour of the thing . . . was pretty well exhausted; and a two years' and a half existence has been a tolerable duration for a phantom." It is this "half existence" that Lamb goes on to define as natural. Describing the writings of his "friend" (his "familiar," one might call Elia) as "unlicked, incondite things—villainously pranked in an affected array of antique modes and phrases," he asserts that "they had not been *his*, if they had been other than such; and better it is, that a writer should be natural in a self-pleasing quaintness, than to affect a naturalness (so called) that should be strange to him." Quaintness is the natural mode of a strange identity. The duplicitous doubling of Lamb and Elia—the splitting of self into two (or more)—takes this alienation effect a stage further; as Lamb writes, defending Elia against the charge of egotism, "What he tells us, as of himself, was often true only (historically) of another":

> If it be egotism to imply and twine with his own identity the griefs and affections of another—making himself many, or reducing many unto himself—then is the skillful novelist, who all along brings in his hero, or

[47]Ibid., II, 200–202. See *Five Miscellaneous Essays by Sir William Temple*, ed. S. H. Monk (Ann Arbor: Michigan University Press, 1963), pp. 20–21, 25.
[48]Lucas, *Works of Lamb*, II, 29.

heroine, speaking of themselves, the greatest egotist of all . . . And how shall the intenser dramatist escape being faulty, who doubtless, under cover of passion uttered by another, oftentimes gives blameless vent to his most inward feelings, and expresses his own story modestly.[49]

The modesty of fiction is the mask of egotism. Dispersing his identity among many or reducing many unto himself, Elia becomes the chameleon poet—"the least of an egotist," in Hazlitt's phrase.[50] The dead humorists of the South-Sea House, like Wordsworth's "Old Humourists . . . Of texture midway betwixt life and books" (*Prelude* III, 610–13) are "persons of a curious and speculative turn of mind. Old fashioned . . . Humourists . . . Odd fishes" who form a gallery of eccentric phantoms conjured out of the past as surrogates for Elia himself; so many Uncle Tobies "summon[ed] from the dusty dead."[51]

Temple, then, is an idealized version of Elia, and the language of books (his books) doubles for the language of the self. Writing, we know, is already a kind of quotation, and "The Genteel Style in Writing" uses quotation to create a fictional space where the self can be made and unmade. For Schlegel, romantic irony is an ever-present authorial intrusion or self-conscious narrative that draws attention to its own fictionality, as Lamb's writing does by its play of endlessly dividing selves and its motley (Elia's "toga virilis," which sits uneasily on him, making him a humorist in his own right; a Yorick, or even a Hamlet). The irony that Schlegel calls "this amazement of the thinking spirit at itself, which so often dissolves in a light, gentle laugh," is also "the only entirely involuntary and nevertheless completely conscious dissimulation," making everything "at once jest and yet seriousness, artless openness, and yet deep dissimulation. . . . It contains and incites a feeling of the insoluble conflict of the absolute and the relative, of the impossibility and necessity of total communication. *It is the freest of all liberties.*"[52] Quotation as Lamb practices it here is just such a freedom, an ironic disguise that liberates and authorizes self-representation through the dissimulation of writing. More than half the essay is given over to quoting Temple, whose garden pedantry becomes an embowering

---

[49]Ibid., II, 151. The preface was originally published in 1823.
[50]Howe, *Works of Hazlitt*, V, 47.
[51]Lucas, *Works of Lamb*, II, 3, 6.
[52]Friedrich Schlegel, *Dialogue on Poetry and Literary Aphorisms*, trans. Ernst Behler and Roman Struc (Philadelphia: University of Pennsylvania Press, 1968), p. 131 (my italics).

refuge for Elia and whose final words in his own essay *Of Poetry* form the conclusion to Lamb's. Temple's defense of poetry and music against those who despise them "as toys and trifles too light for the use or entertainment of serious men"—as play—culminates in a momentary closure of the teasing gap between mask and actor, Temple and Elia: "'when all is done'", he concludes, "'human life is at the greatest and the best but like a froward child, that must be played with, and humoured a little, to keep it quiet, till it falls asleep, and then the care is over.'"[53] Here ventriloquism speaks with the voice of the ventriloquist. The genteel style puts Elia himself among the skillful beggars whose impositions he defends in his "Complaint of the Decay of Beggars in the Metropolis": "When they come with their counterfeit looks, and mumping tones, think them players. You pay your money to see a comedian feign these things, which, concerning these poor people, thou canst not certainly tell whether they are feigned or not."[54] Lamb's counterfeiting is the same; at once the freest of all liberties and the only entirely involuntary form of disguise, it makes the language of books a necessary fiction for "these things, which . . . thou canst not certainly tell whether they are feigned or not."

III

For Wordsworth in Book IV of *The Prelude,* "Incumbent o'er the surface of past time," the inability to disentangle past from present or depths from surface reflections brings a special kind of perplexity:

> As one who hangs down-bending from the side
> Of a slow-moving Boat, upon the breast
> Of a still water, solacing himself
> With such discoveries as his eye can make.
> Beneath him, in the bottom of the deeps,
> Sees many beauteous sights, weed, fishes, flowers,
> Grots, pebbles, roots of trees, and fancies more;
> Yet often is perplex'd, and cannot part
> The shadow from the substance . . .
>
> [IV,247–55]

---

[53]Lucas, *Works of Lamb,* II, 202; see *Five Miscellaneous Essays by Sir William Temple,* p. 203.
[54]Lucas, *Works of Lamb,* II, 120.

Though the discoveries are "solacing," the office "pleasant," there is also the danger of tumbling in and drowning "in the bottom of the deeps," as Lycidas visits "the bottom of the monstrous world" (l. 158). The submerged image of watery dissolution makes this idly self-reflexive activity more edgy than it looks. The pleasant interfusion of past and present is naturalized by Wordsworth's simile, with its written-in parting of shadow from substance; and if the poet seems to risk total immersion it is because his imagery itself has been too successful in blurring boundaries ("cannot part / The shadow from the substance" after all). Put another way, although Romantic autobiographers characteristically desire to reintegrate past and present selves—or, like Wordsworth, to replace self-mirroring with a natural fusion of image and reflection—the closing of the gap would obliterate autobiography altogether. Attempting to overbridge, not "The froward chaos of futurity" (V:372), but the "Two consciousnesses" of past and present ("conscious of myself / And of some other Being' [II, 32–33], writing simultaneously brings that "other Being" into alien half-existence and makes the split manageable. Parting the shadow from the substance, writing thus becomes the language of temporality, a means of structuring the self in time. Inscribing both temporal alterity and an origin that is always lost, it is at once a form of archaeology and a means of ordering the past. What is salvaged is also "managed" so that the burden of the past can neither swamp the present nor be swamped by it.

De Quincey's famous image of a palimpsest in *Suspiria de Profundis*—the "membrane or roll cleaned of its manuscript by reiterated successions"—purports to be a multilayer inscription in which the successive writings of the past are simultaneously present and eternally retrievable. But the palimpsest is also an image of management, controlling the unruly discontinuities of past experiences as it creates them, and (in theory at least) preventing a perplexed interweaving of texts, since only one can be read at a time. Though De Quincey becomes facetiously digressive about the possibilities of the multilayer book (making sense for one age, nonsense for the next, reread by the one after), he is really preoccupied by the mythic unattainability of origins: "We have backed upon each phoenix in the long *regressus* and forced him to expose his ancestral phoenix, sleeping in the ashes below his own ashes." The infinite regression forces archaeology beyond history into myth and opens up an apocalyptic retrospect. A work not so much of exorcism as of conjuration, it unleashes the demonic hubbub of incoherence and bacchic laughter stored in the human brain:

237

The image, the memorial, the record which for me is derived from a palimpsest . . . is but too repellent of laughter; or, even if laughter *had* been possible, it would have been such laughter as oftentimes is thrown off from the fields of ocean,* laughter that hides, or that seems to evade mustering tumult; foam bells that weave garlands of phospheric radiance for one moment round the eddies of gleaming abysses; mimicries of earth-born flowers that for the eye raise phantoms of gaiety, as oftentimes for the ear they raise the echoes of fugitive laughter, mixing with the ravings and choir voices of an angry sea.[55]

The image is only sublimely laughable, and the laughter that of the mathematical sublime invoked by De Quincey's footnote to "the fields of ocean"—the overwhelming plurality of Aeschylus's "multitudinous laughter of the ocean billows." The mockery of pandemonium installs destructiveness in the depths of the imagination, like the tumult of "Kubla Khan," with its ancient voices prophesying war. For Freud, the instinctual source is "a chaos, a cauldron, full of seething excitations."[56] If id were to swamp ego, if writings were to be overwhelmed by sound waves—the *"fluctus decumanus* of rhetoric"—the tumultuous flood would have the apocalyptic force of the ocean in Wordsworth's dream of the Arab Quixote from Book V ("Books") of *The Prelude*. This is surely the subliminal link between the image of the palimpsest and the episode of the drowning woman (resurrected from *Confessions of an English Opium Eater*) which De Quincey goes on to introduce—another version of simultaneity, in which the past events of the drowning woman's life are flashed before her eyes "as in a mirror," "arraying themselves not as a succession but as parts of a coexistence." The woman of *Suspiria de Profundis* drowns, in effect, in her own depths. For the mind of each individual, De Quincey reminds us (like Freud with his image of the magic writing pad) "there is no such thing as *forgetting*."[57] Like consciousness, the written page (the film of the past?) interposes its surface as a barrier between the present and total recall. The palimpsest, then, "contains" the past in a double sense.

Writing contains: deciphering recovers. The two-way traffic is De Quincey's version of the man hanging over the side of his boat, another attempt at unperplexing the relation between experience

---

[55]Ward, *De Quincey*, pp. 168–69.

[56]*The Standard Edition of the Psychological Works of Sigmund Freud*, trans. James Strachey et al., ed. James Strachey, 24 vols. (London, 1953–74), XXII, 73.

[57]Ward, *De Quincey*, pp. 91, 170; cf. *Works of Sigmund Freud*, V, 621: "In the unconscious nothing can be brought to an end, nothing is past or forgotten."

and reflection. The act of deciphering establishes the gap between consciousness and being ("some other Being") across which meaning is generated. This temporal time lag is the subject of one of De Quincey's most crucial footnotes, inserted in his text after the words "I felt" in an attempt to check an otherwise engulfing visionary experience—his childhood vision of the dying infants borne up to heaven amid the blaze of stained-glass windows and the blare of organs. The fantasy of overcoming death's "dreadful chasm of separation" brings with it a moment when De Quincey becomes at once apocalyptic victim and apocalyptic agent, and when his triumph over separation threatens to turn the dreamer into the dream itself, the visionary into his vision, as feeling annihilates the self: "sometimes under the transfigurations of music I felt* of grief itself as a fiery chariot for mounting victoriously above the causes of grief." This vertiginous merging is steadied by De Quincey's elaborate secondary revision or rereading of his dream text:

> "*I felt*". The reader must not forget, in reading this and other passages, . that though a child's feelings are spoken of, it is not the child who speaks. *I* decipher what the child only felt in cipher . . . I . . . did not, as a child, *consciously* read in my own deep feelings these ideas. No, not at all; nor was it possible for a child to do so. I, the child, had the feelings; I, the man, decipher them. In the child lay the handwriting mysterious to *him,* in me the interpretation and the comment.[58]

It is as if Wordsworth had broken off from a spot of time to footnote the existence of two consciousnesses. "Forgetting" ("The reader must not forget"), or self loss, is of course just what De Quincey's dream visions aim to induce, as the spots of time aim to obliterate the gulf between the two consciousnesses; yet remembering must be invoked to ward off possession by the otherness of dream and by the past itself. Though De Quincey deeply desires to cross the "chasm of separation," to do so would be to enter the boundless eternity inhabited by the dead infants of his vision. The child is written: the adult deciphers; the "other Being" is the text: "I" supply the interpretation and the comment (but am always already written). Meaning resides "anteriorly," one might say with De Quincey's landlady, in the regressive movement of dreams and the unconscious. If Freudianism involves an archaeology of the unconscious, an uncovering of

---

[58]Ward, *De Quincey,* pp. 138–39. For another account of De Quincey as autobiographer, see S. J. Spector, "Thomas De Quincey: Self-effacing Autobiographer," *Studies in Romanticism* 18 (1979): 501–20.

mythic regressions and a deciphering of the ever-prior,[59] so too does writing—a system in which previous layers of text shape the present with their buried structures, as the landlady's "anteriorly" conceals De Quincey's past within it like a time bomb.

For Hazlitt, the attempt to derive the meaning of the present from the writing of the past spells Legitimacy. Burke had founded constitutional rights on documents—wills that transmit inheritance from one generation to the next: "From Magna Charta to the Declaration of Right, it has been the uniform policy of our constitution to claim and assert our liberties, as an *entailed inheritance* derived to us from our forefathers, and to be transmitted to our posterity."[60] Tom Paine contends the opposite in *The Rights of Man* (1791): "I am contending for the rights of the *living*, and against their being willed away, and controlled and contracted for, by the manuscript assumed authority of the dead; and Mr. Burke is contending for the authority of the dead over the rights and freedom of the living."[61] What Burke calls "monumental inscriptions"—"records, evidences, and titles"—guarantee legality on the authority of the past.[62] But for Paine, this is the dead hand ruling over the living; more Casaubon's will than a Bill of Rights. And while Burke's "manuscript-assumed authority of the dead" meant the status quo, books and writing could be for Hazlitt—as Paine's *Rights of Man* had demonstrated—a new form of popular power; a force for liberty rather than Legitimacy. In "The Influence of Books on the Progress of Manners" (1828), Hazlitt defines "public opinion" as "the atmosphere of liberal sentiment and equitable conclusions" brought about by books. "The reading public," in his view, is "a very rational animal, compared with a feudal lord and his horde of vassals." Perhaps because the essay was unsigned, Hazlitt opens the offensive with more than usual belligerence: "Books govern the world better than kings or priests. There have always been plenty of the latter with full and undisputed powers, of which they have made as bad a use as possible. It is only of late that books and public opinion have borne much sway . . ." Books are the supreme example of a democratically con-

---

[59]See Paul Ricoeur, *Freud and Philosophy*, trans. Denis Savage (New Haven: Yale University Press, 1970), pp. 439–40. See also Jean-Michel Rey, "Freud's Writing on Writing," *Yale French Studies* 50 (1974):301–28.

[60]*The Works of Edmund Burke*, II, 306. For Burke's use of the family as a central symbol, see J. T. Boulton, *The Language of Politics in the Age of Wilkes and Burke* (London: Routledge & Kegan Paul, 1963) pp. 112–14.

[61]*The Life and Major Writings of Thomas Paine*, ed. P. S. Foner (New York: Citadel Press, 1945) p. 252.

[62]*Works of Edmund Burke*, II, 308.

stituted government, one that modern times alone have made possible; to them are ascribed the curbing of arbitrary power and the transmuting of might to right, with Hazlitt citing as evidence "the way in which books have already battered down so many strongholds of prejudice and power."[63] Neither anarchy nor tyranny, he claims, can exist after the invention of printing. This utopian fantasy is inspired not simply by the wish to make the language of books the enemy of Legitimacy, instead of the means of inscribing ancient authority; nor by the early-nineteenth-century increase in literacy which made it genuinely possible to see books as at once the agents of democratic revolution and the *vox populi*. What lies behind Hazlitt's optimism is a dream of revolutionizing the status of the political writer himself—of turning his writing into direct action.

"On the Prose Style of Poets," though ostensibly a leveling attempt to reconstitute the republic of letters on the basis of prose, had given pride of place to the poet of prose writers ("Burke's eloquence was that of the poet . . . The power which governed Burke's mind was his Imagination")[64]—a personification of the antileveling principle that Hazlitt's essay on *Coriolanus* identifies as that of poetry itself: "The language of poetry naturally falls in with the language of power. . . . The principle of poetry is a very anti-levelling principle."[65] Hazlitt's popularist *jeu d'esprit*, "The Fight" (1822), celebrates a different kind of power in a pugilistic slanging match designed to democratize prose by aligning it punningly with "the FANCY" rather than the imagination ("Truly, the FANCY are not men of imagination").[66] Hazlitt declares himself as a ringside supporter and "lover of the FANCY," that is, prizefighting—the republican symbol in a sporting sketch whose racy colloquialism turns boxing into heroic knockabout, while identifying Hazlitt himself as a lover not just of the FANCY but of fancy's language, slang. Virginia Woolf writes of Hazlitt: "There is always something divided and discordant even in his finest essays, as if two minds were at work who never succeed save for a few moments in making a match of it."[67] "Making a match of it" is just what Hazlitt's popular heroes manage to do—externalizing conflict and containing it within the ring or the fives court (as Lamb confines violence to the card table in "Mrs. Battle's Opinions

[63]Howe, *Works of Hazlitt*, XVII, 326, 321, 325.
[64]Ibid., VII, 302–3 (but cf. VII, 312–13, for Hazlitt's qualification).
[65]Ibid., IV, 214.
[66]Ibid., XVII, 80.
[67]*Collected Essays of Virginia Woolf*, ed. Leonard Woolf, 4 vols. (London: Hogarth Press, 1966–7), I, 158–59.

on Whist"). Hence his envy of the apparently effortless skill of the Indian jugglers and the athleticism of the ace fives player, Cavanagh, whose sporting obituary concludes the essay. "The Indian Jugglers" (1821) is a dazzling tour de force that sets out to beat the jugglers at their own trade, and whose sustained rhetorical metaphor makes writing its displaced subject. Lamenting his own botched efforts, Hazlitt contrasts the effect of seeing the jugglers with "hearing a speech in Parliament, drawled or stammered out by the Honourable Member or the Noble Lord," while turning Cavanagh himself into the opposition writer of the sporting world: "Cobbett and Junius together would have made a Cavanagh." A man of the present as well as the people ("the noisy shout of the ring happily stood him in stead of the unheard voice of posterity"), Cavanagh is said to do more good and make less noise than those who make speeches and answer them. He is the Burke of players, stripped of conservatism and revised as a popular orator whose blows are no longer metaphorical: "As it was said of a great orator that he never was at a loss for a word, and for the properest word, so Cavanagh always could tell the degree of force necessary to be given to a ball, and the precise direction in which it should be sent."[68] Hazlitt has made him the popular winner in the match "People *vs.* Parliament," shifting the arena of power to the fives court and ruling Legitimacy unsporting. But perhaps there is more yet. In laying Cavanagh to rest, Hazlitt kills off the man of action (as Wordsworth embalms the Winander Boy) so that the writer can take his place. If—as Auden has it—poetry makes nothing happen, still, every political writer's most cherished dream is that he may by his writing, so to speak, take the law into his own hands.

Hazlitt attempts to bring writing into the present: Lamb defends against the present by consigning writing to the past. The Elian version of Romantic irony involves not simply disguise, but a splitting of self that simultaneously opens a gap between past and present. In this double time scheme, one dimension is paradoxically lacking.[69] Writing for Lamb is only half Janus-faced ("what half Januses are we, that cannot look forward with the same idolatry with which we for ever revert!"), and the Elian "mental twist" of retrospection prevents the future from having any reality: "The mighty

[68]Howe, *Works of Hazlitt*, VIII, 78, 87, 89.

[69]See Paul de Man, "The Rhetoric of Temporality," in *Interpretation: Theory and Practice*, ed. Singleton, pp. 194–96, for Baudelaire's version of this "dédoublement" or "ironic, twofold self . . . able to come into being only at the expense of an empirical self."

future is as nothing, being every thing! the past is every thing, being nothing!"[70] In "New Year's Eve," Lamb demands rhetorically whether "all good things, even *irony itself*," go out with life ("Can a ghost laugh, or shake his gaunt sides, when you are pleasant with him?"). Not so; for it is death that brings irony into being, as a doubled and affectionate relation to oneself: "Skipping over the intervention of forty years, a man may have leave to love himself," he asserts, writing off his present identity as "this stupid changeling of five-and-forty" in order to make room for "the child Elia—that 'other me,' there, in the back-ground."[71] This is the form of irony that Carlyle calls "the playful teasing fondness of a mother to her child,"[72] the love of the creator for his creation—playful, protective, and characterized by permanent regret, for the defense of irony can be maintained only at the price of life, making the empirical self either an aging changeling or a gaunt-sided ghost. Lamb concludes the Preface to *Last Essays*, his official epitaph on Elia, by claiming that "the key" to his writing lies in "the impressions of infancy." A key to unlock it, or a thread by which it, and Elia too, can be unraveled as a fiction? The same preface mentions "that dangerous figure—irony." For Paul de Man, irony is a dangerous figure because it ushers in what Baudelaire calls "*vertige de l'hyperbole*"; as de Man puts it, "The moment the innocence or authenticity of our sense of being in the world is put into question, a far from harmless process gets under way. It may start as a casual bit of play with a stray loose end of the fabric, but before long the entire texture of the self is unravelled and comes apart."[73] It comes apart, in other words, as writing. This vertiginous unraveling of the text is the far from harmless process that Schlegel initiates in his essay "On Incomprehensibility," in which he envisages becoming entangled in uncontrollably proliferating ironies, his only escape "an irony that might be able to swallow up all these big and little ironies and leave no trace of them at all."[74] Lamb's most poignant essay of lost childhood, "Dream-Children; A Reverie" (1822), is just such an entanglement

---

[70]Lucas, *Works of Lamb*, II, 9.

[71]Ibid., II, 28–30.

[72]Thomas Carlyle, *Critical and Miscellaneous Essays*, 5 vols. (London: Chapman and Hall, 1905), I, 16.

[73]De Man, "Rhetoric of Temporality," p. 197.

[74]*Friedrich Schlegel's "Lucinde" and the Fragments*, trans. Peter Firchow (Minneapolis: University of Minnesota Press, 1971) p. 267; see de Man, "Rhetoric of Temporality," pp. 202–3, and cf. Ehrmann, "Death of Literature," p. 46: "We make and unmake ourselves at one and the same time . . . what is 'made' at one end is unmade at the other—just like a loop of film."

and just such an undoing—a "reverie" into which the writer himself finally vanishes, and in which what is mourned is as much the fragility of fiction as the evanescence of childhood.

If loss gives "Dream-Children" its pathos, it is the ephemerality of representation that makes it ghostly—makes it, in fact, central to Lamb's marginal dream play of spectral selves. Objecting to the 1800 subtitle of Coleridge's *Ancient Mariner* as *A Poet's Reverie*, Lamb told Wordsworth: "It is as bad as Bottom the Weaver's declaration that he is not a Lion but only the scenical representation of a Lion. What new idea is gained by this Title, but one subversive of all credit . . . of its truth?'[75] His own subtitle subverts truth to fiction from the outset. "Narrative teases me," Elia elsewhere confesses, and "Dream-Children" narrates a double story ("Children love to listen to stories about their elders when they were children"). What another essay calls "two stories, with double Time" begins by invoking a prior tale of pathos, the ballad of the Children in the Wood which Wordsworth's 1800 Preface to *Lyrical Ballads* (in the best tradition of eighteenth-century ballad criticism) had singled out for its enduring simplicity. In Lamb's teasing tale—already at several removes from its naive original—the pathetic ballad is reinscribed in the "long *regressus*" (De Quincey's phrase) or fictional perspective of narrative itself. Elia's imaginary listeners are represented as gathered round him to hear about their great-grandmother, who had lived in the great house "which had been the scene . . . of the tragic incidents which they had lately become familiar with from the ballad of the Children in the Wood." Lamb hints delicately at their great-grandmother's housekeeper status by writing that she had lived there "*in a manner as if* it had been her own" (my italics); and everything in "Dream-Children" is "in a manner as if"—even the story of the Children in the Wood is carved on the old wooden chimneypiece, until the carving is replaced by unstoried marble. Like the motif of fictional obliteration, this double inscription (the Children in the Wood: children in wood) is repeated throughout the telling of Lamb's story, placing it in a hinterland between the real and the imagined; the "apparition of two infants" haunting the old house, for instance, doubles with Elia's listeners, who in turn put back a bunch of grapes uneaten when they hear of his childhood restraint in the old garden "the nectarines and peaches hung upon the walls, without my ever offering to pluck them, because they were forbid-

[75]*The Letters of Charles and Mary Lamb*, ed. E. V. Lucas, 3 vols. (London: J. M. Dent and Methuen, 1935), I, 240.

den fruit, unless now and then")—"willing" (we are told) "to relinquish them for the present as irrelevant." The "irrelevance" of the present ushers in the motif of lack in the figure of John L., who is kind to the lame-footed Elia and later becomes lame himself. This crippled alter ego, haunting Elia as the two dead children haunt the fictional house, initiates the unraveling process that finally undoes the entire dream text: "When he died, though he had not been dead an hour, it seemed as if he had died a great while ago, such a distance there is betwixt life and death." The final movement of "Dream-Children" calls up the children's "pretty dead mother" only to collapse reverie into "nothing; less than nothing"; or nothing but text:

> . . . suddenly, turning to Alice, the soul of the first Alice looked out at her eyes with such a reality of re-presentment, that I became in doubt which of them stood there before me, or whose that bright hair was; and while I stood gazing, both the children gradually grew fainter to my view, receding, and still receding till nothing at last but two mournful features were seen in the uttermost distance, which, without speech, strangely impressed upon me the effects of speech; "We are not of Alice, nor of thee, nor are we children at all . . . We are nothing; less than nothing; and dreams.[76]

This is surely the most uncanny moment in all Lamb's writing, as well as the most poignant—the moment when Elia's imaginary world, "receding, and still receding" like a Cheshire cat into the realm of the phantasmal, is swallowed up by his own irony; when the "reality of re-presentment" turns out to be that of a dream.

"Dream-Children" tells us, if we did not know already, that writing is "nothing; less than nothing, and dreams"—a marginal or liminal phenomenon that has no existence beyond the printed page, but one that "without speech, strangely impresse[s] . . . the effects of speech." The spectral effect lies in the very "reality of re-presentment," as the ghostliness of printing ("strangely impressed") lies in the effect of speech—what Wordsworth, in *The Prelude*, calls "the mind's / Internal echo of the imperfect sound" (I, 65). Here, even the writing self is remorselessly discomposed by the spectrality of signs: "Immediately awakening, I found myself quietly seated in my bachelor armchair, where I had fallen asleep . . . but John L. (or James Elia) was gone for ever." Lamb's ironic self-dissolution pre-

[76]Lucas, *Works of Lamb*, II, 75, 226, 100–103.

vents "Dream-Children" from toppling into simple pathos, while opening up dizzying vistas of nonbeing. His vertiginous inversion of creation is the nightmare side of reverie, and only writing as precariously loitering on the edge of ideas and reality as Lamb's could admit both to the same page. Though few Romantic writers go so near the edge as Lamb, his brinkmanship offers a paradigmatic view of what it is that Nature, or music, or direct action, attempts to cover over when Romantic prose—Wordsworth's De Quincey's, or Hazlitt's—confronts the language of books head on. And like Wordsworth's attempt to part the shadow from the substance, De Quincey's deciphering of the palimpsest, or Hazlitt's attempt to hone language to a cutting edge on the substance of things, Lamb's ironic knitting and unknitting of the texture of being reminds us that in each case the "other Being" ("I, the child," the writer as pugilist, or "that 'other me'") is an alienation effect brought into half-existence by the language of books—immune to the present or impotent to alter it because language itself is half Janus-faced or less than nothing. Casting about for an epic subject at the start of *The Prelude,* Wordsworth recoils disheartened from the histories of Britain, myth, Liberty, heroism, or the everyday left unsung by previous epic poets; recoils, in effect, from the history of past writing and from the writing of the past:

> The whole Fabric seems to lack
> Foundation, and, withal, appears throughout
> Shadowy and unsubstantial.
> [I,226–28]

It is not so much the burden of the past that inhibits him as this glimpse of the insubstantiality inherent in all writing—in autobiography as well as epic. The remaining thirteen books of *The Prelude* are an attempt to clothe transparency and provide foundations for fabric that cannot be gainsaid, the history of his own mind. Romantic prose writers remind us what "The Growth of a Poet's Mind" owes to the art of managing books; they tell the one story Wordsworth could not afford to tell at any price—that the language of books can only be the history of itself.

9 /

Of Lips Divine and Calm: Swinburne and the Language of Shelleyan Love

LESLIE BRISMAN

As the pure moon dips into shadow, thou
Camest among us clothed with power and love,
Wearing the kiss of lips divine and calm
Upon the illumined patience of thy brow.
—Algernon Charles Swinburne, "Shelley"

In a peevish footnote to *Modern Painters*, Ruskin disdains to compare "the sickly dreaming of Shelley over clouds and waves, with the magnificent grasp of men and things we find in Scott."[1] Since Ruskin, critical taste has somewhat changed, and most of us would probably rather read Shelley, with his vaunting attempts of soul to clasp the pendulous earth, than Scott, with his "magnificent grasp of men and things." Though our renewed interest in the non-thing-oriented language of Romantic poetry inclines us to value what Ruskin disparaged, his descriptive categories remain useful. They help direct our attention to what Shelley and such Shelleyan poets as Swinburne aimed to do.

A description of men or things as such, a description that does not impel us to read physical attributes as signs of emotion or mind, Ruskin calls *Fancy*. He quotes lines from Suckling: "Her lips were red and one was thin, / Compared with that was next her chin." Ruskin dismisses these lines as "all outside; no expression yet, no mind."[2] Distinct from fancy is imagination, divisible into imagina-

[1] *The Works of John Ruskin*, ed. E. T. Cook and Alexander Wedderburn, 39 vols. (London: George Allen, 1903), vol. 4 (*Modern Painters*, vol. 2), p. 297n. All Ruskin quotations are from this volume.

[2] Ibid., p. 254. The quotations from *Hamlet* and *Prometheus Unbound* follow immediately.

tion contemplative and penetrative. (The third category, imagination associative, is closest to fancy and least concerns us here.) Imagination penetrative yields images that reveal a poet's magnificent grasp of men and things. Ruskin cites *Hamlet:* "Here hung those lips that I have kissed, I know not how oft. Where be your gibes now, your gambols, your songs, your flashes of merriment that were wont to set the table on a roar?" As Hamlet enumerates gibes, songs, and flashes of merriment, he moves from the lips to Yorick himself and the thought of the "things of man" (Hopkins' phrase) that synecdochally represent a man's loving and lovable presence. Perhaps he also moves from Yorick as a thing of man—the king's jester—to the man himself, the king his father. In homage to the depth of human feeling caught in that synecdochal or metonymic leap of the imagination, Ruskin accords these lines his highest praise: "There is the essence of lip, and the full power of the imagination."

For Ruskin, the quotation from *Hamlet* represents imagination penetrative, imagination that penetrates beneath the externals or "outsides" to the heart of the image—or rather the heart of man, for it is not the essence of lips but the essence of Yorick, of affection, of life, that Hamlet apprehends. Though in dismissing Suckling's image as having "no expression yet, no mind" Ruskin does not specifically associate expression with imagination penetrative and mind with imagination contemplative, the implication throughout is that the penetrative imagination takes the things of man and nature as signs ("expressions") of emotion. Ruskin praises Shakespeare's Perdita for going into "the very inmost soul of every flower,"[3] but he means that she makes flowers into flowers of soul, emblems of human meaning and human feeling.

Ruskin has more difficulty defining imagination contemplative, though he is fairly certain who has it, and most certain about his moral mission to subordinate this faculty. In contrast to Scott's "healthy and truthful feeling," for example, "Shelley is peculiarly distinguished by the faculty of Contemplative imagination."[4] Ruskin's first example of imagination contemplative comes from Shelley, and it is given in the chapter on imagination penetrative, right before—and as a foil to—the lines from *Hamlet:*

> Lamp of life, thy lips are burning
> Through the veil that seems to hide them,
> As the radiant lines of morning
> Through thin clouds ere they divide them.

[3]Ibid., pp. 255–56.
[4]Ibid., p. 297n.

Ruskin briefly gives rein to admiration, and then tightens his control: "There dawns the entire soul in that morning; yet we may stop if we choose at the image still external, at the crimson clouds. The imagination is contemplative rather than penetrative." It is not hard to stop with "the image still external" if we read the Shelley lines as Ruskin gives them. But we might be more inclined to move back from the dawn and lineaments of Asia to love and the lineaments of human desire if we remember Shelley's lines as Shelley gave them:

> Child of Light! thy limbs are burning
>   Through the vest which seems to hide them
> As the radiant lines of morning
>   Through the clouds ere they divide them,
> And this atmosphere divinest
>   Shrouds thee wheresoe'er thou shinest.

(As such, the lines are closer to the image from Dante that Ruskin cites as a supreme example of imagination penetrative.)[5] In one sense what is accomplished by Ruskin—or by a combination of bad typesetting and bad memory—is simply an apocalyptic foreshortening of the magnificent Shelley lyric.[6] Shelley's poem begins,

> Life of Life! thy lips enkindle
>   With their love the breath between them.

Stanza 2 moves from lips and smiles—tropes for human emotion—to the limbs of Asia, whose sensual identity is sublimated into the sky and the sunset when her limbs, burning through the vest that seems to hide them, are compared to the red clouds of sunrise. The song heralds the dawn of a new day, a new era of love, and in obeissance to the coming glory, the literal figure of Asia kneels and becomes a rhetorical figure; she fades into the sunrise that announces and symbolizes the actualization of her latent content, her symbolic meaning. In this triumph of love, like that of God's Son in Milton, the individual person is lost in the "indefinite abstraction" of his or her coming.[7] By the fourth stanza (the opening phrase of which

---

[5]Ibid., p. 250.

[6]The 1839 edition does read "lips" for "limbs" (as noted by Ruskin's editors) but this is an obvious misprint. For the text of *Prometheus Unbound* I use that of Shelley's best textual editors (*Shelley's Poetry and Prose,* ed. Donald H. Reiman and Sharon B. Powers [New York: Norton, 1977]).

[7]Wordsworth discusses two processes by which the imagination *creates:* "consolidating numbers into unity, and dissolving and separating unity into number,—alternations proceeding from, and governed by, a sublime consciousness of the soul in her own mighty and almost divine powers." He goes on to cite the passage in *Paradise Lost* describing the Son "going forth to expel from heaven the rebellious angels,

Ruskin assimilated into his quotation) Asia has become all essence, the light of life and love of the world:

> Lamp of Earth! where'er thou movest
> Its dim shapes are clad with brightness.

Given the triumphal progress of the four stanzas, we should not "stop if we choose at the image still external, at the crimson clouds." What is missing from Ruskin's quotation is precisely the gradual process of abstracting Asia *into* the "lamp of the Earth." Yet it may still make sense to distinguish an abstracted essence from a "penetrated" or synecdochally compacted one. Asia's lips, with which the song opens, become the empowering sign of love (the sign that calls into being its significance), while the absent lips of Yorick occasion an intense gleam or flash of memory that burns itself out, leaving us with a renewed sense of loss. In Shelley, lips enkindle not only in that they warm to love but in that the thought of love burns through nature, dissolving the world of appearances for the thought of love. Shelleyan language is thus apocalyptic where Shakespeare's is profoundly, and characteristically, elegiac. In Shakespeare language offers a consolation for rather than a threat of death. The thoughts of Yorick, of love, of Presence that burningly come to Hamlet all at once make the world of appearances more rather than less real. The smell of Yorick's skull, the conversation of Horatio, the funeral of Ophelia—these things, in all their multiplicity (let alone the multiplicity of the occasions for mourning, which also follow "hard upon" one another)—guard against death the way Ruskin's phrase "the essence of lip" guards against the overwhelming abstraction, the essence of loss. In Shelley, on the other hand, a multiplicity of things and images gives way before the coming of the thought of love, and the way all things give way is a tribute to, and proof of, the indomitableness of mind in a world of mutability.[8]

> 'Attended by ten thousand thousand Saints
> He onward came: far off his coming shone,'—

the retinue of Saints, and the Person of the Messiah himself, lost almost and merged in the splendour of that indefinite abstraction 'His coming!'" (Preface of 1815, in *The Prose Works of William Wordsworth*, ed. W. J. B. Owen and Jane Worthington Smyser, 3 vols. [Oxford: Clarendon Press, 1974], III, 33–34).

[8] Shakespeare's is thus a metonymic, Shelley's a metaphoric sublime; where Shakespeare counters the thought of death by suggesting the world of things contiguous with, not out of touch with, death, Shelley restitutes us for the loss we feel (in his own power of repeated abstraction from things) through the power of the overwhelming metaphor of Asia as love.

But it is to Ruskin's terms that I wish to return, and I want to use them to define two limits to the power of poetic language. Imagination contemplative or regardant gives a poet an abstracted stance from which to survey the world of things. Imagination penetrative is said to pierce the world of appearances to get to the heart of the matter. As we have seen, however, Ruskin means by imagination penetrative the faculty for penetrating not the heart of matter (matter has no heart) but the heart of man. Imagination penetrative, the highest faculty according to Ruskin, discovers the world of human meaning, of human feeling, beneath the world of signs. The critic who applauded Hamlet's lines about Yorick's lips would have been equally struck by Wallace Stevens' lines

> Farewell to an idea . . . The mother's face,
> The purpose of the poem, fills the room.

From the perspective of imagination penetrative, poetic language is a veil that half conceals and half reveals the mother's face or the face of Yorick—symbolic as they both are of the most human wish, the wish for perfect presence. Hamlet cannot make Yorick—or his father, or the idealized version of his mother, or *any* version of Ophelia—come back to life; Yorick in Shakespeare's play and the mother in Stevens' *Auroras of Autumn* are the forms of love, felicities from which we are absented, and in the absence of which we make poetry.[9]

Where imagination penetrative penetrates to the heart of man, imagination contemplative contemplates with the eye of God. This alternative mode of transcendence also involves a translation of the material world of signs into a world of significances, but here significance seems that which lies forever far away, like the Lacanian realm of the symbolic with its distance from and reputed priority over the realm of the imaginary and its mother images. If the mother in *Auroras of Autumn* is Stevens' figure of imagination penetrative, the father is the figure of imagination contemplative:

[9]Jacques Lacan focuses on the graveyard scene and the absence of the object of desire (the human presence Ophelia as *O phallos* and the grave itself as a vacancy symbolizing the absence of Hamlet senior and the image of Gertrude as Hamlet would know her). See "Desire and the Interpretation of Desire in *Hamlet*," in *Literature and Psychoanalysis*, ed. Shoshana Felman. Lacan's privileging of the symbolic over the imaginary could lead him to argue, through a different set of terms, for the equivalent of imagination contemplative rather than penetrative. But on all counts this essay is a particular disappointment, and the only "lack" it illuminates is its own insufficiency.

He measures the velocities of change.
He leaps from heaven to heaven more rapidly
Than bad angels leap from heaven to hell in flames.
But now he sits in quiet and green-a-day.

In an act of imagination contemplative, the scholar of one candle opens the door of his house on flames and sees "an arctic effulgence flaring on the frame / Of everything he is."

But I must cut short that quotation and this excursis into Stevens because "the frame / Of everything he is" (as opposed to the frame of everything that is) returns us to the human heart and deconstructs the antithesis between heaven and heart on which Ruskin's thought is based. The rest of Stevens' line makes clear that though the sight as such is the auroras, the significance of the sight is the internal drama of the sublime. The scholar opens the door on flames "and he feels afraid." The two powers of poetic language— the power to lift the soul above this pendent earth and the power to penetrate the veil of things into the human soul—are barely, and perhaps only momentarily, separable. I suspect that it was the desire to avoid this recognition that made Ruskin conflate the stanzas of Shelley's lyric. Shelley leaps from heart to heaven, and in fact believes in no heaven or platonic realm of idealized love except the human heart. But Ruskin is uncomfortable with the urgency of the Shelleyan impulse toward allegory—the way individual images of love or characters in love disappear before the thought of love. The whole purpose of Ruskin's discussion of imagination is to rescue the image from becoming a symbol, and this struggle gains momentum when it marches under the banner of corporeality—as though Ruskin were redeeming the forms of love from the ruinous shadow of Love itself. To wage this war, Ruskin does best to forget that Shelley wrote:

> Life of Life! thy lips enkindle
>   With their love the breath between them
> And thy smiles before they dwindle
>   Make the cold air fire.

Ruskin's Shelley, like his Satan, has to have the external trappings of fire without the heart-flame. Though he understands that in Shelley's lines (as he gives them) "there dawns the entire soul in that morning," Asia remains, for him, a soul as cold and passionate as the dawn. She is the abstraction of love rather than an instance of love,

as Yorick is. Ironically, Asia is a character in *Prometheus Unbound* and
Yorick just a memory in *Hamlet,* but Asia is never given local habita-
tion, never (in language) from incorporeal to corporeal turned.
Though Shelley's Asia is alive and Shakespeare's Yorick is dead,
Yorick emerges as a living soul whereas Asia is, in Ruskin's phrase,
"deprived of material and bodily shape." As Ruskin says about
Milton's Satan, described by the simile "and like a comet burned,"
"the bodily shape of the angel is destroyed, the inflaming of the
formless spirit is alone regarded."[10] Asia, with Satan, traces a comet's path as discerned by the eye of God—or the eye of man could
man imagine himself standing in heaven on God's side. But the
comet's fire is not that of the human heart. Asia moves back to
"realms where the air we breathe is love." Like Ruskin, Satan finds
that element too thin. He cannot feed on thoughts of the radiance of
the mother's face—or Christ's.

Swinburne has been read—when he has been read at all—as committed to the Shelleyan imagination contemplative. His power has
been understood to be that of representing not the particularized
passion of the human heart but what Ruskin, describing Satan, calls
the "inflaming of the formless spirit." As a supreme elegist Swinburne penetrates to—and beyond—the human heart in grief; but
his affinities are less with Shakespeare than with the Shelley of *Alastor* and *Prometheus*—of *Epipsychidion* and *Adonais* preeminently.
Like Shelley he sacrifices identity on the cross of love, and like Shelley's Emily or Adonais or Asia or nameless poet in *Alastor,* Swinburne's characters are borne darkly, fearfully afar. For Swinburne
as for Shelley, individual identities are, no less than material bodies,
"things of man" of which poetry is forever letting go.

I choose *Anactoria* as a paradigmatic text precisely because it purports to be the outpouring of Sappho's all too human and particular
passion. What would Ruskin, the champion of the imagination penetrative, do with the following lines and lips?

> I would my love could kill thee; I am satiated
> With seeing thee live, and fain would have thee dead.
> I would earth had thy body as fruit to eat,
> And no mouth but some serpent's found thee sweet.
> I would find grievous ways to have thee slain,
> Intensive device, and superflux of pain;

---

[10]*Works of Ruskin,* IV, 291.

LESLIE BRISMAN

> Vex thee with amorous agonies, and shake
> Life at thy lips, and leave it there to ache;
> Strain out thy soul with pangs too soft to kill,
> Intolerable interludes, and infinite ill;
> Relapse and relucation of the breath,
> Dumb tunes and shuddering semitones of death.
>
> [ll. 23–34]

Is there anything of imagination penetrative in this exquisite piece of lesbian sadism? Does the reversal into aggression suggest a particularity or depth of human passion previously unspoken in English poetry? Does the *pathos* of Sappho inform these lines, or do we have here simply a piece of technical virtuosity? It may be impossible to specify the physical and metaphysical components of desire behind "shake / Life at thy lips, and leave it there to ache." But whether we are meant to think primarily of something like the life of the Word, burning coallike at the mouth of the prophet Isaiah, or some more corporeal heat at the other lips of Anactoria, life is being shaken from outside, from a source of inspiration or desire external to the self. We do not need to formulate a psychosexual thesis about homosexual love as a less profound rumbling of the human heart; the sheer multiplication of terms seems to satisfy Ruskin's sense of the unimaginative writer who has "never pierced to the heart." Think of Swinburne's *collection* of amorous agonies and one can easily invoke Ruskin's condemnation: "If he has to paint a passion, he remembers the external signs of it . . . he searches for similes, he composes, exaggerates, heaps term on term, figure on figure, till we groan beneath the cold disjointed heap; but it is all faggot and no fire; the life breath is not in it."[11] In one sense this condemnation is entirely appropriate. The thesis of the poem—or at least the thesis by which Sappho as poetess has lived the life of art—is that poetry aspires not to feel more deeply but to play with greater artistry, devising figure on figure. Love, from this perspective, aspires to the condition of music—to the distance from which gasps of passion or pain can

---

[11] Ibid., pp. 252–53. I have omitted the phrase "collects expressions of it from other writers" because despite Swinburne's undisguised debt to several fragments of Sapphic poetry (and his debt to Baudelaire), the imagery of lesbian love is Swinburnian, not borrowed. In Swinburne's own day the issue was the value of his originality of phrase, not the fact of it, and in our own the important questions continue to center on the originality and distinctiveness of particular Swinburnian passages (the way they distinguish themselves from other passages in Swinburne)—however complicated these questions may be by questions of literary influence such as the one about Swinburne and Shakespeare discussed below.

seem "dumb tunes and shuddering semitones of death." In Swinburne's hands lesbian love becomes thus a trope for imagination contemplative, and the very energy that drives love off course from mutuality to music—the energy that perverts the course of love from one capable of fufillment to one capable only of the orchestration of dissonances—drives the poetess to a stance like that of Milton's Satan. It is thus appropriate that the passion of Sappho have about it a satanic spirit of negation, a denial of the monistic valuation of the world of "things," the world created by the hostile divinity in power. In condemning the unimaginative writer's habit of heaping externals, Ruskin continues in the passage just quoted: "It is all faggot and no fire; the life breath is not in it; his passion has the form of leviathan, but it never makes the deep boil; he fastens us at anchor in the scaly rind of it." The ambition of the poet who writes Miltonic similes comparing Satan to leviathan is to do something else with one's life other than to "feel."

At its most intense moment, *Anactoria* rises wholly beyond the occasion of love, the poem's ostensible subject, and confronts its daemonic ambition. Sappho would be the Satan, the eternal Antagonist of the God who made the order of nature as we know it,

> who bade exceed
> The fervid will, fall short the feeble deed,
> Bade sink the spirit and the flesh aspire,
> Pain animate the dust of dead desire,
> And life yield up her flower to violent fate.
> Him would I reach, him smite, him desecrate,
> Pierce the cold lips of God with human breath,
> And mix his immortality with death.
> [ll. 177–84]

Hamlet, standing beside the grave of Ophelia, would pierce the cold lips of Yorick with human breath and mix his death with immortality—or at least with living, human memory. We shall have to return later to the juxtaposition of Swinburne and Shakespeare, but we might hypothesize here that if Shakespeare's Hamlet is a supreme wielder of imagination penetrative, Swinburne's Sappho is a supreme wielder of imagination contemplative. Her desire is as remote as possible from Hamlet's desire to make the cold skeleton (or the questionable shape of his father) put on flesh. Hamlet mourns an absent human presence; Sappho's is the infinitely more abstract desire to demystify the fictions of a particular lover's—and God's—presence. A minor tinge of such passion might motivate a Claudius to penetrate the cold orifices of the godlike Hamlet senior. But beyond good and evil, this passion is the passion for abstraction from, rather than fulfillment of, the human condition. Later in the poem Sappho rails against the ruler of the universe who so separated desire from fulfillment and made unhappiness the motive for metaphor. When she complains against God, who "Wrought / Song and hath lit it at my lips" (ll. 244–45), she seems to move wholly beyond the original erotic subject to a desire of a higher, more prophetic strain. Hers is the paradox of inspiration that in putting on the power one distances oneself from the very identity that called for external reinforcement or redress. The inspired poet breathes in no semitones of death; he or she aspires to the condition of music rather than the acknowledgment of mortality.

Does Swinburne as well as Sappho aspire to the condition of music? Ian Fletcher has characterized *Anactoria* as a poem about "the failure of immortality through art,"[12] and indeed, the more we study the text, the more powerfully we may be struck by the theme of art as a defense against death, against the experiential limits that the poem sadly acknowledges even in its hyperbolic defiance of them. I think it no accident that the passage in which Swinburne quotes Sappho is the one that most poignantly contrasts with song the antithetical theme of the body. Sappho's claim to power is her power of song; because of her power of song, she has been granted a vision of Aphrodite (or the power to think up such a confrontation) in which the goddess urbanely inquires into the complaint of her votary and assures her success:

> She bowed,
> With all her subtle face laughing aloud,
> Bowed down upon me, saying, "Who doth thee wrong,
> Sappho?"
>
> [ll. 71–74]

At this point Swinburne could have followed Sappho more closely and continued with lines 80–81:

> Yet the queen laughs from her sweet heart and said,
> "Even she that flies shall follow for thy sake. . . ."[13]

[12]Ian Fletcher, *Swinburne* (Essex: Longman, 1973), p. 27.
[13]One collection of Sapphic verse with various attempts at English rendition (including Swinburne's) is Henry Thornton Warton, *Sappho: Memoir, Text, Selected Renderings and a Literal Translation* (New York: Brentano, 1920). Swinburne's quotations are from the first poem in Sapphic meter, given various titles such as "Ode to Aphrodite."

What Swinburne does instead, however, is to interrupt the epiphany of the goddess with the equivalent in song of an epiphany of the sensual woman. The thought of supernatural intervention breeds the countering thought of natural physical presence:

> "Who doth thee wrong,
> Sappho?" but thou—thy body is the song.
> Thy mouth the music; thou art more than I,
> Though my voice die not till the whole world die.

The thought is the same as that expressed by Browning's Cleon to Protus: "I can write love-odes; thy fair slave's an ode." For Cleon, the contrast implies envy of those who can get more life out of life: "I get to sing of love, when grown too gray / For being beloved; she turns to that young man, / The muscles all a-ripple on his back" (ll. 297–99). Swinburne, on the other hand—and as he himself pointed out—does not in *Anactoria* further explore the suggestion present in another fragment of Sappho's verse that the addressee is in the arms of a male rival.[14] He concentrates more exclusively on the situation of Sappho and her defensive substitution of art for life. And it is on the grounds of this defense, this sense of the absurd, incredible blindness to literal death, that he moves the poem to its striking conclusion. In declaring that she shall be "one with all these things, / With all high things for ever" (ll. 276–77), Swinburne's Sappho stands with the speaker of *Adonais*, insisting that "the One remains" and lingering before a final, oceanic plunge. Repressing all corporeality as she to incorporeal desire turns, Sappho becomes all poet, at one with her verse, "all air and fire"—and winds aloft to the abode of the eternals, where imagination contemplative aspires to go.

Inasmuch as Ruskin associates imagination penetrative with seriousness and the thirst for truth, perhaps it is not surprising that the turn at the end of *Anactoria* to the thought of an eternal place or posture of contemplation should be accompanied by the high rhetoric of the supreme lie against time: "I say I shall not die" (l. 290). The whole concluding movement of the poem may be regarded as a triumph of imagination contemplative whether we think thema-

---

[14]"I have not said, as Boileau and Phillips have, that the speaker sweats and swoons at sight of her favourite by the side of a man" (*Notes on Poems and Reviews*, reprinted by Clyde K. Hyder in *Swinburne Replies: Notes on Poems and Reviews, Under the Microscope, Dedicatory Epistle* [Syracuse, N.Y.: Syracuse University Press, 1966]); the fragment, suggesting a male rival (printed in the edition cited above as number 2), is the poem imitated by Catullus as *Ad Lesbian*.

tically about the godlike stance or linguistically about "the appearance of a single thing, illustrated and conveyed to us by the image of another."[15] In the largest terms, the tenor of *Anactoria* is the desire to transcend the limits of mortality, and "the image of another" is the vehicle of lesbian love. At this point, however, we might question the distinction between imagination contemplative and penetrative and Ruskin's special valuation of the latter. Granted that the "nature and dignity" of imagination penetrative depend "on its holding things always by the heart,"[16] what is closer to the heart than the desire to transcend the limits of experience, the need to lie against time? And yet Ruskin's terms do describe two different phenomena in poetry or the response to it, and even if we believe that lesbian love is vehicle rather than tenor in *Anactoria*, there remains a profound difference in kind between the imagination penetrative of Hamlet's lines about the lips of Yorick and the countless images of lips in *Anactoria* and elsewhere in the Swinburne canon. One distinction that Ruskin valued will not work: Ruskin says that imagination penetrative "sees too far, too darkly, too solemnly, too earnestly ever to smile."[17] For Sappho at her most radical point of daemonized consciousness, there is still room for the urbanity of perspective on her own present infatuation:

> And they shall know me as ye who have known me here,
> Last year when I loved Atthis, and this year
> When I love thee.
>
> [ll. 285–87]

But there is no less urbanity in Hamlet's perspective on his own meditation about death. The speech quoted by Ruskin concludes with the solemn and the smiling in too close coherence for the term *imagination penetrative* to apply only to half the exchange:

> Hamlet: Dost thou think Alexander looked o' this fashion i' the earth?
> Horatio: E'en so.
> Hamlet: And smelt so? pah!
>
> [V.i.218–21]

More fruitful than the concept of solemnity is the concept of sympathy. Ruskin describes sympathy as a "reciprocal action between the

[15]*Works of Ruskin*, IV, 227.
[16]Ibid., p. 251.
[17]Ibid., p. 257.

intensity of moral feeling and the power of imagination": "On the one hand, those who have keenest sympathy are those who look closest and pierce deepest, and hold securest; and on the other, those who have so pierced and seen the melancholy deeps of things are filled with the most intense passion and gentleness of sympathy."[18] Now sympathy is an emotion properly outside the sublime, and if Swinburne's Sappho begins with a desire to wound Anactoria in her separateness or to obliterate the bounds between their bodily selves, she concludes with a compound of desires—each even further from sympathy than were the opening motions of the poem—to obliterate the distinction between self and nature or self and art. With or without the valuative differential, there is, then, a distinction in kind that can be preserved between a meditation on mortality such as Hamlet's and a rapture on artistic immortality such as Sappho's.

In another sense, too, Ruskin's distinction in kind is reflected in Swinburne's poem. I have hitherto treated Ruskin's concept of "getting to the spring of things" as though "things" were itself a term that drops out; as though when he says of the lines about Yorick's lips "there is the essence of lip," *lip* were a thing representing the emotions with which are associated the memory of kissing lips. Yet it is part of what Ruskin means by imagination penetrative that we cannot dismiss the thing for the emotion behind it. Ruskin's own locutions emphasize that the dignity of imagination penetrative depends on its "holding *things* always by the heart"—because under the eyes of imagination penetrative things themselves seem to have a heart. "There is some*thing* in the heart of every*thing*, if we can reach it, that we shall not be inclined to laugh at."[19] As Ben Jonson said of Camden, "What faith hast thou in things! / What sight in searching the most antique springs!" If any "things" have a heart in *Anactoria*, they are not the throbbing sexual "things" of Sappho and her love, but lips of a different sort apprehended in an extraordinary passage that runs from line 155 through 188. The "heart" of the poem's argument is the poet's quarrel with God, with the creator of limits "who bade exceed / The fervid will, fall short the feeble deed" (ll. 177–78). And what distinguishes this argument from others like it in the Swinburne canon is precisely the corporeality of its climactic images:

[18]Ibid.
[19]Ibid., pp. 251, 257.

Him would I reach, him smite, him desecrate,
Pierce the cold lips of God with human breath,
And mix his immortality with death.

[ll. 182–84]

This piercing is not "at heart" sexual but theological or existential; *pace* David A. Cook, the issue is not cunnilingus but the cunning of the serpent that brought mortal taste into the world and the linguistic prowess of the Word that brought dead matter to life by breathing spirit into Adam.[20] Speaking of Ruskin's moral support of Swinburne, Edmund Gosse remarked that "we may conjecture that he had not studied *Anactoria* or *Dolores* with any very close attention."[21] But I wonder, if he had, whether he could have considered these lines to exemplify imagination penetrative. Swinburne "penetrates" the countenance of God that has not shone upon us and been gracious unto us but has (like Blake's Urizen) symbolized the coldheartedness, the indifference of nature. More important is the reversal of the trope, the reversal by which instead of the breath of godlike life penetrating inanimate matter, the breath of human life is imagined penetrating the inertness of abstraction. The "thing" Swinburne animates is the set of privileged tropes our culture has woven about the idea of God; penetrating into the heart of this rhetorical matter, Swinburne allows such images as dissolution into the sea to stand not for orgasmic, oceanic feeling but for the desire at the heart of lesser expressions of desire, the desire to overgo (troped as the desire to undo) the limits of the Limiter who set bounds to the sea.

In an article about a draft of *Anactoria*, Gosse argued that the absence of the lines we have been considering confirms his sense of their irrelevance:

The text in the Draft stops at the line, "The mystery of the cruelty of things," without any sign that the idea of the impassive harshness of Fate was to be expanded. The 34 lines which now follow have, moreover, a character that distinguishes them from the rest of *Anactoria*, with

---

[20]"The Content and Meaning of Swinburne's 'Anactoria,'" *Victorian Poetry* 9 (1971):77–93. Cooke does read "sexual aberration [as a] common poetic metaphor for cosmic disorder" and "condition of spiritual stagnation," but his interest in the agon of the poem is in agony as "muscular contraction," and his illuminations of structure and image center on "veiled allusions to cunnilinguic orgasm, manipulated with the exquisite verbal wit so characteristic of Swinburne's finest work."

[21]Edmund Gosse, *The Life of Algernon Charles Swinburne* (New York: Macmillan, 1919), p. 155.

which they are not quite in keeping. They leave the individual passion of Sappho entirely out of sight, and they are instinct with an order of theological ideas which occupied Swinburne in 1864 and 1865, when he was writing *Atalanta in Calydon* and the earliest of *Songs before Sunrise*. They are on a higher philosophical plane than the melodious ravings of the love-sick poetess, and the more we read them, the more may we be persuaded that they are an after-thought.[22]

If these lines are an afterthought, they are an afterthought like God's inbreathing of dead matter with the breath of life—or rather an afterthought like the belated creator's trope on that quickening power, the breathing of human life into dead abstraction. Regardless of when the lines were composed, they constitute the heart of the poem, without which the whole would indeed be the ravings of a lovesick poetess. To borrow Gosse's Miltonism, the lines are instinct with spirit, but if we are still inclined to distinguish contemplative from penetrative spirit, we might pause for a moment on the lines with which the draft breaks off: "For who shall change with prayers or thanksgivings / The mystery of the cruelty of things" (ll. 153–54). These lines are quintessentially Swinburnian, but if "things" here means not the limitations of sexual organs or desires but things in general, then human imagination, depending on the "single glorious faculty of getting to the spring of things" is here apprehended in getting not just to fundamental issues but to the source of the image itself. In *King Lear,* at a moment Ruskin would have probably identified as a highlight of imagination penetrative (though the scene is a contemplation of prison as heaven), Lear imagines an ultimate godlike perspective:

> So we'll live,
> And pray, and sing, and tell old tales, and laugh
> At gilded butterflies, and hear poor rogues
> Talk of court news; and we'll talk with them too,
> Who loses and who wins; who's in, who's out;
> And take upon 's the mystery of things,
> As if we were God's spies.
>
> [V.iii.9–15]

Perhaps one reason these lines are so poignant is that Lear is Lear still, contemplating the majestic assumption of godlike knowledge ("And take upon's the mystery") rather than human sympathy

[22]Edmund Gosse, "The First Draft of Swinburne's 'Anactoria,'" *MLR* 14 (1919):277.

("And weep upon the sorrows that we see"—or some such line). The indifference of the leisurely option, "and pray, and sing, and tell old tales," becomes in Swinburne's poem the urgency of the rhetorical question "For who shall change with prayers or thanksgivings?" "The mystery of things" becomes, in an act of literary clinamen like a rape or desecration through insertion or penetration, "the mystery *of the cruelty* of things." If the poem in any sense breaks off at this point, it does so to be rapt into higher contemplation of its more penetrating theme. It is a theme close to the heart of the poet—the indifference of nature troped as the cruel heart of things.

Imagination penetrative gives us our greatest songs or poetic moments of human feeling; imagination contemplative gives us songs that aspire, in the words of Wallace Stevens, "beyond human meaning, beyond human feeling." The limit of imagination penetrative is the point beyond which song expressing desire for human presence would actualize the godlike power of creating another soul under the ribs of death. The limit of imagination contemplative is the bourn beyond which lies the realm of the gods—not under the ribs of death but aloft, far from the world of life and death. These are the limits of language in relation to which any actual poetic language must define itself. Imagination penetrative, though it can never actually pierce the cold ribs of death, can penetrate all abstraction to uncover—or recover—the fundamental human desire for idealized human presence. Imagination contemplative, though it can never wholly abstract the imaginer from the condition of earth to the condition of fire, can—like the kisses of Sappho on the lips of Anactoria—"brand them with immortality."Both forms of imaginative desire, both aspirations for Romantic language, are all involved with love and death. It was the genius of Shelley, and I think his greatest legacy to Swinburne, Browning, and others who yearned to follow in the comet's course, to recognize that the two modes are polar opposites that nonetheless touch. The darkness aloft *is* the darkness of the human heart, and "burning through the inmost veil of Heaven," as Shelley says in *Adonais,* the soul of the poet "beacons from the abode where the Eternal are." Keats wanted most to penetrate more deeply into the human heart; Shelley, to contemplate the form of love. But there is only one realm of the Eternals, and there Shelley and Keats beacon together. Men scarce know how beautiful fire is, and we are equally surprised by the manifestations in poetry of the soul's human feeling and its (often concomitant) desire to burn with a gemlike flame.

10 /

"To Autumn" and the Music of Mortality: "Pure Rhetoric of A Language without Words"

RICHARD MACKSEY

In flights of eye and ear, the highest eye
And the lowest ear the deep ear that discerns,
At evening, things that attend it until it hears

The supernatural preludes of its own,
At the moment when the angelic eye defines
Its actors approaching in company, in their masks.
　　　　　　—Wallace Stevens, "The Auroras of Autumn"

After the leaves have fallen, we return
To a plain sense of things. It is as if
We had come to an end of the imagination,
Inanimate in an inert savoir.
　　　　　　—Wallace Stevens, "The Plain Sense of Things"

What mattered was that they should bear
Some lineament or character

Some affluence, if only half perceived,
In the poverty of their words,
Of the planet of which they were a part.
　　　　　　—Wallace Stevens, "The Planet on the Table"

I

In the poignantly brief space between 1816 and 1819 the trajectory of Keats's literary language describes an extraordinary

This essay has been abstracted from a longer study on the development of Keats's last poems, which is itself a part of a projected volume on "terminal cases," the poetry of mortal endings. An earlier version of the essay was delivered under the auspices of

development, a unique performance in the history of English that replays many of the abiding themes of English poetics in compositions that orchestrate the native epistemological and emotional climate of English Romanticism while offering—at the very end—a final punctuation to the moment they have defined. The last poems point to a music and a poetics that lie beyond Romanticism as the term is commonly used by English literary critics; they inhabit a poetic space to be comprehended not in terms of what Keats had learned from his literary masters but most fully in the perspective of Keats's literary heirs—poets of the succeeding century who, like the old Wallace Stevens, suggest "after the leaves have fallen" a new and "impersonal" knowledge beyond all the antinomies and disjunctions of Romantic poetry.

From the chatty archaism of Keats's earlier verse, from the deliberate literarity of the "Cockney style," to the chaste language of "To Autumn" and the uncanny shift of diction that marks the final, chillingly apostrophic line of that "private poem," "This living hand now warm and capable," the poetry records an immense effort of assimilation, transposition, and—ultimately—renunciation. There is a fatal tendency among the poet's critics to record the changing styles as instances of anxious retrodiction—the minor affectations of

---

the Edward H. Butler Chair at the State University of New York at Buffalo. I am grateful to my hosts for their patience with its longueurs and for their suggestions toward its improvement.

For a poem that in its "flawless surface" supposedly resists interpretation, "To Autumn" has elicited a considerable body of commentary. I can only suggest some of my debts to these readers in the notes that follow, but from the store of Keats criticism harvested over the last three decades I am particularly and generally indebted to the work—and the dialogues—of Earl R. Wasserman (*The Finer Tone: Keats' Major Poems* [Baltimore: Johns Hopkins Press, 1953, 1967], as well as his return to Keats during the last two years of his life); I also acknowledge my gratitude to the work of Harold Bloom (*The Visionary Company* [Garden City, N.Y.: Doubleday, 1961], and insights from his later criticism), Walter Jackson Bate (*John Keats* [Cambridge: Harvard University Press, 1963]), Karl Kroeber (*The Artifice of Reality* [Madison: University of Wisconsin Press, 1964]), Paul de Man ("Introduction" to *The Selected Poetry of Keats* [New York: New American Library, 1966]), Ian Jack (*Keats and the Mirror of Art* [Oxford: Oxford University Press, 1967]), John Jones (*John Keats's Dream of Truth* [London: Chatto & Windus, 1969]), Charles I. Patterson (*The Daemonic in the Poetry of Keats* [Urbana: University of Illinois Press, 1970]), Stuart M. Sperry (*Keats the Poet* [Princeton: Princeton University Press, 1973]), Geoffrey H. Hartman ("Poem and Ideology: A Study of Keats's 'To Autumn,'" in *The Fate of Reading and Other Essays* [Chicago: University of Chicago Press, 1975]), Virgil Nemoianu ("The Dialectics of Movement in Keats's 'To Autumn,'" *PMLA* 93 [1978]), and Paul H. Fry (*The Poet's Calling in the English Ode* [New Haven: Yale University Press, 1980]). To this diverse company should be added an unpublished essay by Arden Reed ("The Harvest Hook and the Scythe of Time") of special relevance to my topic. Finally, as I hope my essay suggests, the most responsive reader of Keats's "To Autumn" may still be Wallace Stevens.

Leigh Hunt and the mighty legacies of Spenser, Milton, and Shake-speare. Keats himself, even as he is renouncing the Miltonic inheri-tance of the *Hyperion* fragment in the autumn of 1819, relates his poetic evolution to the larger and more "impersonal" question of the English language itself and the perennial temptations of enrichment from the classical South. Chatterton, with all his fabrication and invented past, may seem a peculiar anticlimax to Keats's earlier gal-lery of masters; the lines from *Aella* that Keats allusively recalls in "To Autumn" hardly vibrate in the collective memory. But the pred-ecessor poet dead at seventeen clearly stands, in the native purity of his Northern diction, as an emblem for the persistence of the En-glish language whose history he pretended to rewrite. Geoffrey Hartman, in his capital essay "Poem and Ideology," has suggestively argued the "ideological" burden of Keats's last attachment to Chat-terton: a conscious turning away from the "Eastern" or epiphanic model of the cult hymn, vacillating between imagined presence and absence, toward a "Northern" or Hesperian poetry of a less rap-turous and visionary tone.[1]

What I argue here is that the poem that concludes the "living year" of Keats's genius does indeed mark a turning toward a more temperate climate of the imagination, but one that was dramatically prefigured in the unresolved tensions of the earlier "sublime" poet-ry. The harvesting of "To Autumn" marks in its own serene closure the repetition "in a finer tone" of the elusive grasping at experience and art vainly sought in the more feverish language and crisis rhet-oric of the great poems that immediately preceded it. This mastery is achieved, however, only through the renunciation of the double quest that inflamed these poems and inspired, in its failure, their sense of the inevitable loss connatural with the most intense encoun-ter. The emotional resolution and the new poetics that this renuncia-tion breeds are intrinsic to a newly achieved temperateness of lan-guage. We have been instructed since Earl R. Wasserman's magister-ial study of Keats's major poetry to associate the "temperature" of the diction with the intensity of the poetic energy, and, depending on the letter to John Taylor of January 30, 1818, to recognize the way in which the metaphorics of temperature calibrates the familiar Keatsian pleasure-pain continuum.[2] The perilous involvement in human passions brings in its wake the "burning forehead" and the

---

[1]Hartman, *Fate of Reading*, pp. 126–46.
[2]Earl R. Wasserman, *The Finer Tone: Keats' Major Poems* pp. 22–26. My debts to Wasserman's readings of Keats, early and late, are pervasive and, I trust, obvious in this essay.

"parching tongue"; the empathic union with objects opens a new modal intensity of pleasure for the ecstatic poet, but a pleasure that is contingent and subject to time and change.

Coming at the end of the thwarted epiphanies of the earlier odes, "To Autumn" is localized in occasion as well as language. The weather of Winchester, the "warmth" of the stubble fields, and the solitudes of a Sunday evening in September 1819 are all implicated in the progressively abstracted situation. Just as clearly, the poem translates and concludes the major themes of the four great odes that precede it—"the songs of spring." Thus all of the odes are profoundly touched by the sense of transience, by the realization that art can claim to be a stay against the deeply felt sense of change and passing away. But in "To Autumn" we are at last beyond the familiar disjunction of "warm love" and "cold pastoral" of the Grecian urn ode or the forlorn awareness of flight as the nightingale's song disappears in the distance of the imagination. We have arrived instead through a seemingly effortless effort at a native, temperate, idiomatic place of mellowing in which the light of day and the ripeness of the season pass imperceptibly away; we have achieved the serene tone of a new music and the poetics of a new poetry. The genesis of this achievement is deeply rooted, however, in Keats's earliest impulses to write lyric poetry, the vocation that he effectively set aside at the end of September 1819.

We find in nearly the earliest of Keat's surviving letters a verse picture that might serve as an emblem of the English Romantic temper. Outstretched on the grass, the poet seeks to "pry 'mong the Stars," straining to "think divinely and hear Apollo's song." Keats professes that if only he could "cleave the Air," bid the world adieu, and glide far, far away "from all sorrowing," he could snatch "spher-ey strains" from the heavens and experience and supernal perfection he tended to call "Poesy" or "Romance.[3] For to his mind the realm of "Poesy" is not our human world but the domain of Apollo, the god of poetry who is also the sun, transcendently above. The posture and the solar myth that informed so much of Keats's development are characteristically proleptic. His yearnings, "on the wavy Grass, out stretched supinely," are recurrently upward: the "Cliff of Poesy," he feels, "Towers above me," and so does his "high Idea" of poetic fame; flight to Apollo is a fleeing of the soul "To high above

[3]*The Letters of John Keats*, ed. Hyder E. Rollins (Cambridge: Harvard University Press, 1958), I, 105–9. All references to the letters are to this edition, which is cited hereafter as *LJK*.

our head," into Poesy's "wide heaven"; it is "upon the night's starr'd face" that he beholds the "Huge cloudy symbols of a high romance"; and to fail in this vocation is to be Phaeton, who tried, with disastrous results, to prove his divine lineage by driving the sun chariot of his father, Apollo.[4]

But even while Keats dreams of peering beyond heaven's enchanted portals in this earliest manifesto, he is conscious that he is pressed against "this dull, and earthly mould," a transcending spirit bound down in mortal clay. At best, man is, like Leigh Hunt, confined in prison but spiritually "as free / As the sky-searching lark." And yet Keats also *fears* transcendence because it flaws the singing of the nightingale. On the one hand he rejoices that, although the poet may see beyond the heavenly gates, "no mortal Eye can reach the Flowers" within the gardens of the poetic empyrean because "well Apollo knows / 'Twould make the Poet quarrel with the Rose." If only Keats could smother his "made ambition" to transcend the world, he is confident he would be "Happier, and dearer to society." On the other hand, to peer too deeply into the waters of our world is to see the "eternal fierce destruction."[5] It is sad that our "prison / Of flesh and bone curbs, and confines, and frets / Our spirit's wings"; it is equally sad that our fleeting visions of the poetic heaven transform the world's "deepest shades" into "deepest dungeons" and carry our souls to "nothingness" in the realm of transient "real things."[6] Strain though we will against our earthly bonds, they shackle our visionary powers; yet visionary flights devalue the sublunary world, shrink it into a prison. Thus Keats yearned for both the world and the dream; but because they undermine each other, he also dreaded them with giddying alternation.

The English Romantic poet, no longer willing to accept Edward Young's location of man "Midway from nothing to the Deity," finds himself psychologically divided. Because his aspiration to heavenly perfection is destructive of his private identity, he can be only nothing or godlike. His human, earthly self becomes nullified because his creative persona is godlike; and, paradoxically, he is humbly self-effacing because he is infinitely and vaingloriously solipsistic.[7]

---

[4]*LJK*, I, 141, 169; "God of the Meridian," l. 10; "Sleep and Poetry," l. 49; "When I have fears," ll. 5–6; *LJK*, I, 139. Texts of Keats's poetry are cited from Jack Stillinger, ed., *The Poems of John Keats* (Cambridge: Harvard University Press, 1978).

[5]"To My Brother George," ll. 71, 44–46; "To John Hamilton Reynolds," l. 97.

[6]*Endymion*, IV, 20–22, and I, 692–93; "Sleep and Poetry," ll. 157–59.

[7]Among the most analytical expressions of this fundamental Romantic dilemma are the so-called "Hymns" that Shelley assigned to Pan and Apollo in their Ovidian

The two poles of this dilemma are the points on which Keats tipped the various webs of most of his poems. In a moment of enthusiasm he may scorn earth's pleasurable wine and drink instead from the sunny bowl of the poetry god's sky until his mind fuses with "the glory and the grace of Apollo"—even though it causes the racking "Delphian pain" of inspiration.[8] But when his soul does ascend toward the god of poetry, he becomes aware that his "body is earthward press'd," leaving a "terrible division" filled with "worldly fear" that leads to madness.[9] Blessed and cursed with imagination, man needs only a few steps to pass "Beyond the sweet and bitter world." Whereas on one occasion Keats urges that we break the leash tethering the idealizing fancy to the human heart, on another he rejoices that our "worldly heart" tugs us back into human relations lest we forget our "mortal way" and "lose" our minds in what he sometimes called "abstractions."[10] Keats was as aware of the astronomer-like insanity of transcendence as he was of the unhealthiness of some of his poetic efforts to attain Apollonian vision, an experience precisely beyond language. The imagination that composed some of his greatest poems was racked by the same tension that orchestrates the divided thematics of so many of them. But how sad it is, Keats wrote of Burns, "when a luxurious imagination is obliged in self defense to deaden its delicacy in vulgarity, and riot in things attainable that it may not have leisure to go mad after things which are not." Neither the human condition nor the "abstraction" of "Romance" will do: ". . . out of sufferance [i.e., patient suffering] there is no greatness, no dignity; . . . in the most abstracted Pleasure there is no lasting happiness."[11]

---

singing contest. His earth god sings of the frustration of desires by the world's inadequacy; his god of poetry and the sun sings of the transcendent ideal, which proves so solipsistic as to preclude contingent human experiences and relationships. The choice Shelley leaves the reader is an unresolvable one between a human self so battered by a recalcitrant world as to lose almost all value and a godlike self so absolute and absorptive as to be unrelatable to the human. His god of human experience identifies himself only by the relational "we" but finds all relations failures; his god of heavenly perfection, only by an "I," an ideal mask that, being everything, can have no relations. Such reaches for a perfection that is "above" are hardly new in man's interior history, being but another mode of the tradition of forbidden knowledge. There are similar aporiae for Swift's Laputans and Johnson's astronomer, who, by insanely assuming knowledge and mastery of the heavens, alienate themselves from human society. Yet the difference between the two historical stances is essential, for Swift's and Johnson's exempla were the pretext for corrective moral advice, whereas Shelley and the Romantics could confront only the obstinate fact of human nature's divided and contradictory affiliations.

[8]"Hence Burgundy, Claret, and Port."
[9]"God of the Meridian."
[10]"Lines Written in the Highlands," ll. 29–46; "Fancy," ll. 89–90.
[11]*LJK*, I, 320.

This oscillation between the human (the unexpressed) and the ideal (the unexpressible), between the immediate and the dream, is almost unremitting in Keats's poetry as now one and now the other wins qualified preference, but in his radical state he experiences only their irresolvable feud. "My spirit is too weak," he wrote on seeing the Elgin marbles:

> —mortality
> Weighs heavily on me like unwilling sleep,
> And each imagin'd pinnacle and steep
> Of godlike hardship tells me I must die
> Like a sick Eagle looking at the sky.

Although it is dangerous to trust Benjamin Bailey's thirty-two-year-old memory, such a confession lends authority to his report that Keats felt deeply the following lines from Wordsworth's Immortality Ode:

> Blank misgivings of a Creature
> Moving about in worlds not realized,
> High instincts, before which our mortal nature
> Did tremble like a guilty thing surprized.

"The last [two] lines he thought were quite awful in their application to a guilty finite creature, like man, in the appalling nature of the feeling which they suggested to a thoughtful mind."[12] Keats intuitively sensed the "fearful summons" of the great turning that marks stanza 9 of Wordsworth's ode (with its metaleptic translation of *Hamlet*, I.i.148, from a world of paternal spirits to the "blank misgivings" of an encounter with the "fallings" and "vanishings" of mortal change). But if Keats felt the encumbering weight of his mortality and finitude, if his mortal nature trembled with guilt before his "high instincts" to transcend the world, he did not relinquish his faith that the artist's distinguishing attribute is, eagle-like, to fly higher than all others of his kind and to strain toward the sun god of poetry.[13]

---

[12]*The Keats Circle*, ed. Hyder E. Rollins (Cambridge: Harvard University Press, 1965), I, 275.

[13]The natural Wordsworthian and Shakespearean insights into the world and the human heart, or the Miltonic and Spenserian imagination's godlike straining to mount the pinnacles of the ideal, transcendent, Apollonian realm of vision—Keats yearned for both and would abandon neither. The desire to be *both* dreamer and "Physician to all men" is the subject of the poet's dialogue with Moneta in *The Fall of Hyperion*. He figures this desire in terms of the dialectic of light and dark: since the imagination strives beyond its human limits and yet is confined by them, what Keats

RICHARD MACKSEY

This indecision between the claims of finite earth and the eagle's flight accounts for the oscillating movement of so many of Keats's speculations. Poesy and what he terms "philosophy" alternately exert their dominion because the human heart (the province of "philosophy," whose "axioms . . . are proved upon our pulses") and poesy or romance (the realm of visionary "abstractions") make equal claims on him. He is attracted equally to Spenser's serene and summery Romance (a seductively treacherous "Syren" who is "Queen of far-away") and to Shakespeare's wintry *King Lear*, which invites man in his home country to its "fierce dispute / Betwixt damnation and impassion'd clay." Put another way, on reading the "Prospectus" of *The Recluse*, where Wordsworth adopted Milton's high style to spurn Milton's theological subject for the theme of man, nature, and human life, Keats is stirred into nervous indecision by the equal greatness of the two rival poets. Keats is left only with "surmises": Milton's indifference to the human heart may mean either that he has passed beyond it or that he did not rise to it; and Wordsworth may have the genius to transcend the human but "martyrs himself" to it by adopting it, as he himself announced, as the "main region of his song"—he may thus be "an eagle in his nest," not "on the wing" (*LJK*, I, 278–79, 280). Keats's letters reveal him ceaselessly shifting around the two terms of his dilemma, the actual and the visionary, as he indecisively explores all their possible combinations and oppositions.

Instead of remaining trapped, like Shelley, in his dilemma or, like Byron, raging against it, Keats sought an existential resolution to his

prays for is neither the soul's "daytime" nor the world's "dark void of Night," but "Sunset," when the two blend and the "material" world joins the "sublime."

In his verse epistle to John Hamilton Reynolds he acknowledges that he is asking for the impossible. Our imaginative visions beyond our mortal "bourn" flaw the singings of the earthly nightingales; between the imaginative ideal and the experientially real there is no meeting point, no mental cottage of which they are adjacent gardens, but only a "Purgatory blind" to which the laws of neither heaven nor earth apply. The consequence is Keats's poetry of ambivalence, as in "Lamia," "La Belle Dame sans Merci," and the "Ode to a Nightingale." The Elfin Lady leads the Knight-at-Arms to the fairy Otherworld, but from the point of view of the mortals who irresistibly intrude into the knight's dream, she has imprisoned him, exiled him from the human. On the other hand, those invading and dissipating his dream are disfigured by their mortality: they are "death-pale" and their "starved lips" are "With horrid warning gaped wide." From the point of view of human life, the Elfin Lady is a Circe; from that of the transcending imagination she unlocks the visionary world. Lamia is equally ambivalent—a beautiful and magical woman who is also a serpent. Apollonius, the worldly "philosopher," is both right and wrong: as Lycius' tutor, he is bound to preserve the youth "from every ill / Of life" by dispelling the visionary Lamia; but thereby he destroys the envisioned perfection that had sustained Lycius' life. Value is relative to our arbitrary choice of the laws of heaven or the laws of life, for there are no laws powerful enough to unite the two.

predicament. If the human world and the literary domain of Romance cannot be reconciled, perhaps the imagination can be the stage for a recuperation of the struggle. Perhaps, then, existence so enacted yields essence, and perhaps Wordsworthian insight into the heart opens the doors of the mystery's dark passages, passages that ultimately give access to the transcendent vision. Perhaps Romance is the ultimate amalgam of our questing flights and life in this "vale of soul-making." Although longing for the "summer" world of Spenser's Romance, Keats faced the fact that we are all inhabitants of a "wintry earth" and cannot make the disjunctive leap from one climate to the other. Characteristically, both the temptation and the sobering realization are played out in terms of literary influence and preempted language: "It is impossible to escape from toil / O' the sudden and receive thy [Spenser's] spiriting," for only the sun god of poetry, with his "golden quill," can rise over the wintry earth, "Firewing'd, and make a morning in his mirth." Keats speculates, however, that in the sublunary world there can be a summer bloom if the winter has been endured; the experiences of our immediate sweet and bitter world can, like the germinating seed, be translated into the "far-away" world of Romance. "The flower must drink the nature of the soil / Before it can put forth its blossoming."[14] The rhetorical flower is both earth and heliotrope.

Whereas Romance, like Endymion's moon goddess, is "Queen of far-away," man is a plant rooted in his native soil, not an exotic; he must be nurtured by what is experientially at hand and develop in accordance with his indigenous climate. English Keats must make his way through "the old oak forest" that is Shakespeare's *King Lear*,[15] an old legend of native history. He must make his way through traditionally oak-forested England, rather than Romantic far-away—such as "France and Italy and the Andes and the Burn-

---

[14]Similarly, the hero of *Endymion, A Poetical Romance*, despite his impulse to spurn the human and leap to the ideal, cannot attain the moon goddess of his visions, whom he conceives of as the "completed form of all completeness," until long after he has learned the partial truth that the world is

Meant but to fertilize my earthly root,
And make my branches lift a golden fruit
Into the bloom of heaven.
　　　　　[II, 907–9]

He is therefore finally "spiritualiz'd . . . from this mortal state" only through his love of the human, sorrow-singing Indian Maid, who thereby becomes transfigured into the ideal moongoddess. By ardent pursuit, in this early and willfully optimistic version, the human becomes the ideal; the ideal is realized through its human form; and a gypsy evolves into Cleopatra, a rogue into Helen of Troy (I, 320).
[15]A manuscript variant of the sonnet reads, "Chief [i.e. Shakespeare]! what a gloom thy old oak forest hath."

ing Mountains"—not only because it is *his* native soil, but because England's gloom is the natural climate of all men: the theme of *Lear*—"the fierce dispute / Betwixt damnation and impassion'd clay"—is begotten by ancient Albion's darkening clouds. The danger of disjunction, however, remains, for after passing through that old oak forest, Keats fears he may again merely wander in an unrelated "barren dream" of pure romance, like the fanatic's and savage's dream of heaven that he writes of in *The Fall of Hyperion*. In consequence of "burning" through the theme of *King Lear*, he must be consumed, annihilated, by the fire of that fierce human contest; he must by that means be reborn out of his own ashes with the vigor to mount to the transcendent realm of his visions, like the phoenix, that bird of the sun, emblem of Apollo:

> But, when I am consumed in the fire,
> Give me new Phoenix wings to fly at my desire.[16]

In this manner Keats set out to fashion for himself a quasi-religious scheme that would accomplish what Christianity had failed to do for him—that is, to mediate some significant connection between this "dark void of night" and the "soul's daytime," between the laws of earth and those of heaven. Read in the light of this system of heaven-making, Keats's *Hyperion* is a quasi-theological poem premised on the seductive impossibility of uniting heaven and earth, essence and existence. Keats's Titans were created as gods, powerful and aloof from human passions; but when they topple into the human world they leave behind them their "strong identities," or absolute existences; they lose their divine creative powers and enter in ungodlike impotence into finite human experience.[17] The Titans are, in fact, sublated by the poem's hero, Olympian Apollo, who is not divine by birth but must generate his own status as the sun god

---

[16]The autograph and the transcript make it evident that "at my desire" was felt as equivalent of "to my desire."

[17]"Fate / Had pour'd a mortal oil upon [their heads], / A disanointing poison" (*Hyperion*, II, 96–98). "Divine ye were created," they are told,

> and divine
> In sad demeanor, solemn, undisturb'd,
> Unruffled, like high Gods, ye liv'd and ruled:
> Now I behold in you fear, hope, and wrath;
> Actions of rage and passion; even as
> I see them, on the mortal world beneath,
> In men who die.
> [*Hyperion*, I, 329–35]

of poetry.[18] Receiving from the goddess of memory and the mother of the Muses knowledge of the entire range of man's earthly experiences and assuming unto himself the whole mortal burden, the human Apollo becomes the poet deity of the solar myth. It is this "Knowledge enormous," he says, that "makes a God of me."[19] As Wasserman has persuasively argued, Keats's Christ figure is not an incarnate divinity who takes on human suffering to expiate man's fall, but a human being who becomes divine as a consequence of accepting that burden. It is telling that in *The Fall of Hyperion* Keats transferred to himself, as the human narrator of the poem, Apollo's death-into-life. Through increasingly "Richer entanglements" in the natural and human world, Keats speculated, we are, like the sun, conspiring in the life of organic process, eventually are "Full alchemiz'd"—transmuted into our perfect state—and, instead of being imprisoned in the world's occluded dungeon, become "free of space," that is, have unrestricted access to it.[20] (And somehow, in the metaphorics of "Richer entanglements," the burden of suffering is transmuted and elided.) In the erasure of the original and the accumulative economy of substitution, we can recognize "the double compass of the word *usure*," which Derrida situates in the metaphoric process at the root of language itself.[21] For Keats, the libera-

---

[18]Like the early, recumbent Keats striving to catch "spherey strains" and like the sick eagle looking at the sky, he experiences the human condition:

> I strive to search wherefore I am so sad,
> Until a melancholy numbs my limbs;
> And then upon the grass I sit, and moan,
> Like one who once had wings. . . .
> . . . why should I
> Spurn the green turf as hateful to my feet?
> . . . Point me out the way
> To any one particular beauteous star,
> And I will flit into it with my lyre,
> And make its silvery splendour pant with bliss.
> [*Hyperion*, III, 88–102]

[19]*Hyperion*, III, 130, 113.

[20]For a discussion of the solar myth and the figural implications of light and dark that, in turn, illuminate the metaphorics of the Hyperion poems, see Jacques Derrida, "La Mythologie blanche," in *Marges de la philosophie* (Paris: Minuit, 1972), pp. 247–324.

[21]"La Mythologie blanche," p. 250 (my translation):

> . . . we may make out the double compass of the word *usure:* as "wear and tear," the effacement by friction, exhaustion, weathering, to be sure; but also "usury," the supplementary product of invested capital, the exchange that—far from losing the original stake—would have the original wealth bear fruit, would increase the return in the form of revenues, of additional interest, of a kind of linguistic value added; the histories of the two meanings remain indissociable.

tion and usury of his sun god into process is the optimistic version of the freedom of the poetic text.

Broadly put, this formulation provides the plots of most of Keats's most familiar poems. Through increasing intensities the poet is progressively absorbed into the ideal scene on the Grecian urn, where love is forever war ; Lycius enters the Otherworld of Lamia's magic palace; the Knight-at-Arms is translated into that of the La Belle Dame's elfin grot; and the poet yearns to enter with ease the intensely ideal world of the nightingale. But, putting aside *Endymion,* with its obviously contrived happy ending, the *Hyperion* and *The Eve of St. Agnes,* which evaporate at the climactic point when the human melts into the visionary and ideal, these poems do *not* precisely enact the fulfillment of Keats's mythogony. Rather, because of the insistent intrusion of human limitations and the unraveling of the text, they are dramas of the thwarting of the formulation. The poet is tolled back from ideal vision to his "sole self"; Lamia and her magic palace are destroyed by the "philosophic mind"; the Knight-at-Arms is awakened by his mortality to find himself sojourning on the world's bleak hillside. Since metaphor is flawed in its very nature (in Derrida's prime example, a turning away at the same time as a turning toward), Keats never successfully completed the poem that would fully embody his conception of the world and the human heart as the elements of soul-making. He could not do so, so long as he was honest enough to take account of man's mortality, of life's restraints and of the duplicity of the text that would mediate them. We rightly relish many of his poems for the very quality that their impending thematic disintegration so acutely elicits: the exquisite intricacy and the intense pressure toward formal coherence with which Keats strove to sustain the world of the poem under threat of its imminent thematic collapse—or, as the poet weak on his deathbed thought back on that exhausting creative stress, "the knowledge of contrast, feeling for light and shade, all that information (primitive sense) necessary for a poem."[22] The "Ode on a Grecian Urn," straining progressively toward a superhuman perfection, cracks thematically in mid-career under its own amazing formal tension and then places the poet under the duress of trying to reintegrate the consequent fragments into a meaningful synthesis. In fact, the poem's very resistance to an integrated interpretation is finally enacted in the paradoxical circularity of its legend. The "Ode to a Nightingale" is, from its beginning, a continuous thematic unraveling that imposes on the

[22]*LJK,* II, 360.

poet the extraordinary strain of working counter to that movement and so weaving into a dramatic and artistic whole materials that repel each other.

The artistic greatness—the formal brilliance of these poems and the powerful aesthetic energy that they release—are beyond doubt. Yet the same straining intensity that is responsible for their greatness makes it necessary to question their authenticity—to question whether they express, to use Keats's touchstone phrase, "the true voice of feeling."[23] To examine that question is to explore the experiential and textual substrata on which Keats's poems ultimately rest, however disparate the poems are among themselves—to locate his "selfhood," or identity, and his various attempts to contain it in language.

One of Keats's most striking characteristics is that of all persons and poetic voices he is among the most selfless, the most outgoing.[24] His sympathy with and generosity to family and friends distinguished him as a man; tolerance and disinterested fellow-feeling were his overriding ethical code. He had the self-knowledge to see that, although conscious of commanding great resources, he presented in society the image of a child, an idiot, a nothing, an *in-fans,* vacuous for lack of definable character.[25] This inner blankness and passivity, this absence of self-directed interest with which to respond to experience in a personal way, was no pose. Earnest accounts recur in his correspondence of periods during which he lacked the interior equipment to carry on personal transactions with the world of others. For example, in a letter devoted in part to his conviction that the man of genius has not "any individuality, any determined Character" or "proper self"—a conviction that increased his "Humility and capability of submission"—he writes of his confinement to the immediate moment of existence, of his self-projection into the life of a sparrow outside his window.[26] Yet this unsparing analysis of his

---

[23]*LJK,* II, 167.

[24]My debt to Paul de Man for his penetrating analysis of this theme will be evident to those who have read his preface to the Signet edition of *The Selected Poetry of Keats.*

[25]Even among his intimate friends, Keats recognized, "I give into their feelings as though I were refraining from irritating a little child—Some think me middling, others silly, others foolish" (*LJK,* I, 404).

[26]"If a Sparrow come before my Window I take part in its existence and pick about the Gravel" (*LJK,* I, 186). He speaks in this letter, too, of his cold acceptance of the misfortune of his friends as but their opportunity to test their spiritual resources. This last, he explains, is the result not of "heartlessness but abstraction," that is, the annihilation of his human self as he is existing selflessly or self-forgetfully in an ideal imaginative realm: "I assure you I sometimes feel not the influence of a Passion or

selflessness follows directly upon his option in the same letter for the "Heart's affections" and "a Life of sensations" in the programmatic belief that "we shall enjoy ourselves here after by having what we called happiness on earth repeated in a finer tone and so repeated." The oscillation here between random access and repetition makes suspect the authenticity of his theory of an ascent to absoluteness through real experiential intensities; it suggests that Keats actually may have lacked any individuated emotional equipment except as he *imagined* sensation.[27]

Nor does Keats's poetic voice have any definable personality or interiority; it is constantly dissolving into the rich texture of "globed peonies" and other "entanglements" that are "self-destroying" as he yearns for dissolution of his identity into otherness, into the nightingale, into the life on the urn's frieze, the instinct of wren or eagle. (In the same way, he is able to lose his own language in the rival voices of the poets whose curriculum informs his evolving work.) It is an unmistakably Keatsian voice mainly in its tone and rhythm of intensely outgoing eagerness to be other than the voice of a distinctive personality. Keats lampooned subjectively oriented poetry as "the Wordsworthian or egotistical sublime," and more than once he ridiculed the title Wordsworth gave to a group of his poems, "Moods of My Own Mind." Keats not only would not but could not have performed the self-constituting introspection that generates Wordsworth's *Prelude*. He is, it is true, intensely introspective in his letters, but only to carry on a quarrel with his interior vacancy or to fret over threats to it. The evasion of self-consciousness is consequently a compulsion as generative of Keats's poetry as self-examination is of Wordsworth's.[28]

Affection during a whole week—and so long this sometimes continues I begin to suspect myself and the genuineness of my feelings at other times—thinking them a few barren Tragedy-tears" (*LJK*, I, 186)

[27]This, the "Adam's Dream" letter, is somewhat confusing, and I have deliberately oversimplified it. It may well be that Keats himself could not distinguish between real and imaginative experience. He expresses faith in both "the holiness of the Heart's affections and the Truth of Imagination," implying that they are distinct; but he also writes that "Imagination and its empyreal reflection is the same as human Life and its spiritual repetition," equating life and imagination. At any rate, since his nominal subject is "the Authenticity of the imagination," it appears that the sensations of which he writes are not responses to actuality but are imaginary, as his illustrative use of Adam's dream suggests.

[28]When to Endymion, locked underground, "thoughts of self came on, how crude and sore / The journey homeward to habitual self" (*Endymion*, II, 275–76). No doubt Keats means "habitual self" in Hume's and Hazlitt's sense: selfhood is not a metaphysical reality, but a mere notion acquired from our habitual attachment of sensations and emotions to a single being. To look within the self is, for Keats, "a mad

This absence of a defining identity is, then, potentially ambivalent. Although the emptiness of the self cannot bear contemplation, it is functional to one's existence in otherness. It is also the key to the poet's extraordinary facility in adopting (and discarding) the stylistic imprint of his predecessors. If complete empathic experience is assumed to be the goal, then annihilation of identity is the means to that end, and the potential horror of self-consciousness can be converted into the ecstasy of consciousness-in-another. Because I am nothing in particular, I can be any other. The true poet, pressing necessity into prescription, Keats claimed, is required to have no self, no identity, no peculiar character or "unchangeable attribute," so that he may be "continually infor[ming] and filling some other Body." "When I am in a room with People," he confessed, "if I ever am free from speculating on creations of my own brain, then not myself goes home to myself"—that dreaded journey homeward to habitual self—"but the identity of every one in the room begins so to press upon me that I am in a little time annihilated."[29]

Mere empathic experience, however, was not enough. The unrestrained Romantic reach for the limitless and ideal—the Apollonian flight—also exerted its pressure; and through his doctrine of empathy, Keats sought not only to justify the absence of identity but also to heal the Romantic disjunction between the actual and the ideal. It is easy to step beyond the bourn of care, to cross the threshold that the poems explore: "Every man has his speculations. . . . Many a man can travel to the very bourne of Heaven. . . . Sancho will invent a Journey heavenward as well as any body."[30]

The processes of most of Keats's major poems, then, are expressions of his underlying urge to make capital of his repugnant selflessness by proposing a progressive unselving as the means of

---

pursuing of a fog-born elf," an illusory will-o'-the-wisp that "Cheats us into a swamp, into a fire, / Into the bosom of a hated thing." When Endymion then reaches the "goal of consciousness"—that is, consciousness of self—he experiences the "deadly feel of solitude" and only "a noisy nothing" rings in his ear (*Endymion*, II, 277–80, 283–84, 321). In the same way, the poet, when fully desublimated from his projection into the nightingale, is tolled back to his "sole self," summoned from vital existence in another to the death of self-awareness and self-containment.

[29]*LJK*, I, 184, 387. The curious expression "myself goes home to myself" belongs to a type of locution that is frequent in Keats's writings and suggests an awareness of two selves, one of which is an empty and available lodge; the other is the agent of active experience. "I nearly consented with myself" (*LJK*, I, 139): "I ask myself—and myself has not a word to answer (*LJK*, II, 291); "I and my conscience are in luck today" (*LJK*, II, 94); "in my dream capacity . . . but in Propria Persona" (*LJK*, II, 174); "I and myself cannot agree" (*LJK*, II, 234).

[30]*LJK*, I, 223–24.

achieving the absolute. In this manner he sought to resolve the Romantic division of the human and the ideal. In the empathic loss of private selfhood through its imaginative assimilation into the essences of the experiential world, the absolute self emerges in the text. Correspondingly, the world, instead of being categorically separated from the divine, becomes, as we have seen, intensely refined into it. In proportion, as the speaking consciousness becomes absorbed into the world on the frieze of the Grecian urn, that world is transformed, in theory at least, from a mutable earthly landscape into an ideal where trees can never bid the spring adieu, where love is forever warm and forever to be enjoyed. It is this transformation of the state of consciousness with respect to its object that is responsible for the corresponding imaginative transformation of the state of reality. A principle of Keats's psychology becomes the clew to his poetics, for only by tightly weaving the texture of language can he hope to realize that transfigured, "distill'd" reality.

But conversion of selflessness into a free absolute self and a poetics of transcendence are doomed for Keats by the nature of things to failure, except through imaginative evasion. Keats is too honest (save in *Endymion*) to superimpose happy endings on his poems. Mortal man is not Apollo; the earth is not heaven. The situation of the poet, like that of his language, is one of continual "usury" in the erosive and fragmenting as well as the additive sense. The radical—and ineradicable—fact in Keats's mind is the mutual incompatibility of the human and the ideal climates, of "life" and the "legend," of experience and the language that would comprehend it. Such poems as the "Ode on a Grecian Urn," "Lamia," and the "Ode to a Nightingale" therefore recount tragedies and not triumphs.[31]

Yet even in the face of inevitable failure, Keats cannot put down the urge to ascend to Apollo's heaven. The vital spirit operative in these poems is motivated not by Lycius' human vanity, but by the

[31]Like Apollonius, the mortal figures who intrude into the Knight-at-Arms' dream and shatter it are an integral part of the human mind; their warning that he is enthralled in the visionary is evidence that transcendence is not reality alchemized but is distinct from it. Only when the door shuts out the real world can Porphyro "melt" into Madeline's idealized dream of him. Lamia's palace is unrelated to the world, and Lycius could have remained there only if he could have "forsworn" the world utterly. But it proves impossible to abandon the human self, however empty it is of identity: Lycius had only "almost forsworn" the noisy world, and he cannot be deaf to the sound of the world's trumpet of Fame. His is not the "Pride and egotism" of the Apollonian self, but the vanity of private identity, and he cannot resist the shattering desire to proclaim his visionary attainment to his fellow men—as though Keats were imagining with horror the consequence of his own vanity were he to proclaim his poems of Romance to the human "herd."

hubristic desire of a mortal to exceed his nature; and the intense struggle the poems enact of a language striving to attain transcendence is the manifestation of Keats's own strenuous but vain exertion to gain his own creative freedom. That enormous but baffled creative energy consistently overflowed into a superhuman heat, a fever; and Keats the former student of medicine was acutely conscious of its unhealthiness. Escaping the menace of selfhood by plunging into "abstract images," "I now live," he says, "in a continual fever," a pathological state induced by his "artificial excitement."[32] The word *artificial* carries the sense both of "unnatural" and of "contrived by art." He is obliged, he says, "to be continually burning of thought as an only resource" against the self-awareness of solitude; haunted by the threatening image of a woman, he seeks "the fevrous relief of Poetry."[33] ("Thought" is, of course, inextricable

---

[32]*LJK*, II, 137.

[33]*LJK*, I, 139, 370. It is understandable, if medically inexcusable, that his doctor attributed his final illness in part to "the too great excitement of poetry" (*LJK*, II, 287). Merely thinking about poetry is an excitement that prevents sleep, while poetic composition exhausts that excitement and makes sleep possible (*LJK*, I, 138, 133). Even the "faint conceptions I have of Poems to come brings the blood frequently into my forehead," for to Keats the sun-god's lyre is "hot" (*LJK*, I, 387–88; "God of the Meridian," l. 21) In a jingle prophesying that George Keats's child would be a poet, Keats wrote, no doubt alluding to the holy lambent fire about the head of the infant Ascanius that prophesied his kingship (*Aeneid*, II, 679–91) and then associating that flame with Apollo's fire:

> See, see the Lyre, the Lyre
> In a flame of fire
> Upon the little cradle's top
> Flaring, flaring, flaring
> Past the eyesight's bearing—
> Awake it from its sleep
> And see if it can keep
> Its eyes upon the blaze.
> Amaze, amaze!
> It stares, it stares, it stares
> It dares what no one dares
> It lifts its little hand into the flame
> Unharm'd. . . .
>
> [I, 399]

Like all his fellow Romantics, Keats yearned to unite divinity and humanity and to temper Apollo's hot lyre with the "staid philosophy" of mortal life:

> An extensive knowledge is needful to thinking people—it takes away the heat and fever; it helps, by widening speculation, to ease the Burden of the Mystery. . . . The difference of high Sensations with and without knowledge appears to me this—in the latter case we are falling continually ten thousand fathoms deep and being blown up again without wings and with all the horror of a bare shouldered Creature—in the former case, our shoulders are fledge, and we go thro' the same air and space without fear. [*LJK*, I, 227]

from the processes of sympathy and empathy that command the poet in this state.)

This unnatural creative heat was not confined to Keats's act of composition; it is contagiously manifested in (and coextensive with) the fever that evolves within his poems. When, in the "Ode on a Grecian Urn," the progressive intensities annihilate the speaker's identity until he is absorbed into pure existence, the passionate warmth that marks that ideal condition ("forever warm") suddenly flares into the "burning forehead" and "parching tongue" of the human state. And that burning forehead then induces the contrary awareness of the sacrificial altar of mortality and the gulf between the world's "little town" and the realm from which no soul "can e'er return." Keats was painfully aware of the abnormality of efforts to exceed human limits and win the freedom of union with a Cynthia or of entrance into Lamia's palace: the apotheosis of the human Apollo takes place with a "fierce convulse" and "a pang / As hot as death's is chill." ("Abnormality" perhaps needs qualification: what seems abnormal in *Endymion* becomes something approximating a "normal perversion" in "Lamia.") The phoenix that would fly heliotropically to the god of poetry must first be consumed in the fire of experience. The goddess Moneta defines the poet who spurns the human and dreams of heaven as "A fever of thyself," an overwrought finite self striving hectically to become absolute.[34] For Keats, poetic composition was the febrile act of a would-be creator-god, and that fever was the superhuman energy he recalled, in deathbed exhaustion, of shaping those remarkably intense, tightly interwoven, and nearly, but not quite, self-containing worlds that are his major poems. In speaking of composition, Keats tended to elide aesthetic and moral judgments in the language of a physician watching the course of a disease. Poesy, abstraction, Romance, the imaginative transmutation into an absolute self—these may have rescued him momentarily from the threatening imprisonment in a blank private identity, but Keats recognized that his poetic struggles not only were doomed to fail but were "unhealthy" (in the same radical sense that Moneta, his Muse, suffers in the great thwarted vision of *The Fall of Hyperion* from "an immortal sickness that kills not"). Wisely assessing the costs of any breakthrough, he knew that

---

But as the murderous effect of Apollonius makes clear, the hope of tempering the creative heat with human knowledge was in vain, and at best the fever was a momentary catharsis that restored him to human health.

[34]*Hyperion*, III, 128–29; *The Fall of Hyperion*, I, 169.

the consequent poetry, however glorious, was by his own diagnosis both etiologically and nosologically morbid.[35]

Finite identity is a prison, a death of being tolled back from abstractions to one's "sole self"; and self-consciousness is the horror of perceiving one's inner emptiness, a "hated thing." On the other hand, a frustrated struggle for freedom and transcendent self-sufficiency is febrile and sickly, an act against the grain of human nature. Language, despite its sensuous "entanglements," ultimately repeats this dialectic of vacancy and fever. (*The Fall of Hyperion* takes Keats closest to a tragic enactment of this predicament, but in the same Winchester letter that reports the genesis of "To Autumn" he announces that he is putting it—and Milton—aside. What, then, remains? Much of the history of Keats's attempts to articulate his consciousness and style obviously is a repeated, intense, and contravening wavering between selflessness and those hot, frustrated flights.[36]

In the wavering, however, Keats has nearly achieved a negative definition of self-existence. "Interior emptiness" is not merely the condition for the empathic absorption creative of absolute selfhood; if one may stave off the fever by striving to be nothing, the emptiness is itself the autonomous and healthy state of human consciousness. Keats's poetic persona is at this extremity close to the ascetic condition of Stevens' Snow Man. Even his humorous comments in the letters about eating as a guarantee of his diminutive identity point to this need to be filled—his blank, perceptive emp-

---

[35]Harold Bloom's later, "revisionary" reading of *The Fall of Hyperion* in *Poetry and and Repression* (New Haven: Yale University Press, 1976) eloquently argues that this poem presents Moneta as the "final form of romance, and sees in her more-than-tragic face the Beautiful Necessity. Of what? Of a mode of repetition in self-destroyings, I think, and a repetition also in the redefinition of romance" (p. 141).

[36]Even that astonishingly egotistic assertion of his creative self which so disturbed Taylor finally broke down at its climax, so that at the point when Keats claimed the solipsistic adequacy of his own soul, the threat of the consequent human fever hung over him, and at once the eagle became aware of its mortal sickness: "I think if I had a free and healthy and lasting organisation of heart and Lungs—as strong as an ox's—so as to be able [to bear] unhurt the shock of extreme thought and sensation without weariness, I could pass my Life very nearly alone. . . . But I feel my Body too weak to support me to the height" (*LJK*, II, 146–47). The only tolerable alternative turns out to be the opposite of unhealthy poetic excitement and subjective absoluteness: "I am obliged continually to check myself and strive to be nothing" (*LJK*, II, 147). There is no middle ground for a private identity between healthy nothingness and the unbearable struggle for solipsistic transcendence. But there is also no resolution of the oscillating as now one and now the other of his unsatisfied impulses surges to the surface and displaces the other: even after acknowledging the need for self-annihilation, he longs for the intolerable "state of excitement, . . . the only state for the best sort of Poetry—that is all I care for, all I live for" (*LJK*, II, 147).

tiness that anticipates Stevens' "nothings."[37] The empirical self is a vacuum and is known to be such by its capacity to receive. I can be occupied; therefore I am. Although he cannot tolerate contemplation of his inner "hollowness" and cannot, without unnatural fever, sublimate that unpleasantness with the rationale that subjective annihilation is, phoenix-like, the means to a creative, ideal identity, there is another Keats who can calmly resign himself to the emptiness of his human ego and make a poetic virtue of it. For if the self is a void, it is also pure receptivity, capable of occupation by everything and anything.

This is what Keats means by "Negative Capability," not to be confused with the doctrine that the poet has no identity. The latter is the basis for empathic extension, for "filling some other Body," not for being filled; it is therefore the opposite of Negative Capability, which is rather the power of not asserting the will, taking a stand, or creating, the power of totally passive and indiscriminate receptivity—or, as Keats defined it, the ability to be "in uncertainties, Mysteries, doubts, without any irritable reaching after fact & reason" because the sheer "sense of Beauty . . . obliterates all consideration."[38] Both empathic projection and Negative Capability require the absence of identity; but empathy is a power to inhabit, while Negative Capability is a capacity, a capaciousness. "The only means of strengthening one's intellect," Keats wrote in opposing C. W. Dilke's desire for personal identity, "is to make up ones mind about nothing—to let the mind be a thoroughfare for all thoughts. Not a select party. . . . Dilke will never come at truth as long as he lives; because he is always trying at it."[39] As opposed to both empathy and the struggle for transcendence, Negative Capability is both a rejection of teleology and an uncritical acceptance of the immediate, a readiness to be content and rich "in the simple worship of a day." In

[37] Always sensitive about his stature—"I being somewhat stunted am taken for nothing"—Keats writes of never feeling "more contemptible than when I am sitting by a good looking coachman," and the coachman's huge florid face "says eat, eat, eat." "One is nothing," Keats adds. "Perhaps I eat to persuade myself I am somebody." He is writing in self-defensive jest, of course, and the coachman, a "Hercules Methodist," does not in fact owe his size to "bread alone"; yet Keats has opened up the possibility of an adequate selfhood defined solely by its vacancy (*LJK*, II, 169). For his running commentary on his stature, see also *LJK*, I, 342; II, 61, 275.

[38] *LJK*, I, 193–94. It is precisely the lack of Negative Capability that Keats disliked in his friend C. W. Dilke, who feels he must have a "personal identity" and for that purpose makes up "his Mind about every thing," just as Coleridge lacks it because he is "incapable of remaining content with half knowledge," or Bailey because he hungers after Truth (*LJK*, II, 213; I, 194, 185).

[39] *LJK*, II, 213.

the area of human relations it manifests itself in those sporadic moments when, subsiding from energetic striving, Keats expresses remarkably generous tolerance.[40]

Few moods are more obsessively recurrent in Keats's letters than a peculiarly acute passivity and indolence, related to his spirit of tolerance and summed up in such statements as "My sensations are sometimes deadened for weeks together" and "I am in a sort of qui bono temper."[41] Although he felt that this spirit especially characterized his "1819 temper,"[42] these "indolent fits" in fact recurred sporadically throughout his career, because they were the most radical manifestations of his lack of inner responsive equipment, not (it seems) because of any evolution or crisis in his history of consciousness. What is striking about these periods is not only their frequency, duration, and severity, but also Keats's vivid awareness of them and his objective analysis of their significance. For his indolent lack of subjectivity, when it did not result in introspection or incite flights to Romance, was not merely a blank but an actual *sensation of that emptiness.* Like its opposite, the transcending loss of self empathically in essence, which can be a "drowsy numbness" that pains, this other state can be "an unpleasant numbness" that "does not take away the pain of existence." Or it can be so total a submission that, like Glaucus when forgetful of "self-intent" on entering Neptune's kingdom, Keats feels that "if I were under Water I would scarcely kick to come to the top."[43] But under any circumstance it is a positive awareness of vacancy, like the "feel of not to feel it," which is Keats's description not of insensate numbness but of nature's wintry sensation of the absence of any sensation recollective of its "green felicity" of spring.[44]

[40]Reynolds, he complains, "has no powers of sufferance; no idea of having the thing against him" as he should (*LJK,* I, 205). "Men should bear with each other; . . . know a Man's faults, and then be passive" (*LJK,* I, 210).

[41]*LJK,* I, 325; II, 42.

[42]*LJK,* II, 116, 122.

[43]"Ode to a Nightingale," l. 1; *LJK,* I, 287. On the transumptions of the Romantic "blank" (itself a Miltonic legacy) from Coleridge to Stevens, see Harold Bloom's suggestive discussion in *The Breaking of the Vessels* (Chicago: University of Chicago Press, 1982), pp. 85–99.

[44]"In a drear-nighted December." Even when he willfully compensates for his passivity with factitious though earnest counteractive doctrines, it persists in surfacing. In the same letter in which he opted for a "Life of Sensations" as generative of its postmortal repetition, he confessed to periods of such insensitivity as to "suspect myself and the genuineness of my feelings at other times." Again, directly before describing the energy and intensity in which poetry consists, he reports, "This morning I am in a sort of temper indolent and supremely careless: I long after a stanza or two of Thomson's Castle of Indolence—My passions are all asleep. . . . This is the

These oscillations between indolence and excitement are, of course, functions of his characteristic waverings between resignation to selflessness and feverish efforts to transcend it. Indolence is nevertheless the authentic state of his consciousness—and it is in its own way uniquely creative. For it is in that state of Negative Capability that the mind acts as a thoroughfare for everything, however foreign, and, by passively accepting what *is* instead of actively striving for ends, grants that freedom Keats so vainly sought through empathic transcendence. "It seems to me," he writes in this mood of "Idleness,"

> that we should rather be the flower than the bee—for it is a false notion that more is gained by receiving than giving—no the receiver and the giver are equal in their benefits—The flower I doubt not receives a fair guerdon from the Bee-its leaves blush deeper in the next spring—and who shall say between Man and Woman which is the more delighted? Now it is more noble to sit like Jove than to fly like Mercury—let us not therefore go hurrying about and collecting honeybee like, buzzing here and there impatiently from a knowledge of what is to be arrived at: but let us open our leaves like a flower and be passive and receptive— budding patiently under the eye of Apollo and taking hints from every noble insect that favors us with a visit.[45]

Thereupon (in this 1818 letter to J. H. Reynolds) he illustrates his principle with the poem the thrush had told him: "O fret not after knowledge—I have none / And yet my song comes native with the warmth." For those who endure the winter of Apollo's absence, some will come instinctively with indolent receptivity to the spring warmth of the sun god's poetry—warmth, not fever. Selfless indifference makes possible a "native" poetry that evolves "as naturally as the leaves to a tree," a poetry that is almost categorically different from Keats's hectic, self-annihilating ascents to new countries. For passive receptivity is also creative, as the thrush—in a significant variation on the paradox of Adam's dream—told the poet:

---

only true happiness" (*LJK*, I, 78–79). The "Ode on Indolence" is forming in his mind at the very time he transcribes "Why Did I Laugh Tonight?," which accepts as fundamental values the intensities of verse, fame, beauty, and death (*LJK*, II, 78–81).

[45]*LJK*, I, 232. Characteristically, Keats, feeling that he may merely have been rationalizing his own indolence and not yet ready to accept it as a creative power, then ends the letter by reversing himself and claiming that the decision is an indifferent one; just as a week later he offers it as an axiom that poetry should come naturally and passively—and then admits that his own impulse is to "ascend the brightest heaven of invention."

"To Autumn" and the Music of Mortality

> He who saddens
> At thought of idleness cannot be idle,
> And he's awake who thinks himself asleep.

The best gloss on the thrush's song and the creative pathos of indolence is Keats's earlier commentary on Wordsworth's "Gypsies."[46] Like philanthropy, philosophy, the search for truth or for private identity, and the knowledge of what is to be arrived at, all of which violate Negative Capability, *thought* is prospective, teleological, and thus can destroy diligent indolence, which is the acceptance of the immediate. Wordsworth's complaint against the gypsies' idleness was the result of some shallow thought in the midst of his own indolence, the creative potential of which would have been dissipated by deeper thought. Saddened by the thought of idleness, he was not idle but opened himself thereby to the admission of the total "picturesque" scene; the result was the creation of the poem not as an objective picture but as a presentation of the scene upon its being received into mental space, an "intellectual landscape," or what Wordsworth himself called "a prospect in the mind."

Indolence, in the sense of unselfconscious acceptance of one's hollowness, leaves one free to admit everything. And Keats associates this state with the reader's encounter with the text: "I'd [like to] sit and read all day," he writes in one of his indolent moods, suggesting mental receptivity. But the sentence continues: "I'd sit and read

---

[46]Keats is writing with the disturbing awareness that it is his own nature to "lie dormant a whole Month" and consequently has been brought up short by a sudden accession of human sympathy with Bailey's troubles: "I wish I had a heart always open to such sensations" (*LJK*, I, 173). The result is a self-searching debate between such "uncomfortable hours" of "philanthropy" and his more natural "indolent enjoyment of intellect," a debate that leads him to Hazlitt's protest against Wordsworth's disapproval of the gypsies' laziness. As usual, both positions alternately make their claims on Keats's mind. Wordsworth, keeping "watch on Man's Mortality," is right to object to the gypsies' indolence, but Hazlitt is also right to prefer "wise passiveness" (ibid.). Yet "Wordsworth is rightest," not for preferring activity, but for actually having engaged in the creative poetic act that Keats elsewhere called "diligent Indolence," the work of the "otiosus-peroccupatus Man" (*LJK*, I, 231; II, 175).

> Wordsworth had not been idle[;] he had not been without his task—nor had the Gypseys—they in the visible world had been as picturesque an object as he in the invisible. . . . if Wordsworth had thought a little deeper at that Moment he would not have written the Poem at all—I should judge it to have been written in one of the most comfortable Moods of his Life—it is a kind of sketchy intellectual Landscape—not a search after Truth. . . . it is with the Critic as with the poet[:] had Hazlitt thought a little deeper and been in a good temper he would never have spied an imaginary fault there. [*LJK*, I, 174]

all day like the picture of somebody reading."[47] Nothing could be more detached, more selfless than that: given his divided consciousness, he has abstracted his living self so that what is left is only a picture of himself reading, an absorbed emblem of receptiveness. And, paradoxically, "receptiveness" is here qualified and undone by the emblematic frame of the pictorial similitude, an impression distanced by the framing. In the same way he saw as "picturesque" not only the poetic description of the indolent gypsies but also his vision of Wordsworth indolently composing the poem. Indolence, then, is also the acceptance of the constitutive function of mere unprospective being (in Stevens' late formulation, "One feels the life of that which gives life as it is"). In such a context the selfish desire for fame becomes, on the contrary, self-destructive and, like all unnatural, superhuman efforts, a morbid fever:

> How fever'd is the man, who cannot look
> Upon his mortal days with temperate blood,
> Who vexes all the leaves of his life's book,
> And robs his fair name of its maidenhood.[48]

Such a person is like a mere dreamer of heaven, who thereby "envenoms all his days."[49] Worse, such self-centering implies a subject that violates itself: "It is as if the rose should pluck herself, / Or the ripe plum finger its misty bloom."[50] Indolence, rather, is not merely a forgoing of the striving for absoluteness; it is the generous acceptance of outward reality, together with its mutability, which the unnatural transcendent flights had sought to overcome—an acceptance made possible by Keats's recognition that the poet is a void into which reality can be received and in which reality has its life for us.

---

[47]*LJK*, II, 46.
[48]"How fever'd is the man," ll. 1–4.
[49]*The Fall of Hyperion*, I, 175.
[50]In contrast to the transcending phoenix, which rises out of its own fiery destruction, the epigraph of the poem explains that "you cannot eat your cake and have it too," for the alternative to self-consumptive desire for fame is simply to *be* and passively receive. The self should be like a watery surface, which, because of its empty clarity, its "crystal space," can mirror everything else; but the desire for fame is "As if a clear Lake meddling with itself / Should cloud its pureness with a muddy gloom," unlike the receptive rose, which "leaves herself upon the Briar / For winds to kiss and grateful Bees to feed." The epigraph of the poem is from Luke's words acclaiming the bounty we are given gratuitously by God: "Consider the lilies how they grow: they toil not, they spin not; and yet I say unto you, that Solomon in all his glory was not arrayed like one of these." The indolent soul does not go naked; it is "besprinkled o'er / With flowers."

In his "Ode on Indolence" Keats envisions three figures passing by like images on a revolving urn—Love, Ambition, and his "demon Poesy," those three forces that constantly menace and torment his selflessness—"and to follow them I burn'd / And ach'd for wings." The "fever" of transcendent flight threatens again. But he now spurns these temptations that would draw him toward a private identity or Romance: "O, why did ye not melt, and leave my sense / Unhaunted quite of all but—nothingness?" (Again, in Stevens' idiom, "As if nothingness contained a métier.") This is a nothingness he now gladly accepts, a blank that has become transparently receptive:

> . . . Ripe was the drowsy hour;
>   The blissful cloud of summer-indolence
>   Benumb'd my eyes; my pulse grew less and less;
>   Pain had no sting, and pleasure's wreath no flower.
>   [ll. 15–18]

In "honied indolence" the empty self is like a blank but receiving lake:

> My sleep had been embroider'd with dim dreams;
> My soul had been a lawn besprinkled o'er
>   With flowers, and stirring shades, and baffled beams.
>   [ll. 42–44]

Reality is entirely an intellectual landscape; and casements now do not open out to the infinite or to hot Apollo's heaven of invention, but (naturalizing the climax of the "Ode to Psyche") "Let in the budding warmth and throstle's lay."

II

With Keats's happy acceptance of the self's empty availability, the tormenting Romantic concern with subjectivity vanishes—or rather it is tempered and translated into the indeterminacy of a psyche and a language that no longer aspire to Apollo's condition. The tormenting division between the limited and unlimited aspects of the ego, its pull in opposite directions that preoccupies his fellow Romantics and provokes much of their poetry, is no longer relevant if subjectivity is only the "crystal space" in which reality is apprehended. In psychological terms, subjectivity then becomes the carrier of reality, the transparent medium of its presence, not the object of agonizing concern. In linguistic terms, the medium is of course far from crystalline; but the language is no longer feverish in its vain attempt to transcend itself, to fuse the sensuous and the visionary. The authentic, unfevered, selfless Keats eschews the questing poetry of "heaven's bourn" for a more modern, immanent "poetry of earth," and his triumph in that emergent mode is the ode that concludes the "living year," "To Autumn." (It was, incidentally, immediately before transcribing this poem for Richard Woodhouse that Keats wrote, "One is nothing—Perhaps I eat to persuade myself I am somebody.") A recognition that all of Keats's poetry is grounded in selflessness clarifies why, on the one side, "To Autumn" is felt to be as truly Keatsian as any of the major poems and why, on the other, readers feel its startling difference from the rest of the canon. It also suggests why so many critics with "modern" sensibilities consider it his most nearly perfect work despite the obviously greater artistry, range, and vigor of others of his poems. Close textual readings have already patiently unfolded the internal activity of "To Autumn."[51] What remains in order to grant the poem its fullest dimensions is to situate it accurately in the rhetorical and linguistic structure of its authorial consciousness. (Contemporary readers will, of course, recognize how exactly consciousness itself is a linguistic structure.)

Before considering the dynamics of the poem itself, I should like to examine the remarkable letter to Reynolds in which Keats mentions having just composed it.[52] The pervasive mood of this Winchester letter is one of pure receptivity and unassertiveness. "I have no meridian to date Interests from, or measure circumstances," he writes in a state of Negative Capability. All things occupy the same level of his mind, and they are equally interesting, equally acceptable on their own grounds: "To night," he says, "I am all in a *mist*" [my italics]; this mist, which is here at once the indeterminacy of a psychological moment and the perennial instability of language itself, is also the figural epithet countering, in the poem, the firmness of the season's "mellow fruitfulness." Keats realizes that he has long had "No anchor—and I am glad of it." His subjectivity makes no comment on reality, no comparative or normative judgments, but simply admits it for what it is. In that spirit he tells of an episode that seems to have curious importance for him and to call for interpretation. The occasion is his jesting determination to side with neither Reyn-

[51]Among the most helpful of these explications is that of Karl Kroeber in *The Artifice of Reality*, pp. 115–16.
[52]*LJK*, II, 166–68.

olds nor Woodhouse in their next dispute but to persist in a position "just half way" between them, simply as a way of fending off the restricting pressure of their urgings. Then he offers an episode to explain his temperament: "In my walk to day I stoop'd under a rail way that lay across my path, and ask'd myself 'Why I did not get over.' Because, answered I, 'no one wanted to force you under.'" In a sense, no Leigh Hunt was there, intent on amputating *Endymion* until seven thousand lines were ablated to four. It had been the irresolvable conflict between the mind's unbounded aspiring and reality's inadequacies that, pressuring the Romantics to accept human limitations—to stoop under the railing—had stirred up their rebellious questing for the absolute, for surmounting the railing. By accepting the value of the empty, receptive consciousness and a language tempered by its own economy rather than fevered by a rhetoric of transcendence, Keats has rescued himself from the urgency to flight and willingly accepts the finite world at his feet. These remarks in the letter of September 21, 1819, follow from his mentioning that two days earlier he had composed a poem on autumn because he had seen (or perhaps more exactly *felt*) a "stubble plain" that somehow had looked "warm"-warm, not fevered. "Warm in the same way," he adds, "that some pictures look warm"; and again, as in conceiving of himself as beholding a picture of himself reading, he has distanced all subjectivity from the scene. Significantly, he renders the "scene" not through verbal description of the landscape, but as a series of preverbal, thermal responses to the climate and the place ("temperate sharpness" of the air, warm "look" of the fields).

The initial experience of autumn in the letter has the atemporal shape of a picture (like the earlier analogy, once removed) and the immediacy of a tactile experience. But exactly what autumn means to Keats evolves as he ruminates on his "gaping after weather": "I always somehow associate Chatterton with autumn. He is the purest writer in the English Language. He has no French idiom, or particles like Chaucer—'tis genuine English idiom in English words."[53] It

---

[53]This curious idea was fixed in Keats's mind. On the same day as this letter, he wrote: "The purest english I think—or what ought to be the purest—is Chatterton's—The Language had existed long enough to be entirely uncorrupted of Chaucer's gallicisms and still the old words are used—Chatterton's language is entirely northern" (*LJK*, II, 212). The notion of "uncorrupted" obviously is not originary but requires the passage of time. Geoffrey H. Hartman has written on the "northern" or Hesperian element in the essay noted above. The original dedication to *Endymion* (March 19, 1818) reads, "To the memory of the most english of Poets except Shakespeare, Thomas Chatterton."

RICHARD MACKSEY

is telling that Keats focuses on language to characterize Chatterton, for it is with words and *in* words that Keats had earlier striven to pass the threshold separating him from the transcendent. His earlier appropriations of new and rival "kingdoms"—Spenser and Shakespeare, Milton and Wordsworth—were linguistic, as were his earlier aporiae. And in situating Chatterton's claim to purity of language he introduces the question of historical priority by reaching for origins in Chaucer, "the well of English" already in a sense defiled by foreign temptations. Further, as he makes clear in the inception to *The Fall of Hyperion,* even his notion of imaginative experience is mediated by language; it is not enough to dream,

> For Poesy alone can tell her dreams,
> With the fine spell of words alone can save
> Imagination from the sable charm
> And dumb enchantment. . . .
> Since every man whose soul is not a clod
> Hath visions, and would speak, if he had lov'd
> And been well nurtured in his mother tongue.[54]

But more important (and critical to the dismissal of *The Fall* itself in the same letter), for Keats being true to one's Englishness, as we have seen, had always a special and pressing significance. Two years earlier he had published a sonnet in which he had wavered between content with England's "artless daughters" and their "simple loveliness" and a desire to forget "world or worldling" for an Alpine throne, Italian skies: "I often warmly burn to see / Beauties of deeper glance, and hear their singing."[55] Although the realm of far-away is that of Romance, he had come to see that Albion's clouds beget the true human theme, the struggle of this "vale of soul-making." In that sense "England" is the real human condition, the one into which we are all born and to which we must be faithful if we are to be authentic, rooted in a native soil of occluded language. The final choice is not for the foreign world of our dreams and fevered imaginative journeys; and it is this realization that leads Keats to reject a "foreign idiom" like Milton's mighty "corruption of our language" for Chatterton's "native music."[56] (The implied opposition here between cosmopolitan language and native music is already a clue to the final lines of "To Autumn.")

[54]*The Fall of Hyperion, LJK,* I, 8–15.
[55]"Happy is England! I could be content," ll. 12–13.
[56]*LJK,* II, 212.

It was for these reasons that Keats had earlier opened the last book of *Endymion* with an invocation to the "Muse of my native land," who had faithfully spurned the successive appeals of faraway Hebrew, Greek, Latin, and Italian poetic voices and had waited for her "native hopes" and for "home-bred glory." She is the muse not only of pure Englishness but also of what that means to Keats—the necessary despondency and limitations inherent both in mortal life and in the life of language. Once he had thought her the muse of Romance:

> Long have I said, how happy he who shrives
> To thee! But then I thought on poets gone,
> And could not pray. . . .
> [*Endymion* IV, 26–28]

For he felt it the fate of the English poet, like Burns, Chatterton, and Henry Kirke White, to be plunged into the wretchedness of the human state. Chatterton especially stood in Keats's mind as the example of the poet suffering the unkindness and neglect of the country to which he remains faithful and pure.[57] (The irony of Chatterton's career as a tragic *original* and the *forger* of a precedent language and history suggests yet another insight into the duplicity of language itself.) On rejecting a plan to go abroad in an Indiaman, Keats wrote in June 1819:

> One of the great reasons that the English have produced the finest writers in the world; is, that the English world has ill-treated them during their lives and foster'd them after their deaths. . . . [Boiardo] had a Castle in the Appenine. He was a noble Poet of Romance; not a miserable and mighty Poet of the human Heart. The middle age of Shakespeare was all clouded over; his days were not more happy than Hamlet's who is perhaps more like Shakespeare himself in his common every day Life than any other of his Characters.[58]

The invocation of Book IV of *Endymion*, then, is not unrelated to the narrative that it introduces and that in turn introduces the resolution of the poem, for hard upon it follows the Indian Maid's lament for her "dear native land," a land of sorrow she has abandoned to join Bacchus' rout to faraway countries. But, "Alas! 'tis not for me," she laments; and her longing for her native land is a desire to return

[57]*LJK*, I, 382, 384. See also Keats's sonnet "To Chatterton" ("Oh Chatterton").
[58]*LJK*, II, 115–16.

to the natural human circumstance, which she describes in her song "O Sorrow." The vocation to preserve the purity of the English idiom and to be genuinely English are therefore Keats's full acceptance of the true human state, with no longer any hankering after France and Italy and the Andes and the Burning Mountains. In this sense, autumn is honestly native, the climate of his late poetry, accepting its earthly circumstance for what it is. Like Chatterton with his "native music," it need not yearn for the Romantic songs of spring; it has its own "music." The season when the fruition of life passes imperceptibly but inexorably into death, it is the authentic state of the sublunary world.

Autumn suggests Chatterton to Keats, then, because it is genuine, not a matter of artifice, free from striving to be other than what it is or to borrow from some condition foreign to its character. Unlike the restless searcher after truth, or the bee impatient "from a knowledge of what is to be arrived at," or Dilke, who will never come at a truth because he is always "trying at" it, autumn is not prospective, fretful, or teleological. It is, instead, authentic experience, an access to reality confined by the reticences of its native tongue. This is the transaction with local reality that Keats's empty, transparent consciousness—like Stevens's poet as "man of glass"—needs to sustain itself. Finally, it is authentic to Keats's new askesis precisely because it is marked by its proximity to absence and death, the same mortality that so quickly claimed Chatterton. Against autumn and Chatterton, Keats proceeds to measure his own Hyperion project, in which the deification of the human Apollo requires a "fierce convulse" and "a pang / As hot as death's is chill." "I have given up Hyperion," he writes in the same paragraph, "there were too many Miltonic inversions in it—Miltonic verse cannot be written but in an artful or rather artist's humour."[59] It is Keats's poems of questing transcendence, such as "Lamia," the "Ode on a Grecian Urn," and *Hyperion,* that are the acme of artfulness—intensely complex, interwoven poetic worlds shaped by the feverish poet-creator vainly staying their impending unraveling. "I wish," he continues, "to give myself up to other sensations," or "another sensation,"[60] that is, to the "temperate sharpness," the calm, warm, selfless presence of the genuine reality that is autumn. No moon goddess, no striving for transcendence and a heavenly afterlife, no sitting ashore and longing to "visit dolphin-coral in deep seas," no Miltonic sublimity and

[59]*LJK,* II, 167.
[60]*LJK,* II, 212.

artfulness, not even the repeated promises to "temper" the fever with "staid Philosophy," but only acceptance ("give myself up to" is te telling phrase) of what is within the horizon of experience. (This is part of the scenario for Harold Bloom's late, revisionary reading of the *concluding* vision of *The Fall of Hyperion:* "Keats had reached the outer threshold of romance, and declined to cross over it into the realm of tragedy. Poised there, on the threshold, his stance is more retrospective than he could have wanted it to be. but there he remains still [at the last lines of *The Fall*], in a stance uniquely heroic, in despite of itself.")[61] In the three letters that he wrote on the day he transcribed "To Autumn" the entire syndrome of the Keats of "another sensation" comes together: passivity, diligent indolence, submission, a recognition of selflessness and the limits of language, a desire for temperate warmth, and a determination to be faithful to his "true voice of feeling," to his "native idiom," and to the mixed circumstances native to man.

With the "Ode to a Nightingale" Keats came to the realization that intense empathic projection into a realm unacquainted with the "weariness, the fever, and the fret" is not natural to man, born as he is "for death"; he recognized that he cannot experience that ideal realm with the nightingale's enviable and unselfconscious (hence "immortal") ease but can only strive after it hectically. It is a valid and valuable experience with "ease" that Keats is now addressing, an experience within man's natural limits and connatural knowledge. Shortly before "To Autumn" he had resolved to write in "a more peaceable and healthy spirit," to "look upon the affairs of the world with a healthy deliberation," and to abandon those unnatural eagle flights "to far above our head": "I have of late been moulting: not for fresh feathers & wings: they are gone, and in their stead I hope to have a pair of patient sublunary legs. I have altered, not from a Chrysalis into a Butterfly, but the Contrary, having two little loopholes, whence I may look out into the stage of the world."[62] "Some think I have lost that poetic ardour and fire 'tis said I once had," he wrote on the day of transcribing "To Autumn," recalling the heat of Apollo's lyre:

> the fact is perhaps I have: but instead of that I hope I shall substitute a more thoughtful and quiet power. I am more frequently, now, contented to read and think—but now & then, haunted with ambitious thoughts. Quieter in my pulse, improved in my digestion: exerting

[61]Bloom, *Poetry and Repression*, p. 142.
[62]*LJK*, II, 106, 128.

myself against vexing speculations—scarcely content to write the best verses for the fever they leave behind. I want to compose without this fever. I hope I one day shall.[63]

Feverish poetry may be the "best," but the temperate is healthy and genuine; and "To Autumn" is Keats's major warm, unfevered poem of earth, an expression of "the true voice of feeling." The discrimination has been phrased with precision by one of Keats's most sensitive and perceptive readers: the "Ode to a Nightingale," W. J. Bate writes, choosing but one example, is "a greater poem" than "To Autumn," but "less 'perfect,'" "perfect" meaning that "the whole is 'perfected'—carried through to completion—solely by means of the given parts . . . with nothing left dangling or independent"—or, I would add, undetermined.[64]

Unlike, let us say, spring, autumn is endowed with Chattertonian authenticity because it looks forward anxiously to no higher state than itself. Not prospective, it is as close as we can come (in experience or language) to indwelling presence, the immanent completeness that Endymion thought to find only in transcendence. It is the absolute fullness of being's existence, when Nature can scarcely endure any extension of its inherent principle of maturation. Reality is strained by the weight of its own fruits; its forms are filled to bursting; its natural containers, like Keats's verse lines, overflow. (While this is, with "On Melancholy," which anticipates its sense of transience, the shortest of the odes, Keats here extends his own perfected ten-line strophe with a supplementary, overflowing eleventh line.) But, as many readers have testified, the initial fullness of the poem is not a static experience. The successive stanzas breed their own sense of movement, a growing awareness of the inexorability of natural process, and passage from richly clustered images of enclosure to a widening horizon of sensation as the poem traces its course—the course of a declining day and declining season—from kinesthetic to visual and finally to auditory traces. The first stanza, which conjoins the palpable pleasures of the season's abundance with the illusion of timelessness, stands closest to Keats's earlier poetry. In the *conspiracy* (suggesting both "a joining in a secret agreement" and a literal "breathing together") of the sun and the as yet unnamed season, the poet evokes only to displace his

[63]*LJK*, II, 209. For Keats the word "speculation" occasionally carried its sense of "star-gazing"; e.g., "Full in speculation of the stars" ("I Stood Tip-Toe," l. 189).
[64]Walter Jackson Bate, *John Keats* p. 581.

heliotropic mythology of an earlier mood.[65] In the same way, there is a subtle tension between the two parts of the first epithet—"mists" suggesting the irreducible indeterminacy of the text and process itself, while "mellow fruitfulness" introduces the extraordinary abundance that loads the stanza. Time itself is, however, mooted: the only "season" actually mentioned here is the "summer" of the mystified bees; and the four sets of counterpoised infinitives that depend upon the "conspiracy" seem to hold time in suspense:

> Season of mists and mellow fruitfulness,
>> Close bosom-friend of the maturing sun;
> Conspiring with him how to load and bless
>> With fruit the vines that round the thatch-eves run;

Intimacy is here (*philia* now, rather than *eros*) and a growing sense of luxuriant plenitude as the two conspirators continue to load the cornucopia, still in the infinitive mood,

> To bend with apples the moss'd cottage-trees,
>> And fill all fruit with ripeness to the core;

---

[65] Jacques Derrida discusses the sun as a philosophic metaphor that "opens up" the "space" of language in "La Mythologie blanche" (noted above), especially in the fourth section, "Les Fleurs de la Rhétorique: L'Héliotrope." Thus:

> What is the property of the sun? . . . We have constantly been carried along, without willing it, by this movement that makes the sun revolve in metaphor; or attracted by what turned philosophic metaphor toward the sun. Is not this flower of rhetoric (like) a sunflower? indeed—though it is not an exact synonym— similar to the heliotrope? [p. 298]
> Heliotropic metaphors are always imperfect metaphors. They give us too little knowledge because one of the terms directly or indirectly implied in the substitution (the perceptible sun) cannot be immediately known. . . . Now the sun . . . is the perceptible object par excellence. It is the paradigm of what is perceptible *and* of what is metaphoric: it regularly turns (itself) and hides (itself). Like the metaphoric trope, it always implies a perceptible nucleus or rather something that, like that which is perceptible, may always be not present in act and in person. And since the sun is in this regard, par excellence, the perceptible signifier of what is perceptible, the perceptible model of the perceptible (the Platonic Idea, paradigm, or parable), the orbit of the sun will always have been the trajectory of metaphor. [p. 299; my translation]

He concludes that metaphor means heliotrope—both movement turned toward the sun and the turning movement of the sun. And he quickly adds another observation consequent on Aristotle's claim that we can never be sure of the sun's sensible characteristics; this being so, the sun "is never present in its nature in discourse. Each time there is a metaphor, there is without doubt a sun somewhere; but each time there is the sun, metaphor has begun" (p. 300). Derrida concludes that if the sun is "already and always" metaphorical, it is not completely natural, it is almost an "artificial construction" (if such a statement could have any meaning, he adds, in the absence of nature).

> To swell the gourd, and plump the hazel-shells
> With a sweet kernel; to set budding more,
> And still more, later flowers for the bees,
> Until they think warm days will never cease,
> For summer has o'er-brimm'd their clammy cells.

There is intensity and warmth here, but not the fevered quest for transcendence of the earlier odes, where images are intensified until they are refined beyond their objective and natural character. This scene signifies only itself and fills the sensorium of the poet (who, like the bees, has lost his sense of the passage of time, the agency that is actually effecting the ripening of all).

Nor, as many readers have remarked, is there any of that subjectivity that elsewhere in Keats progressively wrestles with the object—nightingale or urn—to attain transcendence, the catalysts of conversion to the sublime. There is none of that consecrating "ardent pursuit" by the mind requisite to transform natural objects into "etherial things."[66] Selfhood is unassertive because it is only the receptive medium, the naked awareness, not part of the subject matter. The first person has been at last banished from the diction of the ode. Indeed, by means of the personification of Autumn in four suspended, naturalized tableaux, the poem enacts in its second stanza the recession of subjectivity into pure receptivity, like Keats's abstracted emblem of himself as a picture of someone reading. The four domestic avatars of Autumn—as winnower, as reaper, as gleaner, and as guardian of the "cyder-press"—are "stationed" (to use Bate's helpful term) between their harvest activities and a momentary stay of will and movement, between a liminal consciousness and becoming a part of the allegorical landscape. The tempi and verbal music of this stanza conspire in this effect of *Dauer im Wechsel:*

> Who hath not seen thee oft amid thy store?
> Sometimes whoever seeks abroad may find

---

[66]*LJK*, I, 242–43. For an anticipation of this autumnal mood of acceptance see the 1817 sonnet "After dark vapors," a poem that concludes with "a Poet's death":

> The calmest thoughts come round us—as of leaves
> Budding,—fruit ripening in stillness,—autumn suns
> Smiling at eve upon the quiet sheaves,—

In the early sonnet, however, this sense of resignation in process is achieved only after the native clouds, which "bloom the soft-dying day" in the final orchestration of the last ode, have been banished by a Mediterranean sun, "a day / Born of the gentle South." Mist and the maturing sun cannot yet coexist in this heliotropic vision.

> Thee sitting careless on a granary floor,
>   Thy hair soft-lifted by the winnowing wind;
> Or on a half-reaped furrow sound asleep,
>   Drows'd with the fume of poppies, while thy hook
>   Spares the next swath and all its twined flowers:
> And sometimes like a gleaner thou dost keep
>   Steady thy laden head across a brook,
>   Or by a cyder-press, with patient look,
>   Thou watchest the last oozings hours by hours.

Unlike the traditional personification, as in Collins' Evenings or the Seasons of Blake's four poems, which artificially translates an aspect of nature into the outward pictorial form of its presiding deity with appropriate emblematic equipment,[67] Keats's Autumn is a multi-faceted, experiencing consciousness, a prism through which we are invited sympathetically to feel the season, and yet this emptied consciousness is almost identical with the objectivity personified. All of Autumn's postures, moreover, are of passive, indolent acceptance, even of last things—the last of the harvested grain, the final, expressed drops of the fruit: she keeps steady her head laden with gleanings (marvelously arrested by the line break) and patiently watches by the "cyder-press . . . the last oozings hours by hours." The measure of time here appears in this stanza, but is held in almost hypnotic suspension by the interwoven sound and meter and the indifferent precision of "sometimes." Autumn reposes "careless," "sound asleep," "drows'd," "watching": consciousness is relaxed, attenuated, almost swooning away under the smothering weight of the harvest. While the first stanza suggested a mystified sense of unending fruition, here process is moving toward its close: in autumn all potentiality is fulfilled, perfected, accomplished—hence a perfect end.

In two of Autumn's passive poses the potential subjectivity that receives all this abundance is nothing more than a "crystal space" filled with the objectivity it reflects, so that, instead of the self empathically living the essence of others, we see ambient reality usurping the self: one may find Autumn "sitting careless on the granary floor, / Thy hair soft-lifted by the winnowing wind." But of course it is the grain that is lying on the granary floor, and the "hair" of the

---

[67]Cf., for instance, Collins's "Ode to Evening":

> . . . Winter, yelling thro' the troublous air
> Affrights thy shrinking train.
> And rudely rends thy robes.

wheat that is winnowed by the wind. Without Autumn's being any
the less an awareness instead of an objective personified form, all
possibility of an autonomous responding identity engaged in an
epistemological transaction with the world is nullified by filling her
empty self with proximate nature. The only subject is the object, and
awareness is to be defined by what it is aware of. So, too, Autumn is
pictured as "on a half-reap'd furrow sound asleep, / Drows'd with
the fume of poppies" ; for it is the reaped grain that lies "asleep" on
the furrow. What results from these naturalizations of consciousness—these representations of the experiencing self as "a lawn besprinkled o'er / With flowers, and stirring shades, and baffled
beams"—is not an attempt at a starkly objective description of reality
or nature anthropomorphized, but a world in all its bursting fullness
felt as being received into a consciousness generously resigned to be
whatever occupies it. Although rich in pictorial details, the poem
does not "paint" a picture at all. (In the central visual images of
stanza 2, despite the exactness of the "program," the reader remains
in fact in doubt as to the gender of the figure.) Rather, as the poem
moves through its three "moments," it enacts the very process of
experiencing, and so of knowing, immanent reality in its absolute
sense.

The Keats of fevered Romance sought to transcend sublunary
reality precisely because of the transience of the realm "Where
youth grows pale, and spectre-thin, and dies," where "Beauty cannot
keep her lustrous eyes," and where autumn's abundance "Cloys with
tasting."[68] (The poem paired with "To Autumn" in the 1820 volume, the "Ode on Melancholy," summarizes these images of tran-
sitoriness and mutability.) In short, what Keats earlier sought was an
immutable eternity of absolute being. As the poet of autumn, however, he must not only accept mutability and death but also acknowledge their constitutive function. "To Autumn," therefore, is not
about the tumescent plenitude of reality only; it is also about its
constituting polar opposite—emptiness. As Karl Kroeber has observed, the "mellow fruitfulness" of stanza 1 becomes the "half-
reap'd furrow" in stanza 2, and then the "stubble-plains" in the final
stanza. (The stubble-plains are both the pretext of the poem, as the
letter to Reynolds attests, and, as the etymology suggests, an emblem
of the text itself—*stipulae*, surviving stalks of grain and marks or
tokens of an agreement, the bits of straw broken as signs of an
agreement or covenant between two absent parties.)

[68]"Ode to a Nightingale," ll. 26, 29; "Fancy," l. 15.

In the opening stanza time is an endless pressure working from within and enlarging nature beyond the limits of its containing capacity, swelling the gourd and plumping the hazel shells. The stanza evokes an intensely kinesthetic response, suggesting the tension in Keats's earlier poems that strain after the transcendent absolute. The first stanza, in effect, is of the order of the taut climactic middle stanza of the "Ode on a Grecian Urn," and the autumnal bees that "think warm days will never cease" are like the mystified, belated poet who strove for a state in which love is "forever warm and still to be enjoyed"; for to the fevered Keats the ultimate intensity of the sensuous verges on the transcendent absolute. The similarity is not casual, and in a telling way "To Autumn" is the mental course of the Grecian urn ode transposed from transcendent aspiration to proximate reality. The shaping process of Keats's mind remains constant, but the transposition from one domain to the other results in vastly different consequences. The bees that expect endlessly warm fullness are of course deluded, like the poet of the "Ode on a Grecian Urn," who cannot sustain a condition of eternally warm love and must transfer the burden to the neatly circular interpretive riddle of the legend. Both of the poems lapse at this point (the earlier ode, however, only after passing through the purging fever) from symbolic intensity to a subdued, quiet acknowledgment of the world of death and transience. But whereas the abrupt transition from an ideal realm that cannot "bid Spring adieu" to man's composed but transitory world of mortal life sets up a polarity in the "Ode on a Grecian Urn" that can be resolved only by a conclusion that defines reality in the light of postmortality (or posttextuality), the strict temporal progress in "To Autumn" moves from an apparently endless process of intense, almost insupportable kinesthetically felt plenitude in stanza 1 to an entirely "patient," relaxed, almost indifferent acceptance of time's languid falling off through the suspended harvesting of autumn's excess in stanza 2, arriving at last at the moment of the impending disappearance of the outer world and its sounds in the final stanza.

By the end of the second stanza the process of the gradual acceptance into an empty and passive subjectivity of the absoluteness of reality has been serenely completed. The poet's presiding consciousness, etiolated from the beginning, has been displaced by the half-conscious personification of Autumn (an androgynous figure partaking of the attributes of both Ceres and Bacchus in a postmythological world). Keats is here "stationing" the last and most purely receptive of his tutelary goddesses. But mere receptivity is insuffi-

cient, and the final stanza introduces the remaining element of
Keats's synthesis, the acknowledgment of absence and death (prefigured in the reaper's hook), because they are precisely constitutive
of our apprehension of absolute presence. The very notion of "patience" that informs the ripening of the poem conceals a crucial
ambiguity; the passive-active tension of the deponent verb *patior* at
the root of the word is reflected in the reciprocal senses of patience
as (mere) receptivity and as (actual) suffering; this is a familiar if
submerged duplicity in Keats's lexicon. Time winds down into near
irrelevance in the final orchestration of the ode; and autumn, unlike
the ideal state in the poem on the urn, proves a condition that *can*
"bid Spring adieu" without regret. In the earlier poem the first
riddle generated is why no one can return from afterlife to ask the
reason the world's "little town" must be emptied of its folk and left
desolate; "To Autumn," by limiting itself to the mutable world,
calmly accepts emptiness and death—accepts them as defining
human life rather than as enigmas standing in lamentable opposition to the absolute that was the earlier goal. Thus "To Autumn," as
we have seen, is a late gathering both of Keats's psychology of the
imagination and of his poetics; but, in its return to native soil and
idiom, to "the plain sense of things," it is also a new beginning, an
opening of a field that will be fully harvested only by the poets of our
century.

The final stanza begins, then, with the last of the poet's odic inter-
rogations and an apostrophe that is, in fact, an unregretful valedic-
tion to his own achievement:

> Where are the songs of spring? Ay, where are they?
> Think not of them, thou hast thy music too,—

The frustrated ideal of the "Ode on a Grecian Urn," an eternity of
becoming, has not been repudiated—the beauty of the songs of
spring is acknowledged. But another kind of music is being ex-
plored, an apprehension of being, which can be defined only by an
ensuing nonbeing. If the earlier stanzas, notably purified of the
diction of Romance and Miltonic inversion, still record a lingering
farewell to the sensuous excess of Spenser and the sustained personification of Milton, we have in the last stanza returned, as Middleton
Murry long ago suggested, to the native soil of Shakespeare and the
hard truths of *Lear:* "the fierce dispute / Betwixt damnation and
impassioned clay," "The bitter-sweet of this Shakespearean fruit."
The "music" that supplants "songs" of "Golden-tongued Romance"
is that of nature itself harmonized in the very act of passing away:

> While barred clouds bloom the soft-dying day,
>   And touch the stubble-plains with rosy hue;
> Then in wailful choir the small gnats mourn
>   Among the river sallows, borne aloft
>   Or sinking as the light wind lives or dies;
> And full-grown lambs loud bleat from hilly bourn;
>   Hedge-crickets sing; and now with treble soft
>   The red-breast whistles from a garden-croft;
>   And gathering swallows twitter in the skies.

The day and the season have reached full measure and are softly dying. The mighty originary metaphor of Apollo's sun has been displaced in a final metalepsis by its own reflection "blooming" the "barred clouds." And as the musical orchestration of this final symphonic moment builds, we realize that even the apparently visual image of "barred clouds" may also suggest "barré" to the touch of the musician. The oscillating movement is between life and death itself, between sound and its reverberations. The small gnats are "borne aloft / Or sinking as the light wind lives or dies," wavering between presence and absence. The reciprocating, contradictory movements of rising and falling, the paralleled fluctuation between life and death, uncannily anticipate the master figure of loss and recuperation in Rilke's *Neue Gedichte* [*Flug und Fall*] even as they look forward to the triumphant submission of the last two of the *Duineser Elegien*. Fruition and death are there unexpectedly reconciled in the final orchestration of paradoxical movement ("Und wir, die an steigendes Glück / denken, empfänden die Rührung, / die uns beinah bestürzt, / wenn ein Glückliches fällt" [X, 111–14]).

"Full-grown lambs," to be sure, are sheep, not lambs; but the phrase is right because it calls attention to the natural consummation of the process of becoming; and if we hear a pained cry in the "loud bleat" of the full-grown lambs, death is busy in the completion of maturation.[69] (And, as in the earlier image of the grain about to be cut down but twined with flowers or the "bloom" of the twilight clouds, life is still implicated in that which is about to die.) The emblem of death's constitutive relevance is the image of the small gnats whose droning is part of autumn's terminal music. They are *Ephemerae*, life compressed into the briefest of moments, in life declaring their own mortality: "Then in a wailful choir the small gnats mourn." Their natural living song, beyond any language, is a dirge,

---

[69]For reflections on the "full-grown lambs" I am grateful to a paper read by Earl R. Wasserman to the Johns Hopkins University Philological Association in 1972 and to subsequent discussions with the author.

and death invades, inhabits, is even coextensive with their moment of life. Keats is not merely tracing here the passage from life to death; at this moment he has come to see death as functionally defining life, absence as giving graspable form to presence. The gnats are joined by the other creatures of the waning season. The poem therefore ends not only with postharvest autumn but with the sounds of the close of day, for at the point of nothingness there is plenitude. It is at the verge of night that day most conspicuously blooms and the chatter of the hedge crickets (mediating summer and winter) seems most multitudinous. Correspondingly, in the course of the poem reality has been increasingly disengaged and distanced from the reader. First we sympathetically *feel* the intense, almost muscular pressure of maturation from within natural objects, then lazily *observe* the stations of the harvest from without; but in the final stage we *hear* only a scene hardly any longer visible. And yet, paradoxically, it is in this stage, when the reader's relation to the scene is most attenuated, that we are most vividly aware of its innumerable activities and transitory life.

Although many traditional readings of "To Autumn" have recognized, in one guise or another, the supremely *temperate* quality of its diction and the absence of those personal tensions that orchestrate the conclusions to the odes of spring, none seems adequately to have accounted for the paradoxically *rhetorical* character of this poem. A poem so serene in its calm acceptance of inexorable process that it seems almost willing to renounce the mature resources of language now at the poet's command, it is in an irreducible sense a complete review of the figural possibilities open to the Romantic lyric. The three "moments" figured by the three strophes correspond, in fact, to the three major rhetorical strategies, early and late, of Romantic nature poetry. The progression is, simply stated, from symbolic to allegorical to ironic. The last stanza, however, points the way to a new landscape whose music has displaced the more familiar linguistic disjunctions of subject and object, of inside and outside, of simultaneity and succession. If Keats is supremely a liminal poet, he crosses here three thresholds, the last of which admits of no return. For this reading of the figural evolution of the poem, Paul de Man's discussion of the "rhetoric of temporality" is a capital text.[70] A thoroughgoing application of his rhetorical theory would, of course,

---

[70]"The Rhetoric of Temporality: I. Allegory and Symbol; II. Irony," in *Interpretation: Theory and Practice*, ed. C. S. Singleton (Baltimore: Johns Hopkins University Press, 1969), pp. 173–209.

have devastating consequences for an attempt to read "To Autumn" in any easy analogic or totalizing way. While he links allegory and irony in their common discovery of "a truly temporal predicament," he also argues that they are linked in their common demystification of an organicism "postulated in a symbolic mode of analogical correspondences or in a mimetic mode of representation in which fiction and reality could coincide."[71] Read in such a perspective, this poem of correspondences and conclusions would retain a final openness that would defy either totalization or termination.

The first stanza of "To Autumn," with its rich, tactile sense of plenitude in its smallest parts, its abundance of "pseudo-objects" intricately linked in a syntax of suspension, images that figure an eternal moment of fruition, corresponds to de Man's characterization of the *symbolic* mode, a totality of parts "reflecting" totality, a simultaneity of effects, and a mystified, "misty" sense (like that of the bees) that the warmth and fullness of the scene will "never cease." This is a world akin to the perennially ripe, never-never climate of the Phaiakian gardens in *Odyssey* VII, a world of unpunctuated fruitfulness that Homer's hero significantly enters in "a wondrous mist" (ll. 41–42). Keats himself, in demystifying the atemporal assurances of the first stanza through the growing awareness of time and process, serves as an adroit deconstructor of this vision.

The intense, tactile immediacy and symbolic "conspiracy" are succeeded by the complex personification of the second stanza, a series of homely, arrested autumnal narratives that recall the *allegorical* disposition of the landscapes of Poussin and Claude.[72] Framed by seemingly casual temporal markers ("oft . . . Sometimes . . . sometimes . . ."), the activities of this native harvest are deployed "abroad" in attitudes that are emblems of threshold activities at the extremities of human life. Most specifically, this stanza evokes two panels from the last synthesis of Poussin's art, "Summer" and "Autumn" in the *Four Seasons*, the only documented and completed work to survive from the last five years of the painter's life. There the allegorized biblical narratives are constructed with a deceptive simplicity that through images of the everyday captures a world of process—the cycle of the seasons, the passage from day to night, and the stations of human mortality. Poussin employs a series of familiar stories (which have their parallels in Keats's own itinerary): Ruth with Boaz under a noon sun in the alien corn, the spies returning in the long shadows

[71]Ibid., pp. 203–4.
[72]See Ian Jack, *Keats and the Mirror of Art*, especially chap. 15.

from Canaan with a great cluster of ripe grapes. (There is here, as in Keats's poem, a tacit overlay of pagan mythography, of Ceres and Bacchus.) In describing this rich harvest of Poussin's last years, Anthony Blount speaks of the *Four Seasons* in terms that could equally well apply to Keats's poem: "Now a balance has been struck; the artist is at one with nature and understands her ultimate purpose. . . . By his absolute humility, by his effacement of himself, by his refusal to use any tricks or to overstate anything, Poussin has succeeded in identifying himself with nature."[73] The poem, like the painting, prefigures in its pastoral details held in indolent suspense the unveiling of an "authentically temporal destiny." The allegorical figures inscribed on the landscape are of course not nature but signs of the temporal process moving through it, threatening the myth of self-containment dramatized in the preceding stanza. (In their evocation of moments in the earlier poetry they are also signs of the poet's career at the moment of harvest.) The consciousness is "drows'd," but the separation has already been made from the mystified dream of the bees. In the poem as in the painting, "time's hook" is a necessary instrument of the harvest allegory and of human existence.

The final stanza of "To Autumn," so different from the aporiae of the "songs of spring," at first describes an abrupt parabasis in the repeated question that introduces the recognition of belatedness. (The rhetorical questions that characteristically organize the ode have become increasingly more overt, from the latent "how" of the first stanza to the traditional "who" of the second to the elegiac "where" of the last.) The often noted reference to Keats's own poetic oeuvre in the "songs of spring" is, of course, the sign of heightened *ironic* implication. And the "songs" have been displaced by another "music," this time *without words*. It is this stanza that registers the signature of the poet's new voice, a voice almost completely separated from the empirical situation that inspired and vexed the earlier poetry. The poem has moved from unthinking receptivity through the progression of the season to an awareness of time at work in its dissolution.[74] The reader has moved at the same time—

[73]Anthony Blount, *Nicolas Poussin* (New York: Pantheon, 1967), I, 336.

[74]For a discussion of the maturing awareness of time in the poem, see James Lott, "Keats's 'To Autumn': The Poetic Consciousness and the Awareness of Process," *Studies in Romanticism* 10 (1970):71–81. Two other essays have useful things to say about the enactment of time in this poem: Arnold Davenport, "A Note on 'To Autumn,'" in *John Keats: A Reassessment,* ed. Kenneth Muir (Liverpool: University of Liverpool Press, 1958), pp. 95–101; and B. C. Southam, "The Ode 'To Autumn,'" *Keats-Shelley Journal* 9 (1960):91–98.

like the sun—from sensation to reflection. The rhetorical mode here, as the now absent sun blooms the soft-dying clouds, is clearly then ironic, a separation of the empty poet from his empty text in a way that paradoxically textualizes the finitude of both poet and poem. The movement of the parabasis, like its classical model, is at first forward (with the insistent question) and then aside, to let the represented sounds of the natural world, at once marks of closure and of cyclic repetition, conclude what is both an ending and an acceptance of a transpersonal continuity defined by death and absence. The strophic turn of the poetic voice is a mortal reminder that autumn, while repetitive in terms of natural process, is final for the individual. This is not the irony of the deliberate dislocation of fictional effects by a fictive author, but—in the sense first developed by Friedrich Schlegel and later more extravagantly elaborated by K. W. F. Solger—a recognition of the author's implication not only in fiction-making but in time. It is the irony of objectivity and detachment that Schlegel speaks of in his praise of *Wilhelm Meister*.[75] It is a rhetorical mode that is "no longer inventing," a "new myth of nature" (*ein hierglyphischer Ausdruck der umgebenden Natur . . . eine indirekte Mythologie*).[76]

This is, then, not a temporary interruption of the discourse but a recognition for the reader of the essential negativity of all linguistic constructs and the permanence of the repetitive cycles that they can never successfully enclose. If it is, in the stepping forth and laying aside of Romantic masks, a dramatic parabasis, it is also (in Schlegel's 1797 definition of irony) the act of the end of the imagination where the displacement is permanent, a poetry dispossessed of the old antinomies and disjunctions. The poet, at the extremity of his theatrical space, has become merely a figure in a demystified natural hieroglyph, not so much a reader of nature as an element subsumed within the composition, "like the figure of someone reading." (The break is not as abrupt and spectral as the shift in "This living hand now warm and capable / Of earnest grasping . . ." where the apostrophic shift from "thou" to "you" throws the whole burden back on the reader; but the extraordinary achievement of "To Autumn" lies in the fact that the rhetorical transitions are effected with the same subtlety that marks the passing of the season.) Rising and falling

---

[75]*Friedrich Schlegel, 1794–1802: Seine prosaischen Jugendschriften*, ed. J. Minor, 2 vols. (Vienna, 1882), II, 171. On the "disinterestedness" of the ironic author, see ibid., II, 187, where the ironist is presented as having passed beyond "invention." On irony as a consciousness of an overflowing, chaotic nature, see ibid., II, 296.

[76]Ibid., II, 361.

with the "light wind," the sounds of the final stanza achieve a feverless expansion. To cite Paul H. Fry's summary: "Every ragged threshold merges with the others, and each threshold gives forth a sound; without shape or harmony, the landscape and its voices hum in unison, a vocal scrawl."[77] Fry speaks of this "audition" as "the sound of being"; it is equally the sound of mortality. While the choir of life in the fading day is reabsorbed into death and absence, the "empty text" into which the poet's voice has inscribed him achieves a kind of life as elegiac fiction that will renew itself in the work of his poetic successors.

Despite some hypothetical interpretations of "To Autumn," the poem projects no further after the season of harvest, only death and the nothingness of absence. In his fevered state, as we have seen, Keats conceived the end of life as the beginning of a higher mode of existence; he valued mortal existence not for itself only but for what it leads to postmortally, so that it seemed "rich to die." Now, however, death and absence, instead of being vacancies to transcend, are indispensable to an apprehension of that absoluteness of nature the open mortal self can experience; a calm acceptance of them makes possible one's authentic existence. "There are four seasons in the mind of man," Keats wrote; and he rejoiced that they include man's "Winter too of pale misfeature, / Or else he would forget his mortal nature."[78] This would be a forgetting that distorts the true character of human existence; it would be a forgetting of the lesson of *Lear*. Something remains, perhaps, beyond autumn to give reality a continuity: the redbreast, still enclosed, that "whistles from a gardencroft" will (in England) remain through the winter. But the thread of continuity is attenuated by the singular number of this treble, and the ultimate emblem of reality is the "gathering swallows" that "twitter in the skies." The gathering of the innumerable birds (with their resonance of Dante) is the amplitude of their presence, but the cause of their gathering is, of course, that they may depart in migration.[79] Encroaching absence is less the terminus of existence than the necessary condition for poetic presence. "Gathering" is also a harvest term—the version sent to Woodhouse reads "gather'd Swallows"— and it suggests that in this final "granary of sounds" (Hartman) the birds, like grain, have been reaped in their moment of plenitude,

[77]Paul H. Fry, *The Poet's Calling in the English Ode* (New Haven: Yale University Press, 1980), p. 271.
[78]"Four seasons fill the measure of the year."
[79]For the autumnal flocks of migratory birds in Dante, see *Inferno*, V, 40–49 (marked in Keats's copy).

that the absoluteness of their being is defined for man not by their being "abstracted" or translated into heavenly birds that sing "divine melodious truth" but by the fact of their immanent nonbeing.[80] This is a rite of passage to a new poetry.

By recognizing his emptiness as potential receptivity instead of struggling to overcome it, by translating this emptiness into the void of the text, and by turning from his vain, superhuman striving for the transcendent to the calm acceptance of the natural condition, Keats succeeded at the end in creating a poem that marks the crossing from the poetry and poetics of Romanticism. Like his inheritor, Wallace Stevens, he found in the abundance and poverty of the cycling seasons an allegory for his poetics.[81] And like Stevens he was drawn in the progression of the seasons to a meditation on what impends in the very moment of natural abundance, a meditation that involved an evolution in style and rhetoric. At the extremity of this meditation the objects of experience, in Stevens' winter words, "do not transcend themselves, / In the absence of fantasía, without meaning more / Than they are in the final finding of the ear."[82]

---

[80]"Bards of Passion and of Mirth," l. 19.

[81]For a discussion of the reciprocating relationship of the cycles of the creative imagination and the corresponding cycles of the natural seasons in Keats's successor, see my essay "The Climates of Wallace Stevens," in *The Act of the Mind: Essays on the Poetry of Wallace Stevens*, ed. R. H. Pearce and J. H. Miller (Baltimore: Johns Hopkins University Press, 1965), pp. 185–223; for a more recent discussion of the weather of the poet's imagination, see Harold Bloom's magisterial study, *Wallace Stevens: The Poems of Our Climate* (Ithaca: Cornell University Press, 1977). Both works have discussions of "The Course of a Particular" that shed some light on the extremities of "To Autumn."

[82]*Opus Posthumous* reads this line "in the final finding of the *air*" (p. 97), which makes for a very different poetic universe. The reading used here conforms to that of the poem's first printing in the *Hudson Review* (Spring 1951); I argue its significance in the essay noted above (pp. 216–17). Although I am not sure that I would today insist so heavily on the Heideggerian elements in the poem, the comments on "The Course of a Particular" conclude on a note that is also relevant to Keats's late poem:

> In the merciless stripping away of all that would clothe the particular object and the particular subject, all the resources of language and imagination, we have a search for a discourse before (or beyond) the poetry of *fantasía*. And in the reciprocal fates of the two dying particulars, we have integral enactment of how death appears to *das Man* and to *Dasein*. From this double analysis arises the final paradox: out of his ultimate solitude, the extremity of a less-than-human extinction, Stevens has built his most "human" poem.

I regret that I encountered Helen Vendler's finely observed essay, "Stevens and Keats' 'To Autumn,'" in *Wallace Stevens: A Celebration*, ed. Frank Doggett and Robert Buttel (Princeton: Princeton University Press, 1980], pp. 171–95), only after this essay was completed. Although it is primarily concerned with the resonances in the successor poet, Vendler concludes with an apt summary of the persistence of "To Autumn" in Stevens' mind and verse:

Thus "The Course of a Particular," so much more diminished in its weather, could be taken as a deeply felt commentary on "To Autumn." Alternately, in "Not Ideas about the Thing but the Thing Itself," the paradoxically figurative words with which Stevens concludes his own gathered poems, celebrating another gathering of birds, might have served as an epigraph for Keats's ode: "It was like / A new knowledge of reality." A somewhat less chilly version of the same insight, in a season still warm with the sun, might have been harvested from Stevens' favorite section of his most serene poem, "Credences of Summer." There, in a native valley of eastern Pennsylvania, of which he remarked in a letter, "An accord with realities is the nature of things there," the season had already grown to autumn—

> There the distant fails the clairvoyant eye
>
> And the secondary senses of the ear
> Swarm, not with secondary sounds, but choirs,
> Not with evocations but last choirs, last sounds
> With nothing else compounded, carried full,
> Pure rhetoric of a language without words.

Everywhere we hear Stevens meditating on Keats, whose fashion of beholding without comment must have seemed to Stevens uniquely modern. Stevens sensed that the poem of presentation is the poem of earth: just to behold, just to be beheld; what is there here but weather. These are the assumptions that Stevens found and grasped for himself in the most untranscendental of the great Romantic odes. [P. 195]

CONTRIBUTORS

TIMOTHY BAHTI is Assistant Professor of German and Comparative Literature at Northwestern University. Author of articles on Benjamin, Auerbach, and others, and translator of Hans Robert Jauss, he is completing a book titled *Allegories of History: German Literary Historiography after Hegel.*

LESLIE BRISMAN is Professor of English at Yale University. His publications include *Milton's Poetry of Choice and Its Romantic Heirs* (1973) and *Romantic Origins* (1978), both published by Cornell University Press, as well as articles on Romantic and post-Romantic poetry. He is writing a book on the conversation of Scripture.

CYNTHIA CHASE is Assistant Professor of English at Cornell University. She has published articles on Wordsworth, Freud, George Eliot, Rousseau, and Baudelaire. Currently she is at work on a book about intertextual relationships in Romantic writing.

JEROME CHRISTENSEN is Associate Professor of English at The Johns Hopkins University. He is the author of *Coleridge's Blessed Machine of Language* (Ithaca: Cornell University Press, 1981) and articles on the poetry and poetics of Coleridge and Wordsworth. At present he is writing studies of Hume and Byron.

FRANCES FERGUSON is Associate Professor of English at the University of California at Berkeley. She has written *Wordsworth: Language as Counter-Spirit* (New Haven: Yale University Press, 1977) and articles on the eighteenth century and the Romantics. Currently she is writing on the sublime and on ideologies of education in eighteenth- and nineteenth-century England.

Contributors

MARY JACOBUS is Professor of English at Cornell University. Formerly Fellow and Tutor in English at Lady Margaret Hall, Oxford, she is the author of *Tradition and Experiment in Wordsworth's Lyrical Ballads* (Oxford: Oxford University Press, 1976) and of articles on nineteenth-century prose writers and feminist critical theory, and editor of *Women Writing and Writing about Women* (London: Croom Helm, 1979). She is currently working on books about Romanticism and writing, and about Thomas Hardy.

RICHARD MACKSEY is Professor of Humanistic Studies at The Johns Hopkins University, where he teaches comparative literature and film studies. Volumes he has written or edited include *Florilegium anglicum, The Structuralist Controversy, Velocities of Change, Richard Wright,* and two collections of poetry. Currently he is working on studies of *Tristram Shandy,* of "last words," and of contemporary filmmakers.

REEVE PARKER is Professor of English at Cornell University. He has written *Coleridge's Meditative Art* (Ithaca: Cornell University Press, 1975) and articles on Wordsworth and Blake. His current projects concern dramatic and narrative form in Wordsworth and British literary responses to the French Revolution.

ARDEN REED is Assistant Professor of English at Pomona College. He is the author of *Romantic Weather: The Climates of Coleridge and Baudelaire* (Hanover, N.H.: Brown University Press and University Press of New England, 1983) and articles on Kant and De Quincey. At present he is writing studies of digression and narrative form and of De Quincey.

SUSAN WOLFSON is Assistant Professor of English at Rutgers University. She has completed a book-length study of the poetry of questioning in Wordsworth and Keats and is the author of articles on Romantic poetry and prose. Currently she is working on a study of letter writing among the English Romantics.

SELECTED BIBLIOGRAPHY

Aarsleff, Hans. *From Locke to Saussure: Essays on the Study of Language and Intellectual History.* Minneapolis: University of Minnesota Press, 1982.

———. *The Study of Language in England, 1780–1860.* Princeton: Princeton University Press, 1967.

Abrams, M. H. "The Correspondent Breeze: A Romantic Metaphor." In *English Romantic Poets: Modern Essays in Criticism,* ed. M. H. Abrams, pp. 37–54. New York: Oxford University Press, 1960.

———. "How to Do Things with Texts." *Partisan Review* 44 (1978):566–88.

———. "The Limits of Pluralism: The Deconstructive Angel." *Critical Inquiry* 3 (1977):425–38.

———. *The Mirror and the Lamp: Romantic Theory and the Critical Tradition.* New York: Norton, 1958.

———. *Natural Supernaturalism: Tradition and Revolution in Romantic Literature.* New York: Norton, 1971.

———. "Structure and Style in the Greater Romantic Lyric." In *From Sensibility to Romanticism: Essays Presented to Frederick A. Pottle,* ed. Frederick W. Hilles and Harold Bloom, pp. 527–59. New York: Oxford University Press, 1965.

Arac, Jonathan. "Repetition and Exclusion: Coleridge and the New Criticism Reconsidered." *boundary* 2 8 (1979):261–72.

Austin, J. L. *How to Do Things with Words.* Ed. J. O. Urmson and Marine Sbisa. Cambridge: Harvard University Press, 1975.

Bahti, Timothy. "Coleridge's 'Kubla Khan' and the Fragment of Romanticism." *MLN* 96 (1981):1035–50.

———. "Figures of Interpretation, the Interpretation of Figures: A Reading of Wordsworth's 'Dream of the Arab.'" *Studies in Romanticism* 18 (1979):601–28.

———. "The Indifferent Reader: The Performance of Hegel's Introduction to the *Phenomenology.*" *Diacritics* 11 (1981):68–82.

Barthes, Roland. *Critical Essays.* Trans. Richard Howard. Evanston, Ill.: Northwestern University Press, 1972.

———. *Critique et vérité.* Paris: Seuil, 1966.

———. *Image-Music-Text*. Trans. Stephen Heath. New York: Hill & Wang, 1973.

———. *S/Z*. Trans. Richard Miller. New York: Hill & Wang, 1974.

Bate, Walter Jackson. *The Burden of the Past and the English Poet*. New York: Norton, 1972.

———. *From Classic to Romantic*. Cambridge: Harvard University Press, 1947.

Béguin, Albert. *L'Ame romantique et le rêve*. Paris: Corti, 1939.

Benjamin, Walter. *Charles Baudelaire: A Lyric Poet in the Era of High Capitalism*. Trans. Harry Zohn. London: New Left Books, 1973.

———. *Der Begriff der Kunstkritik in der deutschen Romantik*. Frankfurt: Suhrkamp, 1973.

———. *Illuminations*. Ed. Hannah Arendt. Trans. Harry Zohn. New York: Schocken, 1969.

———. *The Origin of German Tragic Drama*. Trans. John Osborne. London: New Left Books, 1977.

———. *Reflections: Essays, Aphorisms, Autobiographical Writings*. Ed. Peter Demetz. Trans. Edmund Jephcott. New York: Harcourt Brace Jovanovich, 1978.

Blanchot, Maurice. *La Part du feu*. Paris: Gallimard, 1949.

Bloom, Harold. *The Anxiety of Influence: A Theory of Poetry*. New York: Oxford University Press, 1973.

———. "The Breaking of Form." In Bloom et al., *Deconstruction and Criticism*, pp. 1–38. New York: Seabury, 1979.

———. "Freud's Concepts of Defense and the Poetic Will." In *The Literary Freud: Mechanisms of Defense and the Poetic Will*, ed. Joseph H. Smith, pp. 1–28. New Haven: Yale University Press, 1980.

———. *Kabbalah and Criticism*. New York: Seabury, 1975.

———. *A Map of Misreading*. New York: Oxford University Press, 1975.

———. *Poetry and Repression*. New Haven: Yale University Press, 1976.

———. *The Visionary Company: A Reading of English Romantic Poetry*. Ithaca: Cornell University Press, 1961.

———. *Wallace Stevens: The Poems of Our Climate*. Ithaca: Cornell University Press, 1977.

———, ed. *Romanticism and Consciousness: Essays in Criticism*. New York: Norton, 1970.

Brenkman, John. "Narcissus in the Text." *Georgia Review* 30 (1976):293–329.

Brisman, Leslie. "Coleridge and the Supernatural." *Studies in Romanticism* 21 (1982): 123–59.

———. *Milton's Poetry of Choice and Its Romantic Heirs*. Ithaca: Cornell University Press, 1973.

———. *Romantic Origins*. Ithaca: Cornell University Press, 1978.

Brisman, Susan Hawk. "'Unsaying His High Language': The Problem of Voice in *Prometheus Unbound*." *Studies in Romanticism* 16 (1977):51–86.

Brown, Homer Obed. "The Art of Theology and the Theology of Art: Robert Penn Warren's Reading of Coleridge's *The Rime of the Ancient Marriner.*" *boundary* 2 8 (1979):237–60.

Brown, Marshall. *The Shape of German Romanticism.* Ithaca: Cornell University Press, 1979.

Bruns, Gerald. *Modern Poetry and the Idea of Language: A Critical and Historical Study.* New Haven: Yale University Press, 1974.

Burke, Kenneth. *A Grammar of Motives.* Berkeley: University of California Press, 1969.

———. *Language as Symbolic Action: Essays on Life, Literature, and Method.* Berkeley: University of California Press, 1966.

———. *The Philosophy of Literary Form: Studies in Symbolic Action,* 3d ed. Berkeley: University of California Press, 1973.

———. *A Rhetoric of Motives.* Berkeley: University of California Press, 1969.

———. *The Rhetoric of Religion: Studies in Logology.* Berkeley: University of California Press, 1970.

Burt, Ellen. "Rousseau the Scribe." *Studies in Romanticism* 18 (1979):629–67.

Chandler, James K. "Romantic Allusiveness." *Critical Inquiry* 8 (1982):461–88.

Chase, Cynthia. "The Accidents of Disfiguration: Limits to Literal and Rhetorical Reading in Book V of *The Prelude.*" *Studies in Romanticism* 18 (1979):547–66.

———. "Paragon, Parergon: Baudelaire Translates Rousseau." *Diacritics* 11:2 (1981):42–50.

Christensen, Jerome. *Coleridge's Blessed Machine of Language.* Ithaca: Cornell University Press, 1981.

———. "Philosophy/Literature: The Associationist Precedent for Coleridge's Late Poems." In *Literature and Philosophy: New Perspectives on Nineteenth and Twentieth Century Texts,* ed. William E. Cain. Bucknell, Pa.: Bucknell University Press, 1983.

———. "Politerotics: Coleridge's Rhetoric of War in *The Friend.*" *Clio* 8 (1979):339–63.

———. "The Sublime and the Romance of the Other." *Diacritics* 8 (1978):10–23.

———. "The Symbol's Errant Allegory." *ELH* 45 (1978):640–59.

———. "Wordsworth's Misery, Coleridge's Woe: Reading 'The Thorn.'" *Papers in Literature and Language* 16 (1980):268–86.

Compagnon, Antoine. *La Seconde Main ou le travail de la citation.* Paris: Seuil, 1979.

Conrad, Peter. *Shandyism: The Character of Romantic Irony.* New York: Barnes & Noble, 1978.

Cooke, Michael G. *Acts of Inclusion: Studies Bearing on an Elementary Theory of Romanticism.* New Haven: Yale University Press, 1979.

Crawford, Walter B., ed. *Reading Coleridge: Approaches and Applications.* Ithaca: Cornell University Press, 1979.

Culler, Jonathan. "Apostrophe." *Diacritics* 7 (1977):59–69.
———. *Ferdinand de Saussure.* New York: Penguin, 1977.
———. *On Deconstruction.* Ithaca: Cornell University Press, 1982.
———. *The Pursuit of Signs: Semiotics, Literature, Deconstruction.* Ithaca: Cornell University Press, 1981.
———. *Structuralist Poetics: Structuralism, Linguistics, and the Study of Literature.* Ithaca: Cornell University Press, 1975.
De Man, Paul. *Allegories of Reading: Figural Language in Rousseau, Nietzsche, Rilke, and Proust.* New Haven: Yale University Press, 1979.
———. "Autobiography as De-facement." *MLN* 94 (1979):919–30.
———. *Blindness and Insight: Essays in the Rhetoric of Contemporary Criticism.* New York: Oxford University Press, 1971.
———. "The Epistemology of Metaphor." *Critical Inquiry* 5 (1978):13–30.
———. "The Intentional Structure of the Romantic Image." In *Romanticism and Consciousness,* ed. Harold Bloom, pp. 65–76. New York: Norton, 1970.
———. Introduction. "The Rhetoric of Romanticism." *Studies in Romanticism* 18 (1979):495–500.
———. "Literature and Language: A Commentary." *New Literary History* 4 (1972):181–92.
———. "Madame de Staël et Jean-Jacques Rousseau." *Preuves* 190 (1966):35–40.
———. "The Resistance to Theory." *Yale French Studies* 63 (1982):3–22.
———. "The Rhetoric of Temporality." In *Interpretation: Theory and Practice,* ed. Charles Singleton, pp. 173–209. Baltimore: Johns Hopkins University Press, 1969.
———. "Shelley Disfigured." In Harold Bloom et al., *Deconstruction and Criticism,* pp. 39–74. New York: Seabury, 1979.
———. "Sign and Symbol in Hegel's Aesthetics." *Critical Inquiry* 8 (1982):761– 75.
———. "Symbolic Landscape in Wordsworth and Yeats." In *In Defense of Reading,* ed. Reuben A. Brower and Richard Poirier, pp. 22–37. New York: Dutton, 1962.
———. "Wordsworth und Hölderlin." *Schweitzer Monatschafte* (1966):1141– 55.
Dennett, Daniel C. *Brainstorms: Philosophical Essays in Mind and Psychology.* Montgomery, Vt.: Bradford Books, 1978.
Derrida, Jacques. "L'Age de Hegel." In *Qui a peur de la philosophie?,* pp. 73– 107. Paris: Flammarion, 1977.
———. *The Archeology of the Frivolous: Reading Condillac.* Trans. John P. Leavey, Jr. Pittsburgh: Duqúesne University Press, 1980.
———. *Dissemination.* Trans. Barbara Johnson. Chicago: University of Chicago Press, 1981.
———. "Economimesis." In Sylviane Agacinski et al., *Mimesis Desarticulations,* pp. 55–93. Paris: Flammarion, 1975.

──────. *Glas*. Paris: Galilée, 1974.

──────. "Living On: Border Lines." Trans. James Hulbert. In Harold Bloom et al., *Deconstruction and Criticism*, pp. 75–175. New York: Seabury, 1979.

──────. *Marges de la philosophie*. Paris: Minuit, 1972.

──────. *Of Grammatology*. Trans. Gayatri Chakravorty Spivak. Baltimore: Johns Hopkins University Press, 1976.

──────. "The Retrait of Metaphor." *Enclitic* 2 (1978):5–33.

──────. "White Mythology: Metaphor in the Text of Philosophy." Trans. F. C. Moore. *New Literary History* 6 (1974):5–74.

──────. *Writing and Difference*. Trans. Alan Bass. Chicago: University of Chicago Press, 1978.

Donato, Eugenio. "Divine Agonies: Of Representation and Narrative in Romantic Poetics." *Glyph* 6 (1979):90–122.

──────. "The Idioms of the Text: Notes on the Language of Philosophy and the Fictions of Literature." *Glyph* 2 (1977):1–13.

──────. "The Ruins of Memory: Archeological Fragments and Textual Artifacts." *MLN* 93 (1978):575–96.

──────. "Topographies of Memory." *Substance* 21 (1978):37–48.

Emerson, Sheila. "Byron's 'One Word': The Language of Self-Expression in *Childe Harold III*." *Studies in Romanticism* 20 (1981):363–82.

Empson, William. *Seven Types of Ambiguity*. New York: New Directions, 1966.

Ferguson, Frances. "Coleridge and the Deluded Reader: *The Rime of the Ancient Mariner*." *Georgia Review* 31 (1977):617–35.

──────. "Coleridge on Language and Delusion." *Genre* 11 (1978): 191–207.

──────. "The Sublime of Edmund Burke, or the Bathos of Experience." *Glyph* 8 (1981):62–78.

──────. *Wordsworth: Language as Counter-Spirit*. New Haven: Yale University Press, 1977.

Fletcher, Angus. "'Positive Negation': Threshold, Sequence, and Personification in Coleridge." In *New Perspectives on Coleridge and Wordsworth: Selected Papers from the English Institute*, ed. Geoffrey Hartman, pp. 133–64. New York: Columbia University Press, 1972.

Foucault, Michel. *Language, Counter-memory, Practice: Essays and Interviews*. Ed. Donald F. Bouchard. Trans. Sherry Simon. Ithaca: Cornell University Press, 1977.

Frank, Manfred. *Das individuelle Allgemeine: Textstrukturierung und- interpretation*. Frankfurt: Suhrkamp, 1977.

──────. "The Infinite Text." *Glyph* 7 (1980):70–101.

──────. *Die unendliche Fahrt*. Frankfurt: Suhrkamp, 1979.

Gasché, Rodolphe. "The Mixture of Genres, the Mixture of Styles, and Figural Interpretation: *Sylvie*, by Gérard de Nerval." *Glyph* 7 (1980):102–30.

──────. "The Scene of Writing: A Deferred Outset." *Glyph* 1 (1977):150–71.

Genette, Gérard. *Mimologiques*. Paris: Seuil, 1977.

Griffin, Andrew L. "Wordsworth and the Problem of Imaginative Story: The Case of 'Simon Lee.'" *PMLA* 92 (1977):392–409.

Guetti, Barbara. "The Double Voice of Nature: Rousseau's *Essai sur l'origine des langues.*" *MLN* 84 (1969):853–75.

Hamacher, Werner. "Der Satz der Gattung: Friedrich Schlegels poetologische Umsetzung von Fichtes unbedingtem Grundsatz." *MLN* 95 (1980):1155–80.

Hamlin, Cyrus. "The Temporality of Selfhood. Metaphor and Romantic Poetry." *New Literary History* 6 (1974):169–93.

Hartman, Geoffrey. *Beyond Formalism: Literary Essays, 1958–1970.* New Haven: Yale University Press, 1970.

––––––. "Blessing the Torrent: On Wordsworth's Later Style." *PMLA* 94 (1978):196–204.

––––––. *Criticism in the Wilderness: The Study of Literature Today.* New Haven: Yale University Press, 1980.

––––––. "Diction and Defense in Wordsworth." In *The Literary Freud: Mechanisms of Defense and the Poetic Will,* ed. Joseph H. Smith, pp. 205–15. New Haven: Yale University Press, 1980.

––––––. *The Fate of Reading and Other Essays.* Chicago: University of Chicago Press, 1975.

––––––. "Reflections on Romanticism in France." In *Romanticism: Vistas, Instances, Continuities,* ed. David Thorburn and Geoffrey Hartman, pp. 38–61. Ithaca: Cornell University Press, 1973.

––––––. *Saving the Text: Literature/Derrida/Philosophy.* Baltimore: Johns Hopkins University Press, 1981.

––––––. "A Touching Comulsion: Wordsworth and the Problem of Literary Representation." *Georgia Review* 31 (1977):345–61.

––––––. *The Unmediated Vision: An Interpretation of Wordsworth, Hopkins, Rilke, and Valery.* New Haven: Yale University Press, 1954.

––––––. "Words, Wish, Worth: Wordsworth." In Harold Bloom et al., *Deconstruction and Criticism,* pp. 177–216. New York: Seabury, 1979.

––––––. *Wordsworth's Poetry, 1787–1814.* New Haven: Yale University Press, 1971.

––––––, ed. *New Perspectives on Coleridge and Wordsworth.* Selected Papers from the English Institute. New York: Columbia University Press, 1972.

Heidegger, Martin. *Erläuterungen zu Hölderlins Dichtung.* Frankfurt: V. Klostermann, 1951.

––––––. *On the Way to Language.* Trans. Peter D. Heritz. New York: Harper & Row, 1971.

––––––. *Poetry, Language, Thought.* Trans. Albert Hofstadter. New York: Harper & Row, 1971.

Hertz, Neil. "Freud and the Sandman." In *Textual Strategies: Perspectives in Post-Structuralist Criticism,* ed. Josué Harari, pp. 296–321. Ithaca: Cornell University Press, 1979.

––––––. "The Notion of Blockage in the Literature of the Sublime." In

Psychoanalysis and the Question of the Text, ed. Geoffrey Hartman, pp. 62–85. Baltimore: Johns Hopkins University Press, 1978.

———. "Wordsworth and the Tears of Adam." *Studies in Romanticism* 7 (1967):15–33.

Homans, Margaret. "Eliot, Wordsworth, and the Scene of the Sisters' Instruction." *Critical Inquiry* 8 (1981):223–42.

Hughes, Daniel. "Coherence and Collapse in Shelley, with Particular Reference to *Epipsychidion*." *ELH* 28 (1961):260–83.

———. "Kindling and Dwindling: The Poetic Process in Shelley." *Keats-Shelley Journal* 13 (1964):13–28.

———. "Potentiality in *Prometheus Unbound*." *Studies in Romanticism* 2 (1963):107–26.

Irwin, John. *American Hieroglyphics.* New Haven: Yale University Press, 1980.

Isaacs, J. "Coleridge's Critical Terminology." *Essays and Studies by Members of the English Association* 21 (1936):86–104.

Jacobs, Carol. *The Dissimulating Harmony: The Image of Interpretation in Nietzsche, Rilke, Artaud, and Benjamin.* Baltimore: Johns Hopkins University Press, 1978.

Jacobus, Mary. "Apostrophe and Lyric Voice in *The Prelude*." In *Recent Approaches to Lyric Poetry,* ed. Patricia Parker and Haviva Hozek. Ithaca: Cornell University Press, forthcoming.

———. "'That Great Stage Where Senators Perform': Macbeth and the Politics of Romantic Theatre." Forthcoming in *Studies in Romanticism.*

———. *Tradition and Experiment in Wordsworth's Lyrical Ballads, 1798.* Oxford: Oxford University Press, 1976.

———. "Wordsworth and the Language of the Dream." *ELH* 46 (1979):618–44.

Jakobson, Roman. "Two Aspects of Language and Two Types of Aphasic Disturbance." P. 2 of R. O. Jakobson and M. Halle, *Fundamentals of Language.* The Hague: Mouton, 1950.

Johnson, Barbara. *The Critical Difference: Essays in the Contemporary Rhetoric of Reading.* Baltimore: Johns Hopkins University Press, 1980.

Keach, William. "Reflective Imagery in Shelley." *Keats-Shelley Journal* 24 (1975):49–69.

———. *Shelley's Style.* London: Methuen, 1984.

Kelley, Theresa M. "The Economics of the Heart: Wordsworth's Sublime and Beautiful." *Romanticism Past and Present* 5 (1981):15–32.

———. "Proteus and Romantic Allegory." *ELH* 49 (1982):623–52.

———. "Spirit and Geometric Form in Wordsworth's Arab Dream." *Studies in English Literature* 22 (1982):563–82.

———. "Wordsworth, Kant, and the Romantic Sublime." Forthcoming in *Philological Quarterly.*

———. "Wordsworth and the Rhinefall." Forthcoming in *Studies in Romanticism.*

Kermode, Frank. *Romantic Image*. London: Routledge & Kegan Paul, 1957.

Klein, Richard. "Straight Lines and Arabesques: Metaphors of Metaphor." *Yale French Studies* 45 (1970):64–86.

Kofman, Sarah. *Nietzsche et la métaphore*. Paris: Payot, 1972.

Lacoue-Labarthe, Philippe, and Jean-Luc Nancy. *L'Absolu littéraire: Théorie de la littérature du romantisme allemand*. Paris: Seuil, 1978.

Laplanche, Jean. *Hölderlin et la question du père*. Paris: Presses Universitaires de France, 1961.

Lipking, Lawrence, ed. *High Romantic Argument: Essays for M. H. Abrams*. Ithaca: Cornell University Press, 1981.

Lovejoy, Arthur O. *Essays in the History of Ideas*. New York: Putnam's, 1960.

————. *The Great Chain of Being*. New York: Harper & Row, 1960.

Luke, David. "Keats's Letters: Fragments of an Aesthetic of Fragments." *Genre* 11 (1978):209–26.

Lyotard, Jean François. *Discours, figure*. Paris: Klincksieck, 1974.

Massey, Irving. *The Gaping Pig: Literature and Metamorphosis*. Berkeley: University of California Press, 1976.

McGann, Jerome. "The Anachronism of George Crabbe." *ELH* 48 (1981):269– 88.

————. *A Critique of Modern Textual Criticism*. Chicago: University of Chicago Press, 1983.

————. "Keats and the Historical Method in Literary Criticism." *MLN* 94 (1979):988–1032.

————. *The Romantic Ideology: A Critical Investigation*. Chicago: University of Chicago Press, 1983.

————. "The Text, the Poem, and the Problem of Historical Method." *New Literary History* 12 (1981):269–88.

McGaveran, James Holt, Jr. "The '*Creative* Soul' of *The Prelude* and the 'Sad Incompetence of Human Speech.'" *Studies in Romanticism* 16 (1977):35– 50.

Macksey, Richard. "The Artist in the Labyrinth: Design or *Dasein?*" *MLN* 77(1962):239–56.

————. "The Climates of Wallace Stevens." In *The Act of the Mind: Essays on the Poetry of Wallace Stevens*, ed. R. H. Pearce and J. H. Miller, pp. 185–223. Baltimore: Johns Hopkins University Press, 1965.

————, ed. *Velocities of Change: Critical Essays from "MLN."* Baltimore: Johns Hopkins University Press, 1974.

———— and Donato, Eugenio, eds. *The Structuralist Controversy*. Baltimore: Johns Hopkins University Press, 1972.

Manning, Peter. "*Don Juan* and Byron's Imperceptiveness to the English Word." *Studies in Romanticism* 18 (1979):207–33.

Mellor, Anne K. *English Romantic Irony*. Cambridge: Harvard University Press, 1980.

Michaels, Walter Benn. "*Walden*'s False Bottoms." *Glyph* 1 (1977):132–49.

Miller, J. Hillis. "A 'Buchstäbliches' Reading of *The Elective Affinities*." *Glyph* 6 (1979):1–23.

———. "The Critic as Host." In Harold Bloom et al., *Deconstruction and Criticism*, pp. 217–53. New York: Seabury, 1979.

———. *The Disappearance of God: Five Nineteenth-Century Writers*. Cambridge: Belknap Press of Harvard University Press, 1963.

———. *Fiction and Repetition: Seven English Novels*. Cambridge: Harvard University Press, 1982.

———. "The Still Heart: Poetic Form in Wordsworth." *New Literary History* 2 (1971):279–310.

———. "The Stone and the Shell: The Problem of Poetic Form in Wordsworth's Dream of the Arab." In *Mouvements premiers: Etudes critiques offertes à Georges Poulet*. Paris: Corti, 1972.

———. "Tradition and Difference." Review of *Natural Supernaturalism*, by M. H. Abrams. *Diacritics* 2 (1972):6–13.

Modiano, Raimonda. "Words and 'Languageless' Meanings: Limits of Expression in *The Rime of the Ancient Mariner*." *Modern Language Quarterly* 38 (1977):40–61.

Nancy, Jean-Luc. *Le Discours de la syncope*. Vol. 1: *Logodaedalus*. Paris: Aubier-Flammarion, 1976.

Norris, Christopher. *Deconstruction: Theory and Practice*. London: Methuen, 1982.

Parker, Patricia. *Inescapable Romance: Studies in the Poetics of a Mode*. Princeton: Princeton University Press, 1979.

———. "The Metaphorical Plot." In *Metaphor: Problems and Perspectives*, ed. David S. Miall, pp. 133–58. Atlantic Highlands, N.J.: Humanities Press, 1982.

Parker, Reeve. *Coleridge's Meditative Art*. Ithaca: Cornell University Press, 1975.

———. "'Finer Distance': The Narrative Art of Wordsworth's 'The Wanderer.'" *ELH* 39 (1972):87–111.

Paulson, Ronald. *Representations of Revolution 1789–1820*. New Haven: Yale University Press, 1982.

Pautrat, Bernard. *Versions du soleil: Figures et système de Nietzsche*. Paris: Seuil, 1971.

Pierssens, Michel. *La tour de Babil: La fiction du signe*. Paris: Minuit, 1976.

Poulet, Georges. *Trois Essais de mythologie romantique*. Paris: Corti, 1966.

Rajan, Tilottama. *Dark Interpreter*. Ithaca: Cornell University Press, 1980.

Rand, Richard. "Geraldine." *Glyph* 3 (1978):74–97.

Ray, William. "Suspended in the Mirror: Language and the Self in Kleist's 'Uber das Marionettentheater.'" *Studies in Romanticism* 18 (1979):521–546.

Reed, Arden. "Booked for Utter Perplexity on De Quincey's 'English Mail Coach.'" In *De Quincey: Bicentenary Essays*, ed. Robert L. Snyder. Norman: University of Oklahoma Press, 1985.

———. *Romantic Weather: The Climates of Coleridge and Baudelaire*. Hanover, N.H.: Brown University Press and University Press of New England, 1983.

Regueiro, Helen. *The Limits of Imagination: Wordsworth, Yeats, and Stevens.* Ithaca: Cornell University Press, 1976.

Reiman, Donald H. *Shelley's "Triumph of Life": A Critical Study.* Urbana: University of Illinois Press, 1965.

Riffaterre, Michael. "Interpretation and Descriptive Poetry: A Reading of Wordsworth's 'Yew Trees.'" *New Literary History* 4 (1973):229–56.

————, ed. *Languages of Knowledge and of Inquiry.* New York: Columbia University Press, 1984.

————. *Semiotics of Poetry.* Bloomington: Indiana University Press, 1978.

Rowe, John Carlos. "Writing and Truth in Poe's *The Narative of Arthur Gordon Pym.*" *Glyph* 2 (1977):102–21.

Sabin, Margery. *English Romanticism and the French Tradition.* Cambridge: Harvard University Press, 1976.

Saussure, Ferdinand de. *Course in General Linguistics.* Trans. Wade Baskin. London: Fontana, 1974.

Schaeffer, Jean-Marie. *Le Roman absolu: Romantisme et la théorie du roman.* Paris: Seuil, 1981.

————. "Romantisme et langage poétique." *Poétique* 42 (1980):177–94.

Searle, John R. *Speech Acts: An Essay in the Philosophy of Language.* Cambridge: Cambridge University Press, 1972.

Sherry, Peggy Meyer. "The 'Predicament' of the Autograph: 'William Blake.'" *Glyph* 4 (1978):131–55.

Simpson, David. *Irony and Authority in Romantic Poetry.* Totowa, N.J.: Rowman & Littlefield, 1979.

Spector, Stephen J. "Thomas de Quincey: Self-effacing Autobiographer." *Studies in Romanticism* 18 (1979):501–20.

Spivak, Gayatri Chakrovorty. "The Letter as Cutting Edge." *Yale French Studies* 55–56 (1977):208–26.

Sundquist, Eric J. "Suspense and Tautology in *Benito Cereno.*" *Glyph* 8 (1981): 103–26.

Sussman, Henry. "The Deconstructor as Politician: Melville's *Confidence-Man.*" *Glyph* 4 (1978):32–56.

————. *The Hegelian Aftermath: Readings in Hegel, Kierkegaard, Freud, Proust, and James.* Baltimore: Johns Hopkins University Press, 1983.

Thorburn, David, and Geoffrey Hartman, eds. *Romanticism: Vistas, Instances, Continuities.* Ithaca: Cornell University Press, 1973.

Todorov, Tzvetan. *Les Genres du discours.* Paris: Seuil, 1978.

————. *Symbolism and Interpretation.* Trans. Catherine Porter. Ithaca: Cornell University Press, 1982.

————. *Theories of the Symbol.* Trans. Catherine Porter. Ithaca: Cornell University Press, 1982.

Warminski, Andrzej. "'Patmos': The Senses of Interpretation." *MLN* 91 (1976):478–500.

————. "Pre-positional By-play." *Glyph* 3 (1978):98–117.

Warren, Robert Penn. "A Poem of Pure Imagination: An Experiment in

Reading." Abridged version in *Twentieth-Century Interpretations of "The Rime of the Ancient Mariner,"* ed. James D. Boulger, pp. 21–47. Englewood Cliffs, N.J.: Prentice-Hall, 1969.

Wasserman, Earl R. "The English Romantics: The Grounds of Knowledge." *Studies in Romanticism* 4 (1964):17–34.

————. *The Finer Tone: Keats' Major Poems.* Baltimore: Johns Hopkins Press, 1953; reprint 1967.

————. *Shelley: A Critical Reading.* Baltimore: Johns Hopkins University Press, 1971.

————. *The Subtler Language: Critical Readings of Neoclassic and Romantic Poems.* Baltimore: Johns Hopkins Press, 1959.

Watson, Kenneth. "Coleridge's Use of Notes." *Romanticism Past and Present* 6 (1982):11–22.

Weinsheimer, Joel. "Coleridge on Synonymity and the Reorigination of Truth." *Papers on Literature and Language* 14 (1978):269–83.

Weiskel, Thomas. *The Romantic Sublime: Studies in the Structure and Psychology of Transcendence.* Baltimore: Johns Hopkins University Press, 1976.

Wilner, Joshua. "Autobiography and Addiction: The Case of De Quincey." *Genre* 14 (1981):493–503.

————. "De Quincey's Labyrinth and Thyrsus." *Hebrew University Studies in Literature* 10 (1982):23–38.

Wittgenstein, Ludwig. *Philosophical Investigations.* Trans. G. E. M. Anscombe. Oxford: Blackwell, 1953.

Wohlfarth, Irving. "The Politics of Prose and the Art of Awakening: Walter Benjamin's Version of a German Romantic Motif." *Glyph* 7 (1980):131–48.

Wolfson, Susan J. "The Illusion of Mastery: Wordsworth's Revision of 'the Drowned Man of Esthwaite,' 1799, 1805, 1850." *PMLA,* forthcoming.

————. "Keats the Letter-Writer: Epistolary Poetics." *Romanticism Past and Present* 6 (1982):43–61.

————. "The Speaker as Questioner in *Lyrical Ballads*." *Journal of English and German Philology* 77 (1978):546–68.

INDEX

References to individual works are cited under authors' names.